In the houses,
The little pianos are closed, and a clock strikes.
And all sway forward on the dangerous flood
Of history, that never sleeps or dies,
And held one moment, burns the hand.

W. H. Auden, 'To a Writer on his Brithday' 1936

To my parents
Hugh and Elisabeth Montefiore
and
to the memories of
Claud and Patricia Cockburn

Learning Resources
Centre

Contents

Acknowledgements

I would like to thank the University of Kent for giving me the sabbatical in which to draft the book, and I thank my Kent colleagues, especially Lyn Innes and Rod Edmond, for conversation and advice while I was writing it. I also thank the Departments of English and of Women's Studies at the University of Georgetown in Washington, DC, where I was Visiting Scholar in 1992–1994, for their hospitality, especially Professor Margaret Hall and other colleagues in Women's Studies, for their generosity in letting me use their office space to draft much of the book, and Lesley Byers for helping me when I was puzzled by the computer.

I am very grateful to my colleagues in the English Department and in the Women's Studies Research Seminar at Georgetown University for their responses to the parts of the draft which I presented as seminar papers, especially Professors Leona Fisher, Kim Hall, Margaret Stetz and George O'Brien; also Professor Michael Ragussis, whose stimulating seminar 'The Politics of Literary Form' I was privileged to attend. Leona Fisher, with characteristic generosity, took time to read and comment on two chapters; I thank her for her perceptive and exacting annotations. I also thank Laura Marcus, Sue Wiseman and Rachel Bowlby for reading and commenting on early versions of Chapters 1 and 2, and for many stimulating conversations. I especially thank Laura for commenting on drafts of several chapters at several stages from the primitive to the penultimate, and for telling me to read Halbwachs.

Early drafts of parts of the book were also given as papers to the Women's Studies Research Seminar at Kent, to conferences or seminars at the Universities of Nottingham, Glasgow, Cornell, Oxford Brookes University, and to the Critical Theory Group and the Institute of English Studies in London University. I am grateful to the colleagues and students who responded to my papers there. I also thank Nicola Horton who gave me invaluable help, early on, in the formidable task of 'mapping' Rebecca West's *Black Lamb and Grey Falcon*.

I am grateful to Edward Upward for kindly allowing me to interview him and for answering my queries, and to Naomi Mitchison for generous permission to quote extensively from her poems. I thank Kathleen Raine for taking the time to tell me why she objected to my interpretation of her poem 'Maternal Grief'.

I should also like to acknowledge my gratitude to Virago Press for reprinting so many neglected works by women writers in their 'Modern Classics' series. Its editors and directors deserve the thanks of readers everywhere, and feminist scholars in particular, for putting previously rare or unobtainable books into general circulation; a good effect which remains, thanks to libraries, even when the titles go out of print again. Without Virago's reprints, this book would have been far harder to write.

I also thank my editors at Routledge, first Sue Roe and then Talia Rodgers, for being consistently interested, patient and helpful.

Finally, I thank Patrick for his love and support, and our sons Henry and Alexander for being, almost always, a pleasure to live with. This book is for them as well.

Although I have made every effort to locate copyright holders, I have been unable to contact some of them, to whom I offer my apologies. My thanks to the following: Paul Berry, Literary Executor for Winifred Holtby, and Vera Brittain, for permission to reprint an excerpt from Winifred Holtby's poem 'Trains'; Carcanet Press, for permission to reprint excerpts from 'As Our Might Lessens', and 'Full Moon at Tierz' from the *Collected Writings* of John Cornford; an excerpt from 'To the Wife of a Non-Interventionist Statesman' from *Behind the Eyes: Collected Poems and Translations* by Edgell Rickword; 'Opus 7' and extracts from 'Benicasim' by Sylvia Townsend Warner (*Collected Poems* of Sylvia Townsend Warner); 'Rembering the Thirties' by Donald Davie, from Davie's *Collected Poems*; David Higham Associates, excerpts from Louis MacNeice's poem 'Autumm Journal' and 'Epilogue' to *Letters from Iceland*, from MacNeice's *Collected Poems*; Faber & Faber, for permission to reprint excerpts from W.H. Auden's poems, 'Letter to Lord Byron', 'Meiosis', 'Prologue' to *The Orators*, 'Spain 1937', 'To A Writer on His Birthday', in *The English Auden*, by E. Mendelson (ed.), and excerpts from Stephen Spender's poems 'The Pylons', 'The Funeral', and 'The Express' in Spender's *Collected Poems*; Naomi Mitchison, for permission to reprint excerpts from her poems *The Alban Goes Out*, 'The Bonny Brae', 'Clemency Ealassaid: July 1940', 'Chorus' from *The Fourth Pig*, 'New Verse'; Random House, for permission to quote Valentine

Ackland's poem 'Is the hawk as tender', and excerpts from 'The eyes of body, being blindfold by night'; also excerpts from Sylvia Townsend Warner's poems 'Father, most fatherly in our childishness', 'I, so wary of traps', and 'Since the first toss of gale' from *Whether a Dove or a Seagull* by Sylvia Townsend Warner and Valentine Ackland; Reed Books, for permission to quote excerpts from 'The Hill' and 'Song of the Mud' from Mary Borden's *The Forbidden Zone*.

Introduction

'Were there any women writing then?' The innocent question was put to me in 1983, after a talk about the political–literary context of the thirties which I gave to a class of young women 'doing' the Penguin anthology *Poetry of the Thirties* as one of their set texts for A level English Literature. At the time, a little disconcerted, I came up with Stevie Smith's *Novel on Yellow Paper*, Winifred Holtby's *South Riding* – 'and there's Virginia Woolf, of course.' The discussion had to end there because none of the young women had studied these writers, while I myself had not previously thought to set them in the context of the 1930s. Once the question had been asked, it was obvious to me that I should have done so. The following pages are the result of my attempt to think through both the question itself and its wider implications.

Needless to say, twelve years on, my list of women writers between the wars would have been far longer and would have included poets as well as novelists. But although this book is partly intended to correct the currently available gender-blind accounts of the literature of the 1930s, it does not try to make a comprehensive survey of women writers. In other words, it was not written to answer that sixth-former's question directly, although I remain deeply grateful to her for asking it. True, once I started looking for women writers, I realized that their work had flowered impressively during the 1930s, and was by no means all neglected or out of print, thanks largely to the work of Virago Press. But on the whole, this work was being marketed and read as 'women's writing', abstracted from its historical context. And although this approach (which I used myself in *Feminism and Poetry*) was certainly a necessary corrective to the conventional omission of women, it did not seem a good way to approach the history of a decade. First, it risked lumping heterogeneous authors together, effacing the obvious differences of genre and outlook which separate, say, politically conservative writers of detective fiction like Dorothy L. Sayers or Margery

Allingham from the anti-Fascist historical novels of Sylvia Townsend Warner or Naomi Mitchison. Worse still, such an approach was liable to ignore historical context. To concentrate primarily on the writer's gender would be an unhelpful way of reading texts such as Nancy Cunard's 1934 *Negro* anthology or Storm Jameson's *Mirror in Darkness* trilogy of novels (published 1934–1936), which concern themselves with, respectively, the history, experience and culture of Africans and American Negroes (Cunard), and the political history of post-war England, fictionalized as a Balzacian novel-sequence (Jameson),[1] not with the lives of women. Even when one looks at the poetry of the decade, where gender differences certainly are strongly marked, it is clear that Nancy Cunard, Stevie Smith and Naomi Mitchison all have more in common in terms of theme and style with their 'Audenesque' male contemporaries than they do with, say, Elizabeth Daryush or Laura Riding. To read any of these *simply* as women writers would be to adopt a form of tunnel vision which would only reverse the historians' traditional blind spot for women (and would, incidentally, have irritated the writers considerably had they known of it).

To say that the women writers of the 1930s have been ignored also raises the important question, 'How has the literature of this decade been remembered?'[2] To revive the work of women writers while acknowledging the historical and cultural context in which they wrote implies also examining the ways in which the collective memories of the 1930s have been constructed. This job is both helped and complicated by the fact that much of the writing of and about the 1930s is a self-conscious literature of personal memory. As Virginia Woolf observed in 1940: 'No other decade can have produced so much autobiography as the ten years between 1930 and 1939'[3] – a statement which looks even truer now than it did when Woolf made it. The 'Devil's Decade', as Claud Cockburn named it,[4] inspired such a large and lively literature of retrospect that the 'thirties memoir', whether overt or fictionalized, now amounts to a distinctive sub-species of twentieth-century autobiography. Furthermore, the literary histories of the 1930s inevitably rely on personal testimony; the first accounts by George Orwell, Richard Crossman and Julian Symons were written as memoirs,[5] while later historians have often drawn on writers' reminiscences. And, as Woolf astutely observed, the personal memory of the recent past is central to such canonical 'thirties classics' as Orwell's *Homage to Catalonia* (1936), Isherwood's *Goodbye to Berlin* (1939) or MacNeice's *Autumn Journal* (1939). Less obviously, but almost as pervasively, the memory of the Great War is also an unforgotten shadow in much writing of the 1930s. Auden's early work is full of it. These elements of witness and memory are equally to be found amongst women writers in the 1930s, though often with a different slant. Storm Jameson, Vera Brittain or Sylvia Townsend Warner, who came of age during the Great War, remember it rather differently from the 'Auden Generation' of male writers who experienced it as schoolboys. Similarly, the memoirs of the years *entre deux guerres* include the distinguished contributions of Storm Jameson (*Europe to Let* [1940] and *Journey from the North* [1969, 1970]) as well as Rebecca West's elegiac monument to Yugoslavia, *Black Lamb and Grey Falcon* (1942) – all of which have, regrettably, been ignored by the official historians of the period. Again, however, it seems less useful to discuss these works on their own than to recognize them as part of the literature of collective memory.

That, however, is no simple task, partly because the texts themselves are, unsurprisingly, not very reliable. For example, the detailed accounts of meetings and conversations during the 1930s in Storm Jameson's *Journey from the North*, though presumably based on the diaries she kept during these years,[6] are all written (and, one supposes, edited) with post-war hindsight; they should not be taken as a straight factual witness, any more than Stephen Spender's or Christopher Isherwood's multiple accounts of their lives and friends[7] should be taken as unquestioned gospel. But the problem with these retrospective accounts is not only that it is difficult or impossible to determine their authenticity; they also shift the definition of 'thirties writing' from 'writing in the 1930s' to 'writing about the 1930s'. Rebecca West's *Black Lamb and Grey Falcon* is a problematic text in this way, in both being and not being 'of the thirties'. Published in 1942,[8] it appears to come just outside the decade. On the other hand, it was certainly begun during the late thirties, for it is, on its simplest level, a travel-book describing Rebecca West's journey to and within Yugoslavia in the spring of 1937, much of it being closely based on the diary which she kept during that trip.[9] The book's achievement is to turn the particular moment witnessed by the author into an elegiac monument to *Mitteleuropa* before 1940; and this means contextualizing it within an ever more bloody and distant past. Thus the moment of March 1937 is set within the greater context of the catastrophe of 1914, which is itself determined by the centuries of Austro-Hungarian and Ottoman rule in Eastern Europe; this, in turn, began with the medieval Serbian empire's defeat at Kossovo in 1389, which itself cannot be understood without reference to the world of late antiquity. Not that these long perspectives turn *Black Lamb* into a simple history book. Dedicated to 'my friends in Yugoslavia who are all now dead or enslaved', it is also a monument to the grim years in which it was written, 'while there rages around me vileness equal to that which I describe'.[10] Yet it does not seem right, either, to classify *Black Lamb* simply as a wartime book; its dark yet nostalgic account of the moment *entre deux guerres* has much in common with Louis MacNeice's meditative diary-poem, *Autumn Journal* (1939). To read the literature of and about the 1930s in terms of *memory* – as opposed to the more conventional emphasis on *witness* – thus inevitably blurs the neat traditional boundaries of that decade.

This blurring of boundaries in turn raises the question of whether it still makes sense to discuss the 'writings of the 1930s' at all. Should the years 1930–1939 simply be seen as part of the 'Age of Catastrophe', as Eric Hobsbawm has persuasively defined the period 1914–1945?[11] Certainly Hobsbawm's argument, that the forces which shaped the history of the 'thirties' originate with the Great War and were resolved in the Cold Peace of 1945, is compelling. (On the level of literary criticism, this squares with my own reading of the literature of the 1930s as haunted by the memory of the First World War and the fear of the Second.) But it doesn't follow that any account of that decade must either oversimplify history or collapse under the pressure of acknowledging its 'Age of Catastrophe' context. The memory of the 1930s has remained alive in British culture – and not only because, as the appearance of *Poetry of the Thirties* on an A level English syllabus implies, 'thirties writing' has acquired an accepted place in the canon of modern English literature. The decade also still lives in the public memory because its image is so often invoked in political rhetoric. On the Left, trades unionists plan their marches to protest against unemployment to follow the same route as the Jarrow Hunger Marches did in 1933 and 1934.[12] In foreign affairs, the spectre of the Chamberlain government's policy of appeasing Hitler was reinvoked to discredit anti-nuclear activists in the 1980s and, more recently, the word 'appeasement' has surfaced again in debates about Britain's policy – or lack of one – towards the fate of the multicultural Bosnian Republic.[13] (Indeed, the word has since 1940 acquired such powerful connotations of collusion and cowardice that to be called an 'appeaser' has in British politics been an insult comparable with being called a Communist in the USA). The 1930s are remembered, for better or worse, as an intensely political decade. This is true even (or especially) when that memory is repudiated: 'No Return to the Thirties!'

This book, like most accounts of the literature of the 1930s, focuses on the left-wing writers, though, unlike nearly all its predecessors, it includes and emphasizes women. Precisely because these writers were both political and oppositional, they put into question the standard literary–critical assumption that politics and literature shouldn't mix. This direct political interrogation of the reader is one reason for the persistent fascination of 1930s writing – and also makes it impossible for the reader to pass judgement on it without taking up a political position (my own left-liberal perspective will already be sufficiently obvious). Within this political context, I address two principal questions: 'What part does memory play in the political literature of and about the 1930s?' and 'What were the roles of women in constructing that literature of political memory?'. (The second question includes both women as writers and women as signifiers: see Chapter 3 for a discussion of the latter.)

The book has thus been shaped as an interweaving of these themes of gender and collective memory. The first two chapters deal respectively with writers' memories of the thirties and with the different ways in which male and female writers of the 1930s construct a self through memory in their writings. Chapters 3 and 4, the most straightforwardly feminist part of the book, deal with the representation of women by the canonical male writers, including the weight of class guilt and war guilt which images of women are made to carry, and with women's poetry. Chapter 4 is a survey of the largely forgotten women poets of the 1930s; unlike the rest of the book, this chapter does directly address the question 'Were women writing then?'. Chapter 5, which discusses anti-Fascist historical novels, returns to the theme of the relationship between past and present; this is taken up once again in the final chapter's discussion of Rebecca West's great study of gender, history and memory, *Black Lamb and Grey Falcon*.

I am not, of course, so arrogant as to suppose that this structure includes everything that matters about literature and politics in the 1930s. In particular, I regret the absence of a full discussion of Nancy Cunard's perennially ignored *Negro* anthology. This omission is due partly to the obstacles which I encountered in trying to find an unabridged original edition,[14] and partly to my ignorance of the African art and music which form nearly half its subject matter, for to write usefully about Cunard's coverage of these things one needs to know more about them than my own smattering. Other omissions are more noticeable, but I hope need less apology. I have dealt very selectively with the bourgeois male writers, because their works form only part – though of course an indispensable one – of the classic literature of the thirties. (It is, I trust, needless to add that my fairly sharp criticisms of Auden, Orwell and Co. for their sexual politics do not preclude admiration for and pleasure in their works, especially Auden's poems.) I have also devoted comparatively little space to women novelists, whom I discuss in just two chapters, because my focus on memory led me to consider other kinds of writing as well as fiction. Moreover, interwar women's fiction no longer suffers seriously from neglect; Andy Crofts, Alison Light, John Gindin and Rachel Bowlby have all written illuminatingly on the women novelists of the thirties.

I have also said little about the questions of Empire and of imperialist ideology, apart from an account of the feminist readings of imperialist ideology in the novels of Virginia Woolf and Stevie Smith (Chapter 2) and a discussion of Rebecca West's critique of empires (Chapter 6). This is not because I think these questions irrelevant to English cultural history in the 1930s – not least because Great Britain's status as an imperialist world power meant that its citizens' political commitments and debates in these years were never just storms in literary teacups. But the subject of British imperialism between the wars is far too large to be dealt with in a chapter, or even two chapters. The theme of political memory alone has been more than enough for one woman.

Chapter 1

Remembering the 1930s

Memory is not an instrument for exploring the past, but its theatre. It is the medium of past experience, as the ground is the medium in which dead cities lie interred.

Walter Benjamin[1]

POLITICS AND COLLECTIVE MEMORY

This book is about political memory and the literature of the 1930s: how it has been remembered, how personal and political memories work in the literature itself, and also how much important writing has *not* been remembered: especially, though not wholly, the work of women. In English literary culture, the poetry and fiction of the 1930s are accepted features of the twentieth-century landscape. Established classics of the 'thirties canon' include Robin Skelton's Penguin anthology *Poetry of the Thirties* (1964) and the often reprinted novels of Greene, Waugh, Isherwood and Orwell. The past decades have also witnessed the retrospections of Christopher Isherwood and Edward Upward, the belated publication of texts by W. H. Auden and Stephen Spender, and the republication of many women writers, often reprinted by feminist publishing houses,[2] although women are still not commonly perceived as part of 'thirties history', a fact whose causes and implications I discuss below (pp. 19–25). Literary autobiographies of the 1930s began to be published in 1939, continued well into the 1990s[3] and look set to go on appearing as long as there are survivors. The first accounts of the literature of the 1930s appeared in 1940,[4] to which successors are still being produced – including, of course, this book.

Yet literary history, especially of such an intensely if patchily remembered decade, cannot be tackled on its own. Any useful account of the

1930s must begin with politics. This is a surprisingly complicated matter because there exists no universally accepted version of English political history during these years. No one, of course, disputes the main facts: the Wall Street Crash which inaugurated the Great Slump in 1929, the return of the National Government in 1931, the advent of the Means Test in 1934, the policy of non-intervention in the Spanish War and the Munich Agreement in October 1938, the ascendancy of left-wing ideas amongst English writers, and the 'Popular Front' alliances between Communist and liberal intellectuals. The disagreements are about selection, emphasis and value: what these events meant, whether they were good or bad, even whether they were important. For example, the historians Margot Heinemann and Noreen Branson disagree sharply with A. J. P. Taylor[5] about whether there even was a significant Depression in England. The extent of the disagreement about the thirties appears in the two folk-memories of the 1930s which continue to haunt British public discourse: on the one hand, the protest marches and the International Brigade which fascinate the Left and, on the other, the images of appeasement and/or Red treachery by which patriotic conservatives remember that decade. Related versions of these political memories been played out in the long series of literary histories of the 1930s (discussed on pp. 11–19), which have appeared since the decade ended.

To approach these different, often contradictory versions of history, I find it useful to invoke the concept of collective memory, theorized by the French sociologist Maurice Halbwachs (1877–1945) – himself, incidentally, a liberal victim of Fascism. (An immensely distinguished professor at the Sorbonne, showered with professional honours, he died in Buchenwald after being arrested under the Vichy regime for protesting against the murder of his liberal Jewish in-laws.)[6] In *On Collective Memory* (1939), he argued cogently that memory is not, as is commonly thought, an individual phenomenon but a collective creation, whose patterns are defined by the interpretative frameworks of different social groups. Memory should thus be understood as, by definition, a *social* phenomenon. Individual remembrance is part of, and only made possible by, group memory:

> It is to the degree that our individual thought places itself in these [collective] frameworks and participates in this memory that it is capable of the act of recollection ... Collective frameworks are ... precisely the instruments used by the collective memory to reconstruct an image of the past which is in accord, in each epoch, with the predominant thoughts of the society.

This argument dissolves the rigid conventional distinction between things inside the psyche (thoughts) and things outside (material realities), insisting that because thoughts, perceptions and memories are only made possible by language, which is a system of communication, they cannot be purely individual. Once a memory is verbalized, its meaning is shared with others: 'There are no perceptions without recollections. But inversely, there are no recollections which can be said to be purely interior, that is purely preserved by individual memory.'[7] And since the individuals who remember, and the social context which defines their way of remembering, exist in the 'present moment' in which their past is recalled, their (re)constructions of that past must be profoundly affected by the ideas and values current at that present moment.

Halbwachs defined his 'collective frameworks' of memory as the family, the Catholic Church, and social classes – not, significantly, nations, although he wrote at a time of intense nationalism. But though he was not a literary theorist, his verbal 'collective' model certainly works for written memoirs, since autobiographies are written by members of social groups (Bloomsbury littérateurs, politicians, the working class, journalists, etc.), the characteristic rhetoric and symbolism of whose memories are, as Halbwachs argues, shaped by their perception of the present. Halbwachs' notion, far from defining all memory as part of an ideological consensus, thus helps to situate the memories of people belonging to marginalized or excluded groups. This does *not*, however, mean that particular memories are the product of a group consensus about history, still less that the group characteristically speaks through the individual: ' "It is individuals as group members who remember"; it follows that there are as many collective memories as there are groups and institutions in a society.'[8] It is rather that the defining collective 'frame of reference' drawn on by the individual to make his or her past intelligible derives from a dialogue, actual or implied, within the group. Nor can any individual be defined *only* by the membership of a social group, for each of us belongs to several – as in E. P. Thompson's witty parable of the woman worker whose social identity is constructed by several roles and defined by none.[9] It is nevertheless the dialogue with a significant group which defines personal memories, as with the reminiscences which Virginia Woolf delivered between 1920 and 1936 to the Bloomsbury 'Memoir Club'.[10] A more complex instance of a shared 'interpretative framework' would be Isherwood's memoir *Christopher and his Kind* (1977), whose implied audience includes both Isherwood's then-surviving contemporaries *and* a wider gay readership empowered by the politics of gay liberation with which the older Isherwood identifies himself.

Both the literature of the 1930s and most subsequent writings about that 'moment' are visibly shaped by the dialectical framework which Halbwachs identified as working between the interpretative 'framework' of a present moment and a recalled past. The process can clearly be seen in Rebecca West's great retrospective memorial to liberal Eastern Europe, *Black Lamb and Grey Falcon* (1942), which meditates on how the past determines the present, interpreting the monuments of that past by means of present-day imagery. Describing the mummified corpse of a defeated medieval emperor, she conveys the pathetic sight of his dead hands adorned with exquisitely made rings through a contemporary analogy:

> He is piteous as a knot of men standing on a street-corner in Jarrow or a Welsh mining town. Like them he means failure, the disappointment of hopes, the waste of powers. He means death also, but that is not so important. Who would resent death if it came when all hopes had been realized and all powers turned to use?

The allusion to Jarrow and South Wales, then proverbial for poverty and unemployment, makes the Tsar's historical tragedy intelligible by interpreting him through a classic image of 'present-day' 1930s England.[11] But the 'collective framework' of knowledge and memory which makes Rebecca West's analogy possible is itself political. As often in *Black Lamb and Grey Falcon*, a book well to the left of her post-war writings, the thought is shaped by a liberalism which accepts the image of unemployed men as a sign of the economic and social shortcomings of capitalism – not, as a reactionary might see it, of the men's own laziness or plain bad luck.

The converse of this process of understanding the past by drawing analogies with the present is of course the interpretation of new events in terms of the known past. This process is far more common; it is, indeed, the way in which people make sense of politics. And, as Claud Cockburn pointed out, a proneness to historical analogy may only subject people to 'those events and dates which have reached out a long, paralysing hand to grip and twist future history'.[12] A key exchange about war in E. R. Gedye's history of post-war Austria *Fallen Bastions* (1939) bears out Cockburn's point. Gedye, the *Daily Telegraph*'s Vienna correspondent from 1932 to 1938, wrote as an eyewitness, occasionally invoking the memory of the Great War as analogy or reference point to convey the enormity of what he saw. Thus, describing the ruin of workers' flats in the 1934 right-wing coup that destroyed Vienna's Socialist government, he compared them with the Western Front: 'The building was as shell-shattered and bullet-scarred as anything I had seen in Arras or Albert in 1916'. The image is both personal and collective, at once authenticating Gedye's own witness and invoking a generalized allusion to the brutal, pointless destruction which, as Paul Fussell has shown, the Western Front rapidly came to represent in modern memory. Later on, however, when a British diplomat obliquely invokes a similar allusion to the useless destruction of the Great War, Gedye rejects the anti-war consensus implicit in the man's language. He relates indignantly how a member of the 1938 Runciman delegation deplored the Czechs' eagerness to fight:

'a notion which, thank God, we have grown out of in England'...

'Then England would never under any circumstances defend herself against aggression again?'

'England,' I was told, 'would, thank God, never allow herself to be led into the beastliness of war again under any circumstances.'

Each speaker in this exchange gives a different meaning to the words 'war' and 'never again'. The official's phrases 'the beastliness of war' and 'never... again' clearly allude to the Great War, assuming a consensual memory of that useless waste of life as a justification for England's present policy of appeasement. Gedye, the liberal journalist, does not consent to this memory as valid or legitimate. His 'never... again' points to a hypothetical future: 'would England defend herself?'[13]

LOOKING BACK IN IRONY

No other ten years can have produced so much autobiography as the ten years between 1930 and 1939.

Virginia Woolf[14]

'Eyewitness history' of the kind Gedye wrote has traditionally held an honoured place in thirties literary texts. Classics such as Byron's *The Road to Oxiana*, Orwell's *The Road to Wigan Pier* and Isherwood's *Goodbye to Berlin* each deploy a brilliant rhetoric of authenticity, which hindsight reveals to be the product of deliberate and skilful construction. Orwell's revisions to *The Road to Wigan Pier* were clarified by the publication of his 'Wigan Pier diary'; Christopher Sykes revealed how Robert Byron, who spoke no Arabic or Farsi, spent six months in England polishing the dialogues with native speakers in *The Road to Oxiana*; while Christopher Isherwood's *Christopher and his Kind* reveals in detail how his earlier books caricatured his friends and censored his own experiences.[15] Less noticeably but very influentially, a rhetoric of testimony has dominated the literary histories of the thirties, partly because the first of these, Francis Scarfe's *Auden and After* (1941) and Richard Crossman's *The God That Failed* (1950) were written as memoirs by survivors of the thirties, and partly because later historians tended to rely on memoirs of the thirties, sometimes quoting them as straightforwardly transparent texts.[16]

This rhetoric of memory began very early, with two highly influential accounts of the writers of the thirties: Virginia Woolf's 'The Leaning Tower' and Orwell's 'Inside the Whale'. Both essays appeared in 1940 when Britain and its Empire were still fighting alone against the Fascist Axis powers. The 'Popular Front' alliances between Socialists and Communists in the European and liberal democracies had failed miserably; Communism had been discredited by the 1939 Molotov–Ribbentrop pact. On the literary scene, Auden and Isherwood, the two leading left-wing English writers, had departed for America the previous year and apparently lost interest in the political causes they had been identified with. In 1940 it must have been impossible to read optimistic revolutionary poems like Spender's 'The Funeral' – 'This is festivity, it is the time of statistics'[17] – without irony. It is therefore not surprising that, although Virginia Woolf and George Orwell had little time for one another, they attacked the literature of the thirties, which they defined as the poetry of the 'Auden Group' plus a few prose writers,[18] in remarkably similar terms. Firmly identifying texts with authors, they attack 'Auden, Spender & Co.' (Orwell, p. 512) for being well-off ex-public schoolboys who were flawed by dishonesty because they submitted to Communist control (Orwell) or only pretended to want to give up their own privilege (Woolf). Both writers rather disingenuously represent themselves as outsiders excluded from the privileged lives of those they criticize – a rhetorical move which has been given more sceptical treatment when adopted by Virginia Woolf, daughter of Leslie Stephen, than when used by Eric Blair, King's Scholar of Eton College.[19] This verbal self-distancing is underlined by the way that they represent the writer's relation to society by key metaphors enshrined in their titles. With a pleasing elegant symmetry, these 'title metaphors' both invoke that sex to which the writer does not belong, just as in Lacan's witty fable of heterosexual difference (' "Look," says the brother, "we're at Ladies!"; "Idiot!" replies his sister, "can't you see we're at Gentlemen?" ').[20] Virginia Woolf uses the phallic metaphor of the 'Leaning Tower' – an image drawn, appropriately enough, from Auden's poem *Spain 1937*[21] – to represent the young men's 'eleven years of expensive education' (Woolf, p. 170); while Orwell's image for the impotent passivity of the writer in the leviathan State is the whale that swallowed Jonah, a metaphor which he interprets as 'simply a womb big enough for an adult' (Orwell, p. 521).

Of the two essays, 'The Leaning Tower' wears the better, principally because of Woolf's astute perception of the autobiographical slant in bourgeois thirties writing, which she identifies as its central feature. As in *A Room of One's Own*, she argues that literary achievement depends on material prosperity and a good education, symbolized by the 'tower' of privilege. Because this has begun to lean sideways, the writings of 'Day Lewis, Auden, Spender, Isherwood, Louis MacNeice and so on' sitting inside it are self-conscious and skewed. In other words, the left-wing writing of the thirties displays the consciousness of an insecure class. This explains 'the violence of their attack upon bourgeois society and also its half-heartedness. They are profiting by a society which they abuse' (p. 170). Hence 'the pedagogic, the didactic, the loudspeaker strain that dominates their poetry'(p. 175). Unlike Orwell, however, Woolf doesn't mention the word 'Communist'. Her objection to these writers' left-wing politics is that their commitment is hopelessly self-contradictory, being only the symptom of a lived dilemma. The only virtue she concedes them is the creative honesty of their self-absorption: 'They have been incapable of giving us great plays, great novels, great poems . . . [but] they have had a power which, if literature continues, may prove to be a great value in the future. They have been great egotists'. Because these writers had had the courage to tell 'the unpleasant truths about themselves' posterity might well owe much to 'the creative and honest egoism of the leaning-tower group' (pp. 177–8).

Samuel Hynes has criticized Virginia Woolf for the conventionality of her attack on the young poets: 'She had wanted beauty and fine language, and they gave her politics and experiment'.[22] True, 'The Leaning Tower' contains a surprisingly traditionalist account of English literature, is evasive about the writer's own class privilege, and expresses an open dislike of the angry, rebellious tone of thirties poetry, much as *A Room of One's Own* had rejected anger as 'fatal' to good writing.[23] But its shrewdest point about the 'Auden Generation' writers is that they were only really interested in themselves and their own predicament; and Hynes does not refute this argument, which is in fact not far from his own. For all of those commentaries on the writers of the thirties, including *The Auden Generation*, which interprets their work as responding to the dilemma experienced by middle-class male writers in a time of political, social and economic instability, begins with Woolf's essay.

The implicit political perspective of Woolf's essay is a 'one nation' leftish patriotism, which looks hopefully forward to a post-war 'world without classes or towers' (p. 178). Orwell's equally patriotic but pessimistic 'Inside the Whale', with its well-known observation that 'writers do well to stay out of politics' (Orwell, p. 518), is more conservative, partly because the harrumphing contempt for the left-wing

'Nancy poets'[24] is here comparatively unchecked by an equally emphatic commitment to social justice. Like all Orwell's mature writing, the essay is of course a pleasure to read: clear, vigorous and well written. It is also aggressive, misleading and full of holes.

'Inside the Whale' is written as a memoir-cum-social-history of fashionable literature in post-war England: Housman just after the First World War, T. S. Eliot and Joyce in the twenties, and finally the left-wing poets of the thirties, whose ideological allegiance explains both their attractiveness to readers and their weakness as writers. Though admitting that reform of *laissez-faire* capitalism was long overdue, Orwell explains the allure of Communism mainly as a secular religion; it is 'the patriotism of the deracinated' (p. 515) which attracted middle-class intellectuals too soft and naive to understand what a wicked and ruthless system they had embraced. Because Marxism is incompatible with honesty and imaginative freedom, Communist-influenced intellectuals could only write badly, especially when they attempted prose; hence the singular claim that 'no decade in the past hundred and fifty years has been so barren of imaginative prose as the nineteen-thirties. There [has] been . . . practically no fiction of any value at all' (p. 518). He concedes the poetry of 'Auden, Spender & Co.' (p. 512) some grudging approval for its prophetic qualities, but this concession is promptly undermined by the famous attack on Auden's *Spain 1937*, which quotes out of context two stanzas contrasting the promise of a utopian future with the harsh necessities of the present war:

> Tomorrow for the young, the poets exploding like bombs,
> The walks by the lake, the weeks of perfect communion;
>   Tomorrow the bicycle races
> Through the suburbs on summer evenings. But today the struggle.
>
> Today the deliberate increase in the chances of death,
> The conscious acceptance of guilt in the necessary murder,
>   Today the expending of powers
> On the flat ephemeral pamphlet and the boring meeting.

Orwell comments (p. 516) that:

> the second stanza is intended [*sic*] as a sort of thumb-nail sketch of a day in the life of a 'good party man'. In the morning a couple of political murders, a ten-minutes' interlude to stifle 'bourgeois' remorse, and then a hurried luncheon and a busy afternoon and evening chalking walls and distributing leaflets.

Actually, this 'day in the life of a "good party man" ' is Orwell's own fiction. The sequence 'morning...luncheon...afternoon and evening' is his own, as are the 'chalking walls' and the 'couple of *political* murders' (my emphasis). The focus in these stanzas, as throughout Auden's *Spain 1937*, is on collective rather than individual experience, so that the phrase 'the...increase in the chances of death' balancing the 'necessary murder', especially in its war-time context, implies battle rather than assassination.[25]

These distortions are probably not intentional. Orwell seems to have disliked Auden's poetry too much to read it seriously, for his published references to it are sloppily inaccurate (in the same essay, having conceded that calling Auden 'a sort of gutless Kipling' was spiteful [p. 511], he illustrates Auden's supposedly 'boy-scout' tone with a line from C. Day Lewis).[26] Furthermore, his experience of the suppression of the POUM during the Spanish War probably left him prepared to resent anything written about Spain by anyone associated with the Communist Party. Though Auden was never a Communist, his *Spain 1937* was published as a pamphlet by Nancy Cunard's pro-Party Hours Press, and the independent testimony of Claud Cockburn confirms that he was close to the Party at the time of writing it.[27]

Having made Auden his straw target, Orwell scores by the authority of his own experience. Unlike the fire-eater, 'who is always somewhere else when the trigger is pulled' (p. 516), he cannot take the word 'murder' lightly because he has actually witnessed the bodies of murdered men (he is presumably alluding here to his experiences in the Burma Police). He has therefore seen the sordid consequences of murder, 'the terror, the hatred, the howling relatives, the post-mortems, the blood, the smells' (p. 516). Interestingly, this attack is framed in precisely that 'Audenesque' rhetoric of metonymic noun phrases prefaced by definite articles of which *Spain* has been called the apogee.[28] It is almost as if Orwell were consciously parodying his target.

A rather more questionable invocation of personal experience underpins his description of left-wing British intellectuals during the 1930s. Orwell's account, written from the perspective of a disgusted eyewitness, anticipates Cold War condemnations of 'premature anti-fascists' by lumping all left-wingers together as uniform tools or stooges of Moscow (pp. 517–19; note how persuasively the 'you' invites the reader's identification):

For about three years, in fact, the central stream of English Literature was more or less directly under Communist control...Left-wing thought had narrowed down to 'anti-Fascism', i.e. to a negative, and a torrent of hate-literature directed against Germany and the politicians supposedly friendly to Germany was pouring from the Press...Not everyone, of course, was definitely *in* the racket, but practically everyone was on its periphery and more or less mixed up in propaganda campaigns and squalid controversies. Communists and near-Communists had a disproportionate influence on the literary reviews. It was a time of labels, slogans, evasions. You were expected to lock yourself up in a constipating little cage of lies.

To readers who didn't themselves live through this period and aren't already familiar with its literature – i.e. almost anybody born after 1940 – this testimony looks very convincing. (The library copy of Orwell's essays at Georgetown University has approving ticks all down the margin of this passage, evidently pencilled in by some devout young anti-Communist.) Anyone who actually knows the literature of the late thirties, however, must wonder just how much of it Orwell had bothered to read. A standard sample of anti-Fascist texts published in the late thirties would presumably contain Rex Warner's *The Professor* (1938), John Cornford's poem *'Full Moon at Tierz'* (1937), Spender's *Trial of a Judge* (1938); a more wide-ranging list would include Katharine Burdekin's *Swastika Night* (1937), Storm Jameson's *In the Second Year* (1935), Sylvia Townsend Warner's *After the Death of Don Juan* (1938), and perhaps Patrick Hamilton's *Hangover Square* (1941).[29] To describe these books as 'hate-literature resulting from a political racket' is ludicrous.

Moreover, by denouncing writers for their easy lives ('Hunger, hardship, solitude, exile, war, prison, persecution, manual labour – hardly even words', p. 517), Orwell effaces the efforts and risks undertaken by Socialist writers like Storm Jameson and Naomi Mitchison in order to help European victims of Fascist persecution.[30] He also ignores the fact that the despised 'Nancy poets' knew quite as much as he did about prison, exile and persecution. When Isherwood's German lover Heinz was refused entry to England in 1935, the couple were obliged to live in exile for three years until Heinz was finally caught and imprisoned by the German authorities. Similarly, Stephen Spender seems to have spent most of his time in Madrid trying to get his male lover out of jail for deserting from the International Brigade.[31] Of course Orwell could not have known these details in 1940, but, like everyone else, he did know that male homosexuality was illegal. It seems plain that his hatred of homosexuals led him to ignore the dangers they faced.

I have attacked 'Inside the Whale' more sharply than 'The Leaning

Tower', because Orwell's stature as a master of plain blunt prose has lent its dismissive judgements an influence on later perceptions of the thirties out of all proportion to their merits. (Virginia Woolf's reputation for snobbery has so far prevented her judgements from becoming unquestioned orthodoxies in quite the same way.) The problem with his definitions of 'thirties writing', however, is not only the political oversimplifications I have sketched here, which have been criticized much more authoritatively by E. P. Thompson, but also his gaping omissions. As Andy Crofts has pointed out,[32] Orwell's essay effectively deletes virtually *all* writers other than ex-public schoolboys from the record of the thirties, excluding from the record both working-class writers (no *Love on the Dole*, no *Means Test Man*), and women writers (no Storm Jameson, no Sylvia Townsend Warner, no Rebecca West, no Naomi Mitchison, no Christina Stead). And Woolf's essay does the same thing.

These were not the only hostile retrospects of the 1930s written during the war. The negative view of the 'Auden Group' is echoed in two contemporary social histories, Malcolm Muggeridge's *The Thirties* (1940) and Robert Graves and Alan Hodge's *The Long Week-End* (1940). Francis Scarfe's poetry survey *Auden and After* (1941) is more sympathetic, but its irritable treatment of Auden, its central figure, shows a similarly 'disillusioned' tone. More influential than any of these was the post-war book of ex-Communist memoirs *The God That Failed* (Crossman, 1950; unkindly known when I was at college as *The Sod That Wailed*). In his Foreword, the editor Richard Crossman explains that the book began as a heated argument between himself and Arthur Koestler about why intellectuals joined the Communist Party: 'I said, "Wait. Tell me exactly what happened when *you* joined the Party – not what you feel about it now, but what you felt then." '[33] Yet, as Koestler's own essay acknowledges, the memoirs are of course shaped by the writers' Cold War political perspectives at the moment of writing (pp. 63–64):

> Irony, anger and shame keep intruding; the passions of that time seem transformed into perversions, its inner certitude into the closed universe of the drug addict; the shadow of barbed wire lies across the condemned playground of memory.

The contributors' post-war awareness of prison camps and barbed wire haunts these memoirs, both directly, as in Stephen Spender's remark that 'the Stalinists now present the same threat to intellectual liberty as did the followers of Hitler in 1933' (p. 243), and indirectly, as in Koestler's ironic account of himself naively offering his services to the German Communist Party as an undercover agent, and then equally naively blowing his own cover (pp. 34–47). Spender, Gide and Koestler share this consistently ironic attitude to their own political pasts. The tone of the ex-working class contributors Richard Wright and Ignazio Silone, for whom both the Communist Party's betrayal of its promises and their own breakaway represented the defeat of a precious hope, is more tragic and less knowing.

The first full literary and social history of the 1930s, Julian Symons' *The Thirties: A Dream Revolved* (1960), also took the form of a highly readable memoir-chronicle. Like his political mentor Orwell, Symons wrote as an 'outsider' (Symons, p. 130); he was a poet who edited the little magazine *Twentieth Century Verse* (1937–1939). He took a vigorous part in the literary-political debates of the late thirties, but did not belong with the better-known men like Auden who published in Geoffrey Grigson's widely read journal *New Verse*. More sympathetic than Orwell to the thirties Left, Symons nevertheless shared his ironic attitude towards its literature, gleefully quoting its worst lines, and mocking 'earnest seekers after political and sexual liberation'.[34] His lively survey was followed by D. E. S. Maxwell's 1969 account of selected thirties poets and A. J. Tolley's comprehensive study, published in 1975. Martin Green's *Children of the Sun* (1975) and Paul Fussell's *Abroad* (1980) in different ways chronicled the dandy writers of the period. Apart from the anglophile Fussell, all these critics treated their subject with disapproval, their tones ranging from Julian Symons' and A. J. Tolley's faint praise, to Martin Green's outright censoriousness. This ambivalent mixture of nostalgia and dismissiveness was finely characterized in Donald Davie's poem 'Remembering the Thirties':

> The Devil for a joke
> Might carve his own initials on our desk,
> And yet we'd miss the point because he spoke
> An idiom too dated, Audenesque.[35]

In contrast to this disapproving consensus, Samuel Hynes' influential book *The Auden Generation* (1976) reshaped the accepted version of the 'low dishonest decade' full of scheming Comintern agents or naive dupes of Moscow by its sophisticated account of the relation between the writer and history. Although Hynes followed his predecessors in defining 'thirties writing' as the work of a fairly small number of poets, primarily Auden, plus the prose writers Waugh, Greene, Isherwood and Orwell, he broke new ground both in paying close attention to a much wider range of texts, including novels and autobiographies, than previous historians, and reading these in a way that saw the conjunction 'literature and politics' as fruitful rather than foolish. He interpreted the literature of the thirties as a flowering of 'parable art',[36] a loose term that includes many kinds of moralized but not didactic writing, working through metaphor, myth, symbol or dream to articulate the relation between the public world of politics and the private world of the writer's subjective dream. The opposition 'public' versus 'private', so common in the work of the Auden Generation poets, is thus crucial to Hynes' account of political writing as the product of 'a private self becoming aware of a public situation' (p. 140), or as a personal response to the 'public invasion of the private' (p. 186). Subsequent important studies of the writing of the 1930s by Bernard Bergonzi (1978), Valentine Cunningham (1988) and Frank Kermode (1988) have all relied on this distinction between public and private worlds to make sense of the writers of the 1930s.

'WHAT ABOUT THE WOMEN?': THE SEXUAL POLITICS OF MEMORY

> This, I reflected with surprise, is the first time I have been publicly confronted with my own invisibility.
>
> Storm Jameson, after a PEN dinner[37]

The assumption of all the memoirs and histories of the thirties so far discussed is that 'the writer' means, without question, 'the young bourgeois male writer'. Virginia Woolf's account of the writer's relation to history is as much determined by this assumption as Julian Symons' memoirs or Frank Kermode's recent meditations on the work of Auden and others. Barely one historian discusses women writers, apart from a respectful mention of Laura Riding in Graves and Hodge;[38] and few even acknowledge their existence except as the butts of the young men, or possibly as their reviewers. Richard Johnstone's 1986 study of British novelists of the 1930s omits women altogether.[39] Robin Skelton, whose anthology includes just one woman poet, discusses Edith Sitwell's role as the young men's Aunt Sally; Sitwell also gets some reminiscent mockery from Julian Symons, who admiringly cites Spender's caricature of an unnamed 'Communist lady novelist' (obviously Sylvia Townsend Warner).[40] Samuel Hynes cites five women writers – Bowen, Woolf, Lehmann, Mitchison, Jameson – as reviewers or correspondents of the 'Auden Generation' writers; Bernard Bergonzi cites three middlebrow women novelists, and discusses Greta Garbo at some length. Valentine Cunningham's 1986 anthologies, which do include women writers and journalists, are a welcome exception to this rule of neglect, but his monumental *British Writers of the Thirties* has little to say about women writers except for Elizabeth Bowen.[41] Only John Gindin's elegantly written study of British novelists of the 1930s (1992), which is admiring and perceptive about Bowen and Lehmann, does give significant space to women.

A similar blind spot for women has afflicted almost all those Marxist 'counter-histories' of the thirties which deal with other traditions of left-wing writing than 'mainstream' Audenesque. Out of the 'revisionist' books written or edited by Alick West (1975), Jon Clark et al. (1979) John Lucas (1979), Francis Barker et al. (1978), Frank Glover-Smith (1980), Janet Batsleer et al. (1986), Andy Crofts (1990) and Adrian Caesar (1991), only Batsleer and Crofts pay serious attention to women writers.[42] A woman's place is still, clearly, *not* thought to be in that intersection of public and private life where major literature is constructed.

Meanwhile, feminist scholars and historians of women's writing during this period have not been idle. Rachel Blau DuPlessis's feminist study of modernism (1985) contains brilliant analyses of Woolf and Richardson, and Jane Miller's important study of women's novels (1986) has fine readings of Rhys and Lehmann. Shari Benstock's illuminating account of women writers in Paris (1986), Jane Marcus' account of Virginia Woolf (1987), and Sandra Gilbert's and Susan Gubar's three-volume study *No Man's Land: The Place of the Woman Writer in the Twentieth Century* (1988–1994) should also be mentioned, as should Maroula Joannou's account of inter-war women's writing (1995).[43] But because all of these books concentrate on women's writing primarily for its representation of women's lives and stories, they have relatively little to say about women as historic subjects, and nothing about the political role of women writers between the wars, except in terms of their feminism, which is only indirectly relevant to hunger marches and the Popular Front. Apart from Alison Light's skilful analysis of liberal pacifism in women's writing during the years of 'appeasement' in the late thirties;[44] the only political issues in the women's writing of the 1930s much discussed by feminist literary historians are gender equality and the sexual politics of representation. Of course these are important subjects, but they don't comprise the whole of European history in the early twentieth century. Focusing on them cannot correct the ideological convention that men inhabit the public domain while women represent the home and/or sexuality. This archaic assumption of separate spheres, still deeply rooted in our culture, affects nearly all accounts of the 1930s. It is, for example, subtly present in Samuel Hynes' *The Auden Generation*, whose central opposition between public and private experience 'naturally' effaces women through the implicit but unquestioned assumption that women and their writing are part of the private world.

They therefore cannot be affected by the creative tension between the public world and the private dream which Hynes' book explores.[45]

Yet the achievements of those women writers who responded in their imaginative writing to the historic and political issues of the 1930s are numerous and distinguished. Leaving aside the writers of 'Golden Age' detective stories, the 'middlebrow' women writers surveyed by Nicola Beauman in 1983, and the exemplars of 'conservative modernity' analysed in Alison Light's important 1991 study, and only looking at the left-wing and liberal intellectuals – the same terrain as that mapped by Samuel Hynes and his colleagues – I count at least twenty-three writers: Valentine Ackland, Stella Benson, Elizabeth Bowen, Vera Brittain, Katharine Burdekin, Ivy Compton-Burnett, Nancy Cunard, Margaret Llewellyn Davies, Winifred Holtby, Storm Jameson, Rosamond Lehmann, Marion Milner, Naomi Mitchison, Kathleen Raine, Jean Rhys, Dorothy Richardson, Stevie Smith, Freya Stark, Christina Stead, Sylvia Townsend Warner, Rebecca West, Antonia White, and Virginia Woolf. Few of these names are obscure, thanks mainly to the feminist publishing houses which have reprinted so much mid-century work by women;[46] but they are generally considered to belong to a specialized history of 'women's writing'. One would not know from the standard textbooks on the literature of the 1930s that most of them even existed, let alone wrote.[47]

Why, then, has this galaxy of female talent remained invisible to almost all historians' telescopes? Sexual prejudice is an obvious explanation – and, up to a point, convincing. The historians of the 1930s have been overwhelmingly male; the influential Orwell was an avowed anti-feminist, while Julian Symons, Frank Kermode and Bernard Bergonzi have all appeared distinctly reluctant to acknowledge the achievements of women writers in this period.[48] On the other hand, there is no sign of misogynism in the notably fair-minded Samuel Hynes (who, incidentally, edited an anthology of Rebecca West's writings in 1977: a decision which does not suggest a dislike of feminism). And it is difficult, to say the least, to think of Virginia Woolf as prejudiced against women writers.

Clearly all these accounts of the literature of the thirties subscribe to a consensus about which writers 'counted', which was by 1939 well established in magazines and publishers' lists, principally those of Faber and the Woolfs' own Hogarth Press. Yet between 1930 and 1939, the publishing houses Chatto and Windus, Gollancz, Wishart, Jonathan Cape, Hamish Hamilton, Macmillan and John Murray all published important women writers, while the literary magazines included reviews of women's fiction, poetry, autobiography and documentary writing throughout the 1930s – facts which have somehow passed unnoticed by the literary historians. (Q. D. Leavis' rancorous attacks on upper-class women novelists in *Scrutiny* during the thirties also contributed to a generally dismissive consensus that bourgeois women's contribution to writing in this period could be considered negligible.)[49] The middle-class women writers – and not only they – have been nudged out of view by the unquestioned assumption that the literature of the 1930s belongs only to its young(ish) males, the 'doomed generation', as Francis Scarfe glumly put it, 'raised between wars/Whose boyhood language/Was hunger and loss'.[50]

The claim to represent the consciousness of their generation is central to the work of Spender and Isherwood both in and after the 1930s. It is also explored in complex ways in the poems of Auden up to 1939 – and of course it was constantly made for the 'Auden Group' by Michael Roberts, C. Day Lewis, Louis MacNeice and Cyril Connolly.[51] It is likewise implied in Scarfe's naively gendered identification of a generation's predicament with its 'boyhood' experiences. Underpinning this claim was the unquestioned assumption that history and poetry were male preserves – 'masculine' was a term of strong approval in the Auden Generation's critical vocabulary.[52] The poems and plays of Spender, Auden and Isherwood tend to represent women as projections of a male subject's fears and desires – devouring mothers, dried-up spinsters, vamps, and an occasional pure maiden (see Chapter 3 for a full discussion of these themes). Taking the 'Auden Generation' writers at their own valuation as the universal representatives of a generation, critics and historians have failed to correct this gender bias. Instead, they assign women a few walk-on parts as vamps (Bergonzi on Greta Garbo, Martin Green on Nancy Cunard and Sally Bowles), as silly old bags (Symons on Edith Sitwell and Sylvia Townsend Warner), or, more kindly, as intellectual nannies (Hynes on Elizabeth Bowen, Naomi Mitchison and Virginia Woolf nurturing the Young Hopefuls in the literary reviews).

Another reason for the exclusion of women from the histories is that very few of them fit the standard assumptions about writers' ages. Samuel Hynes defined his 'Auden Generation' as 'the men and women' (in practice, only the men) 'born in England between 1900 and the First World War, who came of age in the 'twenties and lived through their early maturity during the Depression'. The age criterion for Skelton's Penguin anthology *Poetry of the Thirties* was even tighter: a 'thirties poet' had to be born between 1904 and 1914. This identification of the literature of the thirties with one generation of ex-public schoolboys automatically effaces almost all women writers from the record. Similar assumptions also delete all working-class writers from the literary canon; Samuel Hynes, for example, states inaccurately that 'virtually no writing of literary importance came out of the working class in this decade'. I am sorry to say that this exclusion of working-class writers from the canon was emphatically endorsed, well before Hynes, by Virginia Woolf in 'The Leaning Tower', which states categorically, 'Take away all that the working class has contributed to English literature and that literature would scarcely suffer, take away all that the educated class has given and English literature would scarcely exist' (p. 168).[53] And other important writers are ignored on grounds of age: Wyndham Lewis, Edgell Rickword, David Jones, Herbert Read and Hugh MacDiarmid, who all published important work in the 1930s, are almost invariably considered too old to count as 'writers of the thirties'. Of the twenty-three women writers whom I named above, only four meet Hynes' criterion of being born in England after 1900 – Valentine Ackland, Rosamond Lehmann, Kathleen Raine and Stevie Smith – all relatively unpolitical writers except for Ackland, the least talented.

Apart from the Australian Christina Stead (1902–1983), the important left-wing women writers of the 1930s resembled the males in mostly coming from the English upper middle class, sharing its literary culture, and being educated either at home or at cheaper versions of the same sort of school (only a few went on to college). The obvious difference, apart from gender, is their age; almost all were at least ten years older than the young men of the 'Auden Generation' – a difference addressed in Naomi Mitchison's slightly embarrassing poem 'To Some Young Communists from an Old Socialist'.[54] Elizabeth Bowen (b. 1899), Vera Brittain (b. 1893), Katharine Burdekin (b. 1892), Nancy Cunard (b. 1896), Winifred Holtby (b. 1898), Storm Jameson (b. 1891), Naomi Mitchison (b. 1897), Sylvia Townsend Warner (b. 1893) and Rebecca West (b. 1892) were all born *before* 1900, came of age during the First World War, and for the most part established themselves as writers during the 1920s. Their educational experiences fall into four patterns:

- Educated at home: Stella Benson, Nancy Cunard, Margaret Llewellyn Davies, Naomi Mitchison (after puberty), Sylvia Townsend Warner, Virginia Woolf. All these are either of the '1890s' generation or older. Total: 6
- Educated at school: Valentine Ackland, Queen's College, Harley Street; Elizabeth Bowen, Downe House; Katharine Burdekin, Cheltenham Ladies' College; Naomi Mitchison, Dragon Preparatory School, Oxford (until puberty); Jean Rhys, Perse School for Girls,

Cambridge; Dorothy Richardson, Southborough House, Putney; Stevie Smith, North London Collegiate School for Girls; Rebecca West, George Watson's School, Edinburgh; Antonia White, Convent of the Sacred Heart, Roehampton. Total: 9

- Educated at school and college: Vera Brittain, St Monica's School and Somerville College, Oxford (History); Winifred Holtby, Queen Margaret School, Scarborough and Somerville College, Oxford (History); Storm Jameson, Whitby High School for Girls, Leeds University (English) and King's College, London (MA thesis on contemporary drama); Marion Milner, Guildford High School, Gypsy Hill Montessori Training College and University College, London (Physiology and Psychology); Kathleen Raine, Ilford High School for Girls and Girton College, Cambridge (Botany); and Christina Stead, Sydney Girls' High School and teacher training college (University of Sydney). Total: 6

- Educated at home and university: Ivy Compton-Burnett, educated privately and at Royal Holloway College, London (Classics); Freya Stark, educated privately and at Bedford College, London University, and the School of Oriental and Asian Studies, London University; Rosamond Lehmann, educated privately and at Girton College, Cambridge (English). Total: 3

Both the small number of college-educated women on this list (barely more than a third), and the fact that few of the 'privately educated' names went on to college, confirm Virginia Woolf's contention that the 'daughters of educated men' were denied the educational privileges which their brothers took for granted.[55] This pattern is, interestingly, not repeated in the USA, where the middle-class women writers born between 1880 and 1910, including the major modernist writers Gertrude Stein, Marianne Moore, H.D. and Laura Riding, were all educated at famous colleges.[56]

But the English record shows privilege as well as dispossession. Nancy Cunard, Naomi Mitchison, Sylvia Townsend Warner and Virginia Woolf, all privately educated in highly cultivated upper-class homes, were very well-read; Warner and Woolf were probably better educated than most Oxbridge graduates. It is also clear from this list that middle-class girls had by 1900 begun to benefit from the efforts of Victorian pioneers in women's education. The institutions which educated this generation – usually boarding schools for the rich and provincial high schools belonging to the Girls' Public Day School Trust for their less well-off contemporaries – were solidly academic institutions; anyone who attended them got a share, if usually a cheap one, of educational privilege. The high schools educated Storm Jameson and Kathleen Raine well enough to enable them to finance their undergraduate educations by winning publicly funded scholarships.

But though these women writers did in important ways share the class, culture and education of the slightly younger men of the 'Auden Generation', their lives were obviously very different, especially in the ways in which most of them lived through the Great War. The differences in experience between a young woman coming of age during the war and a schoolboy too young to fight are visible when one compares the inter-war writings of Jameson, Brittain, Holtby, Warner and West with the canonical male writers (see pp. 44–58 for a full discussion of this theme). Nor do the literary-political trajectories of the women writers born in the 1890s generally correspond to the standard notion of thirties writers – 'starry-eyed do-gooders', as Claud Cockburn sardonically put it, 'with pink illusions which, when darkness came at noon, blew up in their faces and turned them a neutral grey or else deep blue'.[57] Christina Stead and Sylvia Townsend Warner stayed in the Communist Party until the 1950s, and even after they drifted out, they did not repudiate their left-wing convictions, which continued to inform their writings. Nancy Cunard, who translated for the Free French and edited *Poems for France* (1944), lived and died a left-wing rebel; Vera Brittain was a lifelong pacifist. Storm Jameson, who did become a firm anti-Communist after the war, was also a lifelong Socialist and Labour supporter, as is Naomi Mitchison. Only Rebecca West, whose left liberalism hardened after the war into passionate anti-Communism, and Kathleen Raine, never much of a radical, who became a strong cultural conservative, come close to fitting the usual pattern. This failure to conform to political type may well have affected their reputations; Sylvia Townsend Warner certainly thought it had damaged hers.[58]

MEMORIALS OF THEIR TIME

Literary history is not, of course, made only by literary historians. The rhetoric of memory that dominates the available histories of the 1930s also works more simply through a multitude of memoirs and reminiscences of the decade, the best known of which are probably the memoirs of Stephen Spender, followed closely by Christopher Isherwood. The latter's friend Edward Upward, often omitted from discussions of the 'Auden Generation' because of his comparatively small output (and probably also because of his untypical years of dedicated Communism) uses his own life as subject matter, much as Isherwood himself did.

All these writers are, as Virginia Woolf pointed out, almost obsessionally autobiographical. Their work looked backwards from the start, and has constantly returned to the thirties ever since the decade ended. Spender began with autobiographical poems, fictionalized his childhood in *The Backward Son* (1940), turned his short memoir of the thirties into the full-length autobiography *World Within World* (1951), wrote further essay-reminiscences in *The Thirties and After* (1978) and in 1990 published a revised version of *The Temple*, an early fictionalized memoir of his experience in Weimar Germany. Isherwood, whose novels up to the 1950s are all strongly autobiographical, returned to his youth in the 1970s with two memoirs about his family and his own homosexuality, subjects which his early writings avoid. Edward Upward, whose theme throughout his writing career has been his own struggle to integrate his dual commitments to political activism and to a fantastic dream-life, constantly returns to the 'moment' of the thirties which dominates his long autobiographical novel *The Spiral Ascent* (1977). Louis MacNeice shared this autobiographical tendency, producing a travel-book-cum-memoir *I Crossed the Minch* (1938) and a classic long personal/political poem *Autumn Journal* (1939) as well as a post-war autobiography (1965); C. Day Lewis also wrote a memoir, *The Buried Day* (1960). Auden, the only great poet of his generation, is the sole exception to this autobiographical norm. He never wrote a full-length memoir, only mentioning his past in reviews and asides, nor did he use his experiences in the thirties as the basis of his later work. He dealt with his fellow-travelling past not by writing revisionist memoirs but by repudiating it. Though he did allow five *marxisant* poems to be reprinted in the Penguin anthology of 1930s poetry, he insisted that the editor make it 'absolutely clear that "Mr Auden considers these five poems to be trash which he is ashamed to have written" '. He edited all his early left-wing poems out of the later collections of his poetry.[59]

The less reticent Stephen Spender ended by being better known for his memoirs of the 1930s than for his poetry. The first of these is the account of his pre-war flirtation with Communism in *The God That Failed* (1950), in which Spender represents himself as a typical liberal fellow-traveller, encountering equally typical (not to say stereotyped) Communist personalities. He is interested principally in psychology: why was he attracted to Socialism, but not enough to become a Communist? What moves others, less tender-hearted than himself, who do become Communists? Thus, a verbal exchange with 'Chalmers' (Edward Upward)[60] about the 1937 Moscow show trials becomes the peg for an analysis of the self-deceiving

Communist 'mind-set' which 'Chalmers' is made to represent, untouched by 'pity for the victims of revolution' and hypocritically writing off reports of prison camps in Russia as 'bourgeois propaganda' (pp. 238–239). He finds equally typical Communist hypocrisy and mindlessness at the 1937 Writers' Conference in Madrid, in 'a lady novelist' (Sylvia Townsend Warner) who reproves him for criticizing Russia, and in the 'intellectually torpid' Russian delegates like Mikhail Koltzov who 'never said anything in public or in private which could stimulate discussion amongst the other delegates. They had no views of their own' (p. 252). (Probably Spender irritated these people and consequently saw the worst of them, for other contemporaries remember them very differently. He certainly annoyed Sylvia Townsend Warner, who privately called him 'an irritating idealist, always hatching a wounded feeling'; qualities which would not have endeared him to Mikhail Koltzov, who, according to his friend Claud Cockburn, 'had an attitude of entire ruthlessness towards people he thought incompetent or just plain pompous'.)[61]

These incidents and character sketches all reappeared with elaborations in Spender's autobiography *World Within World*, plus much interesting material about Spender's boyhood, his friendships with Auden and Isherwood, his life in Weimar Germany and his relationships with other men and women, including the ex-guardsman 'Jimmy Younger' and his first wife, Inez. Even more than in most autobiographies, the writer's self here is the be-all and end-all, an effect which is enhanced rather than modified by Spender's constant awareness of European history and his richly varied social life. It is tempting to mock the apparently naive narcissism of statements like 'I submitted my own personality to the same searching analysis as I applied to the official Socialists' (p. 240), yet Spender's fascination with his own motives is clearly political as much as personal. It belongs to the ex-Communist or fellow-traveller in the early Cold War explaining, justifying or apologizing for his own past, so that the implicit question structuring his memoirs is 'How could I – or others – have supported any institutions so wicked and ruthless as the Moscow-based Communist Party?' Certainly, this is a valid and legitimate question. But answering it satisfactorily also means raising, as Spender does not, the question, 'What could I – and others – have done to resist Fascism?' His disinclination to confront the significance of Hitler weakens his account of the 1930s compared with the more 'public-minded' memoirs of Storm Jameson and Claud Cockburn discussed at the end of this chapter (pp. 32–42).

Christopher Isherwood, an equally autobiographical writer, published two late books of memoirs as companions to the reticent *Lions and Shadows*.

Kathleen and Frank remedies the omission of Isherwood's family, particularly his mother, from the earlier book. Its basis is his mother's diaries, interlaced with so much editorial comment and personal retrospect that the book amounts to a memoir of the writer's boyhood and schooldays. It explores the origin of the personal mythologies which haunt Isherwood's early fictions: the stubborn maternal conservatism against which the son must rebel in order to define himself, and the corresponding dream of the absent father as a Truly Strong Man, brave and self-confident enough to repudiate heroics.[62] *Christopher and his Kind* begins even more emphatically where *Lions and Shadows* left off by dealing on its first page with Isherwood's homosexuality; that is, both his own sex life and his place in English homosexual literary culture. The latter includes not only his relations with Spender and Auden, the latter his sex partner as well as his friend (p. 197), but also his friendships with John Lehmann, E. M. Forster, William Plomer and J. R. Ackerley. The book certainly is very open and uncensored compared with Isherwood's early works; but it would be naive to accept without question its claim to tell the whole truth. What it does describe, with great skill, is the past as Isherwood wanted it known in 1977, when he wrote the book.

As in *Lions and Shadows*, Isherwood treats his younger self with an ironic detachment which looks deceptively like objectivity; the late memoirs build this distancing irony into their narrative structures, by representing the young self as a not very admirable character called 'Christopher', not to be confused with the mature 'I' who writes the memoir. In both books, the irony directed at the younger self implies the politically enlightened maturity of a present-day 'writing self'; the change is in the politics, not the attitude. *Lions and Shadows* takes a scornful tone about the apolitical escapism of Isherwood's student days; *Christopher and his Kind*, endorsing gay politics, likewise criticizes the Popular Front liberalism of young 'Christopher' for insincerity. Just as he mocked his own juvenilia in the earlier book, so Isherwood pours cold water on the leftism of his celebrated sketch, 'The Nowaks' (still generally considered a thirties classic), attacking its narrator 'Christopher' for playing to the Socialist gallery, and explaining candidly that he only went slumming for sex with Otto Nowak (p. 45).

Candour, in fact, is the constant theme of *Christopher and his Kind*. Isherwood appears candid, not just about his sexuality and his devious or manipulative dealings with his boyfriends, but about the friends whom he transformed into characters in his fiction. The most important of these are Wilfrid Israel and Jean Ross, the originals of 'Bernhard Landauer' and 'Sally Bowles', who were both far more vigorous and purposive than their portraits in *Goodbye to Berlin* (1939) suggest. Jean Ross, who was actually a tough, emancipated, politically dedicated woman and a lifelong Communist, was a complete contrast to the 'Sally Bowles' in the book and its stage and film adaptations. Isherwood ruefully compares the real woman, grown old like himself, to 'a reproachful elder sister' (p. 51) standing beside the endearingly unsuccessful tart whom later actresses have transformed into a charming air-head. Sarah Cockburn, the daughter of Jean Ross, has cogently argued that Isherwood's distortion of his original is caused by his tendency as a 'realist' writer to represent people in easily recognizable and therefore conventional terms:

> To be 'lifelike' it is neither necessary nor sufficient for a work of fiction to be literally true to life; what is essential is that it should accord with the reader's expectations of life – expectations based not only on experience but on the conventions of existing literature . . . Convention does not permit an attractive young woman to have much in the way of intellectual accomplishments, and Isherwood follows it loyally.[63]

Convention, though of a different kind, also affected Isherwood's representation of his friend Wilfrid Israel, portrayed as the over-civilized Bernhard Landauer of *Goodbye to Berlin* who is murdered by Brown Shirts at the end of the book. As the later Isherwood acknowledges, Israel was actually a courageous and effective opponent of the Nazis, who died in 1943 on a mission to help Jews emigrating from Europe (pp. 57–60). Isherwood ascribes the unfairness of his own portrait to the prejudice felt by the young 'Christopher' against the 'Oriental' aspect of Bernhard/ Israel, who is described in *Goodbye to Berlin* as 'clothed in . . . the arrogant humility of the East'. Bernhard thus subliminally represented to 'Christopher' the disturbing challenge of the 'Oriental' Hinduism to which the writer would eventually convert; hence the young Isherwood's defensive hostility (p. 58).

But a less convoluted explanation for these distortions appears to lie, as with 'Sally Bowles', in the determining power of stereotype; though here the characterization conforms to racial rather than sexual convention. Since Bernhard's passivity virtually amounts to a death wish, he corresponds to the conventional image of the Jew as passive victim. Similar distortions occur, very interestingly, in Rebecca West's compassionate portrait (which I discuss at length in Chapter 6) of the Serbian Jew 'Constantine' (Stanislaus Vinaver) in *Black Lamb and Grey Falcon* (1942), who is represented as collapsing psychologically under the intolerable political and emotional pressures of *Mitteleuropa* in the late thirties: a plight described sympathetically as 'dying of being a Jew' in a hostile world. In life, however, Vinaver opposed his enemies vigorously enough to end up as a prisoner of war in Germany.[64] These distortions certainly do not result from anti-Semitism, which was detested by both Isherwood and West. The reason why these writers turned people who in life proved tough and courageous into self-destructively neurotic characters lies rather in their own liberal sympathies. The death wish of 'Bernhard Landauer' and the breakdown of 'Constantine' both signify the imminent doom of European Jewry.

Edward Upward, Isherwood's friend and literary mentor, is a less charming writer who has tried to be more honest. The theme of all his published fiction, apart from the early story 'The Railway Accident', is the struggle undertaken by a central character, easily identifiable with the author, to establish a satisfactory relationship between his often dangerously attractive imaginative life and a necessary but less alluring life of political action. The surreal world 'Mortmere', which the young Upward and Isherwood created as Cambridge undergraduates, conflates fantasy with actuality: the bizarre extravagances of Mortmere characters' behaviour are always contradicted by the heartily middle-class 'normality' of their speech. But because the fantastic element in 'Mortmere' was overwhelmingly strong, Upward found that he could not use it to satirize the bourgeoisie whom he hated: 'I needed to believe (in order to write) that imaginative writing could tell its readers something about the external world and that the telling could indirectly influence them to take action in the external world'.[65] He therefore came to reject this fantasy world completely; although he did permit the post-war publication of the 'Mortmere' story 'The Railway Accident' (1966), he prefaced it with an expression of strong authorial disapproval, much as Auden allowed his early work to be reprinted while describing it as 'trash'.[66] And although the last part of his trilogy *The Spiral Ascent* covers much of the same ground as *Lions and Shadows*, describing the same undergraduate experiences, such as the collaborative friendship with Isherwood ('Richard Marple'), their experiments with fantasy and obscenity and even one or two of the same anecdotes,[67] 'Mortmere' does not feature in its narrative. The old Upward had nothing to say about it.

But to reject fantasy is not necessarily to exorcize its temptations, and the lure of a dream world remained a constant theme in all Upward's subsequent work, including his retrospects of the thirties. His first novel, *Journey to the Border* (discussed in more detail in Chapter 2), tells the story of a young proletarianized intellectual called 'the tutor' who takes refuge from his oppressive conditions in fantastic reveries which become increasingly uncontrollable until, almost at the point of suicide, his consciousness of reality saves him in the form of a 'voice of reason' which tells him to abandon visions, face reality and change the oppressive world by joining the workers' movement. To the tutor's plea to keep his imaginative life, reason responds that of course he will continue to feel, think and create, though in different terms: reborn out of action, his creations will be 'more normally human... more concerned with the world outside you than with yourself'.[68] Yet the book circles ironically back on itself: the obviously autobiographical 'tutor' obeys Marxist reason, rejects fantasy, chooses action and realism – and, after six dedicated years in the Communist Party, produces a grotesque, introspective novel about the temptations of fantasy.

The Spiral Ascent begins where the 1938 novel left off. The first part, *In the Thirties* (published 1962), is on one level a straightforward realist treatment of the life of Alan Sebrill, a rank-and-file Communist who is pulled between his conflicting allegiances to the 'poetic life' of his consciousness and to the 'political life' which represents his experience as a historical subject. Alan becomes a committed Marxist after a personal crisis resulting, like that of the 'tutor', from his failure to live exclusively from his own imaginative resources. Joining the Communist Party and accepting its discipline, Alan Sebrill engages in all the activities which a revolutionary socialist would normally perform: canvassing elections, attending branch meetings and joining in discussions, marching on a political demonstration (not identified, but probably one of the Hunger Marches), turning up with comrades to protest at a Fascist rally, arguing politics with colleagues at work, trying to enlist their support for left-wing causes, and finally recruiting a member. Rejecting the destructive romanticism of his earlier affairs, he courts and marries – mainly, it seems, out of a sense of duty, and despite many snobbish qualms – Elsie, a schoolteacher with working-class origins. Although few courtships in fiction are less romantic than theirs, the following book, *The Rotten Elements* (published 1969), affectionately celebrates their deeply happy marriage. Alan continues to hanker after the 'poetic life' of creative excitement; but the 'new thinking and new feeling' promised in *Journey to the Border* do materialize in his anxious, self-aware sensitive observations of the scenes he witnesses. Thus, when marching in a big demonstration,

> The thought of his slavery caused him, just when his part of procession was passing a traffic island on which...a sad-faced old man [was] standing, to shout with passionate intensity 'Down with the Means Test'. The old man, though startled, remained sad. But from the four behind Alan heard a jeering laugh. It was Elsie's, and she seemed to be

jeering at him. He recognized immediately that he deserved something worse than to be jeered at . . . True, he had felt a genuine indignation when he shouted, but the political struggle required not that he should express his feeling, however noble, but that he should help to get a message across to the masses. Propaganda was a serious art and had to be learnt.[69]

Alan, constantly alert to what people think of him, reacts with shame partly because Elsie is a comrade whom he respects, and will eventually marry. His political awareness thus works directly through the way he perceives his relationships with other people, even so tenuous a relationship as that between a demonstrator and an uninterested bystander: a combination of vulnerability and sharp intelligence which makes him an effective register of the events he witnesses. At the same time, the ordinariness of his circumstances and his relative failure make him a type of the many people who can never become what they should in a capitalist society.

For, as Alan's passionate shout betrays, he still desires a different life – above all, the world of the imagination which he has abandoned for politics. Its loss is actually felt less during the thirties – when political activity is urgent and its nature clear – than in the post-war world of *The Rotten Elements*, when Alan is torn between writing about his lost 'poetic life', which, as he thinks, means selfish nostalgia, and praising the 'political life' of a Communist Party which has become increasingly misdirected and sterile. The result of this conflict is a massive writer's block and, after Alan's resignation from the Party, a breakdown about which he successfully writes a prose-poem. Having implicitly admitted that his real subject must be himself, he continues to explore his own past in the last part of the trilogy, *No Home but the Struggle*. Told in the first person, this returns to Alan's childhood and youth, and retells the personal crisis that made him commit himself to Communism, thus ending up where the trilogy started; but as the book ends, he completes the poem he has been struggling with from the start. The end of the book, highly praised by Frank Kermode, thus at last synthesizes poetry and Communism.[70]

NEGLECTED CLASSICS: STORM JAMESON AND CLAUD COCKBURN

The first time I travelled on the Orient Express I was accosted by a woman who was later arrested and turned out to be a quite well-known international spy. When I talked with Al Capone, there was a sub-machine gun poking through the transom of the door behind him . . . The first Minister of Government I met

told me a most horrible lie almost immediately.
 These things were delightful . . .

Claud Cockburn

The impulse that turned so many of us into pamphleteers and amateur politicians was neither mean nor trivial. The evil we were told off to fight was really evil, the threat to human decency a real threat.

Storm Jameson[71]

Storm Jameson and Claud Cockburn, distinguished writers of the 1930s, both produced classic narratives of that decade during their rather less well-known old age. These autobiographies, Storm Jameson's two-volume *Journey from the North* (1969, 1970) and Claud Cockburn's memoir *I, Claud* (1967)[72] are neglected masterpieces of thirties memory. They are not, of course, the only such forgotten classics. An obvious rival is T. C. Worsley's admirable memoir *Flannelled Fool* (1967) which, like a warmer, more open version of *Lions and Shadows*, relates the author's intellectual and emotional development from repressed adolescent to self-aware adult. Worsley writes about his own homosexuality and his family's sometimes grotesque history with remarkable candour, elegance and generosity. These qualities are the more impressive in that his family skeletons included an inadequate (to say the least) father who, after a long series of hushed-up sexual scandals, resigned his deanery rather than be unfrocked for adultery, and the death of a younger brother in a drowning accident in which the boy Worsley himself was involved; a horror which Worsley narrates with controlled self-knowledge. Also of great interest are the belated memoirs of the marginalized and powerless in the thirties, such as Ralph Glasser's journey from miserable poverty in the Glasgow Gorbals to Oxford and academic distinction, related in two subtly written memoirs. His intellectual sophistication contrasts sharply with the lively but unliterary narratives of intelligent women who did not get university scholarships, such as Kathleen Dayus, whose memoirs describe poverty followed by modest prosperity in Birmingham, Helen Forrester who wrote of her deprived childhood and adolescence in Liverpool in the late thirties or, on the cusp of the decade, Hilda Hollingsworth, who recently published *They Tied a Label to my Coat* (1991), the harrowing story of her experiences as an evacuee child in South Wales. All these memoirs of working-class childhoods in the 1930s were published long after the decade ended, just as the memoirs of working-class women, published in 1932, evoke remote Victorian childhoods.[73] It is almost as if, forty and fifty years after J. B. Priestley recorded the poverty and misery of Liverpool and Birmingham and Edwin Muir did the same thing for Glasgow,[74] a few of the children glimpsed in the slums by these compassionate observers at last, in old age, arrived to tell their own stories. But only 'almost': for of course these apparently naive texts are as much constructed by hindsight as Isherwood's self-conscious palimpsest of his old selves; the point is simply that working-class women appear to get their say very late, if ever.[75]

My reason for concentrating on Cockburn and Jameson rather than surveying these other autobiographies, important and neglected though they are, is that because these two writers were public activists, their memoirs are political in a way that the others I have named are not. Margaret Storm Jameson, whose reputation as a novelist was at its height during the 1930s and 1940s, put her energies as much into public activism as into her strongly polemical fiction. As chairman of the English PEN from 1938 to 1945, she worked indefatigably to help refugees from Hitler's Europe[76] – a task which meant much speaking at public meetings and joining committees, as well as paperwork. The Communist journalist Claud Cockburn, owner and editor of the 'insider' newsletter *The Week*, was also the diplomatic correspondent of the *Daily Worker* under the pseudonym Frank Pitcairn. These two very different writers, though certainly far from controlling historical events, did exercise some influence on how English readers perceived them, and consequently helped to shape public responses to political issues. When they discuss their own public roles, they do not ask, like Spender and Koestler, 'How could I/we have been so deceived?' but 'What effect did I/we have?'. Like Kipling's characters, they also ask the harder question 'What else could I have done?'[77]

Their memoirs, however, are very different indeed, as the quotations above indicate. Cockburn, a political commentator and master of anecdote, alternates comedy or black farce with political or historic meditations, saying very little indeed about his personal life. Like other good memoirists of the 1930s, he mostly condenses the political divisions of that decade into lively scenes and character sketches, but because he always thought in terms of political and personal relationships, he hardly ever represents people as character types. Usually he sees them as part of a network of friendships, alliances and enmities. An excellent instance of his 'networked' characterization is the bravura account of his friend Otto Katz the Comintern agent, 'that most talented propagandist and intriguer'.[78] Katz first appears at an anti-war congress in 1932 (pp. 186–90):

After the closing session, I found myself at midnight sweating horribly in an hotel bedroom where Mr John Strachey, Mr Gerald Hamilton, a vigorous Hungarian woman and myself were translating the official

German text of the congress into English which must be, all agreed, as jolly popular in style as the *Daily Mirror* and as rigidly exact as the Athanasian Creed. Just how I got into the act I cannot remember, and it certainly was exhausting.

The Hungarian woman knew German so much better than the rest of us that she concluded she must know English better, too, and made this clear. Mr Hamilton, whose natural prose style was Edwardian, became so discouraged that he took off his wig and sat silently nursing it on his knee, his head gleaming like a new-laid egg...

Every so often, a grave smile and a light sigh floated in from the corridor, both brought to us by a smallish, light-footed man with a big head and abnormally broad shoulders hunched in a way to suggest that his burdens were indeed heavy, but he could bear them, and yours too, if you cared to confide them. His smile said that whatever might be the faults of others working for peace that night, our little group was the salt of the earth – so brilliant and devoted that we should certainly produce splendid results, dead on time, if it killed us. He had the air of a stage manager going round the dressing-room of a troupe on the verge of hysteria.

When I asked who he was, they said, 'You don't know who Otto Katz is? Oh!'

The point of this scene, told in Cockburn's characteristic mix of leisurely mandarin rhetoric and sharply pointed slang, is that Otto Katz cannot be understood on his own. To explain the man, Cockburn has to describe a disputatious committee which includes the well-known Marxist theorist John Strachey and the notorious conman Gerald Hamilton, the original of Isherwood's 'Mr Norris'.[79] He goes on to describe Katz as an energetic and effective organizer of anti-Fascist propaganda – 'Almost weekly he brought off the tricky shot of planting a damaging anti-Fascist story in a pro-Fascist newspaper' (p. 191) and as a Popular Front diplomat whose pleasure was to construct alliances between people who naturally distrusted each other (p. 192):

He was as happy welding mutually hateful novelists and poets into a literary League for the defence of this or that, as he was when arranging a couple of Tory Lords and someone from Transport House to turn up on a platform with the editor of *L'Humanité*. The more improbable the *combinaison*, the more it charmed him. Indeed, after the visit to the United States, the Catholic Prince Loewenstein told me that, though prepared for anything, he had, after all, been startled when he saw Herr Simone-Katz 'genuflect three times and kiss the ring of a Spanish

Cardinal to whom he then presented a Marxist professor just out of jail in Rio de Janeiro.'

Again, these details emphasize that Otto Katz cannot be understood outside of the context of the political tensions of the 1930s – to which his own propagandist work of course contributed.

Cockburn writes of Katz that 'he regarded journalism simply as a means to an end, a weapon. In this I found him sympathetic' (p. 192). Here as everywhere, Cockburn takes it for granted that all governments and political movements, including those he supports, routinely lie, cheat and quite possibly murder to achieve their political aims. He consequently insists that all journalism, including his own, is moved or controlled by political interests. He denounces the creed of journalistic objectivity' as at best 'dangerously naive' and at worst hypocritical (pp. 146–7), and describes with evident pleasure how he successfully faked a story of an anti-Franco revolt in Tetuan, an action which he defends as legitimate war propaganda. He regarded with acerbic contempt newspapers' claims to be 'neutral, impartial fact-purveyors, "servants", so help me, "of the public" ' (pp. 192–5).

It is not surprising, given these views, that Claud Cockburn has been written off as a cynic. But it is wrong to dismiss his journalism, as Julian Symons did, as simply lies and propaganda[80] – and not just because Cockburn's Stalinist cynicism about political means was always combined with idealism about utopian or simply humane ends. He attacked the 'myth' of journalistic objectivity on the grounds that it was untrue and produced ineffective writing. Newspaper stories, he said, 'are supposed to begin with the facts and develop from there, but in reality they begin with a journalist's point of view, a conception ... from which the facts are subsequently organized' (pp. 146–147). And he had reason to describe editorial objectivity as a myth: during the years of appeasement, it was. The historian Richard Cockett has shown that, throughout the 1930s, the Press Lobby and the Foreign Office deliberately and very successfully controlled what was said by the BBC and the Press, whose owners, directors and editors submitted themselves with barely a struggle to voluntary self-censorship. During the years of appeasement, the British news media were, almost without exception, willing servants of Chamberlain's government.[81] At a time when the newspapers were 'mere ciphers for Chamberlain's policies, whilst camouflaging their partisanship in the guise of a democratic free press',[82] what made the piratical Claud Cockburn important was his achievement in making public, against the odds, some inconvenient truths. This he did mainly through his

independent newsletter, *The Week* (1933–1945), which published those
stories – and rumours – which did not get into the main newspapers
owned by financial magnates with political interests and controlled by the
Press Lobby. 'I . . . was struck by the fact that what informed people were
saying – and, equally importantly, the tone of voice in which they were
saying it – were scarcely reflected in the newspapers' (pp. 131–2).

Cockburn does not define what he means by the 'tone' in which
informed people talked; but it is, I think, well conveyed by the mocking
exchanges recorded by Storm Jameson between journalists and diplomats, one of which is quoted below (see p. 40). For although Claud
Cockburn was sole editor and owner of *The Week*, it was not a solitary
enterprise. Many of his stories came from an informal weekly discussion
group held by leading correspondents in London, as well as from people
anxious to publicize information 'for motives sometimes noble and quite
often vile' (pp. 148–9); his informants also included the Vansittart faction
at the Foreign Office, who according to Cockett used *The Week* to
'sabotage and discredit' appeasers.[83] Cockburn wrote with pride (p.
141) that his newsletter became

> one of the half-dozen British publications most often quoted in the
> entire world . . . Blum read it and Goebbels read it and a mysterious
> warlord in China read it. Senator Borah quoted it repeatedly in the
> American Senate and Herr von Ribbentrop, Hitler's ambassador in
> London, on two separate occasions demanded its suppression on the
> ground that it was the source of all anti-Nazi evil.

The Week thus partially succeeded in breaking the self-imposed censorship
of the British Press, while managing to exert some influence on the
international scene.

As Cockburn's allusion to Ribbentrop indicates, *The Week* at times
made an appreciable difference to British politics. Its best-known political
achievement was to break the story of the 'Cliveden Set' – 'those powerful
personalities in England who saw Hitler as a bulwark against Bolshevism
and . . . thought friendship with the Nazis both possible and desirable' (p.
178). Cockburn says that he ran the story twice without result until he
thought of naming the villains the 'Cliveden Set', a phrase which sparked
off an explosion of public anger (pp. 179–80):

> Up and down the British Isles, across and across the United States,
> anti-Nazi orators shouted it from hundreds of platforms. No anti-
> Fascist rally in Madison Square Gardens or Trafalgar Square was
> complete without a denunciation of the Cliveden Set . . . Within a year

or so, the Cliveden Set had...acquired a powerful and alarming significance in the minds of people who could hardly have named three of those who frequented Cliveden. The phrase went marching on because it first had dramatized, and now summarized, a whole vague body of suspicions and fears.

The narrative voice of Claud Cockburn, entertaining, talkative and yet reticent, differs as much from Storm Jameson's harsh candour as his sceptical Communist outlook does from her Northern Protestant liberalism. Jameson's text subjects the author's own choices and actions to the same unsparing gaze which it directs at twentieth-century history. In this, it resembles the autobiography of another rebellious North Country Protestant daughter of the same generation – Lucy Boston (1892–1990), author of the 'Green Knowe' books for children who was, like her, the divorced mother of one son. Her memoirs, though narrower in range than Storm Jameson's, similarly articulate a fiercely defended integrity in singularly limpid, unsparing prose.[84] The early part of Storm Jameson's life also bears a striking resemblance to that of the young Rebecca West, whom she seems to have regarded resentfully as an unfairly successful rival.[85] Young, ambitious and brilliant, each woman was 'biologically trapped' (p. 88) at the outset of her writing career, first by pregnancy and then by the responsibility of supporting a small son with little or no help from his father; each was helped out by her family, and after two or three years left the child at school or with relatives in order to make her own career in London. A crucial difference is, of course, that Storm Jameson, unlike Rebecca West, was respectably married – but to such a useless absentee husband that she might almost as well have been single. And she was later divorced for adultery, which was in the 1920s nearly as disreputable as bearing an illegitimate child.

Storm Jameson does also, however, have points in common with her juniors Spender and Isherwood. Like them, she wrote and rewrote her own life in fiction and memoir. The first quarter of *Journey to the North* describes her marriage to an unsupportive husband and her subsequent experience of maternity, salaried work, divorce and remarriage; she had already used this material between 1930 and 1936 in a novel about the War years, an autobiography, and the *Mirror in Darkness* trilogy, discussed in Chapter 2.[86] Similarly, her vivid, bitter reminiscences of Prague and Budapest in 1938 (pp. 367–415) describe the same incidents and characters as her *Europe to Let* (1940), a 'novel' constructed from three or four thematically linked stories of European politics, told by an anonymous observing English 'I', much like *Goodbye to Berlin* though without its linking diaries. Her autobiographical accounts of the doomed moment of liberal exhilaration in Prague in June 1938, and the ominous Budapest visit just afterwards, repeat scenes in the 1940 book with very little changed except for the names.[87] Storm Jameson simply ignores these earlier texts, as if they were draft material like their source; that is, the diary she kept each night from 1930 onwards, recording any memorable conversations she had heard during the day: 'Over twenty years or so I recorded many thousands of spoken words. I shall destroy the lot when I have finished this book. (Destroyed on the 26th of March, 1965)' (p. 291).

This rough treatment of her own earlier work indicates Storm Jameson's ambivalence about her vocation as a writer. Certainly, *Journey to the North* is on one level an artist's autobiography, describing how the writer gradually realized her own powers and transformed herself from an undisciplined storyteller into a controlled artist. But this theme is qualified and obscured by her harsh contempt for her own overproductive career: 'What an ape! What a fool!' (vol. 2, p. 371). It is also undermined by her contradictory attitude to the art of the realist novel to which she dedicated her talents. She expresses reverence for the masters of the form such as Tolstoy, Stendhal and Proust; she also confesses to a 'deep unrealized contempt for novel-writing as a serious use for energy and intellect' (vol. 1, p. 116). In any case, the subject of *Journey from the North* is only partly Storm Jameson's own story as a writer and a woman. Its focus is at least as much on European history as on her personal life, although this was deeply scarred by living through two world wars. Her younger brother was killed in action in 1916; she lost a much-loved sister in a 1943 air raid, and both her marriages were badly affected by the Great War. (Her first husband left her and their baby son in 1915 to be an army instructor, after which he never again took any permanent responsibility for his family – while Guy Chapman, whom she married in 1926, felt that the rest of his life was a postscript to his experiences as an army officer.)

Unlike Spender and Koestler, Storm Jameson did not repent of her left-wing activism during the 1930s: 'I could not have held aloof. No regrets' (p. 344). She was not naive about the causes she joined: 'The fingers of the puppet-masters and the strings jerking us were perfectly visible. I knew I was being used' (p. 292). But in the last analysis, what matters is achievement, not motive (p. 344):

> I refuse to regret the energy spent writing polemics against war and fascism. Still less the energy given to helping a few, too few, men and women to escape the hell of German concentration camps, and then to keep them alive. Nothing in me is fiercer... than my loathing of the

cruelty that issued in Auschwitz, except the sense that exile is only the human condition pushed to its farthest limit.
These images have burned me to the bone.

Her unsparing meditations frame a series of brilliantly rendered scenes of English and European political life, told with an understated but constant awareness of the terrible price to be paid by the Jews and democrats of Europe for the Western democracies' failure to contain Hitler. Three unforgettable pages meditating on drawings and photographs of the living and dead at Terezin camp (pp. 302–304), preface her account of the slow defeat of liberalism in the late thirties and the ascendancy of right-wing appeasers, leading inexorably up to the catastrophic betrayal of Czech democracy by the British government at Munich. The difference between the bitter clarity of her accounts of conversations with Hungarian Jews, Czech democrats and Labour politicians avoiding the gaze of refugees in her late memoir and their earlier versions in *Europe to Let* is the unsaid but ever-present subtext: 'We let these people die.' A constant awareness of the dark history of Europe illuminates Storm Jameson's accounts of well-informed, witty English liberals like H. G. Wells warning Jan Masaryk in 1938, 'If you're relying on us [Britain] to lift a finger to help you you're off your head. We haven't the slightest intention of risking trouble' (p. 372). In one of her best scenes, the horror of the Great War and the threat of the death camps to come similarly dominate a dinner party at which the writer, her husband Guy Chapman, Philip Jordan the journalist and an unnamed English diplomat discuss the future of appeasement:

> 'There will be demands and crises and demands and crises, and a superb operatic performance from Hitler as Wotan – do I mean Wotan? the fellow who sings bass and is a bore – reciting his sad story, and prophesying the downfall of Europe if we don't all join him in crushing the Bolshies . . . What his kind don't know is the point when this will be too much for us to swallow.'
>
> 'Do you know?' I asked
>
> 'Of course not.'
>
> I had an inarticulate sense that this picture of us was short on logic, that dubious continental trick, and saved at the last moment by sound English instincts, was one of our vanities. But I held my clumsy tongue.
>
> 'By the time we reach that point,' Philip said drily, 'there may be nothing left to stand on, and nothing to do but invite Hitler to take over Covent Garden. And I detest Hitler.' His tongue flickered over his lips. 'They say that Landin blubbered like a calf in the Council.'

'My God, how would you expect him to cry? Like a film star?'

Listening to this exchange and fiddling with her wineglass, Storm Jameson is assailed by an involuntary memory (pp. 340–1):

> At this moment, the finger I was running round the stem of my glass came on a slightly chipped edge, and before I could stop myself I was fingering the chipped saucer I had used to float a night-light when my son had diphtheria. I felt deaf and blind with fear and an insane anger. I stammered stupidly,
>
> 'Someone should assassinate Hitler now.' … I must really have looked insane. X. gave me a sweet condescending smile. I drew my shaking hand out of sight and tried to control my mind. … The images in it were such as any woman might see, thinking of her child's brains spilled on the ground.

The men, still wrapped in their discussion of politico-military probabilities, look at her as if she is crazy – which, she concedes, she probably is at that moment. The implication is that it is not possible to be a fully conscious historical subject, emotionally as well as intellectually, and to stay sane. Yet to remain indifferent is unforgivable, as Jameson has already shown in a telling scene which describes a three-way encounter between herself, a German refugee and a leading Labour politician at a Labour Party conference in 1933 (pp. 322–3). I quote it unabridged; it needs little commentary:

> One day at the end of the afternoon session, a gentle guttural voice – during the next few years this voice, in all its varieties, became very familiar – said in my ear,
>
> 'I think you are helping me. You are Storm Jameson, yes? I am' – I have forgotten his name – 'from Berlin, a friend of Miss Linke. I am a lawyer, I have here very important messages and a letter from some Trades Union officials for Mr Arthur Henderson. One of them is his friend for a long time. The letter tells him how he can help. I think you are taking me to him – perhaps now?'
>
> With the desperation of the timid, I marched him across the lobby to the great man.
>
> 'Mr Henderson,' I said, 'this German has messages for you from a friend of yours in Berlin.'
>
> I drew back a few steps and watched. For all I know, Mr Henderson was feeling an agony of grief. Nothing, no emotion of any sort, warmed a face the colour of a fishmonger's slab. I heard him say stiffly,
>
> 'What do you expect me to do?'

This stupidly mean-minded response to a victim's plea for solidarity has a profundity which the speaker surely never intended. It is true that the possible answers to the politician's rhetorical question were never uniform or simple. A Communist and a liberal would each have had a different response to this exile's plight; and, as Storm Jameson constantly reminds her readers, the answers which people of goodwill did find in the thirties were either ineffective or, in the end, violent. The necessarily complex and imperfect ways in which men and women (more generous and intelligent than their political leaders) responded to, wrote about and remembered the history of the 1930s is the theme of the following chapters.

Chapter 2

The pram in the hall
Men and women writing the self in the 1930s

A child may ask when our strange epoch passes,
During a history lesson, 'Please sir, what's
An intellectual of the middle classes?
Is he a maker of ceramic pots,
Or does he choose his king by drawing lots?'
What follows now may set him on the rail,
A plain, perhaps a cautionary tale.

W. H. Auden

On the other side...is nothing but the Oh no, Oh no. No, no, no, of the undeliberate dream that is to be endured and yet resisted, the horror of refusal with no power of refusal, Oh no. Oh no. No, no, no.

Stevie Smith[1]

CASE-HISTORIES VERSUS THE 'UNDELIBERATE DREAM'?

The two quotations above could easily stand for the differences between male and female English writers in the 1930s: poetry versus prose fiction, 'universal' masculinity versus feminine marginality, authority versus impotence, and so on. Auden's lightly handled epistolary verses represent the poet as a typical bourgeois intellectual, whose social construction is part of the story of English culture. Conversely, the protagonist of Stevie Smith's novel *Over the Frontier* lives in reverie and fantasy, lacks the power to define those key institutions such as education which Auden's poem handles so lightly and masterfully, but knows all about powerlessness and marginality.

Certainly, this gendered opposition between masculine case-histories and a feminine 'undeliberate dream' does partly work for 1930s autobiography, or there would be no point in setting it up. But it is also much too simple as it stands. Not all women writers were drawn to fantasy when they wrote about themselves, and not all women wrote as if from a margin. Some, on the contrary, claimed their own experience as representative. Vera Brittain's *Testament of Youth* (1933) famously spoke for the women of the 'lost generation' whose lovers disappeared during the Great War; so did Storm Jameson's *No Time Like the Present* (1932). And the autobiographical narrative that opens *Black Lamb and Grey Falcon*, in which Rebecca West, moving between countries, seeks to understand an ever more distant and complex historical past, implies a subjectivity that is anything but marginal. On the contrary, this interweaving of personal and collective memory defines the writer both as a woman *and* as a universal subject. Furthermore, men as well as women wrote about marginality and fantasy, themes which determine the narrative structure as well as the story of Edward Upward's heavily autobiographical *Journey to the Border* (1938); and women as well as men wrote poetry (see Chapter 4 for an extensive discussion of women poets). Nevertheless, because this opposition is still useful as a way into discussing the large and complex subject of gendered selfhood in the thirties, I shall start there.[2]

CASE-STUDIES FROM THE AUDEN GENERATION

A young man living at a certain period in a certain European country, is subjected to a certain kind of environment, certain stimuli, certain influences. That the young man happens to be myself is only of secondary importance; in making observations of this sort, everyone must be his own guinea-pig.

Christopher Isherwood[3]

Virginia Woolf's observation that 'no other ten years has produced as much autobiography as the ten years between between 1930 and 1939'[4] has, as I argued in Chapter 1, become even truer today than it was when she made it in 1940. And even then, the autobiographical attempt to write the self was not, as she implied, confined to young men like Auden and Isherwood, for those years are equally rich in memoirs and autobiographical novels by other hands, including those of the women writers whom I discuss later in this chapter. It is true that Stephen Spender, Louis MacNeice, Cecil Day Lewis and W. H. Auden all wrote autobiographical poems and plays, that George Orwell adopted the form of personal testimony for much of his non-fiction, that the published fiction of Christopher Isherwood and Edward Upward in the 1930s was all autobiographical, and that Isherwood and Graham Greene sometimes used their travel writings as a way of revisiting their youth. But the number of substantial memoirs by these men published before 1940 is actually very small, consisting principally of Isherwood's *Lions and Shadows* and

MacNeice's diary-poem *Autumn Journal*, Graham Greene's 1934 anthology of schoolday reminiscences *The Old School*, and the autobiographical third part of Cyril Connolly's *Enemies of Promise* (1938).

Far more common is the short memoir of childhood and schooldays citing the writer's own experience as an exemplary 'case-study', to use the term which Louis MacNeice applied to himself. Such a case-history is characteristically inserted into a study of recent literary history, as in MacNeice's 'case-book' in *Modern Poetry* or Connolly's 'A Georgian Boyhood' in *Enemies of Promise*; an account of the social condition of England, as in Orwell's *The Road to Wigan Pier*; a travel-book, as in Auden and MacNeice's *Letters from Iceland*, MacNeice's *I Crossed the Minch* (1938) or Graham Greene's *The Lawless Roads* (1939); or a long poem about contemporary history, as in Auden's 'Letter to Lord Byron'; or MacNeice's *Autumn Journal*.[5] Thus Cyril Connolly's 1938 study of the writer's predicament begins by analysing contemporary forms of rhetoric ('Mandarin' versus 'Vernacular'), then explores the current obstacles to producing great literature, and finally illustrates its account of the difficulties of writing a good book with a long account of the educational experiences at prep school and Eton which turned Connolly himself into a failed poet.

Louis MacNeice's *Modern Poetry* inverts this order, beginning its account of the problems and achievements of contemporary poetry with three 'case-book' chapters describing the writer's own intellectual development and its shortcomings. Although these chapters of intellectual autobiography are much less personal than Connolly's account of his schooldays, they describe a very similar movement, from innocence to an ignorant sophistication of which the mature writer disapproves. The small boy who loved hymns and nursery rhymes is fascinated at prep school by the lure of a sentimental Romanticism, then seduced at public school by Sitwellian modernist fantasies, and ends up as a self-conscious Oxford aesthete. This 'literary evolution... [which] can be seen as a dialectic of half-truths' (p. 74) is used to demonstrate the generally problematic post-war history of poetry. George Orwell similarly illustrates his analysis of reactionary psychology in *The Road to Wigan Pier* with an account of his own social construction as a member of the 'lower-upper-middle-class' (p. 153). And Graham Greene demonstrates the universality of sin by prefacing a study of the persecution of Catholics in Mexico with a memoir of the miserable schooldays, in which 'faith came to one – shapelessly, without dogma, a presence above a croquet lawn, something associated with violence, cruelty, evil across the way' (p. 2).

Two classic long poems of the 1930s, Auden's 'Letter to Lord Byron' and MacNeice's *Autumn Journal*, likewise insert accounts of the poet's own experience into their much more wide-ranging conversational discourses. Auden's memoir of his childhood and education in part IV of his 'Letter' comes after

1　a condensed history of Victorian England – 'Crying went out and the cold bath came in/ With drains, bananas, bicycles and tin' (p. 50);

2　a subtle analysis of the popular psychology of Fascism (pp. 53–4); and

3　a witty account of English poetry's development from eighteenth-century Augustanism, healthily dependent on its patrons, to the alienated self-indulgence of the *rentier* Romantic artists who 'sang and painted and drew dividends/ But lost responsibilities and friends', thus inaugurating the 'Poet's Party' which has now petered out into a bad post-Modernist hangover (pp. 105–7).

All five parts of the poem are sandwiched unevenly into an eclectic travel-book whose usually lighthearted tone is qualified by its authors' intermittent but sharp awareness of holidaying on the edge of an increasingly threatened Europe. The book's last words are MacNeice's foreboding 'Still I drink your health before/ The gun-butt raps against the door' (p. 261).

This self-aware relationship between personal testimony and public crisis is even more marked in MacNeice's *Autumn Journal* (1939). The poet represents himself both in terms of his unique memories, dreams and hopes and, like the reader, as an ordinarily powerless citizen, anxiously reading the newspapers (p. 23):

> The cylinders are racing in the presses,
> 　The mines are laid,
> The ribbon plumbs the fallen fathoms of Wall Street,
> 　And you and I are afraid.

Against this moment of writing in London during and after the Munich crisis in October 1938, MacNeice brilliantly counterpoints his personal memories of prep school in Dorset, undergraduate life in Oxford and marriage in Birmingham twenty and ten years back.

Almost all of these 'case-histories' begin with a brief glimpse of a nursery Eden when the author was free to contemplate 'wild freesias... with their long thin stems and wayward creamy blossoms' (Connolly), to enjoy nursery rhymes, hymns and ballads (MacNeice) or to admire 'working-class people, because they always seemed to do such interesting things, such as being fishermen and blacksmiths and bricklayers' (Orwell).[6] Such innocent idylls lead inevitably to the more or less oppressive shades of the educational prison-house – that is, preparatory school and middle- or high-ranking public school during the Great War, followed (usually) by three years at Oxford or Cambridge in the early 1920s.[7] This was *not*, as Virginia Woolf pointed out, the typical educational career of middle-class girls, however gifted; nor even for all middle-class boys. The 'Auden Group', however, seem to have taken this route for granted as the normal apprenticeship for writers of their generation – a notion which Woolf herself unequivocally endorsed in 'The Leaning Tower': 'Almost every writer who has practised his art successfully has been taught it . . . by about eleven years of education – at private schools, public schools and universities.'[8]

Although they mostly deal with the period 1910–1925, these educational case-histories are very much of the thirties. The writer's autobiographical gaze moves in them between the years of his growth and the ominous moment of writing (usually 1936 or 1937); while, in the familiar doubled perspective of memory, his awareness of writing at a 'present moment' of political crisis retrospectively illuminates his youthful illusions. Even when these narratives describe an expensive education or a world of privileged security, they are thus bounded by a knowledge of historical catastrophe. MacNeice's *Autumn Journal* is perhaps the finest instance of this dual focus, which is shared by nearly all his colleagues.

Much of the intellectual energy of these memoirs therefore lies in the writers' ironic awareness of themselves as historical subjects, whose comparatively sheltered lives are obviously small beer compared with the European war, revolution and counter-revolution which has defined the history of their time. Their representations of their own educations as 'case-histories' are at once modest and arrogant: modest because this structure assumes the determining importance of the writer's social environment rather than his intrinsic genius, and arrogant in that it implicitly claims a universal status for exceedingly privileged modes of social construction. As later commentators on the left-wing writers of the thirties have observed,[9] a writer's rebellion against public-school values only defined his identity more sharply as an ex-public schoolboy – particularly if, like most of these writers, he was a brilliant student with a record of scholarships and prizes.

These 'case-book' memoirs, then, describe the writer's social construction in order both to explain where his ideas came from and to show a practical example of history's effect on a (comparatively) innocent subject. This can be seen in one such 'exemplary memoir' which is very short indeed: Michael Roberts' Introduction to the influential left-wing anthology *New Country* (1933), which starts with a personal anecdote:

To me, 'pre-war' means only one sunny market-day at Sturminster Newton, the day I boldly bought a goat for 1s.9d and then . . . went out into the country and, finding a gatepost for a table, cut out from the *Express* a picture of a dozen Serbian soldiers (we spelt it Servian then) in spotless uniforms one sunny afternoon before 1914.[10]

Looking back to that lost summer afternoon in Dorset, Roberts represents pre-1914 England as a rural idyll, much as the hero of Orwell's slightly later *Coming Up for Air* (1939) is to dream of the steak-and-kidney puddings and fishing expeditions of his vanished country boyhood. Both texts invoke the English pastoral tradition in order to mourn its loss. Nothing follows from the story, whose point is simply that this memory is *all* that the writer possesses of life before the Great War. The experience thus becomes a synecdoche for the dispossession of a generation; it explains why young men in 1933, with 'no memory of pre-war prosperity or a settled Europe', feel they have little or no stake in English tradition: 'Others have even less than a one-and-ninepenny goat for their share of pre-war prosperity' (p. 9).

The implicit conservatism of this anecdote does, nevertheless, contrast oddly with the revolutionary aspirations of *New Country*.[11] Roberts' nostalgia for the lost idyll of 'before the war' belongs, as the more self-aware Isherwood remarked of himself in *Lions and Shadows*, to 'a daydream about my Youth – *le vert paradis*, from which I felt myself, as did my great army of colleagues, to be hopelessly and bitterly excluded' (p. 74). The story also carries another, probably unintended resonance, in that its image of 'boldly' possessing a proverbially dirty and lecherous animal also symbolizes the bourgeois man mourning his adult exile from his childish, undisciplined enjoyment of his own bodily appetites. Consciously and unconsciously, the memory thus signifies the collective experience of those educated men of the English middle class who were 'born between 1900 and 1914, were at school during the First World War and came to adulthood in the 1920s and to their early maturity in the 'thirties'[12] – in other words, the Auden Generation in its Leaning Tower.

The assumption that the writer's own experiences represent those of a whole generation underpins all these young men's memoirs – partly, of course, because these are overwhelmingly preoccupied with education. Even Graham Greene, who writes in religious rather than sociological terms, insists that his horrible schooldays at Berkhamsted showed the fallen human condition in its characteristic wretchedness: 'Hell lay about them in their infancy' (p. 2).[13] The left-wing memoirs of Isherwood and his colleagues emphasize how the public schools taught their pupils the reactionary values of their class, nation and Empire as well as the skills and knowledge that would enable them to become officials, administrators or teachers; the same point is also made repeatedly by the contributors to Greene's 1934 anthology, *The Old School*. The story of these writers' educations is thus, as in Joyce's *Portrait of the Artist as a Young Man*, one of youthful subjection to false values from which the maturing man painfully struggles free.

This shared narrative structure does not of course mean that all the memoirs tell exactly the same story. Isherwood, for example, represents his young self as a failed artist and a moral coward who writes bad novels because he cannot bear to face the emotional conflicts that inspire his writing: both sexually and artistically, his is a case of what Auden had called 'the distortions of ingrown virginity'.[14] Connolly diagnoses himself in related but different terms as a pathological example of 'romanticism in decline' complicated by 'the virus of good taste' (Connolly, pp. 218, 318) rather than as a victim of repression, while Orwell describes his adolescent snobbery as a typical symptom of the reactionary psychology bred in the 'lower-upper-middle-classes' by their shabby-genteel background: 'When I was fourteen or fifteen I was an odious little snob, but no worse than other boys of my own age or class' (Orwell, p. 169). All of these self-descriptions are shot through with a mixture of anger at the teachers' false values or brutality, pity for their victims, and irony at the youthful self's gullibility, snobbery or cowardice. This complicated irony can also be found in later books by members of this generation, such as Roy Fuller's novel, *The Ruined Boys* (1956), set in a minor public school, or Maurice Richardson's memoir of his prep-school days, *Little Victims* (1976).

Christopher Isherwood's *Lions and Shadows* is, however, the classic example of these ambivalent ironies. As in his later memoirs (discussed in Chapter 1, see pp. 27–30), Isherwood treats his younger self with a kind of affectionate contempt. He constantly deflates the young man's pretensions to heroism by exposing his timid conventionality, as when he and his friend 'Chalmers' plan to challenge the order of things at a college feast (pp. 114–115):

> Exactly what we were going to do, we didn't know. Perhaps Chalmers would simply jump up on the table and shout: '*J'en appelle!*' – whereupon, we said, the earth would open, and the dons, the silver heirloom plate, and the college buildings themselves would be immediately engulfed ... Once the bluff had been called, we liked to imagine, the whole academic 'blague' became bankrupt and would automatically collapse.

Needless to say, what really happened was that we had an excellent dinner and that I got drunk.

The book is full of these anti-climactic self-ironies – usually, as here, prefaced by the phrase 'needless to say'[15] – which emphasize the young man's subjection to the institutions against which he ineffectively rebels. This structure of superior ironic knowledge works particularly effectively in the subtle passage where Isherwood analyses his bad first novel, also called *Lions and Shadows*, 'less a work of art than a symptom . . . a very typical specimen of the "cradle-to-coming-of age" narrative which young men like myself were producing in thousands of variations' (p. 74) The pathology represented by this symptomatic text is, Isherwood explains, the neurotic anxiety which his generation felt about the Great War, in which they had been too young to fight: ' "War", in this purely neurotic sense, meant the Test. The test of your courage, of your maturity, of your sexual prowess: "Are you really a Man?" ' (pp. 75–6). If the young Isherwood had been willing or able to write about this anxiety instead of trying to evade it, his book 'might have become a genuine, perhaps a valuable work of art. But I didn't. And thousands of others didn't, either' (p. 75). His autobiographical novel says nothing about the war; its climax is the illness which prevents its hero from entering the public school which he had longed for and dreaded: 'Thus it was that "War" dodged the censor and insinuated itself into my book, disguised as "Rugtonstead", an English public school' (p. 77).

Although self-ironies such as these earned Virginia Woolf's praise for the young writers' honesty in 'telling the unpleasant truths about themselves',[16] all of these memoirs now look exceedingly reticent. *Lions and Shadows*, for example, is almost completely silent about the writer's family. Isherwood's mother appears occasionally as 'my female relative' (p. 179) or still more vaguely as 'my family' (pp. 198, 307), and his younger brother Richard is omitted altogether. The nearest he comes to mentioning the death of his father is to complain of 'having been emotionally messed about . . . at my preparatory school, where the war years had given full licence to every sort of dishonest cant about loyalty, selfishness, patriotism, playing the game and dishonouring the dead' (p. 13). This reticence about family traumas is entirely typical of the early memoirs of Auden and his friends, all of whose childhoods were darkened by the loss or disappearance of a parent. Isherwood's father was killed at the Battle of the Somme in 1916, Louis MacNeice and C. Day Lewis lost their mothers in early childhood, while Spender's semi-invalid mother died when he was twelve. Although neither Auden nor Connolly was actually orphaned, both suffered severely from their parents' absence; the disappearance of Auden's father from his family's life during the four years of the Great War, when he served as an Army Medical Officer, left the boy with a permanent sense of having 'lost him psychologically', while Cyril Connolly was sent away from home at the age of seven because his father's regiment was moved to Hong Kong. (The Connollys' marriage later disintegrated when the son was in his late teens.[17]) Their autobiographical case-studies barely hint at these traumas. Spender's writings of the 1930s say nothing about his mother's death; MacNeice says nothing about his family background in *Autumn Journal*; Connolly mentions moving to Bath in 1910, where 'my grandmother spoilt me' (Connolly, p. 193), but says nothing about missing his parents. Auden only alludes very obliquely to his father's wartime absence, bracketing it with the food shortages which ended after the Armistice: 'Butter and Father had come back again' (Auden p. 206). Yet even allowing for the numbing effect of boarding school on young boys' family feelings, such traumatic events must have scarred these men.

Very little is said about sexuality either. Although in 1938 discretion was only prudent for gay men, Isherwood's silence about his own homosexuality in *Lions and Shadows* goes much further than Auden's flirtatiously reticent line 'My vices? I've no wish to go to prison' (Auden, p. 203). Even allowing for the real danger of prosecution, his self-portrait as a repressed male virgin 'alone in my single bed' (p. 195) looks very censored indeed when compared with his later cheerful statement that 'at school, Christopher had fallen in love with many boys and been yearningly romantic about them. At college he had at last managed to get into bed with one.'[18] Other 1930s memoirs are almost equally silent about their authors' bodily experiences. The pleasures of adolescent sexuality are unmentioned, apart from Auden's brief admission that, 'like other boys, I lost my taste for sweets/ Discovered sunsets, passion, God and Keats' (p. 208). Desire is occasionally acknowledged, but only in a context of frustration, as in Isherwood's description of his celibate bed-sitting room (p. 222) or Connolly's account of himself at the peak of his Eton career: 'I was eighteen and a half, I had never had sexual intercourse, I had never masturbated' (p. 321). Bodily revulsion also features in Graham Greene's recollections of evil personified in 'Collifax, who practised torments with dividers; Mr Cranden with three grim chins, a dusty gown, a kind of demoniac sensuality' (p. 2) and, more interestingly, in Orwell's confession of his youthful horror at the dirty bodies of labourers (p. 160):

> You saw a great sweaty navvy walking down the road with his pick over his shoulder; you looked at his discoloured shirt and his corduroy

trousers stiff with the dirt of a decade; you thought of those nests and layers of greasy rags below, and under all, the unwashed body, brown all over (that was how I used to imagine it) with its strong, bacon-like reek...And even 'lower-class people' whom you knew to be quite clean – servants, for instance – were faintly unappetising. The smell of their sweat, the very texture of their skins, were mysteriously different from yours.

This testimony to his past obsession with dirty, alien working-class bodies belongs to Orwell's general analysis of bourgeois class-consciousness, and more specifically of the middle-class revulsion from the workers, a social pathology which can be 'summed up in the four frightful words... *The lower classes smell'* (p. 159). Orwell claims to have grown out of this prissiness – 'Nowadays, thank God, I have no feelings of that kind' (p. 163); but the energies of his prose tell a different story. It is not just that *The Road to Wigan Pier*, which begins with a bravura account of a filthy lodging-house (pp. 5–17), is famous for its preoccupation with dirt and smells; the passage quoted above is as full of excitement as of disgust. When Orwell describes his younger self noticing the texture of a housemaid's skin, or imagining a labourer's body within its nest of rags, 'brown all over' – a phrase which contradictorily suggests *both* sexy sunburnt nakedness *and* a repulsively dirty body, the language betraying that fascinating otherness, at once alluring and repulsive, which the sweaty working-class body could hold for the gentry.[19] As Beatrix Campbell has pointed out, Orwell's avowed admiration for the coal-miners with their coal-dusted 'noble bodies' (p. 23) implies an unacknowledged homoerotic streak (this is confirmed, incidentally, by Rayner Heppenstall's complaint of 'Eric Blair, who got a bloody homosexual crush on me, stifled it, let it fester and then, when he had me helpless, went for me with a shooting stick.').[20]

Such omissions and contradictions may well call into question the reliability of these autobiographers. This problem is articulated in slightly different terms, by Louis MacNeice, in a witty passage in canto 12 of *Autumn Journal*, attacking the hard complacency inculcated by privileged educations like his own. These

> May lead to cushy jobs
> But leave the men who land them spiritually bankrupt
>   Intellectual snobs.
> Not but what I am glad to have my comforts;
>   Better authentic mammon than a bogus god,

If it were not for Lit. Hum. I might be climbing
   A ladder with a hod.[21]

Such frankness did MacNeice no good with Virginia Woolf, who treated it
as a mere symptom of the insecurity and guilt which bedevilled all the
young writers of the thirties. But although her verdict that *Autumn Journal*
was 'feeble as poetry' was certainly myopic and unjust, her *ad hominem*
critique of the 'Leaning Tower' poets for 'profiting by a society which they
abuse'[22] remains useful because it does put into question the reliability of
the speakers. The writers themselves are apt to dodge this question by
assuming their own authorial objectivity, as when Orwell simply asserts
that he has now got over his 'middle-class squeamishness' (Orwell, p. 163).
More ambitiously, Connolly and Isherwood both stake their claims to
impartiality by prefacing their self-analyses with a self-conscious rhetoric
of 'scientific' objectivity. Cyril Connolly draws on the imagery of
calibration to introduce himself – 'The critic is an instrument which
registers certain observations; before the reader can judge of their value he
must know sufficient of the accuracy of the instrument, and allow for the
margin of error' (p. 186), while Isherwood defines himself still more
emphatically in terms of the laboratory as 'a young man . . . subjected to a
certain environment, certain stimuli. That the young man happens to be
myself is only of secondary importance; in such matters, everyone must be
his own guinea-pig' (p. 7).
   Yet these claims to impartial self-judgement are clearly questionable,
not least because of the assumption, shared by all the 'Auden Generation'
writers, that their case-histories represent the experience of a whole
middle-class generation. This can only be true if the women writers don't
count. This blind spot about gender flaws even Isherwood's otherwise
admirable analysis of his own obsession with the 'Test' (discussed above,
see p. 50), in that he implicitly defines as universal the specifically
masculine and middle-class[23] anxiety about the War by which 'we young
writers of the middle "twenties" were haunted' (Isherwood, p. 74). That
assumption of 'universal' masculinity is pervasive both in the other 'case-
histories' and in the discursive texts in which they are embedded. It can be
seen in the stanza from 'Letter to Lord Byron' quoted at the start of this
chapter, which introduces the poet's own experiences as those of a typical
'intellectual of the middle-classes'. The imaginary child of Auden's future
utopia has never heard of class hierarchies and thinks monarchs are
democratically chosen, but calls his teacher 'Sir' and knows that all
societies consist of men – 'Is he a maker. . . Does he choose his king?' (p.
201). Auden's lighthearted, masterly summings-up of Victorian social

history, the psychology of the Average Man, the post-Romantic hangover and the poet's own education in 'Letter to Lord Byron' all imply that history and literature are men's business. Apart from the poet's mother, who is mentioned on page 204, the feminine gender only appears as comic abstractions like the poet's Muse – 'Because it's true Art feels a trifle sick,/ You mustn't think the old girl's lost her kick' (p. 107), or the Motherland – 'England my England, you have been my Tutrix/ The Mater, on occasions, of the Free' (p. 233). In *The Road to Wigan Pier*, Orwell's notoriously conservative views on gender are matched, needless to say, by an unquestioned assumption that 'the worker' means 'the male worker'. Given observations like (p. 81):

> In the working-class home it is the man who is master and not, as in a middle-class home, the woman or the baby... a man would lose his manhood if, merely because he was out of work, he developed into a 'Mary Ann',

not to mention Orwell's indiscriminate dislike of unconventional folk such as sandal-wearers, nudists, Quakers, feminists and pacifists (p. 206), it is perhaps predictable that his justly famous description of coal-miners omits any mention of the women miners who worked in the Wigan pits.[24]

Less defensive than Orwell, Louis MacNeice admits in *Modern Poetry* to having been influenced at school by Edith Sitwell's 'little jazz fantasies' (p. 52), though he explains that he has now grown out of her. He discusses no other women apart from a passing reference to Stevie Smith, whom he wrongly brackets with Dorothy Parker as 'hard-boiled Americans' (p. 148); and he assumes throughout that poetry is properly a man's domain, claiming that 'After the feminine writing of most of the nineteenth century... we are working back towards the normal virile efficiency of Dryden or Chaucer' (p. 152). Connolly's *Enemies of Promise* is relatively unprejudiced against women writers, acknowledging Virginia Woolf (p. 62) and Gertrude Stein (p. 75) as important figures, and including titles by nine women authors in its 'production chart' of important modernist writing (pp. 79–80).[25] But, apart from a brief appreciation of *The Waves*, all Connolly's close readings are of male writers. Most tellingly of all, his account of the obstacles to good writing represents Woman as one of the writer's problems – or, at best, as an unselfish wife who understands that 'there is no more sombre enemy of good art than the pram in the hall' (p. 153).

WOMEN IN AND OUT OF HISTORY

> In 1934 an American reviewer, a woman, complained that 'like so many English writers, Storm Jameson seems unable to outgrow the war'. I retorted that the war we could not outgrow was not the one we had survived but the one we were expecting.
>
> Storm Jameson[26]

Storm Jameson produced important autobiographical writings during the 1930s, as did Vera Brittain, Naomi Mitchison and Rebecca West. (I do not include Winifred Holtby here because although, as Jean Kennard has shown, her novels are often based on the people and relationships which were important to her, she rarely wrote directly about her own life.) All these women were part of the London-based network of English liberal intellectuals. Like the male 'Auden Generation' writers, they were well-educated members of the professional middle class (for full information about their schooling, see pp. 23–4); they all lived in London in the 1930s, held left-wing but not Communist views, supported similar liberal causes such as the Peace Pledge Union, and published in the liberal feminist weekly *Time and Tide*. There were personal links, too: Storm Jameson knew and disliked Rebecca West, and was a friend of Naomi Mitchison and, until 1941, of Vera Brittain (the two were then permanently estranged by a row about pacifism). Naomi Mitchison, whose Hammersmith house was a centre for liberals and intellectuals between the wars, herself knew Vera Brittain, though not intimately.[27] These women do not, however, seem to have influenced one another's novels directly, apart from Vera Brittain's well-documented creative dialogue with the work of Winifred Holtby. Brittain's best novel, *Honourable Estate* (1936), has been described convincingly by Jean Kennard as a rewriting both of her own *Testament of Youth* and of Winifred Holtby's posthumous novel *South Riding* (1935).[28]

Although these women show as much awareness of their historical and political context as their male colleagues, their autobiographical writings differ considerably from the 'case-histories' discussed above. Although both Vera Brittain and Storm Jameson did write full-length memoirs, their preferred narrative form, as with most women writers of the 1930s, was the autobiographical novel, often featuring memories of the Great War. Very few of these novels share the male writers' preoccupation with schooling, apart from Antonia White's classic *Frost in May* (1933), based on its author's experiences at the 'Convent of the Five Wounds' in the 1900s, and Rosamond Lehmann's best-selling first novel *Dusty Answer* (1927), about undergraduate life at Girton College, Cambridge. *Dusty Answer* is also a consciously 'post-war' novel, whose heroine, though only fifteen years old when the Great War ends, is its indirect victim, through her frustrating relationships with young men who have been scarred or subtly corrupted by their wartime experiences.

Narratives written by older women were more likely to deal directly with the experience of living through the War. By 1933, such novels and memoirs included Mary Borden's *The Forbidden Zone* (1929), a brilliant hybrid of sketches and poems inspired by the experience of nursing French soldiers from 1914 to 1919, Vera Brittain's best-selling *Testament of Youth* (1933), Storm Jameson's autobiographical novel about wartime marriage *That Was Yesterday* (1930) and her memoir *No Time Like the Present* (1932), and Irene Rathbone's melancholy novel *We That Were Young* (1932), in which one love affair after the next is blighted by the man's death in battle. Mention should also be made of *Not So Quiet...* (1930) by 'Helen Zenna Smith' (Evadne Price), a highly coloured answer to Remarque's *All Quiet on the Western Front*, which purports to be the wartime autobiography of a VAD (Voluntary Aid Detachment) in Flanders.[29]

Each of these narratives was written to articulate the experience, not merely of the woman who writes it, but of a whole generation. Vera Brittain explains at the outset of *Testament of Youth* that the book originated in a long-held wish to 'write something which would show what the whole War and the post-war period ... has meant to the men and women of my generation, the generation of those boys and girls who grew up just before the War broke out (p. 11). Because the book must relate her own story to the general 'picture of middle-class England – its interests, its morals, its social ideals, its politics', she first tried to write out her experiences indirectly as a 'long novel', and resorted to editing her wartime diary. Both attempts rang false. 'There was only one possible course left – to tell my own fairly typical story as truthfully as I could against the larger background' (p. 12). Storm Jameson makes the same point more succinctly: 'What happened to me happened in greater or smaller degree to the rest of us who in 1914 were the young generation.'[30] Both women emphasize the extent to which the war affected the minds of the civilian non-combatants who lived through it, and often succumbed to the temptations of wartime glamour. Vera Brittain admits that in her pacifist middle age she still feels a nostalgia for 'the heightened consciousness of wartime, the glory seen by the enraptured, ingenuous eyes of twenty-two' (p. 291). A similar point is made by Christopher Isherwood about the 1926 General Strike (p. 179):

'War' was in the air: one heard it in the boisterous defiant laughter of the amateur bus drivers, one glimpsed it in the alert sexual glances of the women ... I [hated] both parties: my female relative announcing briskly at breakfast 'But of *course* I take sides!' – looking fresher and more alive than she'd looked for years; and Rose, gloating over the bus-wrecking in Hammersmith Broadway: 'That'll teach the bloody, damn blacklegs!'

Despite its misogynist tone, this account of women's excitement is surprisingly close to that Storm Jameson's *Company Parade* (1934), whose heroine responds to the 'infection of mass slaughter' with a feverishly sexualized intensity, which the novelist explains as an individual symptom of a general corruption of the spirit (p. 117):

If some quarter of a modern town or city were set apart for the legalised slaughter of human beings, there would spread from it a strange infection through the rest. The very streets, and the children playing in them, would wear an air of listening; what in one quarter ran off in blood would excite in degree the senses of all knowing it ... This impalpable excitement is the reason why delicate women, who could not bear to see a dog run over, can read without turning a hair, 'Our losses were less than three hundred officers and fifteen hundred other ranks.' And why others give away white feathers. Or take to drink or a lover.

Storm Jameson and her colleagues put their own lives into novels as well as, or instead of, writing straight autobiographies during the 1930s. Formally, these female autobiographical fictions are written in two very different modes. On the one hand, there are traditionally written social novels by, among others, Vera Brittain, Naomi Mitchison and Storm Jameson, which use the writer's own experiences of marriage, love and the family as part of a panoramic chronicle of the present or the recent past, which I shall examine first; on the other, there are experimental novels by Virginia Woolf, Jean Rhys and Stevie Smith, which explore the subjectivities of single women, usually through fantasy or reverie. All these novels differ considerably from each other, partly because the writers' collective social range varies from near-upper class (Naomi Mitchison, Rosamond Lehmann, Virginia Woolf) through the moderately well-to-do (Stevie Smith, Vera Brittain) to the hard-up or seedy margins (Storm Jameson, Jean Rhys). Moreover, there are many different versions of the traditionalist writers' general theme of a heroine's experience of sexual love, disrupted by bereavement, anxiety or female emancipation. This general pattern is obviously subject to particular chance variations, especially in a wartime context of hazard and danger.

These realist novels, now largely forgotten, include Naomi Mitchison's *We Have Been Warned* (1935), whose action runs from 1931 to 1933, Storm Jameson's *Mirror in Darkness* trilogy (1934–1936), which begins in 1919 and ends with the General Strike in 1926, and Vera Brittain's *Honourable Estate* (1936), a chronicle novel covering the history of two families from 1890 to the early 1920s; of these, only Naomi Mitchison sets her fiction in the 1930s. Ruth Alleyndene, the heroine of the second half of Brittain's novel, is given exactly the same experiences of working as a VAD in England and then France and losing her lover and a brother in the War as Vera Brittain relates in *Testament of Youth*. In the novel the heroine's brother dies not in battle but, as she later discovers, by his own hand (he has killed himself in order to avoid a scandal about homosexuality). But Vera Brittain was writing from her own experience here as well; for, after publishing *Testament of Youth*, she made the painful discovery that her brother Edward had been about to face a court-martial for homosexuality when he died in battle.[31] After the war, Ruth marries the only son of a talented woman who was destroyed by her marriage to an insensitive would-be patriarch; her wretched story is based on the life of the unfortunate Mrs Catlin, whose son George married Vera Brittain in 1925.[32]

The links between Storm Jameson's *Mirror in Darkness* trilogy, originally intended as a Balzacian *roman fleuve* representing the movements of British political life, and her own story as told in *Journey from the North*, are closer still. The 'mirror' of the trilogy's title is Mary Hervey Russell, the central consciousness of the book, known as 'Hervey'; like Margaret Storm Jameson, she is called by her androgynous middle name. Hervey's early wartime marriage to Penn, an irresponsible creep; the birth of their son; Penn's evasion of his wife's and baby's financial needs; the badly paid advertising work which Hervey undertakes to support the boy, who is looked after by relatives in Whitby; her near-miss affair with an American officer towards the end of the War; her discovery of her husband's adultery; her dithering about divorce; her eventual literary success; her difficult but rewarding affair and second marriage – all these exactly match Storm Jameson's own personal history as she tells it, first in the comparatively reticent *No Time Like the Present* and later, in detail, in the first part of *Journey from the North* (1969). As well as the plotting, many scenes and details about Hervey's experiences in the 1920s, such as her blazing anger about Europe's famished children, her confused response to discovering the letters from her husband's mistress, her physical collapse during the memorial service for the dead of the Great War, and her second husband's permanent nostalgia for army life, match Storm Jameson's later memoirs, point for point.[33]

But Hervey Russell's life is only one among a large and socially varied cast of characters who between them represent the major trends in post-war British politics; that is, the ruling-class Establishment, its victims, opponents and allies. Her story is the main unifying thread in a novel whose principal theme is the slow defeat of the Left by the sinister forces of wealth and reaction. These are represented principally by the newspaper magnate Marcus Cohen, and the industrialist Thomas Harben, who successfully corrupts a Labour MP into betraying his friends and endorsing a corporatist 'national socialism'. Harben later recruits the charismatic thug Julian Swan – obviously representing Oswald Mosley, with his pleasure in violence and his 'womanish bullying mouth' – as the leader of his party.[34]

Dione Galton, the heroine of Naomi Mitchison's *We Have Been Warned*, is even more transparently the author's self-portrait. Like her creator, she is the Socialist daughter of a Scottish landowning family, the mother of five children, the wife of (and canvasser for) an Oxford don standing as a Labour Party candidate in a Birmingham constituency, a critical sympathizer with Communists, a pioneer in sexual liberation, and a visionary Cassandra. Dione's most striking quality is a self-confidence which hardly ever lapses, deriving from her almost unassailable class privilege. (Q. D. Leavis, who loathed upper-class women writers, consequently attacked both Dione and her creator for their 'assumption of authority... grounded, it would appear, on nothing but class'.[35]) Apart from the imagined horrors of the Fascist coup prophesied in the novel's last pages, Dione is remarkably fearless about state control. Questioned by the police about her knowledge of Donald Maclean, a Communist assassin whom she has secretly helped to escape to the USSR, she expects – and gets – respectful treatment and no serious trouble: 'The Sallington police had been very polite; they had recognised her as a lady!' (p. 355). She and Donald write to each other after he has settled in the USSR, and she never appears to worry that openly maintaining a correspondence with a Communist who is wanted for murder might be dangerous. Later, attending a big London demonstration, she reproves a policeman for knocking her down: ' "Look out, my good man!" she said. The rider swerved: "You clear out, ma'am!" he said, irritated but still respectful' (p. 453). Real threats come only from her social equals, who regard her as a traitor whom they would happily see raped or jailed (p. 455).

More sympathetically, Dione's self-confidence also allows her to be sexually adventurous and generous. Sexually liberated and egalitarian, she encourages her husband's affair with Okshana, a lovely Soviet Amazon, begins the repressed Donald's sexual initiation though she doesn't really find him attractive (fortunately for her, he is seduced in the end by an emancipated Russian girl), and survives a nasty experience of rape by a lecherous 'comrade' without much trauma. All of these sexual adventures, which made the book very difficult to publish in the 1930s, are based on episodes in the Mitchisons' pioneering 'open' marriage, though the novelist stops short of letting Dione actually commit adultery, shifting her own affair with an Oxford don to Dione's sister and *alter ego* Phoebe, a married artist and (like Naomi Mitchison's friends, Gertrude Hermes and Agnes Parker) a wood engraver. The Galtons' relations with Labour Party activists are based on the Mitchisons' canvassing activities in King's Norton, Birmingham, contested by Dick Mitchison for Labour in 1931 and 1935; and their visit to the USSR in 1932 is certainly based on the Mitchisons' trip to Russia in that year. Dione's relationship with Donald the political assassin parallels Naomi Mitchison's own rather less erotic experience of helping Socialist refugees escape from Austria and smuggling documents out 'in my thick woollen knickers', when she went to report the death of Socialist Vienna in her *Vienna Diary* (1934).[36]

The fact that Dione's social identity is constituted by a wide variety of social relationships means that her story can also be a panoramic account of liberal England in the early 1930s; and this, indeed, is the book's main interest today. Although the novel consists entirely of Dione's experiences and her running commentary on them, the focus is always on what she sees, not on how she sees it. This is true even of the fantasy dream sequences experienced by Dione and her sister, in which a sinister 'Elephant', together with the 'Campbell Women' who persecuted witches in the Middle Ages, represent the forces of repressive reaction, while progress and utopia are personified as the 'Talking Crow' from Aristophanes' Cloud-Cuckoo-Land, and a powerful tractor driven by Dione herself – an image which is very much 'of the thirties'. A similar image of a beneficent powerful machine occurs in Edward Upward's *Journey to the Border* in which the hero is entranced by the sight of a steamroller (p. 21), while in the Soviet Union, enthusiasts for the Five Year Plans were known to give their babies names like 'Tractor' or 'Electricity'.[37] All these fantasy episodes, especially the prophetic vision of counter-revolution which ends the book, are less explorations of an unknown self than condensed, symbolic representations of the perennial social forces of good versus evil, repression versus liberation, or progress versus reaction.

It is not surprising that heroines modelled so closely on their pioneering originals should all be exceptional women. Mitchison's 'Dione' is consciously adventurous, pushing back the boundaries of acceptable sexual behaviour and engaging in illegal undercover work; Brittain's 'Ruth' achieves the fulfilment in work as well as sexual love of which the previous generation of women could only dream, while the apparent diffidence of Storm Jameson's 'Hervey' masks a survivor's arrogant self-sufficiency. Whereas the 'case-histories' of the male writers defined their authors as subject, 'like other boys' (Auden and MacNeice, p. 208), to a standard process of social construction, these novels insist on their heroines' stubborn refusal to be 'like other girls'.

MARGINAL SUBJECTIVITIES

Good things of day begin to droop and drowse
When night's black agents to their preys do rouse

William Shakespeare[38]

A very different autobiographical tradition, in which subjectivity is not taken for granted but problematized, was established in the 1930s by novelists such as Virginia Woolf, Dorothy Richardson, Stevie Smith and Jean Rhys. Three classics from this period – Stevie Smith's *Over the Frontier* (1938), Jean Rhys' *Voyage in the Dark* (1934) and Virginia Woolf's *The Years* (1937) – all foreground the subjectivities of underprivileged, marginal single women:[39] in *Voyage in the Dark*, Anna the chorus girl turned kept mistress, in *The Years*, the powerless, poverty-stricken Pargiter girls , and in *Over the Frontier*, Pompey the secretary to 'Sir Phoebus', the newspaper magnate, 'that lodestar of official duties, temperately laid, delightfully pursued, not unsuccessfully carried to what conclusions? (A gloss for this bouquet: How boring, how unfree? . . . How *kind* of him to have me?)' (p. 85).

The lives of these marginalized women – bored secretary, downwardly mobile 'kept' woman or spinster on small fixed income – are all determined by their political and economic context. British imperialism is an important, ambivalent theme for all three writers, and Stevie Smith's novel engages with the growing power of Fascism, also noted by Woolf in a brief but telling passage when the ladylike Eleanor angrily tears up a newspaper photograph of a Fascist leader (probably Mussolini), exclaiming 'Damned bully!'[40] But when these women engage with history, with the discourses of imperialism or political activism, they do so not through action, but by means of memory, reverie or fantasy.

This mentally active passivity is particularly marked in *The Years*, Woolf's feminist chronicle of the Pargiter family over fifty-seven years. The female Pargiters are impoverished and marginalized by economic dependence, by lack of access to education and the institutions of British power, and by their father's mean provision for them. Unlike their male relations, who establish themselves as dons, lawyers or colonial administrators, the untrained, unmarried Sara and Maggie have to move from the West End of London to a slum when their father, Digby Pargiter, dies. The only prospect for the Pargiter girls is marriage, which does not necessarily mean escape; the fortunate Maggie marries a nice radical Frenchman, but her cousin Delia, who hero-worships Parnell, marries an Irishman who turns out to be a dim-witted sporting Unionist. And even the poverty-stricken spinster Sara is better off than the Pargiters' servant Crosby (first name unknown), who loses her home of forty years when the family sells their London house, and is last seen in unpensioned old age, about to clean the bath in a grim lodging house because 'there was nowhere else for her to go' (p. 326).

Although *The Years* may sound from this summary like a feminist version of *The Old Wives' Tale*, it is actually a historical novel, but one which contradicts the dominant narratives of recent English history by deliberately marginalizing them. It covers the years 1880–1937 as experienced by an upper-middle-class English family without mentioning the Boer War, the death of Queen Victoria, the rise of the trades unions and the Labour Party, or the collapse of the Liberals. The suffragette movement is touched on – Rose Pargiter is a militant and gets jailed, Eleanor and her cousin Kitty belong to the moderate suffragist lobby – but only in the interstices of reveries and conversations: we are not shown Rose in action. Similarly, the First World War is represented by a single scene, showing a dinner party in London during the Zeppelin raids of 1917.

Clearly, the subject of politics in the traditional, recognizable guise of power struggles between representative individuals, as in Storm Jameson's *Mirror in Darkness* trilogy, is conspicuous by its absence from *The Years*. This lack of public life has drawn serious criticism from Peter Widdowson, who attacks the novel for privatizing history:

> The crippling effects of bourgeois domestic ideology are firmly felt, but the results in the wider culture – the responsibility, say, of the Pargiter culture for the First World War and the subsequent civilization – are not realized, although they are implicit.[41]

And yet, as Widdowson's final concessive clause recognizes, *The Years* is preoccupied, if not with power struggles, certainly with the institutions of power such as the universities of Oxford and Cambridge, the law courts, the colonial civil service and Army – all masculine preserves which uphold the British Empire.

The institutions of imperialism are shown indirectly, not through the minds of their male rulers, but through the medium of silent female minds, whose capacity for imagination far exceeds their knowledge or power. Thus, when Eleanor Pargiter, on her way to watch her brother Morris performing in court as a barrister, reads 'a letter from Martin in India' (p. 113) in the cab. His baldly written account of lighting a campfire in the jungle with his last match, stimulates her mind to imagine rich, vivid images (pp. 114–15):

> A jungle was a very thick wood, she supposed; made of stunted little trees; dark green in colour. . . Flames for a moment danced over the vast funereal mass of the Law Courts. It was the second match that did the trick, she said to herself as she paid the driver and went in.

Later on, she listens with a more detached irony to her erstwhile admirer Sir William Watney telling a similar anecdote (p. 216):

> I found myself in an old pair of riding-breeches standing under a peacock umbrella; and all the good people were crouching with their heads to the ground. 'Good Lord,' I said to myself, 'if they only knew what a bally ass I feel!' He held out his glass to be filled.

Eleanor sardonically observes both Sir William's insecurity – 'He was boasting, of course; that was natural' – and its context within the dinner party, whose anxious hostess has to prompt a clumsy maid to fill his glass (p. 216).

This opposition between male imperial privilege and marginal female vision is brought out still more sharply in the differing responses to Sophocles' *Antigone* of Edward Pargiter the Oxford don and his cousin Sara, materially the most unlucky of her family in being lame and therefore unmarriageable as well as poor. (It is true that the masculine privilege here is not obviously 'imperial', since the gendered difference between the cousins results from men's exclusive access to the upper echelons of education, not directly from the British Empire defended by Colonel Pargiter and administered by his son, Martin. The connection is that both institutions of power and knowledge are part of the British Establishment and male preserves: a point made repeatedly in the novel's 'companion-text' *Three Guineas*.) Edward, a star Oxford undergraduate preparing for the Fellowship examination which will determine his future, reads Sophocles in 1880, with precision, intense concentration and comprehensive textual knowledge: 'He made another note; *that* was the meaning. His own dexterity in catching the phrase plumb in the middle gave him a little thrill of excitement' (p. 52). Edward's form of knowledge implies both authority (the possession of truth) and a Little-Jack-Hornerish delight in his own ability: narcissistic pleasures which are known to most successful linguists. Twenty-seven years later, his cousin Sara absently skims his verse translation of the play while half-watching, out of her window, a garden party to which she is not invited. She is possessed by a vision of the heroine (p. 146):

> Antigone? She came whirling out of the dust-cloud to where the vultures were reeling and flung white sand over the blackened foot. She stood there letting fall white dust over the blackened foot. Then behold! there were more clouds; dark clouds; the horsemen leapt down; she was seized; her wrists were bound with withies; and they bore her, thus bound... where?
> There was a roar of laughter from the garden. She looked up. Where did they take her? she asked... 'To the estimable court of the respected ruler?' she murmured, picking up a word or two at random, for she was still looking out into the garden. The man's name was Creon. He buried her. It was a moonlit night. The blades of the cactuses were sharp silver. The man in the loincloth gave three sharp taps with his mallet on the brick. She was buried alive... Straight out in a brick tomb, she said.

The counterpointing of text and context is even sharper here than in the scene of Eleanor's intense absorption in her brother's letter. And, in some ways, Sara gets the play as wrong as Eleanor does the jungle which she imagines as 'stunted little trees.' She reads *Antigone* vaguely, as a narrative not a drama – 'scenes rose quickly, inaccurately, as she skipped' (p. 145) – and ignorantly, since she can approach the text only through Edward's evidently stilted rendering, from which that quotation 'the estimable court of the respected ruler' (which significantly invokes authority) is presumably taken. The trained classicist Edward knows the words of the play as Sara never can, but her vision of its tragic violence has a power that he never approaches. (When he does slide from mastering the text to thinking about Antigone, he imagines her as a desirable girl whose image rapidly merges into a daydream of his lovely young cousin Kitty [p. 54]). Sara, as her visionary response to the play shows, is a poet *manquée* whose poetry consists only of half-articulated reveries like this one, or else ephemera thrown off in conversation. Her words and fantasies can become art only in the privileged space of Woolf's novel.

Nevertheless, Sara's reading of *Antigone* is shown to be partial, inaccurate and *not*, so to speak, the author's own. Virginia Woolf, who had learnt from Janet Case to read Sophocles in the original, had written elsewhere that 'it is useless... to read Greek in translations', warning readers against glamorizing the classics through their 'haze of associations...reading into Greek poetry not what they have but what we lack'.[42] These criticisms would certainly invalidate Sara's vague, romantic reading.

Moreover, Sara's vision of primitive violence is itself subtly determined by the discourse of imperialism. The scene she imagines, with its vultures, dust-clouds, cactuses and fierce horsemen, sounds more like North Africa than Greece (probably she is mixing up the Hellenic Thebes with the Egyptian Thebes). And Creon 'in [a] loincloth' burying a woman alive is not only a more naked embodiment of male power than Sir William being worshipped in his 'old...riding-breeches' by credulous 'natives'. His image is constructed by an imperialist iconography of alien races as savage, primitive and violent. Whereas Edward imagined Antigone as an idealized girl 'among the marble, among the asphodel' (p. 54), and simultaneously as his desirable cousin Kitty, Sara sees her solely as a victim. Yet her famous defiance of Creon's patriarchal, militaristic authority is singled out for praise in a key passage of Woolf's pacifist-feminist polemic, *Three Guineas*, which originated as a companion-text to *The Years*:

> Consider Antigone's distinction between the laws and the Law. That is a far more profound statement of the duties of the individual to society than any our sociologists can offer us. Lame as the English rendering is, Antigone's five words are worth all the sermons of all the archbishops.[43]

Yet neither Sara nor Edward appears to notice them at all. The creative potential of the powerless, marginal female Pargiters appears in their fantasies of English rule (the colonial jungle) or knowledge (Greek poetry and philosophy), which are dominated exclusively by their male relatives. Yet the terms of their imaginations are defined – and limited – by those same institutions of power from which they are barred.

Unlike Sara's reveries, the daydreams of Anna Morgan, who narrates Jean Rhys' novel, *Voyage in the Dark*, are overtly determined by the facts of imperialism, being based not on fantasy but on her memories of childhood and adolescence in one of Britain's Caribbean colonies. Anna, a *déclassée* single girl without even a small fixed income, is even more socially marginal than the Pargiter spinsters. The English see Anna only as a tart; her true identity, unknowable to them, is represented by the nostalgic memories of her Caribbean home (she is a dispossessed daughter of the planter class). Her private desire for warmth, richness and colour becomes a mental retreat from the cold brutality, hypocrisy and ugliness which she encounters in England; her memories, always prompted by adversity, have the escapist quality of fantasy. As she falls lower socially, reveries and daydreams come to dominate the narrative. She constantly recalls the paradisaical, sensual appeal of her island: the night-blooming lilies, the waterfalls, the sunshine – 'The light is gold and when you shut your eyes you see fire-colour' (p. 43) – and the smells 'of niggers and woodsmoke and fishcakes fried in lard . . . of frangipani and lime juice and cinnamon and cloves, and sweets made of ginger and syrup, and incense after funerals' (ibid.).

But as the blandly racist word 'nigger' implies, people's lives on that glamorous Caribbean island are as much determined by racism and imperialism as in the grim commercialized English towns where people hate 'dirty foreigners' (p. 110). Belonging to the 'fifth generation born out there, on my mother's side', Anna remembers seeing names on old slave-lists (pp. 52–3); and remembers how a textbook defined 'the Caribs indigenous to this island' as 'a warlike tribe [whose] resistance to white domination, though spasmodic, was fierce . . . They are now practically exterminated' (p. 105). Her feelings about black people are an unstable mixture of attraction, envy, superiority and guilt. As a child, she says, 'I always wanted to be black . . . Being black is warm and gay, being white is cold and sad' (p. 31). These oppositions are personified by the two principal female figures in her life: Hester, her cruelly respectable English stepmother, and Anna's best friend, 'that dreadful girl Francine', as Hester calls her (ibid.), a black servant full of sensual vitality and physical strength. (With hindsight, both Francine and her ambivalent friendship with Anna look like a preliminary sketch for the more powerfully handled love–hate relationship between Antoinette Mason and the black servant girl Tia in *Wide Sargasso Sea* [1966].) Anna watches people like Francine with admiration, but always separately. She anxiously identifies herself as white when her stepmother insinuates that she may be of mixed race: ' "You're trying to make out that my mother was coloured", I said. "You always did try to make that out. And she wasn't" ' (p. 65).

The friendship with Francine ends on the day when Anna intrudes on the maid on her own turf, the 'horrible' kitchen where 'there was no chimney and it was always full of charcoal smoke', and realizes that 'of course she disliked me too because I was white' (p. 72). Her alienation from both black and white people is made complete in a final delirious scene when, haemorrhaging and feverish after a back-street abortion, she sees the white English faces around her as masks in the 'Masquerade', a carnival when black people donned costumes 'of all colours of the rainbow' and wore grotesque pink or white masks with their tongues sticking through (p. 185) in mockery of their rulers.

Like *The Years, Voyage in the Dark* is only indirectly a political novel. Although its picture of English culture and English people is wholly negative – the food, climate and architecture are awful, the women are insular and mean, the men contemptuously exploit women's bodies, both sexes are coldly hypocritical and the rich own everything and everyone – Jean Rhys' critique of England is moral and aesthetic, not political. There are no satires on class division, only a deadpan observation of provincial towns consisting of 'rows of little houses, and . . . a Corporation Street or High Street or Duke Street or Lord Street where you walked about and looked at the shops' (p. 8), and no arguments about the morality of Empire, only a jingoistic Englishwoman saying 'Don't you hate foreigners?' (p. 110). Yet the historical institutions of British power have, as the book makes plain, shaped the identity of Anna and of everyone she knows. The slavery which originally enriched her family has left a legacy which everyone inherits as pervasive social and racial inequality: landed wealth and leisure for the white planters, manual labour and unventilated kitchens for their black subjects. The British Empire guaranteed first slavery and then the privilege which Anna's family enjoyed over five generations, though the English themselves know and care little about it. The blank wall of incomprehension and hostility which Anna, the colonial subject, encounters in the mother country is as much determined by Britain's imperialist history as are her own memories of the Caribbean. But history and politics are represented at the level of the subject's consciousness, not as action.

Pompey Casmilus, Stevie Smith's autobiographical heroine in *Over the Frontier*, is more politically aware than either Anna Morgan or the Pargiter women, and less inclined to feel herself a citizen of nowhere. When in *Novel on Yellow Paper* she visits Germany and is repelled by the Fascism she sees there, she muses: 'Germany with its Movements, and Back to Wotan, and Youth Youth Youth, it makes you feel: God send the British Admiralty and the War Office don't go shuffling on with their arms economies too long-o.'[44] Unlike the pacifist anti-Fascism for which Virginia Woolf argues in *Three Guineas*, this is clearly not the response of someone alienated from the institutions of British power; but neither is it the speech of someone who expects to make things happen. Pompey remains on the outside. In *Over the Frontier*, however, she joins the movers of events. Convalescing in a North German castle-sanatorium from a nervous illness caused partly by her unhappiness about a broken engagement, and partly by the intolerable boredom of her life as secretary to a newspaper magnate, she is recruited to the Secret Service by Tom Satterthwaite, an Intelligence officer, and rides with him over a frontier, out of her old life, into another world of war where she becomes a cleverer, more ambitious and merciless spy than Tom himself.

Journey and frontier are of course standard 1930s motifs. In the writings of Auden and his contemporaries, the metaphor of traversing a borderland often represents a subjective progress towards Marxist enlightenment, as in Rex Warner's *The Wild Goose Chase* (1937) or Upward's *Journey to the Border* (1938).[45] But in Stevie Smith's novel, no distinction can drawn between the political and the psychic frontier: crossing the line into committed action means abandoning oneself to a powerful, evil fantasy world. This dual preoccupation with Fascism and fantasy has led Valentine Cunningham to describe the novel as 'curiously muddled',[46] but this is to underestimate its power and subtlety. More than than any other novel of the 1930s, *Over the Frontier* does justice to the 'fantastic realities of the everyday world'.[47]

The key subjects of Stevie Smith's brilliant, obsessive narrative are:

1   the power and cynicism of British imperialism;
2   the threat of its still more brutal Fascist enemies; and
3   the source of these evils in humanity's desire for cruelty.

Less than starry-eyed about the British Empire, Pompey observes drily that 'the parsons who write to the papers to say that England holds commission from heaven to colonize the earth must surely be dottily overlooking the Jameson Raid and the Rand Kaffir business' (p. 98). She compares Italian imperialist propaganda unfavourably with English, not because it is unscrupulous but because it is crude: 'When England plays that game she can play it better than that, more thoroughly more vilely more unanswerably final' (p. 99). She concludes her meditation on imperialism with an appropriately Ciceronian burst of rhetoric (p. 100):

> I understand the motives of my country... That she is astute and on occasion equivocal, I believe. That she has conquered in greed, held in tenacity, explained in casuistry, I agree. But fools asking foolish questions have nothing to expect but folly or casuistry.

These musings culminate in the sceptical Pompey's acceptance of her country's *Realpolitik*, and her decision to clothe herself in a military uniform and a spy's identity.

And yet, from beginning to end of the narrative, Pompey's meditations also constantly pull her towards fantasy. It is the fantastic conjunctions between language, desire and cruelty which haunt her as she listens to a gentle old soldier reminiscing about his experience of battle-frenzy – 'We would have murdered our own grandmothers' (p. 67) – or disgustedly reads a cerebral novel by one of the 'leaders of the intellect' (obviously Huxley) who describes a child's agonizing death from cerebral meningitis in meticulous, sadistic detail (pp. 57–58),[48] or watches a fellow-traveller in her railway carriage furtively absorbed in the *Pleasures of the Torture Chamber* (p. 60). Verbal memory, written text and reader's reverie alike inhabit the 'undeliberate dream that is to be endured and yet resisted, the horror of refusal with no power of refusal, Oh no, Oh no. No, no, no ' (p. 70); their common ground is that 'undeliberate dream' whose repeated, ineffective 'Oh no' may equally well be spoken by a powerless victim or by a torturer unable to resist temptation. When Pompey becomes an intelligence officer with a 'commission' from an unknown source, she enters this dream world of night's black agents. Its fantastic nature is first indicated by allusions to thrillers and other 'unrealistic' literature. Pompey's midnight meetings with Secret Service men, her undercover journeys across harsh terrain, and even her conscious anti-semitism all recall John Buchan thrillers like *Greenmantle* (1916) and *Mr Standfast* (1918). And the name of old Mrs Pouncer, an intelligence agent masquerading as a sweet old lady whom Pompey calls 'my dear Mrs Witch' (p. 193), comes straight from John Masefield's prose fantasy *The Midnight Folk* (1928), in which a little boy discovers that his bossy governess has a secret, midnight identity as Mrs Pouncer the leader of a coven of witches. On a more highbrow level, the blasted heath which Pompey must ride across in order to pass 'over the frontier' (p. 226) resembles the landscape of Browning's nightmare poem 'Childe Roland to the Dark Tower Came', while the Schloss Hotel and her mysterious 'commission' both suggest Kafka.

Furthermore, as soon as Pompey looks in the mirror and realizes with horror that 'I am in uniform' (p. 217), the place and timescale of the narrative begin to change into a timeless region of unending European war. References to the 'Christmas tides' (p. 27) and to the invasion of Abyssinia (p. 99) have previously established the novel's chronology as lasting from late 1936 to the following summer, while the Hotel Schloss Tilstein is said to be situated somewhere on the North German coast, with the university city 'Ool' nearby (p. 196). Once Pompey sets out with Tom, however, she finds herself journeying across a bitterly cold, devastated region where a war of attrition is being fought by vast numbers of exhausted men, 'their faces . . . so tired and quite blank' (p. 232). Troops die in huge numbers because of intelligence failures, and the winter is approaching when 'the slightly wounded will lie . . . on cold battlefields to die from exposure in the bitter dark night' (p. 239).

This territory is the familiar nightmare landscape of the Western Front, known to posterity through such texts as Wilfred Owen's 'Exposure', and evoked in an early Auden poem, 'Ode to my Pupils' in very similar terms to Stevie Smith's: 'Though the bunting signals/ Indoors before it's too late, cut peat for your fires/ We shall lie out there.'[49] Even the unmarked frontier which Pompey crosses, a wide ditch bordered by 'beastly damp soft marsh slime' (p. 225), evokes the trenches. It is as if the War which supposedly ended in 1919 is still being fought in a timeless world where 'we shall win, we shall win . . . and we are right, we are right' (p. 255), but all victories turn out to be local and temporary. Although Pompey certainly blames Germany for 'the infection of arrogance and weakness and cruelty that has spread to our own particular enemy' (pp. 255–6), which suggests Fascism, it is not clear who is fighting whom. Or, as Auden's poem puts it, 'the quarrel was from before your time, the oppressor/ No one you know.'[50]

As Pompey passes into this fantastic territory, her identity changes. Free of her old life as a frustrated, unimportant secretary, she becomes a more ruthless, efficient and ambitious intelligence officer than the man who recruited her, realizing fully her own half-sensed desire for cruelty. When she kills one of the enemy, she acts not just in self-defence but to make an idea real: '*I have the thought* to put the barrel between the long dirty teeth, that open so *invitingly* upon slack lips' (p. 250, emphasis added). In this nakedly phallic fantasy of penetration and destruction, the heroine becomes what she has detested; for in this region of dream, thinking and doing are the same thing. Once Pompey enters the world of military action, she thus consents to be determined by the power of fantasy. Things bad begun make strong themselves by ill.[51]

It would be a mistake, however, to assume that only women wrote about marginalized people engaging with the world through reverie and daydream. Such a person is the unnamed 'tutor' who is the hero – or rather, the subject – of Edward Upward's autobiographical novel *Journey to the Border*. A proletarianized intellectual, 'the tutor' is employed by and dependent on a rich bully whom he loathes. The action of the novel takes place mainly in the tutor's mind, which corresponds exactly to Freud's definition of an artist as a man who seeks in dream the satisfactions he cannot achieve in life:

> He desires to win honour, power, wealth, fame and the love of women, but lacks the means for achieving these satisfactions. Consequently, like any other unsatisfied man, he turns away from reality and transfers all

his interest, and his libido too, to the wishful constructions of his life of phantasy.[52]

Having let himself be pressured into reluctantly accompanying his employers to their day at the races, the tutor turns his mind to attractive but dangerous fantasies which draw him to the borders of insanity. His reshaping of reality can be seen at work as soon as his party arrives at the racecourse (pp. 63–4):

> Single and tall the marquee was here. It was here and it was white and triangular flags flew from its roof and there was nothing visionary about it . . . It might seem to have porthole-shaped dormer windows, but that effect was accounted for by the ventilator flaps on its sloping canvas roof. It might look like an airship; that was because of its rounded ends, its whiteness and lightness. It might remind the tutor of an aviary; that was explained by the birds flying round it, and the resemblance to thin wires which the guy ropes had when seen from a distance. It might remind him of the sea; the canvas billowing like sails in the slight breeze explained that. It might suggest gardens; there were ferns and a vase of flowers on a table just inside the entrance. It might give an impression of leisure and abundance and well-being and freedom: the entrance gave a glimpse of people chatting in easy postures, the interior was filled with cool brightness, the knobs outside which topped the invisible supporting poles were gilded. There was nothing startling about the marquee . . . He felt calm and normal.

The rising excitement in this passage is obvious, from the first Hemingwayesque 'It was here and it was white' to the increasingly fantastic associations, first with images of freedom and transcendence – the airship, the aviary, the sea – and then of the things money can buy: gardens, luxury and leisure. The dominant figure of speech here is metonymy, for these images are determined by the associative logic of contiguity. True, they begin with physical similarity – ventilator holes like portholes in the roof, round shapes like an airship – but the succeeding likenesses are all prompted by contiguous associations: the tent resembles an aviary only in that the birds flying around its ropes remind the tutor of one, while it is his own adjective 'billowing' applied to its canvas which suggests waves and therefore the sea. By the end of the paragraph, the marquee has been entirely transformed into a symbol of the tutor's frustrated desire for 'leisure and abundance and freedom' which are represented by details like 'ferns and a vase of flowers' and 'gilded' knobs atop the tent, which the tutor has obviously invented himself.

The realm of fantasy, however, does not fulfil its promise of *luxe, calme et volupte,* as the tutor rapidly discovers. Samuel Hynes has called his subsequent hallucinatory experiences 'so shifting and ambiguous as to leave the reader certain of nothing except the tutor's deranged state',[53], but this is not true if one reads carefully. Whenever objects or people begin to appear excitingly rich, strange or sinister, it is a sure sign that the tutor is fantasizing about them. Once inside that alluring marquee, the tutor experiences a series of tempting but frightening encounters with his desires and fears. As in *The Pilgrim's Progress,* his temptations are personified by characters who engage the hero in conversation, though unlike Bunyan's portraits of Ignorance or Despair, they are given fairly lifelike names.[54] Each begins by asking the tutor how he likes his life, tempts him by seeming to offer him one of the classic trio 'honour, power, and the love of women'[55] and, having enticed him (for the tutor is a much less heroic figure than Bunyan's Christian), turns hostile and threatening. Thus the tutor's ambivalent desire for the wealth and privilege enjoyed by the upper classes is represented by 'Tod', a pioneer colonist just back from Africa. Tod, whose name signifies both the greedy devourer of rabbits in Beatrix Potter's 'Tale of Mr Tod' and (in German) 'death', looks at first friendly, confident and impressive, but turns out to be a hysterical racist thug. The more modest wish for a good job is represented by a conversation with 'McCreath', a kindly rich man who offers the tutor just that. But, as the man's name suggests, there is something creepy about the offer; the tutor realizes that McCreath, though not homosexual, effectively wants to buy him. The most insidious of all these tempters is the psychologist Mavors (partly based on Auden[56]), who insists that social conflicts derive from frustrated personal desires (pp. 156–8):

> Disease is the result of disobedience to the inner law of our own nature.... There is only one sin, and that is disobedience to our own desires.... Desire has been put in prison and driven wild.... Disease and hatred are warning symptoms of a sickness of the soul. They are desire in disguise. They are God.

These arguments derive from the theories of John Layard, the disciple of Homer Lane (they are also cited almost word for word in Isherwood's *Lions and Shadows,* pp. 300–1). Convinced that he must liberate his Desire, the tutor promptly indulges his longing for sexual pleasure in an encounter with a beautiful, exquisitely dressed girl who attempts to seduce him, first by opening her fur coat to show off her body, and then by a more active approach: 'Her lips pressed, withdrew until their touch seemed as light as the touch of an insect's trembling feelers, pressed again, sucking and warm and heavy. He was in her power, wholly dependent on her, humbled with abject longing' (p. 176). Of course, she is really out to torment and humiliate the poor tutor. Once he is aroused, she evades his response, claiming to be otherwise engaged ('You mustn't look so miserable. I don't like it') and finally dismissing him: 'You poor little swine' (p. 181).

The tutor's fantasies now spin out of control, culminating in a crazy nightmare vision of a Fascist coup. But at this point, the 'voice of reason', at first only a buzzing in his ear, proceeds to save him by arguing him out of his fantasies and into the world of Marxist action and realist writing. Samuel Hynes calls this 'Marxism understood as psychiatric treatment ... [in which] the patient is cured, but his imagination dies',[57] but this is to misread a book which is itself, after all, a monument to the power of fantasy. Even after his dialogue with Marxist reason has ended with his own agreement to abandon his daydreams and take action to change reality, the tutor continues to fantasize. A disturbance among the crowd makes him think that a revolt has begun which may lead to revolution, though it is caused only by the M.F.H.'s (Master of Fox Hound's) horse winning (pp. 239–41), and an encounter with a friendly worker represents the attractions of Communist solidarity, until the tutor realizes that this worker isn't interested in politics (pp. 206–8). His commitment to Marxist action and realist writing is made complete only in the final sentence when, like Paul Morel at the end of *Sons and Lovers*, he turns his back on his old life and journeys out of the book: 'The tutor reached the road and began to walk down the hill' (p. 220).

GENDERING THE SELF: MARION MILNER AND REBECCA WEST

The example of Upward's *Journey to the Border* shows, then, that 'marginal identity' and its accompanying fantasies are far from being all-female preoccupations. True, a certain narrative irony is built into all the tutor's fantasies, which the novel's argument anyway rejects; but this refusal of fantasy has at least as much to do with Upward's commitment to Marxist realism as with his gender. In any case, marginal identities are not the only kind written about by women. It may be true that, as I have argued elsewhere, 'women who wrote about their own experiences ... during the 1930s could not take for granted, as men did, their own universal or representative status';[58] but that did not stop some of them from staking just that claim. It is made, though decidedly not in identical terms, in two utterly different autobiographical classics: the Prologue to Rebecca West's

Black Lamb and Grey Falcon (1942) and Marion Milner's *A Life of One's Own* (1934). The difference between these texts and the autobiographical fictions by Vera Brittain, Naomi Mitchison and Storm Jameson discussed above (pp. 55–61) is that, whereas these realist writers tend to take their own identities as unproblematically 'given', Rebecca West and Marion Milner, in very different ways and to very different ends, explore the implications of a female subjectivity.

Marion Milner's pseudonymously published *A Life of One's Own* is not, despite its obvious echo of Virginia Woolf, a literary autobiography. It is the record of an experiment in self-analysis by 'Joanna Field', a young woman who was also a highly trained psychologist (and later became a distinguished psychoanalyst and theorist of creativity) whose discoveries about the workings of her own mind are presented – and were received – as discoveries about the way minds work in general. The book records a quest for self-discovery, described by W. H. Auden as being as exciting as a 'detective-story',[59] which begins as the writer's apparently simple attempt to find 'what kinds of experience made me happy' (p. 1). This search proves to be a very complex process whereby she comes to distinguish between different kinds of thinking. First, she finds that her mind is frequently dominated by what she calls 'blind thinking', which is unreasonable, egotistical and extremely stupid, being unable either to distinguish facts from its own thoughts or to take into account the existence of other minds; it is therefore impervious to reasoned argument (pp. 112–36). She observes that this childish 'blind thinking' is not peculiar to herself (p. 122) but is a near-universal condition. Her attempt to escape from its constant 'self-centred chatter' (p. 215) leads her to distinguish between two kinds of thought: on the one hand, the hard concentration on a particular object, which she has assumed is the only kind of intellectual discipline, and on the other an openness to perception to which she gradually trains herself. As she comes to think in this way, she perceives – to take an example – an iron air vent not as 'that old iron thing' but as a complex form (p. 187):

> I found myself looking at one side, then at the other – they were symmetrical curves with a pillar in the centre and radiating lines thrust downward like the cloak of a queen – and as I watched, the form seemed to crystallize into a growing equilibrium of movement. Now I knew what painters meant about the movement of lines. If one only stood still and watched, they did move.

This second, receptive form of thought, for which Milner sometimes uses religious language (though she makes her agnostic humanism quite clear), is both self-abnegating and sensuous, a version of Wordsworth's 'wise passiveness' which enables her to 'experience the present with the whole of my body instead of with the pin-point of my intellect' (p. 188). By the end of the book, she comes to identify this open, receptive attitude with the feminine aspect of her psyche, the existence and the needs of which she had earlier ignored because she had only understood the masculine 'objective' aspect of her own mind. This does *not* mean that her mind, being a woman's, must be irrational. On the contrary, she has come to realize that the human psyche partakes of both sexes (p. 232):

> I had realized that the good moments came when I . . . was able to let the thing I was looking at take possession of me . . . But I had not understood that the obsession with purposes which had seemed to keep me from such surrender might be in part the attempt to express an inevitably present maleness.

Although the book is concerned only with her own experience, she argues that everyone, consciously or not, experiences similar balances and conflicts between the masculine and feminine aspects of their identity because the human psyche is bisexual (pp. 226–252). Although she does not actually quote Virginia Woolf here, Milner's argument as well as her title echo *A Room of One's Own* and its theory of the writer's 'androgynous mind'.[60]

As an essay in psychology, 'not concerned with external events, but with my reaction to them',[61] Marion Milner's autobiography says very little about its own historical context. Similarly in the 1937 sequel, *Experiment in Leisure*, she mentions the deteriorating political situation in Europe only briefly, as part of 'those preoccupations with cruelty that had obsessed me of late'.[62] History is, however, the central preoccupation of Rebecca West's *Black Lamb and Grey Falcon* (1942), to my mind the greatest of all 1930s autobiographies. Her twenty-five-page Prologue to the book makes a fitting end to this chapter, even though it was published after the end of the decade and even though I discuss the book at length in Chapter 6.

The brilliance of this Prologue lies in the way it presents the writer's experience of a single moment in 1937 (the supposed date of composition), as a way into that interweaving of present and past which makes up the whole book's account of contemporary history. Rebecca West's narrative constantly loops backwards from the present into an ever-receding past, producing a contrapuntal complexity which needs a summary to make it clear. Thus:

a In the sleeper *en route* for Zagreb, the wakeful RW meditates on her feelings about Yugoslavia, which are surprisingly strong given that 'this was 1937 and I had never seen the place until 1936'.[63] The first time she ever heard the name was on

b 'October the ninth, 1934' (p. 1). Recovering from a surgical operation she had listened to a radio announcement of the assassination of King Alexander of Yugoslavia; and realizing that this would mean an international crisis, perhaps even war, she was horrified to think that 'my life had been punctuated by the slaughter of royalties' (p. 3). She tells an uninterested nurse about

c the assassination of the Empress Elizabeth of Austria in 1898, when RW was five years old. She vividly remembers seeing her mother horror-stricken at this news (p. 3). The personal memory introduces

d a long account of Elizabeth's life from the 1850s until her death in 1898 (pp. 4–11): her beauty, diplomatic initiative and skill, her frustration by the stupid brutality of Habsburg imperialism, and her pointless assassination by one Luccheni, who was called a madman but 'was not mad' (p. 9). RW suggests an analogy between this man and

e the Donatist heretics during the fourth century AD, who exemplify a similar pathology: 'Though these people raved they were not mad. They were making the only noises they knew to express the misery inflicted on them by the economic collapse of the Western Roman Empire'. Like them, Luccheni expressed the misery of a dispossessed existence; in the present century, because economic conditions produce a workless urban underclass, men like him had 'astonished the world with the farce of Fascism' (p. 10).

c We return to RW's lifetime. 'When I was ten years old, on June the eleventh, 1903, King Alexander Obrenovitch of Serbia and his wife Queen Draga were murdered in their palace bedroom and their naked bodies thrown out into the gardens' (p. 12). Peter Karageorgevitch succeeded them, a good king who ruled Serbia well; but his successful reign aroused the mistrust and hatred of the Austro-Hungarian Empire (pp. 12–15). The Habsburgs' deliberate provocation of its Balkan subjects led inexorably to

f the assassination of Franz Ferdinand in June 1914, which RW was too wrapped up in her personal affairs to notice at the time (the story of the Archduke's death will be retold at length, much later in the book). As with her own operation in 1934, 'the pain came afterwards' (p. 14); which returns us to b RW thinking about all this in her hospital bed in 1934: 'Here was another murder, another threat that man was going to give himself up to pain, was going to serve death instead of life' (p. 16). Later (pp. 16–19) she watches the newsreel showing the assassination of King Alexander, noting that it does not seem to surprise the victim. She meditates on the violence of Balkan history, and the general British ignorance of its causes, typified by

c Slavophile British liberals in the late nineteenth and early twentieth centuries, the time of her childhood (pp. 22–23), who failed to understand its real nature and causes: 'To hear Balkan-fanciers talk about each other's Infant Samuels was to think of some other painter not at all Sir Joshua Reynolds, say Hieronymus Bosch' (p. 22). She herself, in

b 1934, knew nothing about the Balkans. And since their history has affected all European lives, including her own, it follows that 'I know nothing about my own destiny' (p. 24). She therefore visits Yugoslavia in the spring of 1936, to give some lectures (p. 24) and, unable to communicate to her husband the fascination of this country, resolves to return with him the next year,

a 'in the spring, for Easter' (p. 25) – thus reaching 1937, the time of her narration, though not, of course, the time of composition.

Such layering of memory through memory recalls Proust, a writer whose work Rebecca West regarded as central to Modernism.[64] Indeed the Prologue and its relationship to the great history that follows it bear a marked likeness to the '*Ouverture*' of *À La Recherche du Temps Perdu*. In both works, an immensely long narrative, loosely based on the author's life,[65] begins with the meditations of a solitary, wakeful narrator at midnight. (In *Black Lamb*, 'my husband' is admittedly present 'in the other wagon-lit' [West, p. 1], but as he is asleep and doesn't answer Rebecca West's voice, her thoughts are, like Marcel's, explored alone.) And, as in Proust's novel, the narrative starts by moving backwards into scenes from the past, introducing some key figures – in *Swann's Way*, Marcel's grandmother and Swann himself; in *Black Lamb and Grey Falcon*, Balkan royalties and their assassins – whose stories will be told, far more exhaustively, later on. Like Proust's '*Ouverture*', the Prologue ends with the narrator and reader about to explore the huge undiscovered regions that lie beyond its initial vivid but limited memories. This 'looping' of the narrative backwards from the history of the writer's self into the history of a nation, and forward again to her consciousness of the 'present', prefigures the method of the whole book. It will be done in the long accounts of Bosnian and Serbian history in volume 1, and more subtly perhaps in 'Old Serbia' (vol. 2, pp. 211–386), where the narrative constantly zigzags between the tragic glories of the medieval Serbian past and the squalor of its impoverished post-colonial present.

For, since *Black Lamb and Grey Falcon* is a book about European history as well as an autobiography, its Proustian interweaving of past and present includes much public history. The political murders of King Alexander, the Empress Elizabeth and the Archduke Ferdinand are only the first of many. Its account of the Empress Elizabeth (pp. 3–11), full of detail, humanity, wit, liberalism and judicious weighing of evidence, nevertheless gives the reader a good idea of the kind of storytelling to come, including Elizabeth's pointlessly violent death. As the book will insist throughout, the story of the Balkan kingdoms is inconceivably more bloody and tragic than Western Europeans have realized, the violent deaths innumerable: 'Murder. Murder. Murder. Murder' (p. 155). Themes which will be orchestrated at length in the book are introduced here: the wickedness and stupidity of imperialism, whether Roman, Habsburg or Ottoman; the twilight of the Western Roman Empire in the section on 'Dalmatia' (pp. 147–58); the evolution of the Serbian kingdom ('Belgrade III–Belgrade IX', pp. 533–637); and the assassination of Archduke Ferdinand in 1924 in 'Bosnia' (pp. 337–93).

Rebecca West's pilgrimage to Yugoslavia is taken in order to redress her own ignorance, not only of history but of her own life: 'I had to admit that I knew nothing at all about the south-east corner of Europe ... that is to say I know nothing of my own destiny' (p. 24) – a scandalous betrayal of her own humanity as one among innumerable 'thinking reeds' whose consciousness alone redeems their crushing subjection to the brutal universe. The fact that Rebecca West is a well-to-do Englishwoman in a time of European tragedy means that her destiny is merely the comparatively comfortable one of belonging to the horror-stricken audience which reads newspapers, listens to the radio, watches cinema newsreels, and waits numbly or apprehensively for its collective life to be smashed up. For citizens of the harsh world of Eastern Europe, history can, as her book will show, mean the unimaginable personal suffering that leaves a bereaved peasant woman asking, 'If I had to live, why should my life have been like this?' And that question is, in the speaker's circumstances, heroic. 'She took her destiny not as the beasts take it ... she not only suffered it, she examined it'.[66] And, according to Rebecca West, this desire to find a meaning in one's own experience is the source of all serious expressive art. A key theme of the book is the relation between art as gesture or symbol and the quality of human consciousness which it expresses.

In the Prologue, the notion of the relation between art and consciousness first appears obliquely, not through any descriptions of artefacts (RW is still in her railway sleeper), but in two acutely visualized historical scenes, one 'private' and one 'public'. The first is a childhood memory of her family becoming aware of the assassination of Elizabeth of Austria (p. 3):

> I remember when I was five years old looking upward at my mother and her cousin, who were standing side by side and looking down at a newspaper laid on a table in a circle of gaslight, the folds in their white pouched blouses and long black skirts kept as still by their consternation as if they were carved in stone.

The intensely visual *chiaroscuro* scene endows the remembered women in their workaday skirts and blouses with the fixed formal grief of sculpture ('*as if* they were carved in stone'). And yet if works of art move their viewers, it is because their stillness also implies that tension of mourning and dismay which is implicit in the women's stricken rigidity. It follows that art is a matter of representing human consciousness: a point to which the book will return.

The second scene is the newsreel showing the assassination of King Alexander at Marseilles, which Rebecca West says she watched several times (p. 16). She reads it like an art film whose theme is the tragedy of Europe, 'as if there lay behind the surface of things a reality which at any moment might manifest itself as a eucharist to be partaken of not by individuals, but by nations' (p. 19). That 'reality' is seen in King Alexander's expression of total concentration on his kingdom and, as he dies, in the helpless compassion of the bystanders whose 'innumerable hands caress him' (p. 17, illustrated with a still from the newsreel on the facing page) and in the crowd, 'rigid with horror and reverence' (p. 18), watching Alexander's coffin being carried back to the warship which brought the king to Marseilles. 'They are intensely surprised that the eucharist was of this nature, but the King of Yugoslavia had always thought that it might be so' (p. 19). As with the mourning women, reality here takes on the intensity and signifying richness of art. But whereas the comfortable English rarely achieve this intensity of feeling and gesture, Slavs are doomed to live constantly on this level of tragic awareness. That is why Rebecca West has to go to Yugoslavia to understand her own life.

The distinction with which I began this chapter, between 'central' masculine case-histories and 'marginalized' feminine perspectives, appears, then, to break down when applied to Rebecca West, because she, like Marion Milner, writes both as a woman and as a representative human being. Conversely, Edward Upward's hero, the 'Tutor', is as much excluded by and dependent upon his employer as Pompey Casmilus is on hers. It therefore follows that there can be nothing *essentially* marginal about the representation of female selfhood.[67] Conversely, the 'case-history' form of autobiography, which does seem to be a 'masculine' genre in the 1930s, has not stayed so. Not only has the 'cradle-to-coming-of-age' novel, which Isherwood saw as the typical symptomatic text of a specifically male generation (*Lions and Shadows*, p. 74), now become a familiar feminist genre;[68] but much recent feminist discursive writing has often been hybridized by the insertion of authorial 'case-histories' as illustrative examples, just as in the books of literary criticism or social commentary which I discuss in the first section of this chapter. These have ranged from the brief personal narratives in *Our Bodies, Ourselves* (Women's Health Collective, 1978) to the sophisticated self-reflexiveness of Valerie Walkerdine's *Schoolgirl Fictions* (1990) and Liz Stanley's *The Auto/Biographical I* (1992).[69] The critic Nancy K. Miller has influentially argued that this form of 'personal criticism' is the quintessentially feminist form of literary theory; though not all feminists would agree.[70] It seems that to read autobiographical texts by either sex adequately one must acknowledge their context in history. To neglect that context is to risk typing women or men according to their class or gender; which is almost (though not quite) as bad as ignoring one sex altogether.

Chapter 3

Vamps and victims
Images of women in the left-wing literature of the 1930s

To be 'lifelike' it is neither necessary nor sufficient for a work of fiction to be literally true to life: what is essential is that it should accord with the reader's expectations of life – expectations based not only on direct experience but on the conventions of existing literature.

Sarah Caudwell

Give me a Muse with stockings and suspenders
And a smile like a cat,
With false eyelashes and fingernails of carmine
And dressed by Schiaparelli, with a pill-box hat.

Louis MacNeice[1]

WOMEN AS SIGNS

To write about the way in which the canonical writers of the 1930s represent women is to apply a 'slantways' focus to their work. Neither Auden, Spender, Day Lewis, Louis MacNeice, Christopher Isherwood, George Orwell nor Rex Warner showed much interest in female subjectivity; and of these, only Isherwood, who in his old age became a public spokesman for Gay Liberation, ever showed any interest in dismantling sexual stereotypes – and then only for his own sex. The left-wing writings which these men produced during the thirties are, as I argued in Chapter 2, both strongly autobiographical and much influenced by the writers' acute awareness of their own overdetermined position as historical subjects responding to events that they did not shape. This autobiographical slant, obvious in the poems of Spender and the prose writings of Isherwood and Orwell, is also present in the poems, novels and verse plays which reshaped these writers' private mythologies of their own lives into public parables. In the verse-play *Paid on Both Sides* (1930), Auden represented his own Oedipal dilemma as the predicament of a generation; and *The Ascent of F6* (1937), which he wrote with

Isherwood, does something similar. The verse-plays of MacNeice and Spender similarly transform the personal into the political, as do Day Lewis' longer poems, such as *From Feathers to Iron* (1931), which commemorates the gestation and birth of his first son, and the sequence *The Magnetic Mountain* (1933), about his own journey to Communism. None of these plays or poems deals directly with women, although female symbolism plays an important part in them all.

These writers' awareness of being subject to history did not stop them from taking gender privilege for granted, with what now looks like a staggering degree of arrogance, as their right and due. They defined thought, politics and poetry as, without argument or question, exclusively masculine preserves. This assumption equally underpins Auden's half-joking Lawrentian dictum that for the healing of England 'all of the women and most of the men/ Shall work with their hands and not think again', Spender's all-male revolutionary rhetoric, and Geoffrey Grigson's dictum that poetry should be written in ordinary speech, 'the language in which one is angry about Spain or pleasant or unpleasant to one's wife'.[2] To recast Grigson's phrase as 'the language in which one is pleasant or unpleasant to one's husband' is immediately to make plain its assumption of privilege, for it could only be spoken by an unusually dominant wife. Most telling of all is the parable with which C. Day Lewis opened his study of contemporary poets, *A Hope for Poetry*:

> In English poetry there have been several occasions when the younger son, fretting against parental authority, weary of work on the home farm, suspecting too that the soil needs a rest, has packed his bag and set out for a far country. Rumours of his doings come to our ears; they are generally unfavourable, and always distorted, for they have had to pass across seas. He is flirting with foreign whores, we hear, or with ghosts: he has wasted his fortune: he has forgotten how to speak English: he has shamed his father: he has gone mad in the desert: he died some years ago. There is a great deal of indignation in the home town. Only his father smiles indulgently, assured of the vigour of his seed. Then the younger son returns, not a broken prodigal, but healthy, wealthy and wise. He has many acres under cultivation over there, we find: he has money in the bank, strange tales to tell us, and some fine children already. We assure him that we had said all along he would make good, but we cannot help feeling a bit small.[3]

In this cheerful parable of a Prodigal Son who makes his detractors change their tune by returning tall, travelled and as splendidly loaded with possessions as the Jumblies sailing back from the hills of the Chankly

Bore,[4] Day Lewis unselfconsciously asserts the virility of modern poetry. The potency of modern poetry – 'the younger son' – is affirmed by work in progress and acclaimed publications (represented by 'acres under cultivation' and 'money in the bank'), creative achievements (represented by 'strange tales to tell') and even a tradition in the making (that is, his 'fine children'). This allegory assumes that 'English poetry' is, exclusively, a man's affair; the patriarchal Spirit of Poetry appears to father his son by the miraculous 'vigour of his seed' alone. This account of poetic tradition is a left-wing version of the genealogy parodied by Cyril Connolly in *Enemies of Promise*: 'There is a natural tradition in English poetry, my dear Tim, Chaucer begat Spenser, Spenser begat Shakespeare, Shakespeare begat Milton, Milton begat Keats, Coleridge, Shelley, Wordsworth, and they begat Tennyson...'[5] Needless to say, Day Lewis' *A Hope for Poetry* does not name a single woman poet.

The imperialist assumptions of Day Lewis' parable are also now as painfully obvious as its sexism. Clearly, the objection that English poets also include daughters and mothers is no more part of its intellectual world than the notion that the successful colonist might not, from a colonial subject's point of view, look like a hero. (The allegorical trope whereby a colonial planter's acquisition of landed wealth represents the tradition of English poetry, is actually rich in unconscious ironies of the kind analysed by Edward Said and Gayatri Chakravorty Spivak.[6]) My object here, however, is not to score points off the 'Auden Generation' male writers for being guilty of patriarchal male chauvinism and unconscious imperialism, features which seem to me too self-evident to need much labouring. A more interesting question, which this chapter attempts to answer, is, 'What sort of meanings did their sexual signifiers carry?'

It is important here to take account of context. Many of the most stereotypical representations of women by the 'Auden Generation' poets occur in the experimental verse-plays which they wrote for the Group Theatre, an association of actors and dancers who were inspired, trained and organized by the dancer and director Rupert Doone, between 1932 and 1938. As Michael Sidnell has shown in *Dances of Death*, his excellent history of the Group Theatre, Doone and his colleagues attempted, with genuine if finally limited success, to change the naturalistic face of English drama by producing deliberately stylized, often avant-garde plays. Dance and choreography played a major role in the Group Theatre productions, which were influenced by the theories and practice of Cocteau and Diaghilev as well as Brecht.[7] It is hardly surprising that, when left-wing ex-public schoolboys wrote and produced deliberately extravagant, non-naturalistic plays that satirized their own class, they represented the females of this species as caricature villains, just as they did with the figures of male authority like the Fascist Leader, the mad Vicar or the corrupt Press Baron. Nevertheless, the representation of women in the Group Theatre plays is done with a venom which cannot be wholly accounted for by their satirical intent and deliberately simplified characterization.

The female characters in the plays of Auden, Isherwood and Spender are almost uniformly threatening and treacherous. Older women represent the deadly power of reactionary authority, either as mothers who give their sons up to death, or worse still as childless women who vent their frustration at their own barrenness in a death wish against young men. Young women, less threateningly, are expensive temptresses or, very occasionally, brides. These images of women represent both the ideological demands and the often illusory rewards with which a reactionary State bullies and tempts the revolutionary hero: a theme also worked by Day Lewis in his sequence *The Magnetic Mountain*, discussed below. Auden's narrative poems also have at times a strong misogynist streak, especially the malicious comic ballads which he wrote in the late thirties, 'Miss Gee', 'Victor', 'James Honeyman' and the posthumously published 'Sue',[8] all of which gleefully culminate in the death of a woman. Married women get killed by their husbands, deliberately by Victor and inadvertently by James Honeyman; single women destroy themselves out of boredom, like Sue, or out of repression, like poor dowdy cancerous Miss Gee. Since almost all members of the Group Theatre were homosexual – including Rupert Doone the director, his lover Robert Medley who designed the sets, and the young Benjamin Britten who wrote much of the music – this aggressive treatment of female characters might be explained as gay misogyny. Yet, however anti-feminist their imaginative writings, in life Isherwood and Auden had warmly affectionate friendships with women.[9] Moreover, almost equally hostile representations of women are to be found in the robustly heterosexual poems of Day Lewis, whose 'Magnetic Mountain' makes the hero's enemies include a murderously possessive mother-figure and a snaky seductress.

DEVOURING MOTHERS AND REVENGEFUL SPINSTERS: WOMEN IN THE PLAYS OF AUDEN, ISHERWOOD AND SPENDER

> He is defeated; let the son
> Sell the farm lest the mountain fall,
> His mother and her mother won.

W. H. Auden

Poor mummy. She really was a *femme fatale*, wasn't she? She killed at a touch.

Evelyn Waugh[10]

All the experimental dramas written by Auden and his colleagues in the 1930s are autobiographical parables about the relation between private and public worlds, in which the hero's life represents the characteristic dilemma of the whole 'Auden Generation'. Though not central to the hero's story, Woman is, typically, important in it. As temptation or threat, she represents part of the hero's problem, while, as reconciling bride, she may also represent a possible symbolic solution.

Clearly I am drawing the terms of this description from Samuel Hynes' influential account of the work of the 'Auden Generation' male writers as creators of non-naturalistic 'parable art', representing public, political issues through a private mythology.[11] The public–private dichotomy tends to efface women as subjects, because the feminine is conventionally associated with the world of private life. This is certainly true of the Group Theatre plays: the mother or maiden aunt is part of a domestic scenario, while the siren belongs in the bedroom, or at best the shopping arcade. (The only woman in these plays who actually enters public life is the wicked Wife in *Trial of a Judge* – who ends up as one of a uniformed Fascist junta.) Yet these 'privatized' female characters also carry a much wider, public significance. The devouring Mother who dooms her son to destruction represents the bitterness famously felt by the younger wartime generation against its patriotic elders in the Great War, and thus personifies a whole blameworthy generation. More than this, she also represents the means whereby the claims of the State get their claws into the young man's psyche. Her near relation, the enraged barren woman who vents her frustration on the young, conversely represents the psychopathology of Fascism. The lovely Vamp is a class signifier as much as a sexual one, for she is the ultimate luxury, affordable only by the rich. Her charm, which resides in her expensive accoutrements as much as in her looks, makes her the prime signifier of the privilege enjoyed by the ruling class, and thus also of their guilt. This notion of female beauty as the incarnation of class privilege is shared by many other Socialist writers of the thirties as well as the 'Auden Generation' poets; a theme which I discuss in detail later in this chapter (see pp. 94–8).

Mothers are the chief culprits of Auden's first play, the 'charade' *Paid on Both Sides*[12], a tragedy of two embattled families, the Nowers and the Shaws, fighting over a 'Northern' landscape. Their feud, like that of Mark Twain's Grangerfords and Shepherdsons,[13] seems to have begun before living memory and looks set to continue for ever. Edward Mendelson describes its imaginary world as having 'a past but no history', yet the play itself is very much of its historical moment. Auden called the play 'a parable of English middle class (professional) family life 1907–1929'[14] – a period which runs from the year of his birth to the year he completed it. Isherwood wrote of *Paid* that its tight-lipped idiom makes its characters into a cross between Icelandic warriors and 'the members of a school OTC'.[15] This is true but misleading, because the play is not about male communities, but about the dynamics of families where fathers vanish and possessive mothers destroy their sons' lives.

Wealthy, powerful, and mutually destructive, the Nower and the Shaw families are mirror images of each other; on each side, the fathers are killed off young, and their widows bring up their orphaned sons to carry on the feud, regarding any attempt at reconciliation as betrayal of the memory of the dead. The 'hero' John Nower is thus the victim of his family's tradition of revenge, right from the moment of his premature birth which is brought on by his mother's shock when she hears that her husband has been assassinated. The bereaved Joan dooms the infant to 'an unforgiving morning' (p. 12), and then disappears from the play – except, crucially, as a forbidding figure in her son's psyche.

The grown-up John, having imbibed his family's gangster ethic, is next seen successfully arranging the assassination of the head of the opposition, 'Red Shaw' and other members of his family. A Shaw survivor is caught and shot as a spy. This leads to a fantasy scene, based partly on the dream of a shell-shocked Army officer recorded by the psychiatrist W. H. Rivers, and partly on the traditional mummers' play,[16] in which the Spy, representing John's own repressed sexuality, is put on trial with 'John as the accuser, the spy as accused and Joan as his warder, with a gigantic feeding bottle'. John's 'evidence' against the Spy, who represents his own repressed desires, consists entirely of a patriotic speech (p. 22):

> I know we have and are making terrible sacrifices, but we cannot give in. We cannot betray the dead. As we pass by their graves can we be deaf to the simple eloquence of their inscriptions, those who in the glory of their early manhood gave up their lives for us? No, we must fight to the finish.

The rhetoric which Auden parodies here does not merely accuse its speaker, by implication, of hypocrisy; more specifically, it identifies him with the bloodthirsty generals and politicians who were responsible for the mass slaughters of the trenches. The later *Dog Beneath the Skin* (1935), which he wrote with Isherwood, contains a feminine version of this cant in the

Queen of Ostnia's speech to the bereaved wives and mothers of strikers ceremonially shot by the King:

> I too have borne the pangs of childbirth . . . I too am a wife and have lain in the strong arms of the beloved. Remember then, in your loss, that in all you suffer, I suffer with you . . . Be comforted, therefore, and abide patiently, strong in the hope that you will meet your loved ones in another and better world.[17]

Prompted by his mother, John shoots the fantasy Spy, more reluctantly than he shot the real one. He is then rebuked for his stunted emotional development, and the corpse is revived by a comic doctor (much borrowing here from the mummers' play). Having acknowledged his own sexuality and discovered emotional liberation in a vision of progress and fertility, John proposes marriage to Anne Shaw of the 'enemy' family. Their betrothal, symbolizing the reconciliation of the warring families, is broken up, inevitably, by Anne's mother who nags Seth, the only remaining Shaw male, into revenging his father and brother (p. 32):

> Have you forgotten your brother's death . . . taken out and shot like a dog? It is a nice thing for me to hear people saying that I have a coward for a son. I am thankful your father is not here to see it.

Though cast in a quite different idiom from the tired 'public' rhetoric of John Nower's 'patriotic' speech in the dream scene, this 'egging-on' directly parallels John's insistence on the duty owed by the living to the dead. Seth obediently murders John, and the feud continues: 'His mother and her mother won' (p. 33). Mrs Shaw and Joan Nower both seem, like the Queen of Ostnia in the later play, to be close relatives of the infamous 'Little Mother' immortalized by Robert Graves, so eager to sacrifice her children and so full, like John Nower, of jingoistic rhetoric: 'The corn that will wave over land watered by the blood of our brave lads shall testify to the future that their blood was not spilt in vain'.[18]

Fathers are conspicuous by their absence from this scenario; John's is killed off at the start of the play, and Seth's never appears at all. John's patriotic speech about 'our duty to the dead' makes him sound like one of those father-figures accused by the war poets: 'If any question why we died/ Tell them, because our fathers lied'.[19] But of course he is *not* one of the fathers, which is the point; he is only their heir. Having repressed his own desires, he lacks words to articulate them; the Spy who represents his imprisoned libido can only groan, not speak (p. 22). John's own language is simply a gramophone record, to use the period simile, reproducing the empty speech of his dead and imagined fathers, like the repressed subject in Auden's contemporary poem in whose mind ghosts must forever 'do again/ What gives them pain.'[20] The psychic cost of the War is thus what Auden would call ten years later the 'dishonest mood of denial' from which patriots suffer, and since the condition affects both families, the price is 'paid on both sides'.[21]

The autobiographical application of Auden's parable of English family life is obvious. The image of the son brought up in a world of murderous conflict, without a father and with a dominating mother, is transparently drawn from the poet's own childhood and adolescence during the First World War.[22] On the other hand, the play ignores Auden's own homosexuality, representing heterosexual love as the solution of the hero's conflicts: 'Now this shall end with marriage as it ought' (p. 31). It may appear odd, on the face of it, that a satire on the bourgeois family should represent the proper solution of its conflicts as the successful attempt 'to bring home a wife' (p. 37) and to found a male dynasty. But as Lucy MacDiarmid has pointed out, the image of a symbolic heterosexual reconciliation appears as a consistent ideal in Auden's plays, though one invariably prevented by adverse circumstances from actually happening.[23] In *The Dog Beneath the Skin*, the successful quester Alan is supposed to be marrying Iris, the 'princess' of the ideal English village: a wedding which is prevented by the rancorous class conflicts which have turned half the village Fascist and have caused Iris herself to marry 'Mr Rudolph Trunnion-James', obviously one of the bosses;[24] and in *On the Frontier*, the frustration of the love between the 'Ostnian' girl Anna and the 'Westland' boy Eric signifies, none too subtly, these warring nations' sickness.

The Ascent of F 6 (1937), which Auden wrote in collaboration with Christopher Isherwood, deals more overtly with the relation between homosexuality, the family, and the needs of an imperialist State, handling the joint themes of Oedipal trauma and the demands of 'England, home and duty' not much less savagely than *Paid*. Its tragic hero, Michael Ransom, leads a doomed British expedition to scale 'F 6', a mountain in African 'Sudoland'. The project is financed by a Press Baron, partly as a publicity stunt but mainly to secure the prestige of Britain as a colonial power. The British Empire in Africa is being threatened by the European state 'Ostnia', which has sent out a rival mountaineering party. This threatens English interests in the region because – a distinctly John Buchan touch here – 'the natives have begun telling each other that the white man who first reaches the summit of F 6, will be lord over *both* Sudolands, with his descendants, for a thousand years'.[25] Michael Ransom knows he ought to have nothing to do with this imperialist con-trick; but, being a Truly Weak Man[26] who has to prove himself by attempting heroic ventures, he is tempted by F 6 as the ultimate challenge to his skill, and finally persuaded to climb it by maternal blackmail. Mrs Ransom (a widow, needless to say), appears as a horridly possessive devourer who, after pressuring her son to risk his life, appears 'talking to herself in a hoarse and penetrating whisper':

> Michael... Michael darling... can you hear me? There's nothing to be frightened about. Mother's with you. Of course she won't leave you alone, Michael, never. Wherever you are, whatever you're doing, whether you know it or not, she's with you with her love: for you belong to her always. She's with you now, at sea, on board the ship with your foolish companions, and she'll be with you on the mountain too... And she'll be with you at the very end.

Her grisly promise is followed by a song which celebrates her conquest of Michael:

> You shall be mine, all mine,
> You shall have kisses like wine,
> When the wine gets into your head
> Mother will see that you're not misled.
> A saint am I and a saint are you,
> It's perfectly, perfectly, perfectly true.[27]

The promise of 'kisses like wine' (it is not said from whom) and of a safe bedtime, clearly mean that the mother wants to possess her son, which she can do most completely by sending him to his death. For the expedition ends, inevitably, in disaster with the death of almost all its members, including Ransom. Having led the others to their deaths, the hero reaches the top of the mountain to confront the fabled 'Demon' who haunts F 6, in a fantasy scene in which all the other characters appear to him as dream versions of themselves, rather as the English characters in Evelyn Waugh's *A Handful of Dust* appear to the delirious Tony Last in the Brazilian jungle.[28]

As in the dream scene in *Paid*, a murder is committed at the mother's command and a trial ensues to decide the guilt. Here, however, the victim is not the hero's repressed libido; instead, it is his brother James who is killed by a veiled Figure (p. 112), who is finally revealed as Mrs Ransom (p. 117). The meaning of this dream seems to be that Ransom's jealous Oedipal desire to have his mother to himself inspires the dream-wish that she would 'kill' his rival James by rejection, thereby saving the dreamer from the guilt of murder. The ghosts of his dead companions, however, are not fooled by this displacement and know very well who is guilty (pp. 114– 15). Thus the dreaded 'Demon' of the mountain is both the hero's own murderous weakness and – of course – his mother.[29] But this is not the whole story, for Ransom dies as much the victim of England and its rulers as of his own Oedipal weakness. At the moment of his death, a chorus composed of the Empire-builders who sent him out there and 'Mr and Mrs A', the average people who wanted him to be their hero, unite to demand that he sacrifice himself:

GENERAL   Die for England!
ISABEL   Honour!
STAGMANTLE   Service!
GENERAL   Duty!
ISABEL   Sacrifice!
ALL   Die for England.
VOICE   Ostnia.
ALL   England. England. England.
MR AND MRS A   Die for us![30]

As Michael Ransom obeys, to the sound of 'thunder and the roar of an avalanche', the Figure/ Demon of his dream turns into 'Mrs Ransom as a young mother' (p. 117)

ANSOM   Mother!
MRS RANSOM   My boy! At last!

This perfect match between the dying Ransom's fantasy of possessing his mother, and his mother's own fantasy of possessing her son in death, indicates that Mrs Ransom is much less a character than a projection of Oedipal desires, fears and hatreds. Yeats, who as an Irishman was acutely aware of the imperialist implications of Ransom's venture, suggested to Rupert Doone that the Group Theatre's production should make Mrs Ransom appear in the final tableau as 'Britannia from the penny':[31] an excellent stage image which would have connected the play's 'private' fantasy of the powerful, devouring mother with the 'public' imperialist iconography of Britannia, the Mother Country who rules the waves by sacrificing her sons.

Mothers may be 'Freudian carnivores'[32] in the Auden Generation's plays, but barren women are a great deal worse. The widow/spinster Mildred Luce in *The Dog Beneath the Skin* is a truly bloodthirsty specimen of this pathology. When the hero Alan is sent off on his quest to restore the missing heir of 'Pressan Ambo', the ideal English village, she appears loudly mourning her two sons who were shot by 'a German sniper' in the war.[33] She hates Alan for being young, but neverthless has instructions for him (p. 204):

> Set off for Germany and shoot them all!
> Poison the wells, till her people drink the sea
> And perish howling. Strew all her fields
> With arsenic, leave a land whose crops
> Would starve the unparticular hyena!

Mildred reappears, even more crazy and hate-filled, at the end of the play where Alan returns, having discovered Francis the missing heir to Pressan Ambo, which is no longer an idyllic Eden but a centre of British Fascism. Revealing himself to the villagers, Francis tells Mildred and the assembly that her public hatred of Germany is a lie; Mildred never had any sons, and her real tragedy is her virginity (p. 287):

> There was talk at one time of your engagement to a young German cavalry officer. But you hadn't the heart to leave your mother alone.
>
> A doctor would say you hate the Germans because you dare not hate your mother and he would be mistaken. What you really hate is a social system in which love is controlled by money. Won't you help us to destroy it?

Francis' appeal falls on deaf ears (not surprisingly, since by his own account Mildred's frustration has less to do with money than with yet another bad mother) – and she shoots him.[34] In *The Chase*, an early version of the play, she then chants a psalm of vengeance:

> Break their teeth, O Lord, in their mouths; smite the jawbones of the lions, O God; let them fall away like water that runneth apace; and when they shoot their arrows let them be rooted out.
>
> Let them consume away like a snail, and be like the untimely fruit of a woman; and let them not see the sun.
>
> The righteous shall rejoice when he seeth the vengeance; he shall wash his footsteps in the blood of the ungodly.
>
> So that a man shall say: verily there is a reward for the righteous; doubtless there is a God that judgeth the earth.[35]

Having successfully used her to get rid of Francis, Mildred's masters promptly dispose of her: 'The woman's a public menace. I'll get her certified. She ought to have been long ago' (p. 291). Her murder of the hero is a caricature-allegory of the way in which the forces of reaction exploit the psychic sickness of English society; she is thus almost (though not quite) as much a victim of her own class as the dead Francis.

Another fire-eating female reactionary, Martha Thorwald of *On the Frontier*, similarly takes out her own frustrations in fanatical devotion to Westland's Fascist Leader. She does, however, become briefly sympathetic, or at least pathetic, when she articulates her pain directly:

You don't know what it's like to be ugly, to see everyone else getting married, to spend your life looking after other people's children! I've sacrificed everything! I had brains! I might have had a brilliant career but I gave it all up for you! I've been more loyal than any of them! If you let me die, there's no point in being good, any more! It doesn't matter! It's all a lie! I've never been happy! I've been betrayed!'[36]

As with Mildred's lunacy, Martha's plight has a wider representative meaning: she stands for all those who take out personal frustrations in blind, romantic patriotism. Both these women become destructive through frustration and denial, displacing their private desires on to false 'public' images. Martha really wants a husband and family and Mildred really wants her German lover; deprived of these satisfactions, one woman worships the Leader and the other indulges in fantasies of slaughter which turn into real murder. Their predicament thus represents a political variant of the 'Miss Gee' syndrome, whereby repressed desires turn lethal. But whereas Edith Gee's cancerous repressions are represented as comic, harming only herself, these much more sinister spinsters represent a symptom of social disorder and at the same time a threat to their disordered society. Yet, unlike Miss Gee, who lives and dies in denial, these two dramatic characters do become briefly sympathetic during the moment of acknowledging their own deprivation – or, in Mildred's case, of being faced with it. Isherwood's slightly earlier novel *The Memorial* (1932) has a very similar moment of sympathy interrupting its otherwise unremittingly ironic portrait of the war widow 'Lily' who devours her son Eric as a substitute for the dead husband whom she really wants. Lily confronts her own loss, for the first and only time, during a memorial service for the soldiers killed in the war, including her own husband (a scene paralleled, interestingly, in the novels of Storm Jameson and Winifred Holtby[37]). Lily's appalled realization that 'Richard isn't here . . . Richard isn't anywhere. He's gone. He's dead',[38] does not alter or excuse her dreadful pious 'niceness' or her destructive influence on her son. Yet her unappeased grief nevertheless represents a core of self-knowledge and therefore a potential, if not actual, redemption.

No such redeeming festures, however, exist in the Wife of the liberal hero in Spender's *Trial of a Judge*. In this tragedy of impotent liberalism, the Judge is compelled to try 'Three Blacks' (i.e. 'Black Shirts', aka Nazis) who have murdered 'Petra' a Communist Jew. He condemns them to death, as the law demands, along with three much less guilty 'Reds' condemned on a legal technicality. His old friend Hummeldorf and his pro-Fascist Wife persuade the Judge to pardon and release the 'Blacks'; he then tries to withdraw his pardon, and is prevented from doing so by a counter-revolution, which results in his arrest and trial for being insufficiently pro-Fascist. By the end, both he and the Reds are all in jail or shot.

The play contains three female characters, the Red 'Fiancée' – pregnant by Petra and representing hope through her fertility – and two older women – Petra's mother, a pious old terror, and the Judge's Wife, who sympathizes with the Fascists and finally joins them, colluding in her husband's trial and death, because she is a frustrated woman who wants to punish the world for her own disappointments. In terms of the play's political allegory, her sterility probably represents the impotence of her elderly husband's liberalism which, unlike the hopeful Communists, cannot construct a future or father a child. But she is also a psychological 'case' whose self-abandonment to the forces of destruction makes her very similar to Mildred Luce and Martha Thorwald. Unlike these, however, she is remarkably self-conscious about her own mental processes, describing them in a long rant which cannot have been easy for the actress to deliver:

Everything has been wrong for forty years
Because I bore no child.
But now the decorated war restores
Men to their sun and women to their night ...
My breasts were starved because they gave no food,
My cries of hatred were as instinctive
As the babe's scream till the nurse brings its nappy.
But now I forget my self-destroying poison:
In the larger hate which destroys the world
The time is redeemed and I am content ...
Let all children be killed, their little dreams
Flake like ashes under the melted girders.
I have waited for this general anger
To lance my crippled soul of poison
Till my hate explodes in war like a bomb. I am glad.
Oh love, I'm cured, I'm cured.[39]

The Wife's moment of liberation leads to a welcome of the 'dear old days' of militarism and discipline (p. 59); and she ends up as one of the ruling élite. Though implausible in naturalistic terms, this plotting nevertheless makes good symbolic sense. The Wife's enthusiastic capitulation to Fascism represents middle-class women's political support for the Nazis, the psychological attraction which Fascism holds for the frustrated bourgeoisie, and the death wish of a whole nation, imaged in her final paean to Fascism and War (Act V, p. 115):

> Our men's faces in uniforms all one face,
> The face of those who enter a wood
> Whose branches bleed and skies hail lead.
> And the aerial vultures fly
> Over the deserts which were cities.
> Kill! Kill! Kill! Kill!

CLASS STEREOTYPES: THE EXPENSIVE WHORE AND THE WASHERWOMAN

> The stockings she wore were six-and-eleven the pair
> But O they were frankly class-conscious and sheer.
> Her shoes were of glacé with a fringed suede tongue,
> Bangles on each arm, as she liked to look young.
>
> W. H. Auden

> I had time to see everything about her, her sacking apron, her clumsy clogs, her arms reddened by the cold. . . . She had a round pale face, the usual exhausted face of the slum girl who is twenty-five and looks forty, thanks to miscarriages and drudgery; and it wore, for the second in which I saw it, the most desolate, hopeless expression I have ever seen.
>
> George Orwell[40]

Although the writers quoted above are usually considered to be opposites rather than parallels, Auden's ballad about 'Sue' whose clothes and possessions incarnate ruling-class luxury and privilege, and Orwell's documentary image of the inarticulate slum girl whose sordid physical suffering represents the general misery of the working class, use the image of a woman's body as a class signifier in very similar ways. The rhetorical trope whereby a woman's body personifies a class is a common feature of the Socialist writings of the thirties – far more so, in fact, than the maternal harpies in the plays of Auden, Isherwood and Spender, which have few parallels elsewhere. Wealthy women especially personify the privilege of the ruling class. Of course wealthy men of the ruling class are also satirized but, despite their far greater power, they rarely seem to carry the same weight of class guilt as their expensively dressed ladies, whose very stockings are 'frankly class-conscious and sheer'.

The classic example of the upper-class vamp is Sue, the eponymous heroine of Auden's cheerful, malicious ballad. Her character is entirely composed of her possessions, which are catalogued over several stanzas, from her extensive wardrobe, her cosmetics and stockings to her long, low car with grey upholstery, on whose seats 'Were five half-empty boxes of expensive sweets'. Her death from boredom and anomie resembles the fate of 'Prince Alpha', the Truly Weak Man who wearies of his own heroism and dies in the slightly earlier poem 'The Witnesses'. Prince Alpha's adventures are catalogued with similarly ironic brio – 'Where did he travel? Where didn't he travel?/ Over the ice and over the gravel/ and the sea. . . . What did he do? What didn't he do?/ He rescued maidens, overthrew/ ten giants/ like factory chimneys, slaughtered dragons . . .';[41] the difference is that, whereas the man is defined by his achievements, the woman is defined by her possessions. Eventually, 'tired of pleasure and tired of herself', Sue finds that her accoutrements turn hostile:

> She went to the mirror and started to cry,
> The mirror whispered suddenly, 'You're right, die. . . . '

> 'No one will mourn her when she is dead,'
> A fluted robe severely said.
> A pair of directoire knickers agreed,
> 'I think she's a most unpleasant girl indeed.'

> Then a poult-de-soie dress with a taffeta cloque
> Shut in the wardrobe, stirred and spoke:
> 'I disliked her from the moment when I saw her in the shop.
> I shan't be happy till I see her drop.'

A rich woman like Sue is presented as a legitimate target for aggression because her expensively adorned body represents class privilege. Vamps like her also feature in the Group Theatre plays, notably 'Lou Vipond', a famous beauty who is briefly the hero's mistress in *The Dog Beneath the Skin*, and 'Clara de Groot', the film star beloved by the hero in MacNeice's *Out of the Picture*. Auden and Isherwood intended Lou to be not a woman but a mirage, produced by her desirable accoutrements: the stage directions (not followed in Rupert Doone's production) call for 'a shopwindow dummy, very beautifully dressed. When the dummy is to speak, Alan runs behind it and speaks in falsetto'.[42] An affair with this pure essence of commodities is liable to run anyone but a millionaire into debt, costing as she does (p. 269):

> 20 cases of champagne
> A finest pedigree great Dane

Half a dozen Paris frocks
A sable fur, a silver fox,
Bottles of scent and beauty salves,
An MG Midget with overhead valves

... and very much more. When her lover is unable to pay for all this, she is of course unhelpful. In *The Chase*, an earlier draft of this play, she announces candidly, 'My friend/ I do not lend/ I spend';[43] in the final version, she simply fails to answer.

Louis MacNeice's play *Out of the Picture* (1938), also a Group Theatre production, is a differently angled satire on the notion of female glamour. MacNeice's play is far less harsh to women, for in general this poet regards the opposite sex more kindly than any of the other 'Auden Group' poets, not sharing their mocking disapproval of sexy well-dressed ladies. His *Autumn Journal* often celebrates the images of desirable woman, sometimes frankly described as a luxury – 'All I want is an elegant and witty playmate/ At the perfume counter or the cocktail bar', and sometimes seen more generously, like the feminine lover – 'frivolous, always in a hurry, forgetting the address/ Taking enormous notice/ Of hats and backchat', whom the poet nevertheless praises for her qualities of generosity and honesty, in which he finds her superior to himself.[44] And his play *Out of the Picture*, a dramatic parable about the artist's narcissism in a time of imminent catastrophe, comes close to representing women as fellow-humans rather than as a threat or promise. Its hero, the artist Portright (= self-Portrait?), lives by exploiting women: first his landlady, an old family retainer, whose rent he never pays, and second his model Moll O'Hara, whose wages he also never pays. He uses Moll as a lay figure for an inaccurate, idealized portrait, which he then falls in love with, loses and spends much of the play attempting to retrieve. Portright is no great artist: his painting turns the generous, sensible Moll into the image of 'Clara de Groot' the film star, a narcissist who likes to call herself 'she' and whose idea of a romantic evening is to take a lover to 'the pictures', by which she means films starring herself. Clara, who lives by pleasing the gaze – her image fascinates millions, thus endowing her with enormous wealth as well as beauty – is Portright's partner in narcissism. The artist falls in love with the second-hand image he has painted of a woman who lives by reflection in others' admiring eyes. Meanwhile, an all-destroying war is about to break out, making nonsense of everyone's dreams and wishes.

Such empty-headed, evil rich women appear frequently in the left-wing literature of the thirties. The 'First Enemy' in Day Lewis' long poem *The Magnetic Mountain* is a seductress who betrays her manipulation of her lover as she wields a typically feminine luxury object – 'Reach for the powder-puff, I have sinned greatly. *I suppose you hate me, now*'.[45] Similar figures are to be found in prose fiction; the rich ladies in Jack Lindsay's historical novel *1649*, which I discuss in Chapter 5, similarly manifest their evil ruling-class identities in their silk dresses and pearl necklaces, while in Winifred Holtby's *Mandoa, Mandoa!* (1933) the luxurious decadence of the English upper classes is personified in the exquisitely nasty Felicity Cardover, beautifully dressed and 'irresistible to both sexes'[46] The parasitic, charming Brenda Last in Waugh's *A Handful of Dust* is another of the same breed. But the most powerful representations of sirens are probably the unnamed girl desired by the hero of Edward Upward's *Journey to the Border* and her near relation Sally Bowles in Isherwood's *Goodbye to Berlin*. In Upward's novel the *luxe, calme et volupte* for which his hero longs is personified in the beautiful, tempting girl who invites his advances (pp. 169–70):

> Her hands rose towards her throat, gripping the edges of her fur coat. The coat fell open, exposing a silk-covered bosom. Her small blue scarf pointed downwards between her breasts. He was not deceived, knew without the least doubt that her action was a deliberate trick. But there was no trickery, nothing artificial, about what she had to show him.

Of course, the girl is only playing with him, for these vamps in their fur coats and silk-covered bosoms never really want sex, only power. (Day Lewis' seductress similarly regards the male as her 'trembling prey', getting her pleasure from contemplating his surrender, not from 'the harsh friction, the gritted teeth of lust'.[47]) Having hooked the tutor, she promptly informs him that she is engaged to another man – 'What bitches women are. I don't know why I did it. You are the only man I've ever cared for' (p. 172), flirts, humiliates and then dismisses him: 'You mustn't look so miserable. I don't like it. . . . You poor little swine' (p. 183).[48]

In her flirtatious sexiness, expensive clothing, coarse language and inconsequent behaviour, Upward's girl resembles the most famous vamp of all, the wicked-innocent Sally Bowles in Isherwood's *Goodbye to Berlin*. Sally, who plays amateurishly at being an actress and a tart, is for ever defined by her first appearance, at once glamorous, 'dressed in black silk, with a small cape over her shoulders and a little cap like a page-boy's stuck on the side of her head', and sordid, with her 'emerald green fingernails call[ing] attention to her hands, which were stained by much smoking and as dirty as a little girl's' (p. 27). Like all these representations of sexy upper-class girls, Isherwood's portrait is remarkably stylized, effectively representing the girl as a doll.

An interesting exception to these relentlessly negative portrayals of bourgeois women in thirties writing is John Betjeman's poem 'Oxford: Sudden Illness at the Bus-Stop',[49] a poem about a middle-aged don's wife who collapses and perhaps dies (the poem is ambiguous) while waiting for a bus on a summer evening. The poet, passing by in his 'sweetly-running' car, imagines the life of this momentarily glimpsed woman, standing at the bus-stop in her dowdy 'velvet gown with a rose pinned neatly', moving outwards from this moment into a bleakly compassionate vision of a woman trapped in an oppressive marriage. The poem belongs to that genre of inter-war writing which Alison Light has usefully defined as 'conservative modernity'.[50] Traditional in form, it uses the same anapaestic quatrains as Cowper's 'The poplars are felled, farewell to the shade'; but it is full of contemporary references to things like cars, plate-glass windows and tinned peas, none of which would be out of place in an Agatha Christie detective novel. And its very unpoetic title, which reads like a news caption from the *Oxford Mail* (from which Betjeman may well have taken it), is left unexplained, in a typically Modernist way, for the readers to work out the link with the poem.

Into his four quatrains, Betjeman compresses a singularly bleak short story. For the details given in the poem, if read attentively, expand the moment when the woman collapses into a capsule account of her dismal married life. The 'don's wife' in her evening gown is evidently taking the bus from North Oxford into the centre of town in order to attend a dinner party in one of the colleges, probably her husband's. She is travelling by bus because she can't afford a taxi (owning a car was still relatively uncommon in the thirties). Since she is travelling alone, her husband must already be in town, in his college rooms. This implies that he not only works in college all day, but habitually dines there, too, at the dons' High Table; otherwise he would have had to go home to change into evening clothes. His wife's pinched existence is indicated by her elderly 'velvet gown', which dates from the Great War. The last lines of the poem also tell us that her financial anxieties have sadly increased since the years when 'Jack' was a only junior don, 'and rents were lower in Rawlinson Road'. Since Jack is evidently now a senior professor, his wife's dowdy appearance cannot be blamed on his low earnings; clearly, he is mean about money, skimping on the housekeeping, leaving her to worry about the rent, and never buying her a new evening dress in twenty years. The poem imagines her life since then:

> What forks since then have been slammed in places?
> What peas turned out from how many a tin?

From plate-glass windows how many faces
Have watched professors come hobbling in?

The domestic existence evoked here is one of cheap and nasty food prepared by discontented, most likely underpaid, servants whose bad temper is suggested by the 'slamming' of forks. (In English middle-class households of the 1930s, it was the wife's job to supervise the servants, not to do the housework.) The language of the line 'What peas turned out from how many a tin?' has a formal, Latinate elegance and an air of slightly pedantic exactness, in marked contrast to that unattractive wet mass of tinned peas which, as often in bourgeois inter-war writings, represent the essence of modern squalor.[51] Worse still are the apprehension and distaste evoked by the faces (of children? of servants?) watching from behind windows while 'Jack' and his aged, unattractive colleagues approach.

A. J. Tolley has illuminatingly likened the tinned peas and forks in this poem to Wallace Stevens' line, 'These are the measures destined for her soul',[52] a comparison which points up the bleakness of Betjeman's poem. The 'don's wife', fearfully watching her husband from behind a blankly reflecting 'plate-glass window' and doomed to live and die without help or comfort, is herself watched by the compassionately knowing poet. This is not a feminist poem; and yet in form, as well as in theme, it enacts the woman's entrapment within the institutions of male authority.

Betjeman is unusual not only in his preparedness, here and elsewhere, to imagine a woman's subjective world,[53] but in seeing a middle-class woman as a victim. Far more common in thirties writing is the figure of the oppressed working-class woman doomed to drudgery, who often appears in 'realist' prose, her bodily degradation representing the dumb misery of her whole class. The most famous of these images of victimized women is the appearance of the slum girl in *The Road to Wigan Pier*, quoted at the head of this section, whose 'round pale face' is glimpsed by Orwell from a railway carriage as she clears a drain in a back yard. Such images of women's bodies as class signifiers are a marked feature of the fictions published as 'Writing in Revolt' (1937) in the fourth number of the left-wing magazine *Fact*. This magazine is remembered, when it is remembered at all, only for Storm Jameson's essay 'Documents',[54] a passionate defence of documentary realism as the significant form of Socialist writing, which appeared in the first section of 'Writing in Revolt', devoted to 'Theory'. The second, much larger section entitled 'Practice', consists mainly of realist short stories, two of which deploy the trope whereby a woman's physical degradation represents working-class oppression: Fred

Urquhart's 'Sweat', whose heroine lacks a bathroom to clean herself after her work in a tailor's sweatshop, and James Hanley's 'An Episode', in which an exhausted charwoman is cheated of her hard-earned wages.

Both these women are clearly near relatives of the girl clearing the drainpipe in *The Road to Wigan Pier*. But whereas Orwell's slum girl is seen to suffer with complete consciousness of her 'dreadful destiny',[55] even if her dumb awareness can only be articulated by the bourgeois male writer's eye and mind, the women in *Fact* represent the misery of their class without understanding it. The stories do enter the subjectivities of the suffering women, but always from a superior vantage point. Jeanie in Fred Urquhart's 'Sweat' becomes obsessed with the idea of her body being repulsively smelly, and in a desperate attempt to please her boyfriend, she plasters herself with 'Flowers of Passion', only to provoke a disdainful response: 'Why the hell d'you put on all that cheap scent?' (p. 53). Jeanie herself sees no further than her own embarrassment and humiliation: it is the reader, not she, who realizes that she is in a trap. James Hanley's charwoman is reduced by her monotonous labour to mindlessness (p. 60):

> She had become the slave of the infernal rhythmical movements of her hands, and as long as the brush made great circular movements, she could not stop her hand from moving. . . . The floor became a world, the world became warder of her life.

This exhausted, miserable woman can't stop herself from nagging her unemployed husband, who is clearly about to leave his family. When he does try to talk, she rebuffs him brutally (p. 64):

> 'Why are we always tormenting the souls out of one another lately?'
> 'Lately', again the woman was sneering. 'Oh, go and bury your head.'

Whereas the stories about working-class men, both in 'Writing in Revolt' and elsewhere, characteristically emphasize their growth to class-conscious enlightenment,[56] the female victims can only signify misery, not understand it. Their used, degraded bodies represent the suffering of their class, just as their narrow minds represent its emotional deprivations. (And they are unattractively parasitic on their men: Urquhart's 'Jeanie' tries to seduce her boyfriend although she finds him physically unattractive, simply because marrying him would mean escaping from her hated sweatshop, while Hanley's charwoman is a nagging scold who punishes her husband for her own frustrations.) Conversely, the desirably pampered body of the upper-class vamp represents the privilege of the ruling class. This assumption is made particularly clear in Leslie Halward's unpleasant, haunting story 'On the Road', also published in 'Writing in Revolt', about an abortive encounter between an unemployed man 'on the tramp' and a well-to-do girl. Caught in the rain, the man is invited by a woman's voice into a ruined house where she is sheltering. Despite this potentially romantic meeting, no sexual encounter follows; the two talk, initially at cross-purposes because the girl assumes that he is of her own class, and when the shower ends, he leaves. At the end of their conversation, during which he has become increasingly enraged, she gives him a pound: 'He looked at her, at her doll's face. Then he said, "Oh well," screwed up the pound note and, still clutching it, strode down the path' (p. 58).

Yet the girl is not at all insolent. On the contrary; she is at first friendly, then apologetic for mistaking his class – 'You must have thought me very silly' (p. 56) – and finally placatory. However, the man, whose subjectivity dominates the story, is less conscious of her words than her body (p. 56):

He lit a match. She leaned forward, pouting, the cigarette between her lips. Twenty-two or three she would be. Her mouth was made up. Her finger-nails were lacquered.

'Thanks.' She breathed out smoke.

He could see her clearly now. She had a face like a doll's. And a mind, he thought.

This 'doll' is seen as a walking incarnation of luxury and privilege, a commodity which the unemployed man can't possibly afford, and so the more desirable to his hungry awareness of her painted mouth and fingernails, her doll's face and her 'slim leg in its silk stocking, swinging' (p. 57). Both the sound and the sense of that final phrase, with its repeated sibilants and its fetishized visual image of a single leg, subliminally suggest the image of a fascinating snake. As in some medieval paintings, the tempting girl is both Eve and the serpent; yet she is so secure in her class privilege that she does not fear or even notice the desire she arouses. Everything about her thus inverts the traditional power relations between men and women, and is an insult to the hero's male pride. If she were poor, those sexy silk stockings and lipstick would define her as a prostitute, and therefore as contemptible. In her extravagant gift of a pound note (which in 1937 represented more than a week's dole money for a single man), she upsets the 'normal' balance of power when money changes hands between the sexes. No wonder he takes symbolic revenge on her by crumpling her money. She is evidently lucky to escape the encounter without being raped or beaten up – punishments which, so the story implies, she deserves simply for being, like Sue, a 'doll with everything money can buy' (p. 57).

But it is not only the male writers in *Fact* who stereotype women by representing their bodies as class signifiers. Storm Jameson's well-known defence of realism in 'Documents' itself turns on this trope when she considers the problems for Socialist writers of dealing with misery which they have not experienced (p. 10):

> The middle-class writer... discovers that he does not even know what the wife of a man earning two pounds a week wears, where she buys her food, what her kitchen looks like to her when she comes into it at six or seven in the morning. It has never happened to him to stand with his hands in greasy water at the sink, with a nagging pain in his back, and his clothes sticking to him. He (or she) actually has to take a look into the kitchen to know what it looks and smells like; at that he does not know as much as the woman's finger knows when it scrapes the black out of a crack in the table or the corner of the shelf.

Both the bodily misery and the domestic enclosure described here were certainly real enough experiences for many working-class women in the 1930s. The testimonies collected in Margery Spring Rice's *Working-Class Wives* (1939) make it clear that a married working-class woman was only too likely to spend most of her days in a squalid kitchen: 'The working mother is almost entirely cut off from contact with the world outside her house. She eats, sleeps, "rests" on the scene of her labour, and her labour is entirely solitary.' As one woman wrote grimly: 'My life for many years consisted of being penned in a kitchen 9 feet square, every fourteen months a baby'.[57] So the image of the woman trapped in domestic dirt is 'realist' in the empirical sense of corresponding to verifiable fact. On the other hand, the autobiographies of working-class women that I have read do not match these visions of women as passive, trapped victims. On the contrary, one gets an impression of vigour, intelligence and courage against the odds.[58] Furthermore, the way in which women's physical misery is turned into a metonym for class suffering implies some powerful, specifically bourgeois fantasies about gendered bodies and knowledge. In the passage from Storm Jameson quoted above, both the argument and the imagery oppose bourgeois male intellectualism – the enquiring but ignorant eye – to a working-class woman's experience of concrete particulars: the sweaty and aching body, the finger exploring grime.

Both the woman's experience of dirt and the man's inadequate perception of the woman are thus represented as synecdoches for class experience and class relationships: one could easily read this passage as a gloss on the mute interchange between Orwell and the unfortunate girl whom he glimpses out of a passing train (see p. 94). (As Storm Jameson mentions *The Road to Wigan Pier* [p. 12], she may well have had Orwell in mind.) Her vignette emphatically points to the different destinies of the male writer and the woman he watches: the freedom to poke one's nose inquiringly into a kitchen, as opposed to being trapped in it; the freedom from bodily discomfort that lets one attend to smells and sensations, as opposed to nagging pains in the back and dull discomfort – in short, the freedom to think, as opposed to the compulsion to endure. And since the argument also contrasts the man's abstract ignorance with the woman's familiarity with sordid crevices ('he does not *know* as much as the woman's finger knows'; emphasis added), the image also implies different, gendered forms of knowledge.

In their chapter on the place of the female domestic servant in Freud's case-histories, Allon White and Peter Stallybrass show how the working-class women who did the servicing of bodies in middle-class households – washing dirty linen, emptying chamberpots, changing nappies and wiping children's bottoms – became the objects of specifically bourgeois desires and fantasies associating working-class women with degrading bodily knowledge of dirt.[59] Storm Jameson, who was no fool, hinted at this structure of feeling when she sarcastically described the typical bourgeois writer's narcissistic voyeurism: 'What sights I am seeing! What smells I am enduring! There is the woman raking ashes with her hands and here I am watching her!' ('Documents', p. 11). The labouring woman is thus subjected to a masculine gaze which is fascinated by its own repulsion and desire for the knowledge which her fingers horribly have of dirt and discomfort – a knowledge which the male viewer can only imagine. The relationship between the woman's fingers scraping the table and the observing man is not, then, just the familiar opposition of woman as suffering material body versus man as speculative, active mind. The dirty cracks also imply a fantasy of the female genitals as repulsive, fascinating crevices, not fully knowable by the man. The image is directly comparable to the cold, filthy drainpipe penetrated by Orwell's 'slum girl'.

It is noticeable that Storm Jameson's argument represents the privileged class – i.e. the writer – by a masculine point of view. In this, she is simply following the (then unquestioned) convention that 'the writer' meant 'the male writer'. Yet the doubling of class and gender privilege in her example of a typical bourgeois writer also implies some doubt of masculine subjectivity. Whereas Stephen Spender and Arthur Calder-Marshall, writing respectively on poetry and fiction in the same issue of *Fact*, link literary merit to the writer's 'unique and authentic experience' (pp. 24, 44), Storm Jameson is extremely sceptical about the value of the writer's own responses. While she concedes that 'if a writer does not know what poverty smells like, he had better find out' (p. 6), she suspects that writers' interest in their own sensations may be simply a form of narcissism. A writer may well respond with pity or horror to what he sees: 'These emotions are no doubt unavoidable. There is no need to record them. Let him go and pour them down the drain' (p. 12). Yet the demand to abolish one's own feelings by a self-abnegating act of will contradicts itself by the cloacal metaphor which ties 'the writer' back into the same tangle of feelings and fantasies about dirt and class identity which he is supposed to have got rid of. What, anyway, might that 'drain' signify? Pouring one's responses into an unpublished diary? Or just refusing to think about them? So what happens if the drain gets blocked?

POETRY AND THE SYMBOLIC FEMININE: RICKWORD, DAY LEWIS AND OTHERS

> Should not a thinking wife contemn
> The sneaking hand that held the pen,
> And with a flourish signed the deed
> Whence all these hearts and bodies bleed?
> Would not his breath reek of the tomb
> And with cold horror seal her womb?
> Could a true woman bear his brat?
> The millions wouldn't.
>   Thanks, my hat.

Edgell Rickword[60]

The 'Wife of a Non-Interventionist Statesman', whom Edgell Rickword addressed in 1938, may look at first glance like another upper-class Aunt Sally, set up in order to be attacked for her class and gender. Valentine Cunningham has criticized the poem on precisely these grounds, attacking the 'frivolity' of the advertisement on the back cover of *Left Review:* 'Win Over Non-Intervention Statesmen through their wives... Special Offer: We undertake to publish immediately any photographs we receive of little groups of them reading this month's *L.R.*'[61]

I am, like Cunningham, repelled by this public invitation to left-wingers to relieve their own righteous rage and frustration on a female scapegoat, but I think the poem is much more subtle and humane than this anecdote implies. True, Rickword does treat the 'Wife' as his butt in the opening lines, which apologize ironically for invading her privacy: 'Invade? No, that's entirely wrong,/ I volunteered, and came along' – a mocking allusion to Franco's invading volunteer battalions. And the poem's satiric energies are fuelled by misogynist aggression against the female body as a class signifier in a way that is, as I have argued above, depressingly familiar in much left-wing thirties literature. Yet this poem manifests not only crude misogyny, but also subtle imaginative identifications; a paradox produced by the way Rickword speaks both *for* the people who share the poet's impotent anger, and *to* the politically indifferent, 'private' individuals whom he addresses through the 'Wife'.

It is this complex relation to its audience that makes the poem so interesting. For Rickword's poem argues as well as denounces; and its arguments, though addressed to an imaginary Mrs Neville Chamberlain, are really directed at the unknown readers whose anger and compassion the poet seeks to arouse. This wife who inhabits her 'boudoir's private shade', living with power but not exercising it, represents by implication all those private citizens who are not aware, or refuse to realize, that what happens in Spain is anything to do with them. And in arguing that the statesman's complicity in mass murder should make his wife shudder at his touch, the poem is not *only* misogynist, for its prime target is the brutal indifference of the 'non-interventionist statesman' to the suffering which he could prevent. As in Dylan Thomas' contemporary poem 'The hand that signed a paper' in which a faceless, brutal authority is symbolized by an elderly hand whose arthritic fingers 'count the dead but do not soften/ The crusted wounds',[62] the statesman is represented simply as a 'sneaking hand' that 'with a flourish signed the deed/ whence all these hearts and bodies bleed'. His 'thinking wife' is by contrast attributed with at least some sympathetic imagination. When the poet first asks her to recognize what her husband's actions have meant to the Spanish children whose 'little hands and guts and feet' have been scattered by Fascist bombs through his collusion, and then imagines her newly sensitized horror at his touch, the woman is not only endowed with some of the bodily vulnerability of her husband's victims; her imagined revulsion from his brutality also makes her, at least potentially, more human than he is. If the 'Wife' were *only* an Aunt Sally (though of course she is that as well), there would be no point in addressing her.

Rickword's direct invocation of the female body is not common in thirties poetry. The poems of Spender and Day Lewis more often represent the female body indirectly, through the favoured symbolism of a sexualized landscape: 'feminine land indulging its easy limbs'.[63] Auden is, of course, the most sophisticated practitioner of this symbolism, which he often deploys with a disarming camp gaiety, as in the Prologue to *The Orators*:

By landscape reminded once of his mother's figure
The mountain heights he remembers get bigger and bigger.
With the finest of mapping pens he fondly traces
All the family names in the familiar places.[64]

The symbolic equation of mother and place for which Auden is famous
can also be used seriously, as the post-war 'In Praise of Limestone'. It is
also a feature of the beautiful, difficult sonnet 'Love had him fast', written
in 1935 as part of a cycle of meditative sonnets about homosexual love.
The poem, which Auden later called 'Meiosis' (a biological term referring
to cell division),[65] meditates on the origin of the loved one, imagining how

You, the seed to which he was a mother,
That never heard of Love, through Love were free
While he within his arms a world was holding
To take the all-night journey under sea,
Work west and northward, set up building.

In this allegory of conception, the maternal body is a 'world' in which 'he',
the father, plants 'you', the seed of the beloved. The arduous oceanic
journey 'west and northward' appears to mean the sperm making for the
Fallopian tube – although the poem does not mention ovaries, ascribing
conception entirely to the father, whose penis gives birth to the seed that
will become the boy. The mother represents only space and direction: her
contribution to reproduction is simply to be the site where the foetus can
'set up building'. It is fascinating to compare this depersonalized
allegorical treatment of the female body with Hugh MacDiarmid's
beautiful contemporary poem 'Harry Semen' (written in 1934) which,
like Auden's poem, meditates on the mysteries of origin, sexuality and
identity. 'Harry Semen', like 'Meiosis', invokes woman as the means
which makes human origin possible; the difference is that it does not
reduce her to a symbol. The poet celebrates the silent body which teases
him out of thought:

Hoo mony shades o'white gaed curving owre
To yon blae centre o' her belly's flower?
Milk-white, and dove-grey, wi' harebell veins.
Ae scar in fair hair like a stone in sunlicht lay
And pelvic experience in a thin shadow line.
Thocht canna mairry thocht as sic saft shadows dae.[66]

As in Auden's poems, the body is associated with a natural landscape,
for the blue veins the colour of harebells and the scar under the pubic hair

like a stone in sunlight suggest a bare, sunlit moorland scene. But the woman has not disappeared into symbolic geography; on the contrary, her body is lovingly and literally evoked, including its stretch marks from old pregnancies. Such absorbed, painterly particularity is simply beyond the range of the young 'Auden Generation' poets.

Metaphorical female bodies are a marked feature of Spender's early poems about landscape, notably of course the pylons whose girders enclosing a hollow space makes them 'bare, nude giant girls that have no secret' which yet contain the phallic power of electricity, 'like whips of anger/ With lightning's danger'.[67] Spender's industrialized imagery is often bisexual in this way; the railway train in 'The Express' is imagined, once she builds up speed, as at once phallic, hurtling through 'deafening tunnels, brakes, innumerable bolts... Plunging new eras of happiness', and as a girl moving 'entranced' with the beauty of a 'bough/ Breaking with honey buds'.[68] Similarly, in 'The Landscape Near an Aerodrome' the airliner, 'more beautiful and soft than any moth', is called 'she', but its all-seeing movement over the 'feminine land indulging its easy limbs/ In miles of softness', which she passes 'in the last sweep of love', sounds distinctly masculine – one can hardly imagine the young Spender intentionally alluding to lesbians so positively. This oscillating male–female imagery is probably determined less by the poet's own sexuality than by the contradiction between the linguistic convention that artefacts like ships, trains and aeroplanes should be called 'she', and the fact that these powerful artefacts are the result of human purpose, ingenuity and labour – which are conventionally assumed to be male prerogatives.

Day Lewis' early poems deploy a simpler opposition between a passive feminized nature and a purposive masculine culture. In Day Lewis' symbolic world, femininity and nature seem almost interchangeable. His early poems frequently remind me of 'Mr Mybug', the Lawrentian intellectual in *Cold Comfort Farm* who sees sex everywhere:

> He pointed out to Flora that he and she were walking on seeds which were germinating in the womb of the earth. He said it made him feel as if he were trampling on the body of a great brown woman. He felt as if he were a partner in some mighty rite of gestation.[69]

Such invocation of a feminine Nature is most obvious, and perhaps inevitable, in *From Feathers to Iron* (1931), a sequence of lyric poems celebrating and meditating on the conception and birth of a child, which is tentatively made to symbolize wider hopes for England's future. The attempt to marry private and public themes is problematic, because the baby's conception and growth can only represent the nation's desired rebirth in the most general terms. After the birth, when the baby is no longer a symbolic possibility but enters the human world for good, the poet, after celebrating labour and industry throughout the sequence, significantly commands the nation to 'Take a whole holiday in honour of this', thereby avoiding the question of what form the symbolic rebirth of England might actually take.[70] The sequence, which is full of agricultural imagery, constantly praises the notion of purposive labour, its first poem marrying woman's fertility to man's purpose (p. 92):

> Now our research is done, measured the shadow,
> The plains mapped out, the hills a natural boundary.
> Such and such is our country. There remains to
> Plough up the meadowland, reclaim the marshes.

Though 'our research' and 'our country' suggests the couple's harmonious partnership, this rhetoric also clearly identifies the poet's wife with the landscape, her productive 'meadowland' being fertilized by the phallic plough. The metaphor becomes more elaborate in poem 26 (p. 92):

> My love is a good land. The stranger
> Entering here was sure he need prospect no further.
>   Acres that were the eyes' delight
>   Now feed another appetite.
> What formed her first for seed, for crop must change her.

Woman thus exists as a field to be possessed and cultivated, to please and to nourish. But the symbolism is not stable, partly because elsewhere it allows – and indeed invites – a 'public' application (England as the field waiting to be made productive), and partly because the wife can sometimes be regarded as partner in the task of cultivation. Thus, in poem 12, the couple waiting for the new life are likened to prospectors bringing civilization, an image which has more than faintly colonialist overtones: 'Like Jesuits in the jungle we journey/ Deliberately bearing to brutish tribes/ Christ's assurance, arts of agriculture' (p. 62).

The most persistent image of the woman, however, is as a fertile field or as a tree, symbols which will be repeated in *The Magnetic Mountain*, where the earthbound female complains of the purposive, questing energy of the male 'setting up Art against Chaos, subjecting/ My flux to the synthetic frost of Reason' (poem 6, p. 25). The eventual birthday is represented as an occasion of public as well as private renewal: 'The nine tramp steamers rusting in the port today/ Get up full pressure for a trade revival' (p. 75). This notion of agriculture and industry as straightforward images of progress is very much of its time. Other poems insist on a more overtly political contrast between England beset by industrial slump and agricultural depression and the productive vigour of Communist Russia. Similar assumptions about the decay of capitalism are echoed in Auden's Chorus surveying a sick England: 'I see barns falling, fences broken,/ Pasture not ploughland, weeds not wheat'.[71] This emphasis on ownership, productivity and control is even more strongly stated in *The Magnetic Mountain* (1933), which records the poet's journey towards Communism, represented as a territory within the self (poem 28, pp. 45–46):

> Stake out your claim. Go downwards. Bore
> Through the tough crust. Oh learn to feel
> A way in darkness to good ore.
> You are the magnet and the steel.
>
> Out of that dark a new world flowers.
> There in the womb, in the rich veins
> Are tools, dynamos, bridges, towers,
> Your tractors and your travelling-cranes.

This Comus-like imagery of Mother Earth as a rich mine to be exploited by masculine ingenuity is deliberately ambiguous. The 'rich veins' and their products, and the bridges and tractors of the 'new world', represent both technological progress (probably in Russia) and the poet's own inspiration and achievement, implying that the poet has history with him. Both politics and poetry are defined as exclusively masculine preoccupations, confined to 'Wystan, Rex, all of you that have not fled' (poem 27, p. 44). The women whom the speaker encounters are all enemies, consisting of a mother (poem 7) a wife (poem 8), a seductive vamp (poem 17) and a personification of daydream (poem 23); they each try to possess the hero, who shrugs them off with no trouble. (Male enemies include schoolmasters preaching Duty, clergymen and Press Barons.) Because the poet refuses to contemplate any real conflict between hero and obstacle, *The Magnetic Mountain* is, as Samuel Hynes rightly says,[72] a narrative failure, its interest lying mainly in its lyrical handling of symbolism. Femininity and Nature, throughout the poem, slide in and out of each other: the Eternal Feminine seems to include both Nature as opposed to masculine culture, and the demands of a matriarchal home, symbolized by the trees or fields. Either way, masculinity is firmly linked with freedom and pilgrimage, representing both escape from the bonds of domesticity and transcendence of the home, which makes women's claims easy to shrug off as contrary to the purposive determination of Man. It also essentializes woman as inherently a creature of the home or the bed. Thus the 'First Defendant', a conservative mother deserted by her radical son, laments his growth to consciousness, wishing that he would return to her as dead bodies return to Mother Earth: 'Blessed are they that mourn,/ That shear the spring grass from an early grave,/ They are not losers' (poem 7, p. 17). Envying such straightforward bereavement, the speaker compares herself to a willow-tree threatened by pit-heads and glaciers: an unlikely but very Audenesque combination. Unworried, the hero acknowledges her past role as a maternal presence which is needed no longer – 'Woman, ask no more of me' – following up this echo of Christ[73] by adding that if anyone ought to die, the mother should (poem 8, p. 19):

> Let love be like a natural day
> That folds her work and takes to bed;
> Ploughland and tree stand out in black,
> Enough memorial for the dead.

Although the sense of these lines is both intellectually tangled and indefensibly sexist, they also strike me as rather good verse. As so often in Day Lewis' poems, the metaphors are mixed and confusing, but the general sense is clear: mother-love should fade out once its job of raising children is done. The linking of the visual image of a rural landscape quietly abandoning itself to darkness with the metaphor of the woman folding up her sewing before bedtime produces a puzzling but interesting tangle of gendered metaphors. The meaning of the allegory seems to be that maternal love has had its day and must 'fold her work' at sunset (i.e. death); but the pastoral scenery suggests that the verb 'fold' means something more than putting away needlework, for sheep are 'folded' in the evening. There is a subliminal association here, once again, between maternal fertility and the life-sustaining land, so that the mother's presence is commemorated in the cultivated landscape represented by 'ploughland and tree' whose silhouettes are her lasting 'memorial'. Yet this too is odd, because the moment at evening when objects do 'stand out in black' against the dying light is actually very short.

The last part of *The Magnetic Mountain* consists of lyrics prophesying spring, revolution and the reclamation of England: nature will be harmoniously subjected to masculine toil, and women, 'no longer stale with deferred crisis' (poem 34, p. 53), will know their place – a Lawrentian prescription, mediated no doubt through Auden's influence.[74] The body and its pleasures are to be reclaimed by a society where 'possessions shall be no more part/ Of the man, where riches and sacrifice/ Are of flesh and blood, sex, muscles, limbs and eyes' (poem 34, p. 53) – lines which echo

Spender's command to young men and young comrades to 'Count your eyes as jewels and your valued sex'.[75]

Because his vision of progress is so unrelentingly macho, the task of examining the meanings carried by symbolic femininity in Day Lewis' early poems is, for a Socialist reader, a depressing exercise, not really relieved by its moments of unintentional comedy. The rhetoric of production, industry and agriculture, used interchangeably as a political and psychological symbolic language in *From Feathers to Iron* and *The Magnetic Mountain*, is all too plainly predicated on a sexist and imperialist trope that opposes a feminized or savage nature to European male knowledge and applied power ('Jesuits in the jungle'). These poems also represent females as possessive, dangerous and not to be entrusted with power. When female figures do have influence – or want it – as mothers, wives or lovers, they appear as enemies. The poet concedes no imaginative space at all for women to exist outside of these stereotypes, unless as a vague obedient mass 'mating and submitting, not dividing and defying' (poem 29, p. 46). And this from a self-proclaimed rebel!

John Cornford's long, posthumously published poem, 'As Our Might Lessens', also uses sexual pleasure as an allegory of political liberation, in similar though more egalitarian terms. This poem opposes healthy heterosexuality (= socialism) to the perverse pleasures of a sadistic ruling class:

> For those whose tortured torturing flesh
> Stirred at the body under the lash,
> The painted boy in the praetorian bed.
> For those who were strong to live and love
> Who claimed life had no need to starve,
> Camphor and pincers fouled urine and blood.[76]

As in Cornford's better-known 'Full Moon at Tierz', whose stanza-form is very similar, the central thread of this poem is a vision of Communism's past and future, mediated through vivid imagery. But whereas 'Full Moon at Tierz' meditated on the flux of history symbolized as a moving fluid mass ('history forming in our hands/ Not plasticine but roaring sands'[77]), 'As Our Might Lessens' uses bodily imagery, identifying lovemaking with political praxis: 'Action intervenes, revealing/ New ways of love, new ways of feeling,/ Gives nerve and bone and muscle to the word'. Women, who contain the essence of life and joy – 'all strength moves in the dance of a woman's body' – also represent the potential power and freedom of the working class:

But moving in the masses' blood
Vienna Amsterdam Madrid
The ten years sleeping image of the storm

Shows us what we stand to gain,
If, through this seeming senseless pain
If through this hell we keep our nerve and pride
Where the nightmare faces grinned
We, or our sons, shall wake to find
A naked girl, the future at our side.

Cornford's 'naked girl' symbolizes the new world to be enjoyed in the future, as in MacNeice's 'Tomorrow is a virgin who must be tried again'.[78] At the same time, her nakedness also represents the present dispossession of the men who are to make and enjoy that world. The girl's body is not a class signifier; on the contrary, she represents transcendence, the end of class division. This is Communism imagined as two virginities meeting together, the girl's consent signifying the arousal of the workers, whose revolutionary energies are 'moving in the masses' blood . . . The ten years sleeping image of the storm'. These lines finely rework the numinous language of Auden's 'The blood moves strangely in its moving home', in a poem which also meditates, less joyously than Cornford, on revolutionary disturbance and the uncertain future.[79]

Yet Cornford's own feminine imagery inevitably defines the workers as objects, not subjects of history. The poem asserts that women must 'love as equal not as slave', but its final resolution defines Communism as masculine conquest through which 'we or our sons' will possess the future. As so often in thirties writing, women's subjectivity is effaced by the heavy load of symbolism carried by the female body.

Chapter 4

'Undeservedly forgotten'
Women poets of the thirties

Some books are undeservedly forgotten; none are undeservedly remembered.
W. H. Auden

Have you noticed that those who stirred a finger for Spain are left for the kites and crows to deal with? And she was a poet, too. What can we expect?
Sylvia Townsend Warner, on the memory of Nancy Cunard[1]

A BURIED TRADITION

The consensus among literary historians is that women's poetry in the 1930s doesn't exist. Accounts of thirties writing almost invariably ignore women poets (with the occasional exception of Kathleen Raine, who is noticed in two studies of 1930s poetry: A. J. Tolley's *The Poetry of the Thirties* [1975] and Adrian Caesar's *Dividing Lines* [1991]).[2] Robin Skelton, whose Penguin anthology *Poetry of the Thirties* (1964) has probably done more to shape current perceptions of thirties poetry than any other single book, defined the poets of that decade as 'the men [*sic*] of the 1904–1916 generation'. Certainly, the decision to restrict its membership, with the single exception of Anne Ridler, to bourgeois male poets born between those years, has given *Poetry of the Thirties* a pleasing, unusual coherence which partly explains its lasting popularity. Nevertheless, it produces an oversimplified and skewed version of British poetry as overwhelmingly masculine. This masculinity is emphasized in Skelton's introductory essay, which points out these poets' notoriously 'schoolboyish' tone, and emphasizes their self-definition *against* a woman poet, namely Edith Sitwell.[3] In her aristocratic birth, lack of formal education and theatrical self-definition as a Poet, this writer represented everything the young men detested; she thus became their butt in the influential poetry magazine *New Verse*, which contemptuously dubbed her 'the old Jane' (alluding to her own lines 'Jane, Jane/ Tall as a crane'[4]).

It is probably unfair and anachronistic to blame Robin Skelton's otherwise excellent and useful 1964 anthology for reproducing the anti-feminist received wisdom of *New Verse*. Ignorance of women's poetry is, after all, a feature of all the currently available histories of the 1930s, even the most recent. Thus, Adrian Caesar's recent history of thirties poetry defends its inclusion of 'very few women poets' (i.e. none except Kathleen Raine) on the grounds of 'the infrequency with which their work was published and discussed in the major literary periodicals. The literary world of the 1930s was male-dominated, and this study reflects the fact without wishing to condone it'.[5] It is a pity, however, that Skelton also accepted the notion that the thirties poet must be young as well as male. The exclusion of poets born before 1904 means that his apparently comprehensive selection of political poetry omits Hugh MacDiarmid's First and Second 'Hymns to Lenin' and 'The Seamless Web', Edgell Rickword's satire 'To The Wife of a Non-Interventionist Statesman', and all of Jack Lindsay's poems; while on the Right, it leaves out Wyndham Lewis' satire 'One Way Song,' (1933) and Roy Campbell's pro-Franco 'Flowering Rifle' (1939). The anthology lacks also Nancy Cunard, Sylvia Townsend Warner and Naomi Mitchison, who were all born before 1900; also Kathleen Raine, Stevie Smith and E. J. Scovell, who did fit the age criterion.

In fact, the record for women's poetry in the 1930s is nothing like as slight as these omissions imply. The publication of Laura Riding's *Collected Poems* in 1938 remains a landmark in twentieth-century poetry. Many other women produced interesting and accomplished poems, some of which are classics. Stevie Smith, who first achieved her characteristic voice in the 1930s, published two collections of poems before 1940: *A Good Time Was Had by All* (1937) and *Tender Only to One* (1938). In a different, more traditional idiom, Frances Cornford published *Mountains and Mole-hills* in 1934, and Ruth Pitter published three well-received collections between 1930 and 1939: *A Mad Lady's Garland* (1934), *A Trophy of Arms* (1936) and *A Spirit Watches* (1939). Sylvia Townsend Warner produced two books of poetry: *Opus 7* (1931), a long narrative poem, and, with Valentine Ackland, *Whether a Dove or Seagull* (1934), a collection of love poems, lyrics and meditations. Warner also published a fair number of left-wing political poems in contemporary periodicals and anthologies,[6] which remained uncollected until Claire Harman edited her posthumous *Collected Poems* (1982). And although E. J. Scovell and Kathleen Raine published their first collections after the end of the decade,[7] their poems of the 1930s deserve remembrance and discussion, as do those of Naomi Mitchison and Nancy Cunard. The typography and layout of these books are often distinctive, many of them being illustrated with wood engravings, an art which flourished between the Wars, especially among women artists.[8] Stevie Smith's poems are illustrated by her own sketches from the beginning; Frances Cornford's *Mountains and Molehills* has beautiful woodcuts by her cousin Gwen Raverat; Kathleen Raine's *Stone and Flower* (1943) has lithographs by Barbara Hepworth; and Laura Riding's sequence 'The Life of the Dead' in her *Collected Poems* was written around the surrealist woodcuts by John Arlidge. (Similarly, though in a completely different tradition and idiom, Sylvia Townsend Warner would later write poems as 'illustrations' for the wood engravings of Reynolds Stone in *Boxwood*.[9]) Naomi Mitchison's *The Fourth Pig* (1936) has a frontispiece engraved by Agnes Miller Parker, and her poem *The Alban Goes Out* (1939) has woodcuts by Gertrude Hermès; while her illustrated fantasy story *Beyond This Limit* (1935) was produced in collaboration with Wyndham Lewis, each of them taking turns to invent the story through words (Mitchison) and drawings (Lewis). This use of black-and-white engravings is a distinctive feature of women's poetry, which is not found among male poets of the period – perhaps because Faber, the firm which published most of the latter, was not interested in graphic art. Some of these engravings are straightforward illustrations, but most of the books suggest complex and interesting relations between text and picture.

To say that women produced some fine and much interesting poetry during the thirties is not, of course, to claim that their works constitute a mine of forgotten or undiscovered gems which outshine the poems of Auden and Co. The achievement of English women as prose writers in the 1930s is undeniably much stronger than that of women poets, a rule that seems to apply even when the poet and the novelist are the same person. Of the poetry collections I have named, only Laura Riding's *Collected Poems* seems to me to equal the distinction of such novels as Stevie Smith's *Over the Frontier*, Virginia Woolf's *The Years* or Sylvia Townsend Warner's *Summer Will Show* (not that their excellence saved these books from being slighted either, at least until recently). The works of American women poets like Marianne Moore, H.D. or Gertrude Stein in the same period have a brilliance, ambition and range that go far beyond anything attempted by English women in this period. I claim only that women poets in Britain did, contrary to the received wisdom, write and publish enough fine and memorable poems to deserve serious attention.[10]

TAKING SIDES: WOMEN AND POLITICAL POETRY

In public poetry, the mode most often associated with the Thirties, the record of women is fairly narrow but not without distinction. The women who most successfully attempted a political voice are the extreme left-wingers. Naomi Mitchison and Ruth Pitter, who both wrote good public poems in the 1940s, do not shine at this mode in their pre-war verses. When the forces of evil threaten democracy with bombing raids and 'famine/ Whose other names yet thin the brats: bread, marg and tea fed, nervy' in Naomi Mitchison's prose-and-verse miscellany *The Fourth Pig*, or when Ruth Pitter expresses anger at the status quo in the poem '1938': 'Honour's an ass-head, a bauble,/ The mark of a profitless fool'[11] the liberal indignation may be impeccable, but the language is written to formula and the rhythms are dull. Far more impressive are the Spanish Civil War poems of the anarchist Nancy Cunard and the Communist Sylvia Townsend Warner (though honesty compels me to add that the latter's political verse also includes the interesting but embarrassingly flawed poem 'Red Front'.[12]) The mutual commitment of these two poets to the Spanish Republic was also the bedrock of their lifelong friendship.[13] Neither woman, who had already worked her apprenticeship in different styles, employed the Audenesque rhetoric which is commonly associated with Marxist poetry of the 1930s. Indeed, Auden's poetry did not noticeably affect the work of any women poets of this period, with the partial and ambiguous exception of Naomi Mitchison, discussed below (pp. 125–9); not that women's lack of poetic homage to Auden is surprising, given this poet's semi-serious prophecy that, in a healthy England, 'all of the women and most of the men/ Shall work with their hands and not think again'.[14]

Nancy Cunard, who organized the famous questionnaire 'Authors Take Sides on the Spanish War', wrote comparatively few poems during the 1930s, but those she did produce are fine and memorable. Cunard herself is a much underestimated figure who is usually remembered only as a *femme fatale* of the 1920s, thanks to the caricatures of her as the rapacious Lucy Tantamount in Huxley's *Point Counter Point* and the tragically misunderstood Iris Storm in Michael Arlen's *The Green Hat*.[15] She was in fact a serious writer, identified with the avant-garde in music and the fine arts, and an indomitable fighter against injustice, who dedicated her talents to the cause of those who were unjustly treated. Radicalized by her affair with the black jazz musician Henry Crowder, her political loyalties lay on the Left; in the 1930s, she dedicated herself and her writing to championing first the politics and culture of black people and later the cause of the Spanish Republic; causes to which her loyalty was lifelong. Her principal claim to posterity's attention probably lies in her meticulous, elegant work as editor, publisher and translator. The *Negro Anthology* which she edited, financed by a successful libel suit against the *Daily Express* and published in 1934 by the left-wing house Lawrence and Wishart, is a beautifully produced, invaluable source book. Its scope and variety anticipate the multidisciplinary approach of Black Studies by a generation, by including not only the work of the 'Harlem Renaissance' but accounts of African art and music, as well as the social and political history of slavery and emancipation. Her 'Hours Press' also published (among others) Louis Aragon, Samuel Beckett, and the first pamphlet edition of Auden's *Spain 1937*.[16]

Nancy Cunard wrote prolifically in her youth, producing the title poem of Edith Sitwell's Modernist anthology *Wheels* (1916); her long poem *Parallax* was published by the Hogarth Press in 1928. Her early work is up-to-date in content but fairly conventional in form and style. Her poems were greatly improved by her friendships and affairs with jazz musicians from the mid-1920s, which educated her sensitivity towards syncopated rhythms and vernacular English. The few published poems which she wrote in the 1930s are free and inventive in rhythm, with an energy that comes partly from political anger and partly from an ear for spoken voices. Her successful political poems include the vigorous, angry satire 'Southern Sheriff', a dramatic monologue in end-stopped free verse which was published in the *Negro Anthology*:

> We run them International Labor Defense attorneys out the town,
> They nigh got lynched on the train, huh.
> Know what them agitators of 'Equal Rights' is askin'?
> 'Self-determination for the Black Belt'.
> Well, farmer over there'll show you an old lynched nigger's tooth,
> Kinda lucky he thinks, on his fob,
> Holds it up when a cropper hands him sauce
> Askin' for wages...
> That's the kind o' 'Self-Determination' *we* got,
> Don't need no interference,
> That's why we're shooting so many niggers jes' now
> Ain't we gotta protect our white women?
> *Naw,* ain't no rape, why, a nigger wouldn't dare,
> Jes' our word, sorta slogan...
>
> *That* is the Southern justice,
> Not lynch-mobs, but part of the Law speaking.[17]

The Spanish War inspired Cunard's memorable poem 'To Eat To-Day' (1938), which, like 'Southern Sheriff', angrily mimics the speech of the oppressors. It is addressed to the Fascist bombers, 'sons of Romulus or Wotan' who have just destroyed a mother, her family, and her carefully guarded olive oil:

> I wonder, do you eat before you do these things?
> Is it a cocktail or a *pousse-café*?
> Are you sitting at less now, saying 'visibility medium . . .
> We got the port, or near it, with half a dozen,' I wonder –
>
> Or highing it yet, on the home run to Mallorca,
> Cold at 5000 up, cursing a jammed release . . .
> 'Give it 'em, puta Madonna, here over Aernys –
> Per Bacco, it's nearly two – bloody sandwich it's made down there –
> Aren't we going to eat to-day, teniente? *Te-niente?*'
> Driver in the clouds fuming, fumbler unstrapping death,
> You passed; hate traffics on; then the shadows fall.[18]

Nancy Cunard also accomplished some excellent translations of Neruda's war poems, especially his 'Almeria' which repeats the theme of inhuman feasts:

> A dish for the bishop, a dish that's well-kneaded and bitter,
> A dish made of iron-ends, a dishful of tears,
> A dish overflowing with sobbing and walls that have fallen,
> A dish for the Bishop, a platter of blood – Almeria.
>
> A dish for the banker, a dish that's contrived from the cheeks
> Of the South's happy children, a bowl of
> Explosions, crazed waters, of ruins and terror,
> A dish of smashed axles, a dish of heads trampled on,
> A black dish, a tray of blood for him – Almeria.[19]

Sylvia Townsend Warner likewise wrote her best political poems about the Spanish War. Like Nancy Cunard, she served Spanish poets well as a translator, for her English versions of *romanceros* admirably communicate the simplicity and immediacy of their originals. Her translation of Felix Paredes' elegy for the washerwoman Encarnaciòn Jimenez, executed by the Fascists for 'washing the linen/ Of wounded militia-men', has her own characteristically distanced, deliberately archaic diction and unobtrusively skilful music:

Her name confessed the Word
made flesh; fate fleshed in her –
curt payment for her virtues –
five times a rifle fire ...
Old and guileless, we greet you
we bare our heads in your honour
and greet on your tattered carcass
each springing gillyflower,
each gout of blood blossoming
under the metal shower.[20]

Her own lyrics are no less patriotic, but much grimmer and more
foreboding; particularly 'Benicasim', which contemplates a rest home for
the wounded:

And it seems to me we have come
into a bright-painted landscape of Acheron.
For along the strand
in bleached pyjamas, in rope-soled tread
wander the risen-from-the-dead,
the wounded, the maimed, the halt ...

But narrow is this place, narrow is this space
of garlanded sun and leisure and colour, of return
to life and release from living. Turn
(Turn not!) sight inland:
there, rigid as death, stand
the mountains – and close at hand.[21]

Sylvia Townsend Warner's lover, the poet Valentine Ackland, was also
moved by the Spanish War to write a crisp epigram about the stolid
indifference of the English public:

Note nothing of why or how, inquire
no deeper than you need
into what set these veins on fire;
note only that they bleed.

Spain fought before and fights again,
better not question why;
note churches burned and popes in pain
but not the men who die.[22]

'THE MEN WHO DIE': WOMEN POETS
REMEMBERING THE GREAT WAR

Dead, maimed or dying soldiers are a constant haunting presence in the poetry of the thirties. To read at all deeply in the literature of the inter-war years is to realize that collective and individual memories of the First World War continued to be important, living issues in politics and literature right up to 1939 and beyond. Retrospective poetry of the Great War appeared all through the thirties, most notably of course in Herbert Read's poignant sequence *The End of a War* (1934), which contains his bitter anti-war poem 'The Happy Warrior' and David Jones' great poem *In Parenthesis* (1936). The writings of the men who were too young to fight are full of the legacy of the Great War. In *New Signatures* (1932), the anthology that launched the poets of the 'Auden Generation', the War is invoked in W. H. Auden's ambiguous 'Ode' ('Though aware of our rank and alert to obey orders') collected in *The Orators*, as well as Julian Bell's lesser-known verse satire 'Arms and the Man'.[23] It is the subject of Isherwood's novel *The Memorial* (1932), of Auden's play *Paid on Both Sides* and, indirectly, of *The Orators*.

The invocation of Wilfred Owen by Auden (' "The poetry is in the Pity," Wilfred said') and Day Lewis ('Some of us claim Wilfred Owen as an ancestor') is another sign of the War's effects.[24] The war poets' influence was not just thematic, though both Spender and Day Lewis echo them: Day Lewis using the imagery of trench warfare ('In this sector when barrage lifts and we/ Are left alone with death') to describe the tension of waiting for a birth, while Spender's 'the inexhaustible anger of the guns' in the Spanish War poem, 'Two Armies', repeats Owen's 'The monstrous anger of the guns'.[25] There is also a stylistic influence, in that the widely copied 'Audenesque' style partly draws its characteristic imagery of derelict industrial landscapes and its consciously youthful, rebellious stridency from the war poetry of Owen and Sassoon. Even Louis MacNeice, whose poems are not in the 'Audenesque' style, was affected by these war poets. Their influence can be seen in a famous passage from *Autumn Journal*, part 15:

> And now they reach the gates and line up opposite
> The neon lights on the mediaeval wall
> And underneath the sky-signs
> Each one takes his cowl and lets it fall ...
> But something in their faces is familiar;
> Where have we seen them before?
> Was it the murderer on the nursery ceiling,

Or Judas Iscariot in the field of blood
Or someone in Gallipoli or Flanders
Caught in the end-all mud?

MacNeice's last line echoes Sassoon's 'I fell/ Into the bottomless mud, and lost the light', while his image of the ghosts may also echo Owen's famous vision of a gassed man's 'hanging face, like a devil's sick of sin' in 'Dulce et Decorum Est'.[26]

Revulsion from these memories of death was understandably widespread in this decade, inspiring the Oxford Union's well-known resolution in 1936 that 'This House would in no circumstances fight for its King and Country'. At one end of the anti-war spectrum are the disillusioned post-combatant generation of young men for whom 'War was a brutal bungle. They at any rate were not going to be taken in by it.'[27] A more idealistic and politicized expression of anti-war feeling found its expression in the peace movement of the middle thirties, which inspired anti-war books like Engelbrecht and Haighan's *Merchants of Death* (1934), Beverley Nichols' *Cry Havoc!* (1933), and Aldous Huxley's pacifist pamphlet 'What Are You Going to Do About It?' (1936), the last of which made enough impact to get a reply from the Communist Day Lewis, *We're Not Going to Do Nothing* (1936).[28] Campaigning pacifists like Vera Brittain and (before 1940) Storm Jameson worked for the Peace Pledge Union, an influential pacifist organization with more members than the Communist Party. The Peace Ballot, a referendum organized in 1935, collected ten million signatures affirming collective action to reduce armaments; two million of its respondents also affirmed their rejection of settling international disputes, in any circumstances, by 'military methods'.[29] The memory of the Great War's horrors certainly also strengthened middle-class liberals' acceptance of the Foreign Office's policies of non-intervention in Spain and appeasement of Hitler. This can be seen from the published diaries of Virginia Woolf and Naomi Mitchison, the former of whom expresses intense relief at the Munich settlement in 1938, 'which is soberly and truly life after death ... Now suddenly we can travel & move & use our usual faculties. No slaughter of the young beneath us.' In 1939, Naomi Mitchison looked forward without enthusiasm to 'a long and increasingly horrible war, effectively smashing all that we care for ... The ending of a civilisation, and above all the killing of people, the extermination of a generation'.[30]

Memories of the Great War haunted women's poetry as well as men's in the 1930s. As well as her famous *Testament of Youth*, Vera Brittain published *Poems of the War and After* (1934), which includes the well-known

poem 'To my Brother' ('Your battle-wounds are scars upon my heart').[31]
Her friend Winifred Holtby's 1931 poem 'Trains' is full of the impotent
sympathy which so often characterizes women's war poetry:

When, through the darkness, as I wakeful lay
I heard the trains
The savage, shrieking trains,
Call to each other their fierce hunting-cry,
Ruthless, inevitable, as the beasts
After their prey.
Made for this end by their creators, they,
Whose business was to capture and devour
Flesh of our flesh, bone of our very bone.[32]

To my mind, the best of these late war poems by women are Mary
Borden's, published in her little-known classic of war reminiscence *The
Forbidden Zone* (1929). Mary Borden, a well-known and prolific novelist,[33]
served from 1914 to 1918 as a volunteer nurse for the French Army, for
which she was awarded the *Croix de Guerre*. She dedicated her book to 'the
Poilus who passed through our hands during the war', adding that 'The
book is not meant for them. They know, not only everything that is
contained in it, but the rest that can never be written' (p. v).

The Forbidden Zone is a difficult book to classify. It was published in 1929
and consists partly of work written during the War and partly of new
material written 'from memory' (p. v), so its 'thirties status' is questionable,
though hardly more so than that of Auden's *Paid on Both Sides*. It consists of
a mixture of stories, prose sketches and, in the final section, five
remarkably powerful longish poems written in the style of Walt Whitman
– not, as one might expect, the Whitman of 'Drum-Taps' but the early,
visionary poet of *Leaves of Grass* (1855).[34] Adopting the voice of this
fervently democratic lover of young men was a brilliant strategy for an
American civilian writing about the sufferings of ordinary, anonymous
soldiers, though not all of the poems are fully achieved; sometimes their
rhetoric is strained, and sometimes their Whitmanesque form is over-
repetitive. At their best they are very fine indeed, and ought to recognized
as classics of the Great War. 'The Hill', for example, contemplates the
surrealist lunar landscape of a battlefield: 'There was no shelter for field
mice or rabbits, squirrels or men./ The earth was naked and on its naked
body crawled things of iron.../ And iron rivers poured through the
wilderness that was peopled with a phantom host'.[35] Best of all is Borden's
'Song of the Mud', which moves through irony and compassion to an
unwilling fascination (pp. 179–80):

This is the song of the mud, the uniform of the poilu.
His coat is of mud, his great dragging flapping coat, that is too big for
    him and too heavy.
His coat that once was blue and now is grey and stiff with the mud that
    cakes to it.
This is the mud that clothes him.
His trousers and boots are of mud,
And his skin is of mud,
And there is mud in his beard.
His head is crowned with a helmet of mud.
He wears it well.
He wears it as a king wears the ermine that bores him.
He has set a new style in clothing;
He has introduced the chic of mud.

Mary Borden's list successfully imitates Whitman, both in her detailed free-verse catalogue of the muddy *poilu*'s accoutrements and in the way in which she directs an increasingly intent gaze at her imagined object. Moreover, Whitman's all-inclusive, visionary Romanticism enabled this woman writer, who as a nurse was constantly meeting the horrors of trench warfare and trying to patch them up, to make her own unwilling, pitying voyeurism into a mode of poetic articulation. But her use of Whitman is also ambivalent, for her 'Song of the Mud' has elements of aggressive parody. While its title and style both invoke his 'Song of Myself', her poem's vision of the mud as a mass grave is a sinister recycling of his optimistic paean to the grass:

Tenderly will I use you curling grass,
It may be you transpire from the bodies of young men
It may be if I had known them I would have loved them . . .

O I perceive after all so many uttering tongues
And I perceive they do not come from the roofs of mouths for
    nothing.[36]

This visionary optimism is both invoked and contradicted by Mary Borden as she contemplates (pp. 181–2) 'the vast liquid grave of our armies which has swallowed up

Our fine men, our brave, strong, young men;
Our glowing red, shouting, brawny men.
Slowly, inch by inch, they have gone down into it,
Into its darkness, its thickness, its silence.

Slowly, irresistibly, it drew them down, sucked them down,
And they were drowned in the thick, bitter, heaving mud.
Now it hides them, Oh, so many of them!
Under its smooth glistening surface it is hiding them blandly.
There is not a trace of them.
There is no mark where they went down.
The mute enormous mouth of the mud has closed over them.

This is the song of the mud,
The beautiful glistening golden mud that covers the hills like satin . . .
Mud, the mantle of battles;
Mud, the smooth fluid grave of our soldiers:
This is the song of the mud.

Whitman's verbal transformation of the grass-stems into 'uttering tongues', whose growth out of the ground speaks of resurrection, is horribly transformed here into a vision of the ground as soft speechless lips, insatiably sucking in the living, just as his invocation of the plants sprouting from 'the faint red roofs of mouths' is bitterly recalled in Borden's image of the 'mute enormous mouth' of the mud swallowing the 'young' and 'glowing red' men. Yet there is nothing explicitly gendered about this implied critique of Whitman; far from speaking 'as a woman', Mary Borden's poem shares his Romantic inclusive humanism. (Her unconscious symbolism is another matter; her image of the mud as a soft, greedy, formless mouth exactly matches those fantasies of the female body which Luce Irigaray has classically analysed in *Speculum* and *This Sex Which is Not One*.[37])The only overt sign of the poet's feminine identity is her fondness for imagery of expensive fabrics, as when the gleaming surface of the mud is seen 'like satin', or the soldier is said to wear his mud-encrusted uniform elegantly, 'as a king wears the ermine that bores him'. These contrasting images of valuable garments intensify the poem's intense concentration of the battlefield's naked squalor, producing the effect of bitter paradox which is concentrated in the irony of the filthy soldier who 'has introduced the chic of mud'.

Sylvia Townsend Warner's long narrative poem *Opus 7* (1931) also articulates the experience of mass slaughter through the medium of poetic pastiche, but in a very different style and to different ends. The poem is set in post-war England, but includes a 'crippled Anzac soldier' contemplating the mother country after the war – 'She's as rotten as a cheese,/ her women bitches, and her men C3s'.[38] The poem ponders the War in a long metaphorical passage that virtually equates patriotism with cannibalism. Sylvia Townsend Warner's irony here is, one might say, biting (p. 7):

When grandees feasted have, to see the abhorred
heeltaps and damaged dainties to the board
come cringing back, agrees not with their taste –
eat they will not, and yet they would not waste.
Then to the butler's or the cook's discreet
beck comes the charwoman on stealthy feet,
and in a bag receives, and bears away
the spoiling relics of a splendid day...
I knew a time when Europe feasted well:
bodies were munched in thousands, vintage blood
so blithely flowed that even the dull mud
grew greedy, and ate men; and lest the gust
should flag, quick flesh no daintier taste than dust,
spirit was ransacked for whatever might
sharpen a sauce to drive on appetite.
From the mind's orient fetched all spices were –
honour, romance, magnanimous despair,
savagery, expiation, lechery,
skill, humour, spleen, fear, madness, ennui...
Long revel, but at last to loathing turned,
and through the after-dinner speeches yawned
those who still waked to hear them. No one claps.
Come, Time, 'tis time to bear away the scraps!

The fluent witty symmetries of these heroic couplets; the elaborate
opening simile; the witty chiasmus 'eat they will not, and yet they would
not waste'; the deliberate inversions of 'feasted have' and 'to loathing
turned'; and the archaisms 'gust' for 'greed' and 'heeltaps' for 'dirty
glasses' – all these make a point of their own artificiality. The poem, which
is modelled on Crabbe's narratives in 'The Parish Register', is thus
accomplished with a certain Modernist irony which serves to distance the
poet from the horrors she condemns. More angry than pitying, the poem's
attitude to the war is best characterized in the writer's own phrase: 'no
compassion... but a massive intellectual repudiation'.[39]

WOMEN POETS AND THE AUDENESQUE STYLE: NAOMI MITCHISON AND STEVIE SMITH

Naomi Mitchison's poems form a paradoxical exception to the rule that
women poets always ignored Auden. Her angry poem 'New Verse' is,

most unusually, both a feminist and an 'Audenesque' poem, addressed to
'Young men, haters of women, begetters of no real thing':

> We who have laid with men in grass fields, under hedges,
> Hearing the lambs bleat on the hillside, or the twisting water,
> Aware of golden oak leaves or noon-gray apple leaves...

> To us the dams and pylons, the fields plowed with tractors,
> To us anode and cathode, to us dyes and test-tubes,
> All delicate adjustments, all new parts,
> The pressing and battering of the half-formed idea,
> To us in silent creation, to us at last
> After centuries freedom. You cannot chain us now,
> You have lost your power, young men. Young men, with freedom we
>   take
> The future also.[40]

This attack is probably not addressed to Auden himself, whom Naomi
Mitchison liked and admired (she immediately recognized the quality of
his *Poems* [1930] and wrote one of its earliest admiring reviews[41]), but
certainly to his disciples. The title indicates that the poem is aimed at the
poets published in Geoffrey Grigson's poetry magazine *New Verse*, the
house journal of the Audenesque poets. Probably the main targets are Day
Lewis, whose solemnly macho long poem *The Magnetic Mountain* prophe-
sies a Lawrentian utopia full of 'Young men proud of their output, women
no longer stale/ With deferred crisis', and Stephen Spender, author of
'The Pylons' and other prophetic poems which invoked an all-male
revolution to create an equally male utopia.[42] Yet the poem itself
addresses its audence as a collective 'you', sexualizes an imagined
landscape, and invokes a metonymic list of new technologies to symbolize
a moment of liberation – all familiar rhetorical strategies of left-wing
Auden-influenced poets, particularly Day Lewis; though at the end,
Mitchison abandons her listing of pylons and test-tubes for a repetitive,
heavily accented chant, the form of verse which came most easily to her.
The poem is not a classic, but it is certainly as good as the kind of poem it
argues with. It is also an interesting proof that angry feminist poetry did
not, as is sometimes thought, spring fully grown out of the corpse of Sylvia
Plath.

Naomi Mitchison achieved her most successful interweaving of
personal and public life in a poem written just after the decade ended,
'Clemency Ealasaid: July 1940',[43] an elegy for a youngest daughter who
lived only six hours. The poem's joint themes are the writer's grief at the

death of her baby and her wider grief, fear and anxiety at the disintegration of Europe into war. Naomi Mitchison writes, very consciously, both as a woman and as a citizen; a combination which, again, became familiar in the feminist poetry of her granddaughters' generation. The poem is, I think, both imaginative and moving, successfully handling the long line developed by Auden and Eliot for their verse plays in order to move flexibly from the map of Europe to her own empty body:

> Roll up the map of Europe.
> The lights have gone out: the concentration camps are full: the men and women
> Who thought themselves safe have been betrayed to the vultures,
> To Himmler, Goering, Franco, to those whose faces
> Express Satanic possession. Paris is dead.
> Only the bones remain. Paris of the Commune
> Dead as the sailors at Oran. This winter we hope to starve
> France, Belgium, Holland, Denmark, Norway, Poland:
> Harvest of dead babies, disease, hatred: no sense.
> My breasts tingle and stab with milk that no one wants,
> Surplus as American wheat, surplus and senseless.
> Not her soft kind mouth groping for me. Useless, senseless.
> If my baby had been starved by England, would I ever forgive?
> Roll up the map of Europe.[44]

The Audenesque chorus is, however, a difficult mode for anyone else to carry off. Without Auden's lexical energy and his control of rhythm, it risks becoming prosy and lolloping – risks to which this passage falls prey in the lines listing Fascist dictators or European countries. A remarkable, slightly earlier long poem, *The Alban Goes Out* (1939), about the Carradale fishing fleet, deals with this problem by varying its rhythms and styles, alternating a 'conversational' free-verse idiom with formal metres and lyrical rhymed passages. This poem celebrates the work of the fishermen of Carradale in ways that have less in common with any long contemporary poems than with documentary films of the thirties about the lives of the workers, such as John Grierson's early documentary about fishermen *Drifters* (1928), or still more his documentaries, *Coalface* (1935) and *Night Mail* (1936), with their accompanying poems by W. H. Auden. (I have no evidence that Naomi Mitchison did see these films, but given her political and cultural affiliations and the fact that she lived in London at the time when these films were being shown, I think it highly probable that she was part of their audience.[45]) By describing ring-net fishing, the poem celebrates co-operation as well as labour, for this method of fishing demands that when one boat in the fleet signals a catch, the crew of the nearest 'neighbour boat' go to help drag in the nets. In her celebration of the risks and joys of this labour, and her way of ringing the changes on a series of strong metrical and rhymed patterns, Naomi Mitchison can sometimes sound like a left-wing Kipling:

> We are working all the season, boat next to boat in the night,
> And danger may come on us quick, no time to stand upon right.
> When all of our hands are as net-cut, and our eyes are sore from the
> spray,
> How can we think of our neighbours except in a neighbourly way?
> . . .
> The circle closes
> To the neighbour boat . . .
> With a great smashing,
> Gunwhale on fender,
> We board her, we board her . . .
> The Viking noises,
> The single glare
> Of the working light
> On oil-skin armour
> On quick limbs heaving
> In a battle turmoil,
> The black-winged Valkyrs
> With screaming babble
> Of snatch and death
> Swoop to the circle
> That lights them up
> As common gulls
> Greedy for herring,
> And the men not angry
> But wise and working.
>
> . . . The Alban stands away now, rocking and dark,
> Sandy alone aboard, in the wheel-house, keeping
> The engine slow . . .
> Men and engines grunting and hauling,
> The nets dropping, the folds falling,
> The spring-rope jerking and the winches creaking,
> Winds up its fathoms from its sea-deep seeking,
> Steady and long like a preacher speaking . . .

Green to green and red to red –
How can we tell our neighbour boat?
Over wet dark acres the lights are shed,
The moon is hidden, the clouds are high,
Thirty couples that shift and float.
But a wife can tell her man in the bed
By little touchings of hand or thigh,
And so we tell our neighbour boat
By the slope of her lights in the blink of an eye –
Perfect safety, go ahead.[46]

As this extract suggests, Naomi Mitchison's best poems often combine strong, regular, incantatory rhythms with erotic imagery, which also feature in her love poem 'The Bonny Brae' which celebrates sexual pleasure: 'This is the dear, the human flesh/ Over bone and muscle the berry-brown skin . . .'[47]

Naomi Mitchison's feminism, though not her uncomplicated celebrations of sexual love, are paralleled in the poems of her friend Stevie Smith.[48] The sexual jibe in her '*New Verse*' about the young men 'out of whose loins come only dry, half-light words' is matched by Stevie Smith's early squib 'Eng.': 'What has happened to the young men of Eng.?/ Why are they so lovey-dovey so sad and so domesticated . . . So sad and without sensuality?'[49] Her angry feminism is also echoed in 'Major Macroo', another, better poem which describes a married homosexual who exploits and neglects his 'patient Griselda of a wife'. The poem begins lightly, the jaunty rhythm of its end-stopped first line ('Major Hawkaby Cole Macroo/ Chose . . .') sounding a little like Edith Sitwell's 'When/ Don/ Pasquito arrived . . .',[50] but its tragicomic sketch of a wretched marriage ends with an explicit denunciation of men exploiting their wives;

Such men as these, such selfish cruel men
Hating what most they love what most loves them
Never make a mistake when it comes to choosing a woman
To cherish them and be neglected and not think it inhuman.[51]

The quotation also shows how different this poet is from Naomi Mitchison – and not only in her characteristically 'anecdotal' focus on a particular couple, as opposed to the other's more personal yet general approach. Unlike Naomi Mitchison's poems, which tend to be weak on rhythm when they depart from traditional stanza forms, the scansion of Stevie Smith's lines is far more skilled than their insouciant irregularity might suggest. The first two lines quoted articulate a post-Freudian awareness of the

Learning Resources
Centre

complexities of a sadomasochistic relationship, through a rhymed heroic couplet which displays the traditional Augustan virtues of neatly doubled binary oppositions – 'hating what most they love what most loves them' – and strong, regular metre, only slightly qualified by an unconventional lack of punctuation and the use of a strong assonance – 'men/them' – instead of rhyme. The second couplet adds so many extra syllables before the stresses that its underlying traditional five-stress structure is barely noticeable. This effect probably owes something to Stevie Smith's experience of churchgoing, from which she would have learnt the Anglican practice of 'pointing' psalms, whereby the same tune is sung for each line, but the number of syllables chanted on each note varies according to the number of words in it. 'Pointing' is thus a way of chanting lines of unequal length (as Stevie Smith later became well known for doing when she read her own poems in public). Stevie Smith's final couplet in this way gives two very long five-stress lines:

> Never make/a mistake/when it comes/to choosing/a woman
> To cherish them and/be neglected and/not/think it in/human.

These looping metrical irregularities are buckled together by the final half-rhyme 'woman/inhuman', which is also an ingenious metrical pun. English scanning convention defines monosyllabic line-endings as 'masculine endings', whereas two or more syllables are called 'feminine'. The rhyme 'woman/inhuman' is thus a feminine ending, while the last word, 'inhuman' – beginning as well as ending with an unstressed rhyming syllable – is, so to speak, doubly 'feminine', thus reinforcing the poem's feminism.

'Major Macroo' shows that Stevie Smith had by 1937 achieved her characteristic poetic style, in which pastiche and parody of other styles coexist with a storyteller's ear for conversational voices and a peculiar, individual viewpoint. Another early poem, 'The Bereaved Swan', works in this mode, switching styles and rhythms from line to line:

> Wan
> Swan
> On the lake
> Like a cake
> Of soap.
> Why is the swan
> Wan
> On the lake?
> He has abandoned hope ...

O would that I were dead
For her sake that lies
Wrapped from my eyes
In a mantle of death
The swan saith.

The first stanza, with its repeated 'Wan/Swan...swan/Wan', comically sends up its own self-consciously 'poetic' register while ingeniously repeating the 'doubled' effect of the bird's reflection on the lake's still water. It moves from the Sitwellian near-nonsense of the 'cake of soap' simile to an elaborate Tennysonian rhetoric of mourning whose archaism – 'the swan saith' – is hardly camped up at all. The effect, as so often in Stevie Smith's poems, hovers between irony and melancholy in a stylized poetic world of its own, where a barren romantic landscape forms a bleak setting for a single lonely consciousness. The swan is not seen as a living thing existing independently of the poet; it is an emblem evoked – to cite a favourite Stevie Smith quotation – 'to point a moral or adorn a tale'.[52]

Stevie Smith's originality, quirkiness and peculiar brand of allusiveness are fully achieved in these highly individual poems. Yet, while her style owes nothing to Louis MacNeice, W. H. Auden or C. Day Lewis, she has a surprising amount in common with all of these poets. In her habit of alluding to hymns, she resembles Auden and Day Lewis. Her funny-bitter 'Fair waved the golden corn/ When I was stepping out' sends up its original in much the same way as Auden's hymn 'Hail the strange electric writing/ Alma Mater on the door' parodies the hymn 'Lead us, Heavenly Father, lead us'.[53] Elsewhere she uses hymn-tunes as 'backings': her poem 'In a shower of tears I sped my fears' is to be sung 'To the tune of "Worthy the Lamb" ' while the title of 'The nearly right' is 'To the Tune of the Coventry Carol'.[54] Though deployed for very different ends, these serious parodies of Anglican hymns resemble C. Day Lewis' rewriting of 'Away in a Manger' in 1935 as a protest poem: 'The stars in the bright sky/ Look down and are dumb/ At the heir of the ages/ Asleep in a slum'.[55] And, like Louis MacNeice, she was also influenced by Edith Sitwell's jazz poems and by popular songs. Like his justly famous 'Bagpipe Music', Stevie Smith's poem 'Freddy' intercuts conversational almost-free verse with the fast thumping rhythms of music-hall songs like 'My Old Man Said, Follow the Van':

I don't love him so much in the restaurants that's a fact
To get him to hobnob with my old pub chums needs too much tact
He don't love them and they don't love him
In the pub lub lights they say Freddy very dim.

But get him alone on the open saltings
Where the sea licks up to the fen
He is his and my own heart's best
World without end ahem.[56]

The tone of Stevie Smith's poems also has a surprising amount in common with Auden's poems of the 1930s, being full, like them, of semiparodic allusions to literature, popular music and the Anglican liturgy. Randall Jarrell astutely wrote of Auden's 'set piece' pastiche poems that 'the poem exists on two levels, like counterpoint – that is, like a counterpoint in which one of the levels has to be supplied by the hearer'.[57] This could equally well have been said of 'The Bereaved Swan' or 'Major Macroo', poems which depend for their effect on shifting quickly from one tone to another. And, like Auden, Stevie Smith moves easily from an ironic to a numinous register, but in a different, more specialized way and to different ends. Thus the story-lines of her 'Little Boy Lost' and 'Alone in the Forest' resembles Auden's ominous 'Now the leaves are falling fast' in their movement from cosy cliché to spookiness, though the poems do not share Auden's political overtones (and are, I think, the weaker for that). Her fascination with solitary journeys also parallels his. Although the tone, style and rhythm of her poem 'The Fugitive Ride' differ greatly from Auden's 'Doom is dark' and ' "O where are you going?" said reader to rider', their theme of the lonely quest is very similar.[58]

Furthermore, Stevie Smith has, like Auden, a penchant for black humour. In its lighthearted treatment of a grisly theme, her poem 'Bag-Snatching in Dublin', about the refined 'Sisley' who ended up in 'the Liffey's turgid flood . . . Where a bruiser in a fix/ Murdered her for 6/6', resembles Auden's ballad of 'Sue,' the elegant girl who kills herself, as well as his 'Victor' the wife-murderer. It also calls to mind William Plomer's misogynist ballad 'The Dorking Thigh', about a dismembered female corpse, though it does not share Plomer's gloating tone. Her poem 'The Murderer', a four-line version of 'Porphyria's Lover', is also bizarrely funny: its speaker describes murdering his wife, with masterly under-statement, as 'we had an accident'.[59]

In their penchant for gruesome subject matter, Smith, Plomer and Auden belong to a very English tradition of gory comic verse, stemming from those parodies of morality fables which have entertained middle-class English children for the past hundred years: Hoffmann's *Struwwelpeter*, Harry Graham's *Ruthless Rhymes for Heartless Homes* – 'Down the brand-new well/ Which the plumber built her/ Aunt Maria fell./ We must buy a filter' – and above all Hilaire Belloc's *Cautionary Tales*, whose witty couplets describe such unfortunates as 'Matilda, Who Told Lies, and was Burned to Death' or 'Lord Lundy, Who was too Freely Moved to Tears, and thereby ruined his Political Career'.[60] Though Stevie Smith's humour is not limited to this register, it is certainly to be found in her poems of the 1930s.

IRONY AND TRADITION: RUTH PITTER AND SYLVIA TOWNSEND WARNER

Pastiche ... usually implies a real affection for the thing parodied.
George Orwell[61]

The ambivalent relationship of women poets to the English traditions which they 'inherited' as educated women often appears in their fondness for imitating other styles. Such pastiche, as I have shown above, features – though very differently – in the poems of Stevie Smith and Mary Borden. It is also very marked in the poems of Ruth Pitter, who was a skilled parodist of past poets. Her first collection, *A Mad Lady's Garland*, was published in 1934 to considerable acclaim; Hilaire Belloc wrote an admiring preface, praising 'Miss Pitter's perfect ear and exact epithet', while A. E. (George Russell) paid tribute to 'Miss Pitter's ... exquisite artifice' and 'classical perfection of utterance'.[62] It consists mainly of monologues 'spoken' by insects and other vermin, often in a high-flown Renaissance style; there is also a delightful parody of cosmetic advertisements in the alliterative manner of *Piers Plowman*: 'Timelie Tydinges For Loveles Ladyes (& Look Ye Miss Not Ye Speciall Offere)' (p. 43).

Ruth Pitter's early poems are usually light in tone and, unlike those of Sylvia Townsend Warner or Mary Borden, they do not belong to a 'public' realm, do not invoke their own historical context, and appear to be innocent of Modernist ironies. On the contrary, they represent an attempt to preserve a timeless realm of poetry whose wider horizons are not social but religious; Randall Jarrell called her ' "traditional" in the bad sense'.[63] Her talent for skilful pastiche can be seen in 'The Earwig's Complaint', in which the insect looks longingly at a sleeping woman:

I but the bigness of three wheaten grains,
And black withal, and she so great, so fair!
Whole continents of beauty, starry plains,
An universe of love, surveyed I there!
And I will die, but I will share that sleep,
Madly I muttered, and within did creep,

And found myself within a heavenly vale
Whereof the ground was spread with living snow;
Or seemed as close inlaid with lilies pale
Heaved by a zephyr wandering to and fro;
Where, falling prone in an ecstatic swound,
I cried out Love! and kissed the enchanted ground . . .

Ah, fatal boldness! woe, that I forgot
My steely casque, my greaves, my mailed arms,
Which to the silken blossoms of that spot
Did violence, and called forth loud alarms
As 'twere from underground, the mighty fair
Sending melodious thunders through the air![64]

These stanzas invoke the decorative, ornate style of Elizabethan poets
(one of Pitter's models is clearly 'Muiopotmos', Edmund Spenser's mock-
heroic poem about the death of a butterfly). The phrase 'continents of
beauty' also, unmistakably, alludes to the geographical metaphors – 'O
my America! my new-found-land!' – for which John Donne's erotic *Elegies*
are famous.[65] Ingenious and lyrical, these essays in moralized mock-
heroic are very enjoyable and technically impressive; but I am not sure
that they are more than that. I should add that Ruth Pitter's mature poems
of the 1940s show a much more fully achieved voice. When she
contemplates London during the blitz in 'The Cygnet', she successfully
invokes the rhythm and diction of Owen's 'Exposure' to produce a vision
that is not at all second-hand:

The blear smoke crawls, the dawn glimmers, the children
With their wan mothers, creep from dens that hide them
A little from their terror; they turn homeward
To the poor dole of food allotted strictly,
To each his portion, just and insufficient;
To the grey day, labouring on till evening,
Then turning blindly to the earth for harbour
As beasts do, bolting into holes for terror.[66]

The traditionalism of Sylvia Townsend Warner is of a more complex
kind. Her long poem *Opus 7*, from which I have already quoted an extract,
is an exercise in ironic pastoral, originally published as a small book under
the 'Dolphin' imprint of Chatto and Windus. An impressively accomplished narrative in the style of Crabbe, its small rural world represents
issues beyond itself in highly formalized language and metre, as pastoral
convention prescribes. What is unconventional is the high degree of

historical realism with which this world is imagined: 'Love Green', the name of its heroine's village, is very different from the picturesque countryside beloved of Georgian poets. Sylvia Townsend Warner's country-dwellers are not Arcadian shepherds but poverty-stricken small-holders, doomed 'lifelong the same sour clods to grub forlorn' (p.19), or else housewives gossiping in the village shop as they buy 'Empress washing blue, or salmon paste/ or postal orders, or canary seed', while their 'wet umbrellas, ranged in patience glum/ mixed sullen swamps on the linoleum' (p. 13). These villagers are hard-working, conservative, mean-minded people whose lives are dominated by harsh labour and intensely conformist social mores, with no outlet into poetry or fantasy except for the pleasure of malicious gossip.

The poem, however, is not only descriptive; it is also a fable. It tells the story of Rebecca Random, an elderly, green-fingered drunkard, who in the post-war years successfully sells the flowers in her cottage garden to finance her thirst for gin. Scandalously, she plants her flowers at night (p. 25):

> Outlandish her vast shadow prowled and strayed –
> a rooting bear, a ghoul about her trade –
> beheaded, with her rising, into dark.
> Birds scolded at her, dogs began to bark,
> John Pigeon, reeling home to fight his wife,
> checked at the glare, and bellowed out *The strife
> is o'er, the battle done*, to scare the fiend;
> while him forgetting, Mrs Pigeon leaned
> out of the bedroom window in her nightgown
> rapt as a saint at gaze, to track the light down.

On one level, the poem rewrites Sylvia Townsend Warner's first novel *Lolly Willowes* (1926) whose heroine, Laura, a spinster aunt bullied by her respectable family, abandons them all to live in the country and become a witch. Rebecca, regarded by her pious neighbours as a 'fiend' to be warded off with an Easter hymn, finds in gin what Laura found in magic: freedom, intensity of experience, and the courage to defy God. And just as Laura acknowledges her liberation by Satan 'the loving huntsman', Rebecca is blessed by a transgressive, outlawed male deity – not the Devil this time, but Bacchus (pp. 38–9):

> Fill to this guest, Rebecca, drink once more!
> How soft his leopards pad your kitchen floor!
> and with their thick tails buffet you, and thresh

sharp waves of joy along your drowsy flesh.
Lovely they are, and affable and tame,
and fawn and sidle round you, as the flame
fondles the log, owning you one on whom
their lord looks kindly. In your shabby room
how vast and calm a shade his ivy throws!

But unlike Laura Willowes who possesses a patrimony, however depleted,
to fund her escape, Rebecca is really poor – which is why she sells her
flowers. Emphasizing its heroine's straightforward need for cash, this
poem is more materialist than the novel it rewrites, permitting fantasy and
even the play of mind to exist only in its telling – not, apart from Rebecca's
drunken visions, in its imagined world. And her success is due not to
witchcraft, whatever her neighbours say, but to talent and business flair.
She sells her flowers 'extremely cheap' to a thin-lipped lady equipped with
furs and terriers, treating her patron respectfully (on the same principle,
the poet explains, as shepherds sacrificing to Pan) and recouping the loss
by overcharging her 'humbler customers' (p.30). Her capacity for visionary experience (inspired by gin), and her creation of beauty in her garden
may be taken, in a familiar post-Romantic trope, to symbolize the writer's
own artistry. If so, it is an artistry informed by the spirit of Dr Johnson's
well-known saying, 'No man but a blockhead ever wrote, except for
money'.[67]

As Donald Davie showed in his subtle essay on Sylvia Townsend
Warner's poems, the relationship of her poems to the conventions of
traditional English poetry is complex and ironic, characteristically opening up 'a space between the poet and us': a distancing, ironic effect which
Davie illuminatingly compares with those achieved in the poems of John
Crowe Ransom.[68] Her puzzling, playful irony can be seen in many poems
in *Whether a Dove or Seagull*, the collection which she and her lover Valentine
Ackland published in 1934, notably the long, ironic, ceremonial prayer for
the Revd Joseph Staines Cope (p. 69):

Father, most fatherly in our childishness,
Most comprehended in our errors,
Thyself ungirding of terrors
To wear on thy feastday a party dress,
And rustling to eternity in a blue silk petticoat
Stitched to thy praise by holy Mrs. Ferrers;
By thy trinity-blue sky, by thy rustling apparel
Of sheaved sea and wind-wallowed corn,
By all the roses thou hast worn,

With divine coquetry sweetening thy look
To catch man's eye...
We implore thee with due hope
For the soul of thy servant, Joseph Staines Cope.

This very anti-Christian poem parodies the language of formal prayer. Its initial pious-sounding apostrophe to God, 'most fatherly in our childishness', actually identifies belief with immaturity and 'errors'. Piety is further teased by the suggestion that God the Father is a transvestite; the altar cloth embroidered by the devout Mrs Ferrers is His 'party dress' or 'blue silk petticoat' – a very proper garment for one clothed like a lady of the *belle époque* in the rustling garments of seas and cornfields, who wears roses with ambiguous 'divine coquetry' to catch the human eye. It is thus impossible to take the refrain of the poem, 'We implore thee with due hope/ For the soul of thy servant, Joseph Staines Cope' as anything more than an ironic, splendidly sonorous couplet.

Yet the poem's use of religious language is not wholly parodic, either. The lovely lines invoking the Lord's 'rustling apparel/ Of sheaved sea and wind-wallowed corn' uses alliterative phrasing in the manner of Gerard Manley Hopkins, while its theme and imagery echo his visionary sonnet 'Hurrahing in Harvest', which contemplates God through an ecstatically perceived summer scene of stooks 'barbarous in beauty...Up above, what wind-walks! what lovely behaviour/ Of silk-sack clouds!'. Sylvia Townsend Warner's diaries similarly show religious language coexisting with a marked antipathy towards Christianity. Thus, during a period of gloom and dismay about her lover Valentine's conversion to Catholicism, she records how:

> when I woke feeling old & melancholy and clumsy with age ... I looked out the window onto such a glory of stars, solitary, unfrequented, secure *& yet transient*, that I cried out. In wisdom hast thou made them all, and slept again, comforted by that immense transience.[69]

It seems that in order to speak of the beauty of the visible world, Sylvia Townsend Warner needed the intensity and formality of religious language, however ironically she might deploy it.

TRADITIONAL LYRICS: E. J. SCOVELL, VALENTINE ACKLAND AND OTHERS

Kathleen Raine and Laura Riding, who both saw themselves as inheritors of the English poetic tradition rather than Modernists, are the best-known women poets (a description which they have both resented) who published during the thirties. Their work has had more public recognition, if often of a sceptical or hostile kind, than any of the other poets whom I have discussed in this chapter. Significantly, their works were published and reviewed in Geoffrey Grigson's very influential little magazine *New Verse*: Kathleen Raine was the only woman whose poems regularly appeared in its pages, while Grigson himself paid Laura Riding's *Collected Poems* the tribute of a review, though of course a dismissive one.[70] Both certainly deserve a long discussion, which I am not able to give them here. I cannot discuss Miss Raine's poetry here, because she has objected both to my choice of her poem and to my interpretations of it,[71] and I cannot even try to do justice to Laura Riding's *Collected Poems* without devoting this whole chapter to it. To pick out one or two sample poems from this important collection can give no idea of its scope and range; it seems best simply to alert readers to its importance.

The tradition of the English lyric was also maintained during the 1930s with some fine poems by women. These include those of *Whether a Dove or Seagull*, the book of poems which Sylvia Townsend Warner published with Valentine Ackland. This book, which has never been reprinted (its poems were left out of Warner's posthumous *Collected Poems*), consists of 109 poems, 54 by 'S.T.W.' and 55 'by 'V.A.', which are printed without attribution, although page 152 of the English edition lists the respective pages written by each woman. The poets explain in their preface that this arrangement is meant to combine both the pleasure of contrast and the freshness of anonymity. 'The book...is both an experiment in the presentation of poetry and a protest against the frame of mind which judges a poem by looking to see who wrote it' (p. 1). As with many poetry collections of the 1930s, the poems are nearly all untitled. More radically, they are not numbered, either. This is unfortunate, because the lack of clear textual divisions diminishes the effect of contrast which the poets hoped for. The first-time reader sometimes has to turn to the key page at the back of the book to be sure when one poem ends and another starts. This experimental layout has been highly praised by Wendy Mulford in her illuminating study of Sylvia Townsend Warner and Valentine Ackland. She argues that the book is important because it:

> reveals the interaction and growth of feeling between two writers...The poems themselves represent voice speaking to voice in antiphonal dialogue, each voice separate, distinct, clear-toned...the voices of the two women speak to, slide past, touch upon and explore the shifting growth of feeling in their relationship'.[72]

This claim that the book represents a specifically women-centred version of textual erotics is movingly and persuasively put, though the 'unbroken' presentation of the poems does, to my mind, so muffle their dialogue that only a reader who knows the book as well as Wendy Mulford does is likely to hear it. If the book is ever reprinted, the poems ought to be numbered.

The love poems by Sylvia Townsend Warner are more direct and personal than in any other of her published poems (p. 131):

> I, so wary of traps,
> So skilful to outwit
> Springes and pitfalls set,
> Am caught now, perhaps.

The book does not, unfortunately, include the lovely erotic poem to Valentine 'Drawing you, heavy with sleep to lie closer', which must have been written too late to go in.[73] It does, however, include Warner's 'Since the first toss of gale', which represents lovemaking through a transparent allegory of storm: 'Throe shall fell roof-tree, pulse's knock/ Undermine rock'. This is not, I think, an entirely successful poem except in its last lines, perhaps because Warner's talent as a lyric poet was for formal balance and understatement. Strained and overemphatic on the release of sexual energies by the 'hand/ Scattering lightning along thighs', its ending beautifully suggests the tension of these energies, held in by the lovers' outwardly calm appearance, which belies (p. 117):

> What winds, what wrecking
> What wrath of wild our dangerous peace
> Waits to release.

The poems by Valentine Ackland in *Whether a Dove* are sometimes less accomplished, but are, as Wendy Mulford says, 'remarkable in their freshness of feeling and their direct, clear evocation of complex mental states'.[74] She is good at erotic poetry (p. 94):

> Is the hawk as tender
> To be belly of its prey,
> White belly wet with dew
> As I am to you
> In the same way
> My slender?

In the sonnet 'The eyes of body, being blindfold by night/ Refer to the eyes of mind', Ackland invokes a tactile eroticism: 'I order out a hand/ To journey forth, as deputy for sight'. The poem's open lesbian sensuality looks surprising for the period. Obviously it was possible to say things in poetry which would be censored in fiction:

My hand, being deft and delicate, displays
Unerring judgment; cleaves between your thighs
Clean, as a ray-directed airplane flies.

Thus I, within these strictly ordered ways,
Although blindfolded, seize with more than sight
Your moonlit meadows and your shadowed night.

This 'strictly ordered' sonnet, full of erotic energy, deploys some well-known thirties motifs: the map, the body which is also a landscape, and the technological image of the aeroplane (which here doesn't work too well). What makes the poem original and successful, in its use of a standard topographical image (body as map), is the way it recognizes the distance implied in this visual metaphor, confronts it and crosses it.

Other women poets writing in traditional forms often chose themes from the natural world. Ruth Pitter wrote several such nature poems, some of which are very enjoyable, like her 'Thought Against Drought':

Solomon's seal under broad leaves
Hung down the serried flower
And periwinkle under the eaves
Nodded to feel the shower:

And though from the dank cottage-wall
The grinning mildew glared,
What in the dry world might befall
I neither knew nor cared. [75]

The playing off of the inverted stresses in the first stanza against the 'eight-six' metre is finely crafted, achieving an unexpectedly vigorous effect. Less impressive perhaps is the over-allegorical 'grinning mildew' glaring from the cottage wall. As so often, Ruth Pitter is a strongly emblematic poet whose natural or animal images tend, like Stevie Smith's, 'to point a moral or adorn a tale'. Much less allegorical is the work of E. J. Scovell, who published her first poems in the later thirties. Her meditations on 'Bloody Cranesbill on the Dunes' or 'The Swan's Feet' are equally free of moralizing and of the pathetic fallacy:

Like muscled leaves darker than ivy
Blown back and curved by the unvarying wind

They, that thrust back the water
Softly crumple now and close, stream in his wake.

These dank weeds are also
Part and plumage of the magnolia-flowering swan.
He puts forth these too –
Leaves of ridged and bitter ivy
Sooted in towns, coal-bright with rain.[76]

The comparison of the swan's feathers to petals and his dark wet feet to ivy is worked out in complex, associative detail through the lovely phrase 'coal-bright with rain', an oxymoron which is presumably suggested by the previous 'Sooted in towns'. All this detail – of plants with sooty surfaces, coal sparkling in the wet, visual pleasure contradicted by dirt and damp – is deliberately distanced from the actual bird contemplated. The ambiguous line 'He puts forth these too' seems to identify the bird with the figurative plant but actually refers to the movement of its feet; the long simile doesn't occlude the bird's swimming movement but illuminates it. This is remarkable poetry which ackowledges its own verbal processes while subordinating these to the object contemplated. Evidently traditional in form, Scovell's poems at their best have a scientist's loving objectivity.

Chapter 5

Parables of the past
A reading of some anti-Fascist historical novels

One of these stories I saved for you, it was so beautifully Marxian. A Chinese dictator, determined to establish peace in his dominions, took away all the peasants' weapons. The metal thus collected he had melted down and cast into twelve massive religious figures which adorned his palace. In the end the peasants overthrew him with sharpened bamboos.

You will see that this seemed all rather odd to the Dorchester Labour Party.

Sylvia Townsend Warner to Edgell Rickword, 1936[1]

REALISM VERSUS FANTASY?

English Marxist fiction of the 1930s is little read and much criticized; consequently, the Socialist historical novels written in these years are almost unknown. The choice of 'Socialist realism' as the proper form for progressive writers at the 1934 Congress of Soviet Writers has been taken as an ideological whipping-boy by people who don't bother to read Marxist novels, because they already know that these must be either boringly naturalistic slices of proletarian life, or else even more boring glorifications of grain silos in Kiev.[2] Yet the Popular Front alliance of Communist and liberal intellectuals that produced a rebirth of rich and lively European historical fiction had its counterpart in England, where the record of anti-Fascist historical novels is, in fact, surprisingly long and distinguished. It includes Sylvia Townsend Warner's novels *Summer Will Show*(1936) and *After the Death of Don Juan* (1938), Jack Lindsay's *1649* (1938) and other novels set in eighteenth-century England and ancient Rome,[3] Leopold Myers' trilogy *The Root and the Flower* (1934) set in sixteenth-century Mogul India, and Naomi Mitchison's long novel *The Corn King and the Spring Queen* (1931), as well as her short stories collected in *The Delicate Fire* (1933) and *The Blood of the Martyrs* (1939), set in first-century Rome. This chapter discusses a small selection of these titles: Warner's two novels, Lindsay's *1649* and Mitchison's *The Corn King and the Spring Queen*.

To put the writer Sylvia Townsend Warner at the centre of a chapter on forgotten historical novels may look like a doubly perverse way of discussing English fiction of the 1930s. Historical novels are themselves a fairly specialized and obscure variety of fiction, even if undeservedly so; furthermore, Sylvia Townsend Warner looks like an especially eccentric writer to focus on, being largely (if shamefully) neglected, not only by 'mainstream' critics but by most Marxist accounts of the 1930s.[4] In fact, her principled commitment to Marxism and brilliant writing make her an exemplary representative of the honourable tradition of anti-Fascist literature. A publicly identified Communist and a distinguished writer of fiction and poetry, Warner is, as I have argued elsewhere,[5] very close to the canonical 'Auden Generation' male writers in terms of her class, culture and education; but like so many other women writers of the thirties, she belongs to the wrong sex and the wrong generation (she was born in 1893) – to be counted as a 'writer of the 1930s' by the historians. Moreover, the ironized traditional forms which she chose to write in – lyric poems and a pastiche of Crabbe, short stories and historical novels set in unpopular periods – do not fit standard perceptions of thirties writing. (*Summer Will Show*, however, is increasingly considered to be an under-ground classic of lesbian fiction, though it is still quite hard to find in bookshops.) Her work has been noticed and set in a tradition of lesbian fiction by Terry Castle, but at the expense of ignoring its politics and its historical context.[6]

Still, the question remains: why these particular writers, and these novels? It is true, but not enough, to say that Sylvia Townsend Warner's *Summer Will Show* and *After the Death of Don Juan*, Jack Lindsay's *1649* and Naomi Mitchison's *The Corn King and the Spring Queen* are forgotten classics which deserve attention, both for their own sake and as part of the too often narrowly defined literary history of the 1930s. Other revisionist scholars would mostly claim the same thing of the material which they survey and analyse; or if cultural historians, they would say that their chosen books were important evidence for structures of feeling or for dominant and subversive ideologies. I have chosen to concentrate on these particular novels, first because they belong to a distinguished but undervalued tradition of anti-Fascist historical writing whose neglect I hope to redress, and second, because they raise important questions about realist fiction in general through the liminal space which they occupy between history and dream. They exemplify both what remains good and enduring about anti-Fascist fiction and what makes its forms and assumptions different from ours today.

To understand the assumptions underpinning these novels, it is important to grasp the crucial cultural shift of emphasis from realism to fantasy that has occurred amongst writers and readers in the last twenty-odd years: a shift from writing 'what is' to 'what might be', which has affected both fictional narratives and critical perceptions. In the 1980s and 1990s, radical writers imbued with cultural politics do not aim to document the unacceptable realities of their societies or to produce chronicles of suffering and resistance, on the model of Steinbeck's *The Grapes of Wrath* or Storm Jameson's *Mirror in Darkness* trilogy; instead, they have characteristically exploited the mode of fantasy. Angela Carter, Salman Rushdie, the South American 'magical realists' and Toni Morrison all deliberately go beyond the actual, transforming the available means of representation to deconstruct the seemingly ordinary. A radically minded literary critic correspondingly expects to read fiction not for referential 'reflections' of reality, but for symbolism, multiple voices, intertextuality and above all fantasy – the mode which, as Terry Castle puts it, 'dismantles the real, as it were, in a search for the not-yet-real, something unpredicted and unpredictable'.[7]

Although the writers of the 1930s, who were often politically aware post-Freudians, were aware of the relationship between reality and dream (or nightmare), attempting, as Christopher Isherwood retrospectively put it, to do justice to the 'fantastic realities'[8] of contemporary history, they did not share our post-modern disaffection from 'the real'. In 1937, for instance, the Socialist novelist Storm Jameson wrote a passionate manifesto for 'documentary' writing which would use a transparent language to make 'the emotion . . . spring directly from the fact'. Writing itself should, she argued, become a kind of photography in which the writer is *not* Isherwood's famously passive 'camera with its shutter open' but a film editor:

> As the photographer does, so should the writer keep himself out of the picture while working ceaselessly to present the *fact* from a striking (poignant, ironic, penetrating, significant) angle . . . discarding from the mass of his material to get the significant detail which leaves no more to be said.[9]

Left-wing writers of the thirties aimed to tell the truth, whether by large-scale chronicles of the suffering of the masses or by satires which might border on the fantastic in order to sharpen the attack on real targets, as in Christina Stead's caricatures of wealthy Eurotrash in *House of All Nations* (1938), whose characters include a sinister pair of bankers called Rosenkrantz and Guildenstern. A more familiar example would be the semi-surrealist exchanges between the upper-class people whom the tutor overhears in Edward Upward's *Journey to the Border* (1938, p. 132):

> 'She's a character. . . . Born and bred at Southend.'
>   'Luckily the M.F.H. popped out of his library just at that moment.'
>   'Otherwise I'd have been down on my hands and knees – gathering up the fragments that remained.'
>   'She keeps him in order too.'
>   'She does.'

This commitment to reality has been dismissed as an unfortunate result of writers' spineless submission to the tenets of 'Socialist realism' as defined at the Congress of Soviet Writers in 1934. Valentine Cunningham claims that this conference 'helped to smash up modernism especially in the novel, thus pushing the novel back beyond Henry James into the arms of bourgeois naturalism'.[10] But the Congress's decision only directly affected Party writers; and in any case, both Marxist realist writing and the arguments for realism were much more various and artful than is commonly supposed.[11] For, as Brecht pointed out, there is no intrinsic need to identify a commitment to Marxist truth-telling with particular forms of writing. Walter Benjamin demonstrated this point brilliantly by arguing the superior realism of an implausible 'frozen' melodramatic scenario:

> The mother is just about to pick up a pillow to hurl at the daughter, the father is opening a window to call a policeman. At this moment a stranger appears at the door. 'Tableau', as they used to say about 1900. In other words: the stranger is suddenly confronted with certain conditions: rumpled bedclothes, open window, devastated interior. But there exists a view in which even the more usual scenes of bourgeois life appear rather like this.[12]

Benjamin's posed 'tableau' satisfactorily represents the true violence of bourgeois family dynamics, precisely *because* it calls its own plausibility into question by being so obviously stylized. For the terms of that questioning are to be shaped by Marxist theory, which understands the essential truth of social relations glossed over by bourgeois ideology. The scene thus produces a more trenchant realism about family relations than could ever be achieved by the watered-down plausibilities of naturalist writing. This account of realism comes out of the techniques and theory of Brechtian drama, and so can't be transferred directly on to narratives. But serious historical novels are bound to raise the question of truth – or at least, of accurate interpretation – in comparable ways, especially if, like the novels of Warner and Lindsay, they are Marxist. More paradoxically and more sharply than other modes of fiction known to me, the historical novel works the contradictory, liminal ground between realism, with its accompanying claims to truth, and fantasy or daydream. By representing the processes of historical crises in terms of the lives of individuals, the historical novel claims for its characters a representative truth, which is of course implicitly contradicted by the fictionality of the characters themselves.[13] Furthermore, most twentieth-century historical novels use a narrative mode of seemingly uncomplicated realism which, wherever it is employed, tends to efface the frontier between text and world by inviting identification with its main characters, working on the assumption that the characters are knowable by readers in the terms and language (more or less) of the present. Despite Walter Scott's use of dialect and archaism to convey historical, deliberately archaized dialogue ('verily thou art a great loon') is a difficult option for the realist novelist, because this obviously artificial technique inevitably draws attention to its own fictionality; which is why deliberate archaisms tend to appear in parodic postmodernist texts like Peter Ackroyd's *Hawksmoor* (1985) or A. S. Byatt's *Possession* (1990). Conversely, realist historical novels risk anachronism if they represent distant times and places in terms of the language and assumptions of a too-familiar modernity. This is more of a problem in Naomi Mitchison's historical novels of the 1930s, where even slaves speak an educated middle-class idiom, than in Sylvia Townsend Warner's, which use an elaborate formal rhetoric for the speech of grandees and a direct simplicity for peasants and workers. (Mitchison's post-war fiction satis-factorily solves this technical problem, first by using a deliberately stylized Scottish idiom, and later by working the mode of the folk-tale in her later 'African' stories.[14])

Furthermore, the historical novel is itself a notable site of sexualized fantasy. It has a time-honoured association with romance, from popular classics like the novels of Georgette Heyer or Margaret Mitchell's *Gone with the Wind* to Jeanette Winterson's ambitious art novels *The Passion*, set in Napoleon's Europe, and *Sexing the Cherry*, set in seventeenth-century England. There certainly are elements of fantasy and sexualized romance in all the 1930s novels I'm discussing, most notably those of Naomi Mitchison, which use classical settings to stage heterosexual lovemaking, male homosexual declarations of love, the sensual pleasure of breast-feeding, and even group sex: subjects then impossible for 'contemporary' treatment. (She has described how her publishers censored the descrip-tions of sex and contraception in *We Have Been Warned* [1935], whose action occurs in 1931–1933, whereas no one minded the overt sex in *The*

Delicate Fire [1933]: 'Apparently it's all right when people wear wolfskins and togas'.[15]) Sylvia Townsend Warner's *Summer Will Show* has also been read influentially as a lesbian fantasy; and her *After the Death of Don Juan* mockingly exploits the association between exotic historical setting and sexual romance by using Dona Ana's lust for the absent Don Juan as the 'starter motor' for its narrative. And even Jack Lindsay's deliberately unromantic *1649* contains a great deal of (admittedly dismal) sex.

Nevertheless, these elements of sexual romance don't define the novels, which, like their European counterparts, were written in response to and partly shaped by the crises of contemporary history: the economic disruption of the Depression and its accompanying mass unemployment; the facts of successful revolution in Russia and counter-revolution in Italy and Germany; the inescapable politicization of European life, and the steady disappearance of ordinary private lives and choices. John Mair suggested in 1938 that the historical novel was becoming popular because the reality of contemporary dictatorships had become so grotesque: 'School-book history has been given a new lease of life, and the colours, corruptions and cruelties of the more picturesque centuries no longer seem wholly fantastic'.[16] The historical novels are, however, less melodramatic and more intellectual than Mair's remark suggests, interpreting the events of the past in terms of a present need for narratives about surviving defeat. Lindsay's novels especially seem to have been written in response to Dimitrov's warning at the Seventh Congress of the Comintern, that because the Fascists were 'rummaging through history' it was urgent that Communist writers contest their falsifications by 'link[ing] up the present struggle with revolutionary traditions'.[17] The influence of Marxism is crucial here, not simply as a radical inspiration and authority to write the history of the dispossessed losers, but as the totalizing interpretative narrative structure which made the individual narratives intelligible. After all, the *Communist Manifesto* is itself an economic history of capitalism.

LUKÁCS, MARXIST HUMANISM AND OTHER STORIES

No discussion of the historical novels of the 1930s can afford to ignore Gyorgy Lukács' classic contemporary[18] study of the nature and limits of historical realism in *The Historical Novel*. This book remains indispensable both for its analysis of the novel's characteristic creative tension between 'subjective' fantasy and 'objective' materialism, and for its perception of the complex dialectical relationship between the political urgencies of the 'present' moment where the fiction is produced, and the 'historical' dramas which it narrates.

Lukács reads the historical novel as both interpretation and embodiment of historical process. His paradigm novelist is Scott, whose novels respond to the tensions of his own place and time (Scotland, ruled by an English constitutional monarchy at war with revolutionary France and Napoleon's empire) to dramatize history through the creation of a cast of individualized characters from popular life who are also social types, to whom the authenticated 'great men' of history take second place (p. 48). He repeatedly calls Scott 'great' because of this writer's feeling for the contending social forces that propel historical development, his intuitive perception of the 'ceaseless class struggles and their bloody resolution in great or small or abortive uprisings' (p. 32), and most of all for his sympathetic grasp of the ways in which 'ordinary' people come to think and act extraordinarily at moments of political crisis. His novels therefore enable readers to 're-experience the social and human motives which led men to think, feel and act just as they did in historical reality' (p. 42). This classic realism belongs to Scott's particular historical moment; after the failed revolutions of 1848, writers 'no longer have any immediate social sense of continuity with the prehistory of their own society' (p. 244); instead they produce subjective fantasies in decorative historical settings. The paradigm historical novel is now Flaubert's *Salammbô*, in which Carthage is no more than an exotic backdrop for a study of its heroine's psychology; she becomes 'a decorative symbol of the hysterical longings and torments of middle-class girls in large cities' (p. 189). For Flaubert's successors, especially in the early twentieth century, the element of subjective fantasy is strengthened by modernist scepticism about the possibility of representing objective truth, so that the historical novel increasingly becomes a 'subjective' dream or mystical fantasy embroidered with antiquarian detail. The ability to create individuals who are also social types disappears (p. 253).

Recently, however (i.e. from 1930 onwards), the liberal and Socialist struggle against Fascism has, says Lukács, inspired a renaissance in historical fiction: writers have rediscovered the political energies of the form through their 'honest and consistent coming-to-grips with the really burning problems of popular life in the present' (p. 265). A new type of historical novel is produced by refugees from Fascism such as Heinrich Mann or Leon Feuchtwanger, who no longer understand the relation between past and present as (p. 271):

a decorative antithesis between picturesque poetry and grey prose...

Knowledge of the great struggles of the past, familiarity with the great forefighters of progress will inspire men in the present with aims and ideals, courage and consolation, amid the brutal terrors of Fascism. The past will show the way mankind has gone and the direction in which it is moving.

But though he writes warmly about the 'historical novels of democratic humanism', Lukács still sees them as marked to their detriment by a bourgeois alienation which limits the authors' ability to create characters who are also social types (p. 338). Their objective realism is never secure: the 'pliancy of historical material' (p. 244) offers the writer a permanent temptation to subjective fantasy. (One can just imagine what Lukács would have thought of Woolf's *Orlando*.) Where writers have insufficient knowledge of, or feeling for, the material conditions of people's lives, they create inauthentic, anachronistic characters. Marxist novelists too fall prey to this problem. When they lack 'the controlling function of concrete facts of existence which alone can tell the writer the kinds of feelings and thoughts which are possible for a character belonging to a certain period', they reduce individuals to specimens of their class, representing (for example) all merchants in all periods as identical with 'the present-day stock exchange king' (p. 296).

Furthermore, in anti-Fascist novels, argument too often crowds out historical experience: Lukács cites an exemplary passage from Feucht-wanger's *The Jewish War* where a slave points out to the historian Josephus that the real cause of the war lay in the impossibly high taxes imposed on the peasantry by the 'temple aristocracy' and the Roman authorities. This is much too abstract, says Lukács, though he doesn't specify just what he would have preferred (he probably had in mind something like a first-century equivalent to one of Scott's tales of rebellion). He attacks Feuchtwanger's overt didacticism because it substitutes argument for lived experience (p. 294):

> When Marx says that the economic categories are 'forms of existence, determinants of existence', he is not only defining the material character of economic categories philosophically, he is providing a key to the literary portrayal of economic determination. That is, the economic categories must not be seen fetishistically as abstractions... but as immediate forms of existence in human life.

Although Lukács' own words are so shamelessly abstract here as to make him sound like the Devil rebuking sin, his point is shrewdly taken. When historical narratives do not sufficiently realize the past, they can become overloaded with contemporary political allegory. Naomi Mitchison's *The Blood of the Martyrs* (1939), a very decent, deeply felt novel but not her best, is, though not mentioned by Lukács, a good instance of this weakness for 'turning the past directly into a *parable of the present*' (p. 338). The parallel suggested by the title between the Neronian persecution of the Christians and the Fascist persecution of Socialists is explained in Mitchison's Foreword and reiterated in her Hitlerian Emperor Nero meditating on 'Strength through joy! . . . I am the Will of Rome and the people know it, the ordinary people who love me', and underlined too hard in a lengthy discussion of the economic causes of Rome's history since the Punic Wars, entitled 'Difficulties of a United Front'.[19] By turning the events of ancient history into a simple allegory of the present instead of trying to understand it on its own terms, the novel limits itself to reiterating the crisis of the present, rather than exploring its nature and its relationship to the past.

Despite Lukács' shrewdness and his analytic subtlety when dealing with the dialectical relation between past and present in the historical novel, his account is open to many serious criticisms. That overprivileging of traditional narrative methods in fiction which is held against him today by poststructuralist critics like Colin MacCabe and Toril Moi is perfectly defensible in political terms: realism was easily accessible to readers, and therefore had obvious potential for popular influence in a way that avant-garde novels did not. This reasoning also underpinned all the arguments for realism at the Soviet Writers' Congress in 1934 from Stalin's crude saying that 'writers are the engineers of human souls' to Bukharin's more nuanced argument that texts are social objects which 'reproduce and transmit definite group psychologies'. And almost sixty years later, in the quite different political context of 1980s feminism, the critic Rita Felski has used similar arguments to assert the political usefulness of realist feminist novels.[20]

Much more problematic is the fact that Lukács' overvaluation of the term 'objectivity' within his binary 'subjective/objective' dialectic led him, notoriously, to dismiss Modernist texts as 'subjective' without bothering to explore or explain them. Also, like many Marxists, he lacked any understanding or acknowledgement of sexual politics, which meant that his humanism constantly privileged a masculine perspective. (It may look anachronistic to criticize Lukács in 1937 for not admitting feminist insights; but since the Marxist critic Christopher Caudwell did at least acknowledge gender politics as an issue, the problem cannot have been totally invisible to Communists even then.[21]) Most damagingly of all, Lukács' theory of realism implies a curiously unliterary notion of writing. Although he rightly resists any crude explaining of writers in terms of their social class, he consistently argues that the creation of those individua-lized, socially representative characters which are the glory of the historical novel depends on the author's social insight, which itself is determined by his or her relationship to 'the people' (p. 283). Thus, though he acknowledges 'the connection between Scott and Shakespeare' (p. 90), he never explores the way Scott reinvents Shakespearean themes and characters.[22] There is no trace of his contemporary Bakhtin's perception of the multiple languages of narrative, or the significance of irony and parody as means of contesting definitions; nothing at all to show that language, as the medium of narration, demands attention and analysis. Lukács' reading of fiction assumes, or rather insists, that narrative effects have their ultimate source in the Author as historical subject.

This humanist assumption has in the last twenty-odd years been subjected to a searching formalist attack, brilliantly pioneered by Roland Barthes in S/Z (1970), and articulated most influentially in England and America in Catherine Belsey's *Critical Practice* (1980) and Toril Moi's *Sexual/Textual Politics* (1985), for whom 'Lukács' is a Stalinist byword and a hissing.[23] These Socialist-feminist writers criticize both realist fiction and the critics who privilege it, attacking their uniform submission to the authority of bourgeois common sense – an authority not of explicit maxims, but of ideological assumptions about the primacy of the bourgeois individual. These assumptions are, Belsey argues, all the more powerful in that they are not directly stated, but subtly encoded in the 'transparency' of the classic realist text: 'Classic realism constitutes an ideological practice in addressing itself to readers as subjects, interpellat-ing them so that they freely accept both their subjectivity and their subjection' (p. 69). Following Colin MacCabe, she cites a passage from a George Eliot novel to illustrate the way in which classic realism 'points us almost irresistibly to a single interpretation which appears as the product of an intersubjective communication between the author and the reader in which the role of language has become invisible' (p. 72).

Certainly, this account of the way realism appears to compel belief in its ideological world is true of much realist fiction. But to my mind it works much better for interpreting crudely written popular fiction than for complex classic novels, because its method depends on 'fixing' the text as having only one significant meaning, an approach which is demonstrably inadequate to the subtle energies of classic realist prose. Indeed, only a monolithic account of *any* text, from *Middlemarch* to a Mills and Boon novel, could claim that it points its readers 'almost irresistibly' to given conclusions. Although some fictional texts, especially popular fiction written in a 'realist' mode, do point readers in ideologically predictable directions which only a minority of readers may be able to resist, the history of argument and debate about classic realist novels is clear evidence that these do not in fact work in such a straightforward fashion.[24]

Furthermore, this anti-humanist critique of realist fiction addresses only its narrative mode, neglecting the important question of plot. Plotting – and its transformations – have, however, been the target of another highly influential group of cultural critics: those feminists who have been working, mainly in North America, to redraw and enlarge the map of women's writings, emphasizing women's transformations of old plots and invention of new ones. These feminists argue that traditional narratives are ideologically prescriptive in that, without necessarily pointing a moral, their patterns define the limits of (what is thought to be) the possible. Thus Nancy K. Miller's *The Heroine's Text* (1979) showed that the standard stories about a woman's life represent her chief end either as integration in patriarchal heterosexuality (the 'euphoric' marriage plot) or as failure and death (the 'dysphoric' plot). Miller has also shown how, because these normative patterns shape readers' expectations of fiction, women's novels which depart from these plots tend to be dismissed as implausible 'minor' art. Rachel Blau DuPlessis has applied Miller's interpretative model to twentieth-century writers such as Woolf, Richardson or Stein, who refused to struggle 'manfully' with an outmoded realist narrative form, instead inventing new 'female heroes' – collective as well as individual – in quest of a new language.

This notion of a questing 'female hero' has since been used to interpret much more overtly old-fashioned novels, including those of 'Somerville novelists' such as Dorothy L. Sayers, Naomi Mitchison, Vera Brittain and Winifred Holtby, as well as Sylvia Townsend Warner's books. All of these feminist readings interpret works of apparently traditional realism as transformations of old marriage-or-death plots into new exemplary fables of female heroes, whose quest for consciousness is tied not, as in DuPlessis' argument, to new forms of writing, but to the more familiar goals of autonomy and identity. The surface realism of women's fictions is thus read as a 'set' for the staging of mythical narratives of free, transcendent identity.[25] And the gains of this 'mapping' of women's writing in terms of the reinvention of autonomous female selfhood are certainly important. This feminist identity, founded on sexual rebellion and polished by two decades of feminist literary theory, is undeniably impressive; without it, the 'no man's land' of women's writing might still be an uncharted terrain of swamp and jungle. As Virginia Woolf might have put it, I respect and admire that feminist identity from the bottom of my bourgeois heart . . .[26]

For autonomous subjective identity is, of course, precisely that bourgeois fantasy which the poststructuralists have, in the name of a Marxist 'politics of form', attacked realist fiction for affirming. It is true that this critique of realist narratives greatly exaggerates their alleged 'transparency', neglecting both the workings of plot, which feminist critics have shown to be ideologically crucial, and the role of fantasy in these texts. Yet if these elements can be shown to promote the classic bourgeois ideological illusion of free subjective identity, it looks as if Catherine Belsey could be right after all. Indeed, since the novel is by origin a bourgeois capitalist genre, it is not surprising that its textual energies should so easily lend themselves to fantasies of individualist autonomy.

Yet it would obviously be both reductive and politically short-sighted to dismiss the question of female identity as mere capitalist ideology. As Nancy Miller has drily observed: 'Because women have not had the same relation of identity to origin, institution, production that men have had, they have not, I think, (collectively) felt burdened by *too much* Self, Ego, Cogito, etc.'[27] And certainly, the last thing which the institutionally dispossessed need is a dismissal of that identity which they have not been privileged to enjoy as just another ideological illusion. A satisfying interpretation of realist historical novels needs to work with both the feminist critique of narrative as ideology, and to acknowledge with Lukács the dialectic between the present and the past which is implied by historical fictions. Otherwise the reader will be left with the unacceptable, contradictory alternatives of a Marxism which refuses to pay attention to anything that looks like 'subjectivism' (Lukács) or the autonomous Subject (Belsey), and a feminism which seems interested in little else.

THE PRESENT IN THE PAST: JACK LINDSAY AND SYLVIA TOWNSEND WARNER

The clash between Marxism and feminism can be seen, unsurprisingly perhaps, in the historical novels themselves. Both the strength and the limits of the kind of Marxist humanism approved by Lukács can be seen in two highly original novels by Communist Party writers: Jack Lindsay's *1649: A Novel of a Year* and Sylvia Townsend Warner's *After the Death of Don Juan*, both published in 1938. Lindsay's book, whose title alludes to Victor Hugo's revolutionary novel *1793*, narrates the story of a group of characters through the year 1649 from January to December, one chapter per month. It contains 108 sections, of which ten, together with the 'Endpiece', consist of quotations from authentic historical documents.[28] Eleven more are narrated as extracts from private seventeenth-century journals; the scenes entitled 'Arthur Boon' are told as the journal of a Parliamentary official with cautious Leveller sympathies, in a lively stylistic mixture of Pepys and Aubrey. Apart from these, the mode of narration is mainly realist, though with little authorial commentary. Instead, Lindsay uses a free indirect method, naming each scene for the character whose point of view dominates it, and so including multiple perspectives on history. The novel's totalizing Marxist vision is thus implied by the narrative pattern, rather than spelt out in authorial commentary.

The overall theme of the novel, as Lindsay's poem prefacing it insists, is the capacity of the English tradition of libertarian revolt to survive defeat and repression. Lindsay interprets the ascendancy of Cromwell and the grandees as a capitalist takeover of popular revolution, which is represented by the Levellers and Diggers. The only real difference between Royalists and Puritans is the latter's belief in a free market: New Capitalists are but Old Lords writ larger and more ruthless. (The landed gentry is represented by an authoritarian but comparatively decent squire who is reluctant to use the unscrupulous methods of his get-rich-quick neighbour, 'the abominable Sir Lucius': p. 179.) Like Scott but even more so, Lindsay gives minimal treatment to famous historical figures; the opening scene of the king's execution, for example, focuses almost entirely on the gravely watching crowd. Instead, the novel concentrates partly on the revolutionary leaders John Lilburne of the Levellers and Gerrard Winstanley of the Diggers (the latter supported by a distinctly stagey chorus of supporters, who sing a different stanza of their song 'Stand up now, Diggers all!' every time they appear), but more on the fictional characters who follow them. The drama of the narrative turns on the different ways in which these men handle the failure of their revolutionary hopes. Will Scamle, son of a dispossessed yeoman farmer, defies the Parliamentary forces, escapes them and ends up as a class-conscious Norfolk fisherman; Roger Cotton, an agonized Puritan printer, is unjustly gaoled for a time, briefly joins the Diggers, and after much suffering and self-scrutiny becomes a member of a group of activists determined to 'fight on, openly or out of sight' (p. 558); and Ralph Lydcot, son of a reactionary Puritan merchant, moves from being an ardent Leveller to 'unpolitical' capitulation to family values.

Lindsay's representation of the Cromwellian capitalists as counter-revolutionaries has been criticized for historical inaccuracy by the Marxist critic H. Gustav Klaust, who has pointed out that *1649* is anachronistic in showing the ex-revolutionary Ralph Lydcot agreeing to 'withdraw from all politics' (p. 376) as a condition of becoming a successful capitalist. In the context of the Civil War, the free market was itself a revolutionary idea, for 'the Revolution was headed not by the people but by the bourgeoisie'.[29] But Klaust's criticisms, though just, seem not quite to the point, because they imply that Lindsay ought to have written a quite different book about the causes of the English Revolution, instead of a novel about the common people's persistence in retaining libertarian ideals and resisting oppression in the face of counter-revolution. In 1938, those were the lessons an English Marxist would look to learn from his nation's past; and *1649* is very much a book of the thirties. The novel's most lyrical passage describes two Levellers finding themselves (p. 193):

> on a giddy crag of vision from which they saw the mass movements of men suddenly coherent and understandable, a map of man, a land-scape of time, perilous and engrossing, terrific as a burst of storm, yet clear as a page in a printed book.

The splendid rhetoric of this prophetic vision belongs as much to the moment of writing as to the seventeenth-century history which it surveys, echoing as it does the famous opening of Auden's prophetic lines 'Consider this and in our time/ As the hawk sees it or the helmeted airman.'[30]

Lindsay's novel implies many parallels between England in 1649 and in the 1930s: economic crisis and widespread unemployment, bad in London and worse in the North; the steadfast courage of the despised common people; the power both then and now of corrupt, ruthless capitalists and their free-market ideologues; and even the stranglehold of the City on English industry. As Will Scamle meditates, 'he had found one thing constant: the struggle between the poor and the rich. And not only that; also the struggle between the men who were running industries and the men who were trading on the commodities produced' (p. 444). The same point was being made by Socialists who attacked finance capitalism for its reluctance to invest in industry – as when Ellen Wilkinson, Labour MP, showed in *The Town That Was Murdered* how the shipping magnate James Lithgow, head of the National Shipbuilders' Security, Ltd., had manipulated the shipbuilding slump in Jarrow, to the profit of the NSS.[31]

Much more powerful than Lindsay's overt economic didacticism, however, is his implied parallel between John Lilburne's show trial for alleged sedition and the trial of Dimitrov the Comintern agent for allegedly burning down the Reichstag. Lindsay's narrative of Lilburne's trial stays close to his sources, but the connections between England in 1649 and Germany in 1933 are strongly suggested. (Ralph Fox had suggested in *The Novel and the People* [1937] that the story of Dimitrov's trial 'is an epic of our time which demands that the novelist should give it life', and his sketch of a possible scenario may well have contributed to Lindsay's handling of Lilburne's trial.[32]) The Levellers are shown as precursors of the Communists; their committee-sessions, their methods of getting support by producing semi-legal pamphlets, and their networking of the Army via reliable cadres, all sound much like Party activists at work. More importantly, both the trials and their outcomes are remarkably similar; each hero of the people faces a trumped-up accusation, rigged by a hostile government, and manages, against apparently overwhelming odds, to turn the trial around, put the judges themselves in the dock, and walk free. Claud Cockburn wrote that:

> nobody... today can have any notion of what Dimitrov was to us as a symbol, a flame in darkness, a proof that, however bad things seem to be, the courageous, even the apparently foolhardy backers of a sixty-six to one chance may still win.[33]

But *1649* can still give its reader a fair idea.

So far, so admirable; the only problem with the novel is its sexual politics. The poem which prefaces the novel invokes an exclusively masculine tradition of heroic English radicalism, 'Chartist truehearts... all the yeoman stock', the men 'that love England, have our pride in her/ Aye, love of England is the tale we tell,/ We mix with her in toil' (p. vi). The novel that follows correspondingly represents libertarian revolution as entirely a men's affair. However, women are not absent, for the relation between the public history of the aborted English Revolution and the 'private' lives of his characters is articulated through a web of singularly joyless romance intrigues between revolutionary youths and upper-class women. The latter, unrelentingly represented as signifiers of class essences, are a predictably sorry lot: Lucy, a pretty, neurotic heiress who briefly attracts Ralph Lydcot, marries and then murders a royalist rake, relieving the subsequent guilt by having sex with strangers; Aleonora, another heiress, who is raped by Will Scamle, the honest son of the soil, and comes back and back for more; and Mary, an arrogant and selfish farmer's daughter, who seduces the lecher Randol in a cornfield scene which perhaps consciously recalls Ursula Brangwen's aggressive sexuality in D. H. Lawrence's *The Rainbow.* Above (or rather, below) all is Nell, the downwardly mobile gentlewoman-turned-prostitute, who knows no other relationship to men than letting them fuck her, taking their money and hating them for it. Nell nearly destroys the saintly Roger Cotton during their long, destructive affair; he never resolves his political and personal conflicts until she finally leaves him.

Less demonic but even more destructive is Joan, the 'good' bourgeois heiress whom Ralph Lydcot marries, and who carries the main guilt of his withdrawal from politics which she regards as treachery to 'her domestic scheme of things'. The counter-revolutionary Joan thus bullies Ralph into abandoning his revolutionary friends and even into burning his Leveller pamphlets (pp. 514–15). The only character who achieves a healthy balance between sex and politics is Will Scamle who, having escaped from the insatiable Aleonora, elopes with a pure virginal girl who is herself avoiding a wealthy bridegroom, marries her and settles down in a Norfolk fishing community, vowing 'to organize ourselves the way the masters do in the Companies and the Government' (p. 541). All of these character-izations imply a deep suspicion of women in general and active female sexuality in particular, hardly redeemed by the warm description of the working-class Leveller women whose class loyalty and shrewdness impress Ralph Lydcot: 'These clear-eyed women . . . seeing the political facts so much more clearly than the orators of Westminster – they made him feel even greater disgust for Lucy and her kind' (p. 192). Although 'Lucy and her kind' are not actually responsible for the defeat of the English revolution, they are all, particularly the devoutly capitalist Joan, made to seem quite as guilty as Cromwell – perhaps even more so, since they appear in the narrative and he doesn't.

After the Death of Don Juan, Sylvia Townsend Warner's fable of class war in a remote eighteenth-century Spanish village, also deals with a failed rebellion. Its Prologue relates the familiar Don Juan legend – the notorious libertine attempts to rape Dona Ana, a betrothed virgin, is interrupted by her father the Commandant, and kills him. The Commandant is commemorated by a life-size marble statue, which the unrepentant Juan invites to dine with him; it duly appears, adjuring him to repent; he refuses and is dragged off to hell by devils, as witnessed by his servant Leporello 'with every appearance of terror' (p. 2). The plot's action starts here. Dona Ana, now married but ruled by an unadmitted passion for Juan, insists on going to break the sad news to his father, Don Saturno of Tenorio Viejo. The couple, with their hangers-on, journey arduously across 'two mountain-ranges and . . . dried river-beds without number' (p. 17) to reach this remote village, impoverished and plagued by drought. Don Saturno, an elderly liberal, shocks the pious deputation by receiving the story of his son's death sceptically; they nevertheless stay on at Dona Ana's insistence, Don Saturno's disbelief having given her hope for Juan's return. In the village, the peasants, whose poverty has financed the heir's extravagant lifestyle, are divided: some believe that Don Juan 'is off our backs at last' (p. 108), others think this is too good to be true.

True or false, the news brings enough hope to act as a political catalyst. The peasants ask Don Saturno to invest in a desperately needed irrigation project, which Don Juan's expenses have previously made impracticable. Don Saturno is agreeable, and things go well until Don Juan reappears, alive, at the castle. He also has plans for improvement; he means to irrigate the land and turn out the peasants. Negotiation becomes dispute, and the peasants surround the castle, refusing to accept Juan as authentic; the grandees inside manage, despite their mutual hatred, to outwit the peasants, getting a message out to an Army detachment posted nearby. The book ends with the soldiers wrecking the town, and a handful of courageous rebels making a last stand in the old schoolhouse with maps of Spain on the wall (p. 301):

> 'So large a country,' said the dying man. 'And there in the middle of it, like a heart, is Madrid. But our Tenorio Viejo is not marked. . . . It is too small, I suppose. We have lived in a very small place, Diego.'
> 'We have lived in Spain,' said the other.

This exchange, directly echoing the image of Spain as a map and the line 'Madrid is the heart' from Auden's contemporary poem *Spain 1937*, clinches the allegorical parallel between these ill-equipped, outnumbered peasants bravely and hopelessly resisting the allied powers of Church, Army and landed gentry, and the Spanish Republic besieged by its Fascist enemies. Warner described the book to Nancy Cunard as 'a parable if you like the word, or an allegory. . . of the political chemistry of Spain, with the Don Juan – more of Molière than of Mozart – developing as the Fascist of the piece'.[34]

This story of an obscure skirmish of the class war in a remote place and time is not, however, just a differently costumed account of the Spanish War. Warner's fable works quite differently from the naturalism of, for example, Storm Jameson's slightly earlier political novel *In the Second Year* (1935), which also deals with the ascendancy of Fascism, describing a successful Fascist coup in England. Jameson's narrative represents England's political dangers as its unstable economy and corrupt rulers; her dictator 'Hillier' (= Hitler), with his private army of 'National Volunteers', gets his chance because of a currency crisis and a failed General Strike. He then consolidates his power by allying himself with the great financial institutions which he originally promised to oppose. *After the Death of Don Juan* contains no comparably direct representations of contemporary issues. Tenorio Viejo, its microcosmic site of struggle, is too isolated for the opposed forces to have any outside links, apart from the grandees' message to the soldiers. The allegory therefore does not extend to the relations between the Spanish Republic, the International Brigade, Soviet Russia and the 'non-interventionist' governments on the one hand, and Franco's backing by Fascist Italy and Germany on the other.

The prevailing tone of the novel is an ironic realism, typified by Don Saturno musing that the tale of supernatural vengeance is probably just a convenient fiction to enable Juan to escape the debt collectors: 'Duns, without any act of God, seemed as good a reason for the disappearance' (p. 74), and more harshly by the appearance of Tenorio Viejo. Advertised by Leporello as 'a rural paradise' (p. 16), this village proves to be a 'straggle of lime-washed hovels' in a bleak setting (p. 24):

> The olive-trees in their cultivated earth looked like the spots on a leopard's skin, the vineyards were few and poor.... On the higher slopes the colour of the earth, fading from the valley's leopard-colour to an ashen whiteness, showed that cultivation need strive no further.

Every feature of this landscape carries social meanings: the hovels dominated by church and castle, those allied oppressors; the yellow land eroded by overcultivation and lack of irrigation; the few poor spots of cultivated earth – every detail shows that the land is a site of class division, oppression and acute exploitation. All of this implies a parallel with Spain in the 1930s, not yet industrialized, still dominated by Church and gentry, and notoriously cursed by agrarian poverty. Warner's political observations are, correspondingly, both as modern and as 'timeless', as her description of a delegation's reception by its constituents: 'They went out, and met those awaiting them; and like all delegations felt they had done pretty well until the comments of those they had represented made them feel they had done pretty badly' (p. 181).

The relationship between the eighteenth-century moment of the story and the present moment of narration is articulated principally through Warner's narrative *donnée*, the death of Don Juan, arch-oppressor and heir of the estate, which allegorically represents the discomfiture of the Spanish ruling class by the election of a Popular Front government in February 1936. The desperately needed irrigation project represents the reforms needed to bring Spain's undeveloped economy and antiquated social institutions up to date, while Don Juan's resurrection, more virulent than before, corresponds to the ultimately victorious Fascist revolt. For as Ramon, the clearest-sighted of the peasants, points out, while the landlords in the castle still own the estate, the heir's death counts for little: 'Dead or no, what difference do you think it would make?' (p. 117). The reforms will not be in the peasants' interest (p. 149):

'More than water is needed to wash away the Castle. . . . For suppose the water is brought, it will still be theirs. They can turn it away if they choose. It will be another weapon in their hands, and we shall have put it there . . . You have made it seem that everything hangs on the death of this man.'

He frowned with the effort of speaking. Words were not coming easily, exasperated he gave the tree a blow with his fist. The wizened fruit pattered down.

'There!' he exclaimed. 'There fall a dozen Don Juans. But here' – he smote the tree again – 'here is the tree.'

Though Ramon knows nothing of Marx, his hard-won insights articulate the Marxist perception that class control of the means of production, which in a pre-industrial society means the ownership of land, is crucial to political dominance. His speech is thus a parable within a parable, and yet this *mise en abyme* of political allegory seems to arise, by the accident of punching a tree, from the speaker's own experience. The political perceptions are not tacked on to the narrative by means of authorial commentary or 'abstract' anachronistic dialogues, but grow, as Lukács required, out of the peasants' own life and work. Appropriately enough, *After the Death of Don Juan* is the only Sylvia Townsend Warner novel held by the Lenin Library in Moscow.[35]

Warner's characterizations as well as her political analysis also fit Lukács' aesthetic, in that all her characters are social types. Thus Don Gil the sacristan, perhaps the most evil character in the book, represents a clerical Fascism inspired by a vision of cosmic cruelty (p. 155):

A hierarchy of bullying opened before him, fear ran through the social organism as blood runs through man; and behind the social order was God, the source and support of all fear, God like a heart eternally pumping fear into the universe . . . He saw, and adored, and dedicated himself to becoming powerful.

More complex is the sympathetic landlord Don Saturno who, as Wendy Mulford has pointed out,[36] represents the political failures of liberalism. A democratically minded sceptic who believes in progress, he has started up a school in the village to stimulate the peasants to 'a noble discontent' (p. 54), but has never funded it adequately. In his progressive views on behalf of his tenants, combined with his practical neglect of them, he resembles the ineffectual Mr Brooke in George Eliot's *Middlemarch*, except that he is not a comic butt. Unlike Brooke, Don Saturno has real intellectual distinction, good taste, unfailing courtesy to his tenants as well as to his fellow grandees, and quick-witted conversation (p. 32):

> 'You cannot ask me to think that my father's spirit is a superstition,' said Dona Ana with energy.
> 'The souls of the righteous are in the hands of God. And I am positive that your father would not leave such a repose in order to sup at a restaurant.'

But neither his progressive views nor his genuine admiration for the sweated farmers can make Don Saturno's goodwill effective, for he cannot protect his tenants from his son. His aristocratic isolation at the castle leaves the village vulnerable to the sinister Don Gil; and since the villagers pay for his hobbies as well as for his son's extravagances, he is also responsible, though less criminally than Juan, for their miserable poverty. In a final scene which strangely recalls the blinding of Gloucester in *King Lear*, Don Saturno attempts to go out to protect his people from the soldiers, only to find himself prevented by his son, who by now regards him as a traitor: 'No old men leave this house... Sit down in your easy-chair, father. You need a little nap. First I will tie your arms, so...' (p. 286).

The peasants are represented more simply and sympathetically than the grandees. They are not idealized; their courage and solidarity are shown, but so are their prejudice, superstition, credulity, including a naive belief in their enemies' honour, their macho contempt for women, and their mutual divisions. Ramon, the best of them, is praised for his 'steadfast' loyalty to the communal, secular morality (p. 248):

> The world is not so bad as we make it. As we have hands given us to work with so we have wits given us to think with. There should be justice for the poor.... Neighbour should stand by neighbour.

But though respected by his neighbours, Ramon has little influence on them. For all their just rage against the grandees, few other villagers see the issues clearly; supposition rapidly circulates among them as fact.

But, of course, the novel itself is based upon the supposition that Don Juan had actually disappeared in eighteenth-century Seville; and the fictionality of this *donnée* is a crucial part of its own narrative. At the outset, Don Saturno tells his visitors that their story is not new: 'This legend of the wicked Don Juan is one of our family traditions... In fact, the story has passed into literature. Molière wrote a play on the theme, an uneven work but not without merit' (p. 35). The legend belongs also, much more influentially, to the anonymous popular traditions which are invoked in the ballad sung by the villagers (p. 122, 219):

Is it a lady or is it a nightingale
That sings so sweetly, that cries so sadly?
Lady, though you sang to a harp of angels,
You would not fetch Don Juan from hell,
No, would not fetch him.

This popular ballad is a form of communal, subversive art, releasing highly explosive energies, for it rouses the peasants to make their demand for water. Through the song and its effect, the novel shows how, once a story is put into circulation, the truth or falsity of its words matter less than the fact that they are spoken – or, even more powerfully, chanted. The power of language is, however, hard to control or direct, not least because its meaning – and therefore its political effects – vary according to context. The ballad is first mentioned ironically at the peasants' meeting by a sceptic, who sings it to prove that 'this story's a fable. An old fable too' (p. 122). But by the end of the debate, it becomes the hymn of the optimists who want to believe that their lives have changed already (p. 126). When the child Engracia sings it during the confrontation at the castle, irony again predominates (p. 219).

Does this playful instability of meaning, this *mise en abyme* of the Don Juan narrative, mean that the novel's Marxist politics disappear into the play of signifiers? Hardly. The way this novel points up its own fictionality works in much the same way as Benjamin's imaginary stage 'tableau' which tells the truth in a way that more moderate and plausible acting never could, both because its melodrama draws attention to the actual extremities of class struggle and because its obvious fictionality invites debate and scrutiny of the issues raised. The self-conscious fictionality of *After the Death of Don Juan* actually illuminates the problem of ideological struggle in the class war. The unstable meanings produced by the popular ballad clearly show both the power of propaganda and the difficulty of disseminating and controlling it.

But, like Lindsay, though she doesn't share his sexism, Warner represents the class struggle as, overwhelmingly, a men's affair. True, the novel acknowledges and criticizes macho dominance (p. 151), shows Don Gil contemptuously bullying his wife (pp. 83–4) and, more positively, gives space to the verbal vitality of peasant women (pp. 100–4). It also sketches the talented, courageous little girl Engracia, whose singing inspires a rebellious crowd and who manages to warn the rebels that the soldiers are approaching. Engracia might in another time and place be a potential Minna Lemuel, the artist whose revolutionary words are at the centre of *Summer Will Show*, Warner's other historical novel of the thirties.

Here, however, she is only a minor detail in a tragedy fought out between men.

The reasons for Sylvia Townsend Warner's comparative neglect of women in this novel lie, I think, both in her sense of Spanish history and in her technique as a Marxist novelist. Like Lindsay, she relies on free indirect narration, using little or no authorial commentary, her overview being implied by her ironic or sympathetic penetration, as the story unfolds, into all the different minds which perceive it. In Tenorio Viejo, where male authority is everywhere unquestioned, it would clearly be both anachronistic and off the Marxist point to invent a character who questioned gender relations. This (relative) absence of feminist critique, however unavoidable, does make the novel's humanism look a little narrowly defined.

SEXUALITY AND SOCIALISM:NAOMI MITCHISON

In contrast to the deliberately harsh realism of the Marxists Jack Lindsay and Sylvia Townsend Warner, the political strength of Naomi Mitchison's early fictions, set in ancient Greece and Scythia, lies mainly in their feminism and the way in which their narrative energies are enabled by a spring of fantasy. Mitchison's own metaphor for the relationship between her writings and the unknown past is playful and erotic: 'a game of hide-and-seek in the dark... [where] if one touches a hand or face, it is all chance'.[37] Because the ancient world knew a sexual freedom unparalleled even in the relatively emancipated Britain of the 1920s and 1930s, and was also remote enough to demand a great deal of imaginative invention, her pioneering historical novels could use their classical settings to explore sexuality in society in ways that sometimes resemble utopian science fiction (such as her 1962 *Memoirs of a Space Woman*) as much as they do history.

Her novel *The Corn King and the Spring Queen* excels at vividly realized, sensuous narration. The moments of happiness, all shadowed by a grim past and an uncertain future, are intensely realized, as in the idyll of the Spartan games with the boys and young men 'in lovely pale-brown groups, half conscious of their own bodies and the girls in the trees behind them, setting one another off with long legs and straight backs and heads up in the golden sunshine' (p. 219), or the extraordinarily sensuous scene where the heroine breast-feeds her baby (p. 304):

For a moment she teased him, withholding herself; then, as she felt the milk in her springing towards him, she let him settle, thrusting her breast deep into the hollow of his mouth, that seized on her with a rhythmic throb of acceptance, deep sucking of lips and tongue and cheeks.

Even more surprising in a novel published in 1931 is the scene where two men remember the night they first made love (p. 648):

> 'You ducked a little as I took the sword sling over your head... You took your tunic right off and laid it by the sword. I saw no blemish on you, Panteus.'
>
> 'Nor I on you. And I was glad that my body was strong and hard and clean. You were very brown all over, more than I'd thought. I put my hands on to you, on to your chest, and stroked down over your flanks and thighs. I stood up and we kissed one another. You said, "Tomorrow there will be fighting again. Stay with me now." So I stayed.'

In her sympathetic, sexy treatment of male homosexuality, her retelling of classical myth as liberal realist fiction, and her post-Frazer 'anthropological' approach to the ancient world, Naomi Mitchison anticipated and probably influenced the better-known historical novels of Mary Renault, who published her first novels in the late 1930s and, as a progressive intellectual, would certainly have read Mitchison. Not only does Mary Renault's representation of the bloodthirsty matriarchies tamed by Theseus (the hero of her first historical novel *The King Must Die* [1948]), look very like an anti-feminist rewriting of the powers of the Spring Queen; her novel itself is based on Mitchison's own theme of 'Kings who die for the people' in *Corn King* (part 7, pp. 545–653).

As a feminist and Socialist who joined the Labour Party in 1932, Naomi Mitchison has more in common with the liberal feminist novelists of her generation such as Vera Brittain, Winifred Holtby, Storm Jameson and Rebecca West, even though none of these wrote historical novels, than she has with her Marxist contemporaries. The closeness between these writers is cultural and political as much as personal; all four women, living like Mitchison in London, knew each other as members of pacifist and/or anti-Fascist causes, as well as meeting on the pages of the liberal feminist magazine *Time and Tide*, to which they all contributed. Like them, Mitchison is no formal innovator; her historical fictions, which draw on Kipling as well as Frazer,[38] use a fairly old-fashioned realist form to articulate urgent contemporary issues in politics and sexuality, orchestrating these around a central, indirectly autobiographical narrative of an exceptional woman's unconventional life. (See pp. 56–61, for a full discussion of these themes in contemporary autobiographical novels by women.) Her novels, again, lend themselves easily to 'mythical' feminist interpretations like those of her biographer Jill Benton, who draws on Rachel Blau DuPlessis' theories to emphasize the ways in which the lives of her feminist heroes transcend the conventional limits of the 'heroine's story'.

The subject of Mitchison's *The Corn King and the Spring Queen* is indeed the quest of its heroes, Tarrik and Erif Der, to find meaning and identity beyond their culturally prescribed destinies as Corn King and Spring Queen of Marob. Erif Der's five-year search takes her into exile in Sparta and eventually Alexandria, while Tarrik works out his salvation at home. The novel also surveys historical development, moving from archaic, stable 'barbarian' Marob, through Hellenistic Greece self-consciously remembering its glory days, to the rich, multicultural decadence of King Ptolemy's court in Egyptian Alexandria. Marob is a primitive but not tyrannical patriarchy, which includes female witches respected for their magical powers. Its people perceive their own lives as part of a cycle, endlessly renewed and maintained by the seasonal fertility rites. Marob has no temples or priests praying to the gods; the Corn King and the Spring Queen *are* gods for as long as they play their parts during the great open-field rituals at Plowing Eve, Midsummer and Harvest. When the Corn King grows old and loses his divine powers, he is killed and ritually eaten by his heir. Spring Queens, however, are allowed to retire.

But this stable, timeless society is about to enter history through Tarrik and Erif Der (it already has trade links with Hellenistic Greece). Tarrik travels to the Greek states, finding partial answers to his anxieties first in Stoic philosophy and later in Epicureanism. The Stoic philosopher Sphaeros has also influenced King Kleomenes of Sparta, who carries through a briefly successful Communist revolution, bringing back Sparta's ancient laws and customs so that personal wealth is handed over to the State, and some of the helots are enfranchised as Spartan citizens and soldiers. Much of the narrative deals with the 'New Days' of the revolution, as seen by the young aristocratic girl Philylla, an ardent revolutionary who also becomes a close friend of Erif Der and her brother Berris. Philylla later becomes Berris' lover out of pity combined with frustration at her own unsatisfactory marriage to the King's lover Panteus.

The Spring Queen's story, described by Jill Benton as 'a woman's search for self in community',[39] amounts to a feminist-Socialist rewriting of Aeschylean myth. As Agamemnon sacrificed his daughter Iphigenia to ensure that his expedition against Troy could set out, so Erif Der's father uses her life to consolidate his own power, first ordering her to marry the Corn King and then killing their child for being Tarrik's son. When she kills her father with the Spring Queen's ceremonial sickle at the Harvest ritual, this unconscious but willed revenge mirrors Clytemnestra's murder of Agamemnon as payment for their daughter's death. But also, because Erif Der incurs a supernatural curse by committing parricide, her act and its punishment are a cross-gendered re-enacting of Orestes' vengeance on his mother Clytemnestra and of his persecution by the female Furies. The male god Apollo's rescue of Orestes from the claims of the Furies is represented in Aeschylus' *Eumenides* as establishing stable patriarchal forms of order; Erif Der's 'cleansing', conversely, is magically tied up with the death and symbolic resurrection of Kleomenes' revolutionary Socialism. Like Orestes, she appeals to Apollo, whose Delphic oracle responds with a cryptic promise of absolution when certain prophecies are fulfilled (p. 376):

> The Mother must meet the Daughter. The Dead must meet with the Snake.
> A House shall stand in the Cornfield, though it cost five years to make.
> Potters shall paint their vases, Poets shall string their rhymes
> And Kings shall die for the People in many places and times.

In Alexandria, these prophecies are fulfilled, both by the emotional resolution which Erif Der experiences through the rites of the goddess Isis and through meeting the ghost of her own mother, and by her own intimate connection with the death of the Spartan revolutionaries and with the survival of their ideals. King Kleomenes does die for the people as prophesied, when he and a faithful Spartan remnant perish in a last desperate uprising. The remaining Spartan women and children, including Philylla, are then killed by the Egyptian soldiers, who are also ordered to flay and publicly expose Kleomenes' body for three days. During that time Erif Der lies unconscious while a mysterious snake appears to guard the dead king, whom the awed people begin to worship as a god. When she awakes, healed of the curse, a snake is briefly glimpsed by a few watchers (pp. 692–3).

By becoming the supernatural snake which protects Kleomenes' dead body, Erif Der gives the Spartans' revolutionary ideas continued existence. At the same time, their resurrection enables her own return to love and life: a dual resolution which is beautifully manifested in the psychological healing of a lone Spartan survivor, the withdrawn little boy Gyridas. After the execution of his parents, this little boy spends all his time making 'plaits and knots' while whispering to himself (p. 689): an image which seems intuitively to anticipate D. W. Winnicott's interpretation of a child's obsessive string play as a denial of separation.[40] Touched by the 'great coloured snake', Gyridas comes out of the corner where he has been 'plaiting rushes . . . talking rapidly to himself under his breath, as he usually did now'; he re-enters human society, claiming a revolutionary identity: 'When the next New Times comes, I shall take heart, I shall break the laws too!' (p. 689). And the novel's coda (p. 717) shows that Gyridas does indeed grow up to be a lifelong revolutionary.

The king's redemptive death, which of course echoes the Marob fertility rituals, also anticipates the Passion of Christ: a point underscored by Berris Der's narrative pictures of incidents in Kleomenes' revolution corresponding closely (though, of course, none of the characters can know this in 235 BC) to key scenes in the life of Christ, including the Last Supper, the Kiss of Betrayal, and the Crucifixion. These pictures are destined to become the secret iconography of a Greek revolutionary movement, which never wins for long but is never exterminated even by the most violent repression (pp. 713–19). The brother's art and the sister's magic thus both keep alive the idea of human freedom.

All of this sounds – and is – more like myth than history. (Interestingly, the heroine's metamorphosis into a divine snake has several parallels in recent feminist literature, notably Hélène Cixous' 'The Laugh of the Medusa' and Gloria Anzaldúa's 'The Way of the Serpent'.[41]) It is not, however, all invention: Naomi Mitchison drew heavily on classical sources, especially Plutarch, for the story of Kleomenes, including the mysterious snake who protects the king's body. The novel also clearly indicates a parallel between Kleomenes' militarized Communism and the then-recent Russian revolution, not yet hardened into Stalinism. But, unlike Lenin, whose power survived the suppression of the 1919 European revolutions, Kleomenes is defeated, both by the strength of the counter-revolutionary forces arrayed against him and by his own bad judgement in agreeing to go slow on enfranchising the helots. His revolution thus loses its political momentum and alienates its potential peasant allies, who might otherwise have overthrown his enemies, the rulers of reactionary Greek states. Ptolemy's court circle in Alexandria, with its luxurious frivolity and diverse sexuality, also suggests a satiric allusion to the emancipated 'Bright Young Things' of post-war London, whose frivolity has been described by Martin Green in *Children of the Sun* (1975). The court may also have been partly modelled on the Prince of Wales' notoriously fast set. A more sinister analogy with Fascism is suggested by King Ptolemy's sadistic lust for sacrificing others to his own divinity, culminating in his Dionysiac 'new religion' of orgiastic blood sacrifice.

The political strength and weakness of *The Corn King and the Spring Queen* is the exact inverse of Marxist novels: its energy lies in a feminism whose insights Marxists tend to ignore, but its Socialism is much less convincing, mainly because it deals almost entirely with the lives and minds of royalty. Despite its wide ethnic and geographical range, and its focus on the egalitarian ideals of Communism and the social experiences of shared ritual, the novel has little to say about the lives of anybody except kings, queens and their friends. This apparent clash between Marxism and feminism is, however, superbly resolved in the last novel which I discuss: Sylvia Townsend Warner's *Summer Will Show*.

LISTENING TO MINNA: SYLVIA TOWNSEND WARNER AND HISTORICAL REALISM

> No, not a fairy-tale. I have told so many. This, this shall be a true story.
> Sylvia Townsend Warner[42]

A central passage of *Summer Will Show* is the long scene, charged with political and erotic energies, in which a relationship is set up between two women, strangers to each other: a speaker and a listener on the periphery of her audience, through whose consciousness the story is told. Sophia Willoughby, a wealthy bereaved mother and wronged wife in search of her erring husband, Frederick, finds his mistress Minna Lemuel, a profes-sional storyteller, holding the guests in her Paris salon spellbound by her tale of her childhood in Lithuania, climaxing with the pogrom in which her Jewish family and community were killed and scattered. Minna tells her story like a folk-tale full of archetypes: a distant forest, a child standing by a river in torrent, the same child lost in a dark icy wood. Her narrative, at once tragic and exhilarating, has a power, simplicity and immediacy that appear to burn through the barriers of class, race, gender, ideology and even language, creating a miraculous absence of the problems of miscomprehension and opacity that ought to occur when an English-woman listens to a Lithuanian Jewess telling the story of her life in French. The experience of listening to Minna inaugurates Sophia's complete transformation of her own life and identity; the hardheaded, apolitical materfamilias abandons her own class, is recruited as a messenger by the Communists, and fights alongside Minna on the revolutionary side of the barricades in June 1848.

The significance of this scene, as of the novel containing it, is partly a matter of intertextual transformations. Warner's plot corresponds closely to Virginia Woolf's speculative rewriting of a Shakespearean tragedy in *A Room of One's Own*: 'Cleopatra did not like Octavia. And how completely

Antony and Cleopatra would have been altered had she done so!'[43] Sophia, the virtuous wronged wife and mother in search of an irresponsible husband captivated by an exotic, ageing foreign mistress, 'half actress, half strumpet' (p. 31), is a cooler Octavia going to reclaim Mark Antony from a Cleopatra who welcomes her supposed rival into a realm of poverty, pleasure and revolutionary freedom. And Mark Antony – who, of course, doesn't take their desertion lying down – invents a different ending to the tragedy.

Moreover, this Cleopatra is also a revolutionary artist, whose performance witnessed by Sophia reworks the famous opening scene of Germaine de Stael's *Corinne*, much echoed by later women novelists, in which the Englishman Oswald falls in love with the Italian Corinne as she recites her own improvised poems to a fascinated audience. Here, however, it is the artist's fair English rival who plays the part of absorbed listener. The original heterosexual plot, in which the hero wavers between choosing dark, brilliant, forbidden Corinne and a virtuous British blonde, is transformed as the women find Oswald irrelevant to their desires. The artist's political allegiance is, however, made much more extreme and risky in *Summer Will Show* than in de Stael's novel. Whereas Corinne is an idealistic Italian patriot, Minna is a social revolutionary, a 'dangerous woman' (p. 178) whose art, unlike Corinne's, bumps into political realities. For her performance is rudely interrupted by the concierge's grotesquely polite announcement that the February Revolution has actually begun: 'Excuse me, ladies and gentlemen. But the people in the street are demanding the carriages for their barricade' (p. 135).

This interruption of Minna's narrative by the revolutionary energies she has invoked parodically recalls the great chapter in Charlotte Brontë's *Villette* where the Jewish actress Vashti, like Minna 'half actress, half strumpet', speaks with a fiery genius that rouses a literal blaze in the theatre to disrupt her performance and endanger the audience. Moreover, the power of Vashti's acting to sweep the audience off its feet is likened, among other images, to 'a deep, swollen winter river, thundering in cataract, and bearing the soul, like a leaf, on the steep and steely sweep of its descent'.[44] As we shall see, the image of a river in flood is central to Minna's story, while Warner's novel constantly represents the power of women's speech through metaphors of liquidity.

Considerable irony is implied, however, by these allusions to Romantic myths about the power of female art. When Minna finds her narrative cut off and her spell broken by the revolution which she had invoked, she takes on 'the look of a cat made a fool of – a massive sultry fury' (p. 136). The ironic fate of the revolutionary artist is more tragically thematized later, in the story of the composer David Guiterman who cannot get work and dies of consumption and hunger because 'revolutions have no need for symphonies' (p. 200). Moreover, Minna's revolutionary art has serious political drawbacks. She is an undisciplined, romantic anarchist, surrounded by ineffectual bohemian hangers-on. (It is Sophia, not she, who eventually joins the Communists, though she is adept at stealing iron for their weapons.) Her political shortcomings are later spelt out by the Communist theoretician Ingelbrecht (= Engels) in a long, italicized passage from his treatise on revolutions: improvidence, dissipation of political energies in wasted eloquence, lack of discipline and, worst of all, appeal to bourgeois sympathies (p. 270). Given Warner's avowed Communism at the time of writing, these are serious criticisms, especially since contemporary Marxists were extremely sceptical about Romantic artists who praised Liberty. The critic Christopher Caudwell criticized Romantic revolutionary poets like Shelley as bourgeois idealists, while in Rex Warner's surrealist Marxist fable, *The Wild Goose Chase* (1937), the deceptions of Romanticism are personified in the villainous President Koresipoulos, whose hypocritical odes to Freedom serve to send soldiers to their deaths and himself to glory. For these crimes, the poet is, very properly, strangled by a justly enraged peasant.[45]

The many intertextual echoes in Warner's novel, noted by Terry Castle and Sandy Petrey as well as myself,[46] also indicate that Minna's story should not be taken as straightforwardly 'true'. Even factual historical narratives are notoriously hard to authenticate; Warner wrote of researching the 1848 Paris Revolution for *Summer Will Show* that 'Legitimists, Orleanists, Republicans all told incompatible versions of the same events, and several times didn't even agree on dates'.[47] In any case, because Minna is a fictional character, the truth of her story cannot be literal, only representative. The vividness, detail and immediacy which seem to make her narrative 'transparent' are themselves the unobtrusive fruit of a storytelling art whose performative language constructs the reality to which it seems to refer.

None the less, Minna's story deals with a real place and time: a point of crucial importance, since, unless this 'touchstone' narrative has the stamp of historicity, she really does become the 'romantic charlatan' which Sophia once called her (p. 178) – and so, of course, does Warner. Its location can be identified by one bizarre detail: the child watching a thawing river full of 'shapes, men and horses, half frozen into the ice, half trailing in the water' (p. 125). As Minna explains afterwards, her family lived 'in Lithuania. Almost on the track of the retreat from Moscow' (p. 140). Their Jewish community, enlarged and minimally enriched by refugees 'driven out of their homes' (p. 126), presumably by Napoleon's armies, arouses the envy and malice of their Christian neighbours who kill the lot, except for Minna who is forcibly baptised and enslaved by the priest. The story gives an odd, jolting perspective on European history, evoking not the familiar narrative of Bonaparte's military victories and defeats, but the unwritten lives of the obscure victims of the Napoleonic wars, who may never even have known the emperor's name. Its resonances go further still, back into the history of European anti-Semitism, and forward into the 'present' of 1936, for when *Summer Will Show* was published, Jews were again, not long after another European war, being made scapegoats for social disruption. And they would soon be the victims of mass murder on an unimaginable scale.

Wendy Mulford, who has written extremely well about Sylvia Townsend Warner, interprets the revolutionary effect of Minna's story as a powerful manifestation of art's capacity for political agency: 'Art ignores, shoves aside social construction; it cannot transcend it, but can make a space where transformation can occur. That is the measure of its revolutionary significance'.[48] I find this extremely helpful, without quite agreeing with it. Mulford pinpoints admirably the political power of Minna's storytelling, a form which, as Walter Benjamin explained, is a communal art in which the storyteller's voice represents collective experience (in Minna's case, of oppression); and of 'good counsel',[49] which here means rebellion.

Yet both Minna's tale and Sophia's response to it *are*, in fact, socially constructed. The story, we learn later, is actually addressed to Sophia: 'Did you not know I was speaking to you?' Minna asks her (p. 140). And the 'space' of the performance, including an important silent interchange between speaker and listener, is partly defined by prejudice and parody. Early on in the story, Minna pauses for a moment and Sophia thinks how like a Jewish shopkeeper she is in her responses to the audience's attention (p. 127):

> In a moment you should rub your hands, the shopkeeper's gesture.
>
> At that moment the slowly flickering glance touched her, and rested. It showed no curiosity, only a kind of pondering attention. Then, as though in compliance, Minna's large supple hands gently caressed each other in the very gesture of her thought. Sophia started slightly. But answering Sophia's start of surprise there had been a smile – small, meek and satisfied, the smile of a dutiful child. And again there had been no time to look for Frederick.

Sophia's patronizing English irony and mild anti-Semitism are disconcerted by Minna's performance as a 'typical Jewess': one accomplished with an irony more knowing than her own. Though Minna is mocking a stereotype of Jewish, not feminine identity, her teasing parody interestingly anticipates Luce Irigaray's argument that women, dispossessed of the power of definition, inhabit discourse through mimicry, attempting 'to recover the place of her exploitation by discourse, without letting herself be reduced to it...if women mime so well, they do not simply reabsorb themselves in this function. *They also remain elsewhere'*.[50] At the same time the incident reminds the reader that Minna's narrative is not the transparent window on the past which it appears to be, but a superbly accomplished performance.

Yet, despite these many qualifications, *Summer Will Show* represents Minna's art as a profoundly liberating, inspiriting form of political agency. Her spoken words liberate the listening Sophia both emotionally and politically – and we see the book through Sophia's eyes; in a familiar post-Jamesian realist mode the heroine's consciousness bounds the text's horizon. This narrative focus on Sophia is, of course, necessary to Warner's didactic purposes, so that the story of her political education can be both vividly convincing and an educative process for the reader. For the transformation of political consciousness is, as Lukács insisted,[51] both the political role and the proper theme of historical realism.

In the long opening section of the book, Sophia's point of view is oppressively dominant; she lives, and consciously judges everything, by the accepted rules of her class, alertly enclosing all the other characters in a net of drily reactionary definition. Her life, 'policed by oughts' (p. 290), consists of duties, efficiently and joylessly performed, to her family and property. She entertains a fantasy of liberty and solitude, but knows it is impossible: 'It was boring to be a woman, nothing that one did had any meat in it' (p. 53). Her irony, whether applied to herself or to others, is at once amusing and imprisoning (p. 186):

> She looked forward through metaphors of furs laid by in camphor, silver wrapped in green baize, fruit trees released of their fruit and nailed against the wall, to the moment when all these people would go and she would begin to play piquet with aunt Leocadie.

The metaphors are themselves metonyms of Sophia's own life of conscientious housewifely stewardship; more than that, these passive objects are like herself *someone else's property*. The effect of this self-reflexive language is, contrary to some theorists of *écriture féminine*, anything but liberating.[52] No freedom seems possible here, except a play of intelligence that limits itself to inventing witty metaphors while assenting to social construction as if it were Fate.

But as Sophia listens to Minna, her judging, stereotyping habits of mind dissolve. She becomes aware that the other woman's identity is not single nor simple (p. 138):

> Are you the child who ran across the bloodied snow to kill the Christians? Are you the prophetess, the brooding priestess of Liberty, who spoke with such passion of the enfranchised river? Are you the woman so bitterly hated, my rival and overthrower?

This change in Sophia is even more apparent after Minna's narrative is broken off. While the citizens of Paris construct their barricades, the guests in Minna's salon chat desultorily; a young fool blathers about the glorious revolution, and Sophia's husband Frederick (whom she has come to Minna's salon to find), observes humorously that the revolutionaries could do with more vehicles for their barricades: 'Think what an improvement an omnibus or two would be, down there' (p. 142). Sophia immediately grasps that this jibe, framed in what has been until now her own style of amused, superior detachment, is actually aimed at Minna: Frederick is 'using her wifely petticoats as a shield whence to attack his mistress' (p. 143). She refuses his knowing irony, names its malice – 'Jew-baiting. The word rushed into Sophia's mind' – and rejects it; she has become a resisting listener. (Frederick's own obtuseness has already been signalled at the climax of Minna's narrative by his crass exclamation, 'Wolves!', at the moment when the *Christians* are about to start the pogrom [p. 130]: a deaf rather than resisting listener, he.)

Minna's effect on Sophia appears next in a charmed sleep, which means that she wakes the next morning in her own apartment, and then in her discovery of a need and power to speak. While the Revolution continues outside, she spends the entire day telling Minna the story of her life. It is a compulsive outpouring: 'she supposed she must talk herself to death as others bleed to death' (p. 156). Frederick calls – his wife and ex-mistress barely notice him. 'Instantly forgetting him save as a character in her own narrative, Sophia went on talking. Minna's grasp tightened on her hand' (p. 158). She is thus liberated by Minna into the field of language and desire: the sudden freedom of a flood of words.

The transformation of Sophia's consciousness is articulated by a sequence of images of liquidity. Since such imagery has been defined by the feminist philosopher Irigaray as a classic symbol of female identity and desire,[53] it is not surprising to discover that almost all of them are associated with Minna, with political liberty, and with erotic passion. The most powerful and obvious of these images is Minna's account of her childhood vision of a spring flood (p. 123):

> As the river flowed, its strong swirling tongue licked furiously at the icy margins and undermined them, and with a shudder and a roar of defeat another fragment would break away. It was like a battle. It was like victory.... I had never heard the word Liberty. But it was Liberty I acclaimed, seeing the river sweeping away its fetters, tossing its neck under its ruined yoke.

The image of the river haunts Sophia even though she rejects it as pretentious. Looking at the grey Seine later, she thinks that 'only a romantic charlatan, speaking for effect, could pretend, as Minna had done, that the sight of a river could bolster up ideas of liberty' (p. 178). Sophia's thoughts here imply an opposed, reactionary symbolism of force, irresistible necessity which sweeps away human hopes, as in Isaac Watts' hymn – 'Time, like an ever-rolling stream/ Bears all its sons away'.[54] Yet, paradoxically, this 'common-sense' interpretation produces a violent daydream of assault on Minna's body, for Sophia imagines holding the other woman under the Seine 'until, soused and breathless, she had revised her notions about rivers' (p. 178).

Sophia's unconsciously erotic fantasy of literally choking the other woman with her own fluid metaphor is not, of course, the last word. The image of flowing water surfaces again, at the point where the two women turn to each other. Sophia offers Minna money to pay off the Willoughbys' obligations to her; Minna promptly bestows it on the nearest good cause, the Polish Patriots, her voice smoothly quivering in the sun:

> 'And there it goes. *Vive la liberté*!'
> '*Vive la liberté*!' answered Sophia.
> For she was freed, God knows how, and could praise liberty with a free mind... It was as though [she] had seen a fountain spring up, a moment before unsuspected, and now to play for ever, glittering and incorruptible.

The fountain turns, a few lines later, to champagne as 'their words, light and taunting, rose up like bubbles delicately exploding from a wine which they were to drink together' (p. 214). The simile brings together female desire, freedom and sensuality, by invoking not only the freedom and energy symbolized in the fountain's play, but the spiced wine Minna gave her when they first met. The shared pleasure of the wine drunk together thus delicately symbolizes sexual pleasure, like the later 'triumphant cry' and the oyster (p. 274) which Terry Castle has convincingly interpreted to mean orgasm.[55] It also signifies the maternal, nurturing side of their relationship. Their story begins with Minna offering Sophia sustenance – 'You look so tired' (p. 139). Now, in this moment of release, both are 'carelessly joyful' (p. 214).

Less metaphorically, Sophia's political transformation is shown through her response to narratives. Minna's *récit* is the most important, of course, but the book contains two other tragic stories of social injustice, both as 'true' as Minna's, whose significance lies partly in the way Sophia interprets them. The first is the appalling anecdote about Samuel Turvey, a nine-year-old sweep burned to death when his master lit a fire under him to force him up a chimney, which she tells her own children in order to terrorize them into good behaviour (and, less consciously, to vent her own rage and frustration). Her daughter is horrified (p. 47):

> 'What a horrible wicked man!'
>
> 'He had his living to make. And chimneys have to be swept. And some are made so that a brush cannot go up them, so that a boy must go instead. Only it happens that I am rich, and so such things do not happen to you or your brother. . . . On just such a morning as this, some unfortunate child has been driven up a dark chimney. And you – you can find nothing better to do than quarrel like wild beasts!'

Cold and cruel, Sophia uses the boy's death to enforce class values: acceptance of necessary hardships (for others) and appropriately decorous behaviour (for her family). By contrast, towards the end of the novel, Minna relates a more melodramatic, but almost equally harrowing story: the death from tuberculosis and starvation of David Guiterman, a victim of the revolutionary situation and of the ruling class's strategy of starving the rebels out. He has died alone, and the music he wrote down in desperate haste before he died is illegibly bloodstained by his last haemorrhage. Minna describes his hard-up landlady's fury and despera-tion at the damage to her only asset (p. 360):

> ' "And his blood is all over the floorboards, I must buy soap to scour it off and I cannot afford food for my children even." . . . And so I gave her what money I had and came away. I am sorry, Sophia, I ought to have kept it for our own rent, I suppose. I gave her nine francs fifty.'
>
> 'I begin to think we must all be all damned,' said Sophia. 'The way we can endure to hear of these things'.

The point here, however, is not personal salvation or responsibility. Sophia blames herself for the way she wasted her charity, when she did have money, on Bible societies and the like, instead of trying to relieve this kind of suffering and degradation. But Minna, as before, disputes and shifts the terms of her thought, repudiating charity, 'that libertine word!' as sentimental: 'While we cannot give justice, Sophia, it is idle to debate whether we have given charity' (p. 361).

Sophia's responses to these narratives indicates the distance she has travelled, from cold indifference to passionate sympathy. But the story of a political education can never leave the hero(ine) as simply a good student. Sophia, already recruited by Communists to smuggle iron and lead for their underground ammunition factory, is well aware that 'to sit still and listen – that was a child's part' (p. 353). She is only listening to Minna telling the story of David Guiterman because the two women are posing for the artist Dury: 'Sophia must listen, hers was a countenance most characteristic in attention. Minna, to give her something to listen to, must talk' (p. 352). Dury, the only revolutionary artist not baulked by poverty, is a master of realist art: 'I can paint a cheap brocade and make it look like a cheap brocade. It's those blistered highlights' (p. 358). But his pictures imprison Sophia and Minna, whom he calls *Mes Odalisques*, into his own definition of their 'characteristic' expressions and actions.

By the end of the novel, Sophia is no longer a listener. The revolution has been bloodily suppressed; Minna is either dead or, worse still, dying, and out of reach either way; Aunt Leocadie has offered Sophia an amnestied return to her husband and position, and been rejected. Sophia sits down to read one of the pamphlets she distributed for Ingelbrecht. Its opening words are familiar, though not to her: '*A spectre is haunting Europe...*' She is last seen deep in the *Communist Manifesto*, 'obdurately attentive and by degrees absorbed' (p. 406). Storytelling has given way to definition and analysis: Sophia, alert, intelligent and passionate, has turned from a listener to an active reader whose life will, one guesses, be dedicated to making the words of *Communist Manifesto* survive the present defeat.

The fact that *Summer Will Show*, written by a member of the Communist Party, culminates by citing the opening fourteen lines of Marxism's Book of Genesis, does not, however, mean that the novel has suddenly turned orthodox and literal-minded. The italicized *Manifesto* is, as Sandy Petrey has shown, skilfully woven into Warner's fiction, which presents it as a quotation from Ingelbrecht's treatise on revolutions, an extract from which has been 'quoted' earlier, also in italics.[56] The point is the words and the revolutionary hopes they carry, not who wrote them – and readers in 1936 would certainly think of the 1917 Russian Revolution and the Bolshevik state in Russia as certain proof of their abiding power. That certainty may have vanished with the collapse of European and Russian Communism since 1989, but Marx's words are not dead yet.

For some readers, however, *Summer Will Show* has less to do with history than with female desire. Terry Castle has argued influentially that Warner's novel is a deliberately fantastic narrative of lesbian escape from the traditional female destiny of marriage and family. Combatively deploying Eve Kosofsky Sedgwick's notion of the 'triangulation' of homosocial desire, in which the relation between two men is defined through a mediating woman, she shows how Warner first creates and then collapses the alternative wife–husband–mistress triangle into a lesbian dyad, thereby subverting the institution of patriarchal marriage. This, Castle argues, is the archetypally utopian and subversive plot of the lesbian novel, whose nature is always to be improbable and fantastic. Despite its 'framing pretense of historicity', the book is consciously theatrical and unreal; its 'built-in intimations of artifice and romance, of delight and high fakery... work against the superficial historicism of the narrative, pushing it inexorably towards the fantastic'.[57]

Although she oversimplifies Warner's writing in the interests of her own argument, Terry Castle writes with grace and energy, her reading of the book is, in its own terms, very persuasive, especially on Warner's 'retriangulation of desire' (p. 90). Her 'inexorably', however, overstates its case, for the relationship between fantasy and history in *Summer Will Show* is much more sophisticated – and more Marxist – than Terry Castle's one-sided account allows. To read *Summer Will Show* as *only* a lesbian utopian fiction amounts to a postmodernist denial both of its engagement with history and its embarrassing Marxist politics, which her argument dismisses as mere analogies for the lesbian plot, thus taking the history out of this historical novel. Yet Sylvia Townsend Warner's political and erotic plots are, as I have shown, closely interwoven. It is not only that the time of the two women's happiness begins with the February Revolution which interrupts Minna's story, and ends with its bloody defeat in June. 'Though you may think you have chosen me, Sophia, or chosen happiness,' says Minna, 'it is the Revolution you have chosen' (p. 277).

Chapter 6

Collective and individual memory
Black Lamb and Grey Falcon

A 'TYPICAL ENGLISHWOMAN' AND HER HYBRID BOOK

> Nothing in my life had affected me more deeply than this journey through Yugoslavia. . . . This experience made me say to myself: 'If a Roman woman had, some years before the sack of Rome, realized why it was going to be sacked and what motives inspired the barbarians and what the Romans, and had written down all she knew and felt about it, the result would have been interesting' to historians. My situation, though probably not so fatal, is as interesting. Without doubt it was my duty to keep a record of it.
>
> So I resolved to put on paper what a typical Englishwoman felt and thought in the late nineteen-thirties when, already convinced of the inevitability of the second Anglo-German war, she had been able to follow the dark waters of that event back to its source.[1]

Rebecca West's *magnum opus* articulating 'what a typical Englishwoman thought and felt' is notoriously hard to classify. It does, certainly, record a visit to Yugoslavia in the spring of 1937, the last possible moment for an Easter holiday in that country before the War. In March 1938 Hitler's armies invaded and annexed Austria, so that a politically aware person would hardly have gone to neighbouring Yugoslavia for a holiday; and even in 1937, as the book shows, the Yugoslav federation was menaced from within by the rancorous divisions between Croats and Serbs, and from without by pressure from Fascist Italy and Germany. Yet Rebecca West is clearly an exceptional rather than 'typical' Englishwoman. She is, naturally, reticent about her own personal history, and she plays down her own distinction as a writer, never mentioning her own reputation except to characterize one or two people by their responses to it (such as the Montenegrin official who disapproves of her being decorated for lecturing in Yugoslavia when her husband is not so honoured [2, p. 433] or the misguided Viennese woman whose wish to write a thesis on West's books –

'I was naturally appalled' – is represented as a symptom of the decadence of Austrian culture [2, p. 477]). Yet her exceptional brilliance, her knowledge of European culture, including political, theological and art history as well as most of its literature from St Augustine to Proust, her wit and humanity are obvious. Her husband, who apparently shares her easy command of history and European literature, also speaks German like a native (2, p. 387) and likes to read Homer's *Iliad* in Greek (2, p. 433).

Both Rebecca West and her husband Henry Andrews are, indeed, not so much as typical products of English culture as its ideal representatives. Both are highly cultivated people, emotionally as well as intellectually, for they are notably aware of everyone's expressions and gestures and inclined to discuss these together with subtlety and insight. They also have an unshakeable self-confidence, which enables them to acknowledge cultural difference without being put on the defensive by encountering customs and values different from and perhaps superior to their own. The book constantly acknowledges the superiority of Slav values compared to English ones: in Croatia, where Rebecca West wholeheartedly admires the Slav 'relish for life', finding the sanatorium at Shestine, with its good food and tolerance of patients' self-dramatization, far superior to the dreary infantilizing routine of an English hospital (1, pp. 75–82); in Sarajevo where the Jewish intellectuals possess graces of mind and body that are simply unknown in England; and above all in Macedonia, where peasant harshness still flowers into Byzantine rituals and embroideries whose power and beauty are unequalled by contemporary European artists. She frequently criticizes the complacency and arrogance of her fellow-countrymen, contrasting the hospitable Yugoslavs with 'the grey ice that forms on an Englishman's face on being introduced to a stranger', and parodying a typical Englishwoman's ungracious response to the charming gesture of a Bosnian hostess: 'My dear, it was too ghastly, she seized me by the hands and simply drenched them with some most frightful scent, I couldn't get rid of it for days' (1, p. 411). The unattractive, effete young Englishmen also compare unfavourably with their counter-parts in Korchula 'with broad shoulders and long legs and straight hair, and an air of unashamed satisfaction with their own good looks which one finds only where there is very little homosexuality' (1, p. 207. As this quote indicates, Rebecca West is unremittingly hostile and dismissive about male homosexuals in *Black Lamb and Grey Falcon*.[2]) Her criticism of England is political as well as cultural; after praising an English-owned mine, she sharply attacks England's governing class, which she finds 'astonishing in its corruption, in its desire for death, and in its complacency towards its disease' (2, p. 339). The book's long Epilogue similarly denounces the death-grip of 'the obsolete party' (i.e. the Conservatives) during the years of appeasement, and the suicidal passivity of 'conservative, mediocre England' (2, pp. 512, 519).

Yet these sharp criticisms of Rebecca West's own country and its national culture coexist with a loyalty and a pride which are made explicit at the end of the book, where the prospect of Fascist annihilation rouses her to nationalist pride and resistance: 'My civilization must not die. It need not die'. Despite the many faults of the English, their lack of self-knowledge, their economic selfishness and their injustice towards their colonized subjects, 'they are on the side of life, they love justice, they hate violence, and they respect the truth' (2, p. 453). Although her intellectual distinction, her relish for Balkan cookery, her fierce criticism of English inhibition, her dislike of empires and, above all, her uninhibited feminism all combine to make her about as plausible a 'typical Englishwoman' as Virginia Woolf, she is in the last analysis an English patriot. She thus writes both as a woman of her own time and place, and as a kind of everyman or everywoman. This is a point to which I shall return.

Rebecca West first visited Yugoslavia alone in 1936, took her husband for a two month visit there in 1937, and in 1938 went back to research the book, revisiting some of the places mentioned in the narrative, which thus condenses the experiences of three visits into a single account.[3] The book was thus written in the darkest days of the late 1930s and early 1940s, during Hitler's invasion of Austria in 1938, the Munich sellout, the 'phoney war', and the Battle of Britain and the London Blitz. Although it far exceeds those 1940 essays by Virginia Woolf and George Orwell which I discussed in Chapter 1 (see pp. 12–17), it belongs to the same literature of retrospection, looking back at the years of threatened and dubious peace from the context of a war which Hitler at that point looked likely to win.

Rebecca West differs from the others, however, not only in the huge scale of what she attempted and achieved in her retrospective analysis, but in choosing not to focus directly on England. Instead, she surveys Yugoslavia's brief moment of equilibrium within the contexts of

- its own short history as a separate nation;
- the histories of its federated countries from their beginnings as Slav nationalist movements contesting first the Ottoman and then the Austro-Hungarian Empires; and
- the long and bloody history of Eastern Europe since the later Roman Empire.

Into and through these collective histories, she weaves the 'micro-narrative' of her own journey, often moving her focus into the past to explain the present. Both generically, as an autobiography-cum-history, and in terms of its composition, the book is therefore a hybrid text. Published in 1942 (1941 in the USA), *Black Lamb and Grey Falcon* is based on the very detailed travel diary which Rebecca West kept during her 1937 visit – from which, as I show at the end of this chapter, it also differs considerably.

Samuel Hynes says of *Black Lamb*, 'it stands at the end of the 1930s like a massive baroque cenotaph',[4] a metaphor which usefully emphasizes the book's memorial intention, as well as its monumentally large size (it consists of two volumes, respectively 653 and 586 pages in length, or 1158 closely printed pages in the 1982 one-volume reprint). By the time it was published, Yugoslavia had been invaded and was experiencing a bloody occupation by the Nazis, assisted by Catholic Croats led by Pavelic. From the title page recording the dedication 'To my friends in Yugoslavia, who are now all dead or enslaved' (1, p. v) to the last reminder at the end of the 'Bibliographical note' that 'all the people I mention in this book are now either dead or living in a state of misery as yet impossible for us in the West to imagine' (2, pp. 556–67), we are rarely allowed to forget that the vigour, cultural richness and ethnic pluralism which she finds in Yugoslavia are shadowed by the disastrous present in which its grace and promise have been destroyed.

This context of tragic hindsight is only too easy to appreciate in the 1990s. Rebecca West's book is now a memorial in a sense she cannot possibly have intended – not, as when she wrote it, to a defeated, occupied nation which might yet revive, but to a dismembered country which no longer exists. Worse still, the blank-faced xenophobia which she feared and detested in the Nazis has now become 'Yugoslav' ideology. It is now impossible to read her warm accounts of the enchanting beauty of Sarajevo in its setting of hills without a bitter taste in the mouth. Worse, the knowledge that the grandchildren of the heroic Serbs whom she so admires have again and again carried out 'ethnic cleansing' on the bodies of Croat and Muslim Bosnians, gives a particularly nasty twist, two generations later, to her exchange with the pro-Nazi, anti-Yugoslav 'Gerda', who protests (2, p. 31):

'You go on saying what a beautiful country this is, and you must know perfectly well that there is no order here, no culture, but only a mish-mash of different peoples who are all quite primitive and low. Why do you do that?' I said wearily, 'But it's precisely because there are so many different peoples that Yugoslavia is so interesting. So many of these peoples have remarkable qualities, and it is fascinating to see whether they can be organized into an orderly state.' 'How can you make an orderly state out of so many peoples?' she asked. 'They should all be driven out.'

Because of its lengthy and complex combination of different narratives, *Black Lamb and Grey Falcon* is an easy book to get lost in. True, there are certain recurring themes: the evils of empires, Yugoslavia as frontier territory, the story of Slav nationalist resistance to Turkish and Austrian imperialism in the past (and, by implication, to Nazi imperialism in the present), and the necessity of art. But although Peter Wolfe claims that these unify the book into an 'epic',[5] in practice it remains irretrievably hybrid, mixing political history, travel, autobiography, meditation, art history, and even fiction; for the portraits of the most important Yugoslav characters, 'Constantine' and 'Gerda', whatever their basis in real meetings, belong, as I argue below (pp. 204–9) more to fiction than to memoir. It also needs to be read alongside contemporary English accounts of Europe, fictional and otherwise. Three 'period' genres are relevant here: contemporary travel writing of the inter-war period, contemporary 'eyewitness' accounts of thirties history, and contemporary 1930s fictions dramatizing the threat of Fascism.

Travel writing is the most obviously relevant of these genres. *Black Lamb, Grey Falcon: A Journey Through Yugoslavia* clearly corresponds to Paul Fussell's useful definition of this genre as 'a sub-species of memoir in which the autobiographical narrative arises from the speaker's encounter with distant or unfamiliar data, and in which the narrative – unlike that in novel or romance – claims literal validity by constant reference to actuality'.[6] Fussell suggests that travel writing is *the* inter-war genre, citing Samuel Hynes on the journey as parable: 'Travel books simply act out, in a literal way, the basic trope of that [Auden] generation' (p. 215).[7] Travel writing is also an entertainment genre, written by the socially and economically privileged for stay-at-home readers who have never seen the country described, or else are reading the book for nostalgic reasons. The travel writer must by definition be both unusually free and rich enough to get to a foreign country and live there, though not necessarily at a high standard; he or she must also be able to move about in order to sightsee and explore, which usually means having the use of a motor car. In the 1930s, even more than now, all that meant social privilege, shared vicariously by the readers, for one of the major attractions of travel writing, then and now, is the way it seems to enable one to share the writer's experience. Hence the characteristically immediate, authentic, 'literal' style of travel writing, often the result of considerable skill and labour; the classic example of this concealed artistry being Robert Byron's *The Road to Oxiana* (1937), a travel diary whose apparently informal immediacy demanded months of retrospective hard work.[8] Almost all the travel writers of the 1930s were, predictably enough, born in Woolf's 'Leaning Tower' of educational, class and gender privilege, the great majority being Oxford men. (D. H. Lawrence is the only travel writer discussed in Paul Fussell's book *Abroad* who was working class even by origin; he doesn't mention James Hanley, whose novels *Boy* [banned in 1935], *The Secret Journey* [1936], *Hollow Sea* [1937] and others all came out of his own experience as a merchant sailor. The very few women whose names he mentions – Rose Macaulay, Nancy Cunard, Freya Stark, Rebecca West, Edith Sitwell – all belong to the privileged end of the upper middle class.)

Black Lamb and Grey Falcon, though inexplicably neglected by Paul Fussell, obviously belongs to the tradition of inter-war travel writing which he analyses, in that its narrative shares the usual position of social privilege, produces the characteristic travel-writer's illusion of total recall, and has many entertaining moments. Furthermore, both the book's large scale and its multitudinous vivid details actually make the experience of reading it curiously akin to travelling through an unfamiliar country, where the confusing wealth of particular landscapes, townscapes, meals, arguments, and encounters with friends or strangers all make it hard to grasp the whole map of the place. But in its intellectual range, as well as its constant awareness of history, including its own dark present, the book also exceeds the limits of the genre: its energies belong to the literature of witness and of history more than to the pleasures of escape.

As an eyewitness account of a country near the brink of disaster, *Black Lamb* also resembles other books of the late thirties which combine reportage and history, such as Claud Cockburn's *Reporter in Spain* (1936), Esmond Romilly's *Boadilla* (1936), Arthur Koestler's *Spanish Testament* (1937), Orwell's *Homage to Catalonia* (1938), and – especially – G. E. R. Gedye's *Fallen Bastions* (1939). Although Gedye's scope and range are nowhere near as ambitious as Rebecca West's, his lively eyewitness history of Vienna from 1922 to the Anschluss in 1938 resembles *Black Lamb* in situating a present moment of crisis in a European country within the much longer historical context of its national history, representing the latter as a series of vividly personalized scenes-plus-commentaries. Both writers represent Fascism as a deadly, corrosive enemy, far more dangerous than Communism, Rebecca West's 1942 liberalism being well to the left of her subsequent political opinions. An American journalist described the book to me as 'naive about Communism', by which she presumably meant that it represents Fascism, not Communism as the enemy of liberal civilization. Certainly, it dismisses Communism as a serious political factor in Yugoslavia, arguing that its citizens 'would never joyously become subordinate atoms in a vast Marxist system. When they say they are Communists they mean they are for the country against the town, for the village against Belgrade, for the peasant against the industrialist' (1, p. 499). Similarly, the book deplores the reactionary Catholic tendency to blame everything on 'Communists, Jews and Freemasons' as not only wicked but silly (1, p. 623). What is striking here is not the fact that the woman who after 1945 was to become obsessed with Communist infiltration should once have taken the subject so calmly, for this is after all a familiar pattern in mid-century liberal thought. It is more remarkable that Rebecca West did not change these remarks in the later editions of *Black Lamb and Grey Falcon* [1955 and 1977], presumably because she still thought them true of pre-war Yugoslavia.[9])

The tone and purpose of *Black Lamb and Grey Falcon* are, however, quite different from that of Gedye and his journalist colleagues. *Fallen Bastions* was published by the Left Book Club as part of a Popular Front campaign to stimulate informed dissent against the Foreign Office's policy of appeasement, and thus to increase public pressure on the British government to change direction. Gedye is deliberately polemical, addressing his English readers directly (pp. 306, 313):

> At the very moment that you may read these words in such comfort as they may leave you – a little less than you are accustomed to feel, I hope – these peasant or shopkeeping families were rescued, refused any-where an asylum, and are to this day huddled together on an ancient vessel in mid-stream – as are others in filthy, desolate Alpine huts in a triangle of No-Man's-Land...
>
> Plunder, murder, insult, torture, concentration camps, ruined existences, head-hunting, refusal of asylum by the Czechs and brutal handing-over of refugees to the Nazis – 'individually responsible' are those four powers, excluding Czechoslovakia but including Britain.
>
> Does that disturb your sleep?

Gedye's angry eloquence belongs unmistakably to those vigorous post-1937 anti-Fascism writings deplored by George Orwell as a 'torrent of hate-literature'.[10] Similarly, Esmond Romilly wrote about the battle of Boadilla to support the Republican cause, while Claud Cockburn's account of his experiences in the International Brigade was demanded from him by Harry Pollitt for the Popular Front campaign against 'non-intervention'.[11] Though Koestler's *Spanish Testament* was also published by the Left Book Club, it was not backed in the same way by the Communist

Party; still less was Orwell's dissenting account of the suppression of the POUM,[12] which he had some difficulty in getting published. Nevertheless, these 'eyewitness' histories are as much works of polemical journalism as those written for the Popular Front. All these books were produced to make known a truth which the writer felt was being suppressed, to influence public opinion about the political events they describe, and thus to affect the outcome of those events.

Black Lamb and Grey Falcon, which does something related to but different from these books, is not political in the same way. Whereas Gedye writes angrily about Britain's betrayal of the Eastern European democracies, Rebecca West, who very likely shared these opinions, says nothing about England's foreign policies, not even mentioning the Prime Minister's name until the Epilogue. Although the 'moment' of her book is 1937, she never alludes to the Spanish Civil War, then raging at the other end of Europe. (This must be a deliberate omission, for her 1937 travel diary remarks, clearly apropos of 'non-intervention' in Spain, 'we feel Serbs would not respect England over the Spanish business'.[13]) Hers is certainly an eyewitness book, written deliberately as a form of warning – but the writer does not herself witness oppression or slaughter. News of political violence menaces her constantly: her journey through Yugoslavia begins 'on October the ninth, 1934' (1, p. 1) when she heard on the radio that King Alexander had just been murdered, and ends with her friend 'Constantine' telling her about a massacre of suspected anti-Fascists in Albania (2, p. 463); and the thousand-odd pages in between constantly return to the murderous violence that bedevils European history. But, unlike Gedye reporting the machine-gunning of workers' flats in Vienna or Orwell describing street-fighting in Barcelona, Rebecca West comes no closer to witnessing any of these horrors than once being on the fringes of an anti-Serb riot in Zagreb (2, pp. 468–71). Otherwise, she hears about them from 'Constantine' or from the radio, reads about them or watches them on a newsreel. The political purpose of her book is plainly not to galvanize her fellow-countrymen's opinion, but to stiffen their resolve. She represents the fate of Serbia at Kossovo as a cautionary tale whose moral is that England must not go the same way: 'My civilization must not die. It need not die' (2, p. 453). In this sense, *Black Lamb and Grey Falcon* is as much a wartime book as a book of the 1930s.

COLLECTIVE MEMORY AND THE GRAND NARRATIVES

> I had come to Yugoslavia because I knew that the past has made the present, and I wanted to see how the process works.
>
> Vol. 1, p. 54

Commemoration, the central theme of *Black Lamb and Grey Falcon*, everywhere pervades its account of Yugoslavia. Its narrative principle is a deliberate intertwining of individual and collective memory, the actual journey undertaken by West and her husband in 1937 being threaded in and out of a series of historical narratives of Eastern Europe from the time of the Roman Empire onwards, organized around West's own meditations on the Christian grand narrative of sin and redemption. All of these historical narratives have their own shape – usually biographical, as she is primarily interested in personality – but the direction of the writing constantly changes, looping backwards into recent, medieval or ancient history, sometimes briefly and sometimes – as with the bravura account of the Sarajevo *attentat* or the long history of Serbia – over fifty or a hundred pages. There are also small 'sideways loops' describing embroidery patterns, or frescos, or the expressions of women selling their vegetables at market and/or chatting to each other.

This multiple narrative approach is unique in twentieth-century travel writing. Paul Fussell says that:

> like no other forms of writing, travel books exploit the fundamental emotional and intellectual figure of thought, by which the past is conceived as back and the future as forward. . . . Travel books are special because the metaphor they imply is so essential [to thought].

West's book effectively deconstructs that simple linear figure of thought – formally, by its constant looping movements in which the reader is liable to get entangled, and thematically by its constant awareness of the historical forces which shape the present. This complexity probably explains why, though Fussell does twice quote from *Black Lamb*, he never discusses it as a travel book.[14] In the Balkans, it is never possible to walk away from the past.

Appropriately enough, the course of West's literal journey in Yugoslavia fails to follow the travel book's usual route from the relatively familiar frontier to the more primitive, or different, or ancient heartlands. Yugoslavia is defined as 'different' from the start, in ways which horrify Rebecca West's conventionally minded German fellow-passengers; and the early chapters on Dalmatia, which frequently look back to the medieval Venetian Republic and beyond that to the breakup of the Roman Empire, have the most remote temporal scope. The route taken by herself and her husband is itself a confusing series of zigzags: they go by train to Zagreb, then westwards to the Dalmatian coast, first motoring northwest up the coast to Split and then sailing south by way of several islands, including Korchula, towards Dubrovnik; then inland and south-east to Bosnia and Sarajevo; then northeast by rail, right across the country, to Belgrade in Serbia; then far south, also by rail, to Skoplje, and then by road through Macedonia to the Albanian border; then northwest through Kossovo, afterwards bearing westwards through Montenegro and so back at last to the Dalmatian coast, the whole trip taking two to three months. There is no point at which one can say, 'Here they encounter, at last, the heart of Yugoslavia', for, of course, given a nation so multifarious and patchworked as Yugoslavia once was, no single place could claim to be the heart. The Serbs would have said that Kossovo – ('Old Serbia', as she calls it) was their heartland – and certainly this is where she finds the tragic symbolism that defines the meaning of her journey. But, as she recognizes, Kossovo is meaningless for Croats, gypsies, Albanians and Bosnian Muslims.

All this complexity does not make the book shapeless – the phrase 'loose baggy monster' does suggest itself, but only because of the book's inordinate length. A summary of the whole book such as I gave for its Prologue (see Chapter 2, pp. 76–7) would show a constant to-and-fro movement from the individual narrative of the writer and her husband to the collective history of Europe. Though, since she writes the stories of countries mainly in terms of the personalities, choices and policies made by their leaders, those collective histories are themselves partly indivi-dualized. There is also movement sideways, on to the particular detail and its ramifying implications, which may be historical, or aesthetic, or may say something about the relations between the sexes.

For *Black Lamb and Grey Falcon* is, among other things, a strongly feminist text. Rebecca West's feminism is everywhere apparent, in her interest in the unwritten lives of the female relatives of great men (1, p. 429); in her response to the sight of a war memorial: 'I became filled with feminist rage' (1, p. 502); in her observation, apropos of the mental patients at Sveti Naum, that their stay in this monastery is for many 'their first break in a life of continuous overwork, and for quite a number of women it is an escape from male tyranny' (2, p. 117); and in her witty comment on the political influence of the Fascist writer d'Annunzio (1, p. 124):

I will believe that the battle of feminism is over, and that the female has reached a position of equality with the male, when I hear that a country has allowed itself to be turned upside-down and led to the brink of war by its passion for a totally bald woman writer.

Although her travelling companions are all males except for the detestable Gerda, and her historical narratives deal almost entirely with men, her book abounds in portraits and sketches of women: the beautiful Russian playwright in Zagreb, whose vitality and literary cultivation she admires (1, p. 61); the belly dancer in Sarajevo whose 'decency and good sense' (1, p. 314) she appreciates; the woman dentist who turns out be the sister of Chabrilovitch, one of the Archduke Ferdinand's Sarajevo assassins, and who tells her how she and her family survived hardship and imprisonment (1, pp. 429–436); Militsa in Skopje, of whom it is said that 'if there are twenty people like this woman scattered between here and China, civilization will not perish' (2, p. 184); and the many unnamed peasant women whom she sees and admires, sometimes for the artistry of their embroidery, sometimes for their courage and faith.

More than this, Rebecca West makes the well-being (or not) of women the main touchstone of how successful or fortunate a culture is. Thus, the enchantingly graceful society of Sarajevo is represented by the lovely Jewish girl whom 'we called "the Bulbul", which is the Persian word for nightingale because of her enchanting voice... [whose] charm built for grave and innocent purposes on a technique of ingenuity which had been developed in the harem' (1, p. 328). Similarly, the health and resilience of a peasant society are represented by Bosnian peasant women, selling vegetables, who are strong and 'free in the spirit' (1, p. 333) though they pretend subservience in order to please their husbands (p. 336). More ominously, the innocent pride which an old lady of Korchula takes in her own fertility implies a political naïveté which in the circumstances is tragic. In a time of war, 'her womb, which was her talisman, would have been a source of danger, which might . . . one day make her husband feel that the delight he had known with her was not worth the price he must pay for it' (1, p. 217). She has been lucky enough never to know how terribly vulnerable a childbearing woman can be to rape and starvation, and she and her family are all too likely to find out. Conversely, the miseries of Kossovo's rural backwardness are summed up by the sight of a brutalized Albanian wife 'carrying on her back the better part of a plough . . . while [her husband] went free' (2, pp. 276–277); and in Macedonia and Montenegro, the price of the male heroism that freed the Slav nations has been the total suppression of women's energies: 'Nowhere have I seen such settled and hopeless despair, such resentment doubled by the knowledge that it might not express itself, as on the faces of the women of Skopska Tserna Gora' (2, p. 50). Her book thus deliberately writes back into history the lives and experiences of women, whom she avoids reducing to signifiers because she never forgets their actual, if unknowable, lives and experiences.

Nevertheless, as Rebecca West acknowledges, women do not dominate history. Within her massive text, two main kinds of historical narrative can easily be distinguished: on the one hand the 'collective narrative' of European history, told from the perspective of an explicit liberalism to which the writer's allegiance is made plain from the start,[15] and on the other, the personal narrative of West and her husband on their journey, also seen from the perspective of English left-liberalism. This intertwining of individual and collective memories can best be understood in terms of Maurice Halbwachs' theory of 'collective memory' (summarized on Chapter 1 pp. 8–10). This defines memory as a social phenomenon, because individual remembrance is only made possible by group memory, which itself bears the stamp of the historical moment at which the past is recalled. The argument that all memories should be understood as collective might seem to dissolve the obvious difference between West's memoir of her own journey and her narratives of the collective history of the Balkans; but that would be a crude misinterpretation of Halbwachs' idea of 'collective memory', which does *not* argue that the group characteristically speaks through the individual but that the individual draws on a defining, collective 'frame of reference'. The pattern which Rebecca West finds – both in her narratives of ancient and modern histories and in her own journey threaded in and through them – is demonstrably determined by the 'frame of reference' which she shares with other middle-class, educated English liberals like herself. It appears most overtly when she draws analogies between the remote past and the present, calling the medieval Tsar Lazar 'a member of the Peace Pledge Union' when she hears how he consented to his nation's defeat, or suggesting a parallel between Roman and Nazi forms of imperialism (1, p. 168):

> We have no real evidence that the people on whom the Roman Empire enforced its civilization had not pretty good civilizations of their own, better adapted to local conditions. The Romans said they had not; but posterity might doubt the existence of our own French and English cultures if the Nazis destroyed all records of them.

It is difficult to find a proper term to distinguish between the personal and collective emphases in *Black Lamb and Grey Falcon*. The familiar dichotomy private–public, suggested by Samuel Hynes as the structuring model of 1930s literary discourse, does not work because the whole movement of West's book is towards dissolving this distinction. This is the point of her opposition between 'idiocy' and 'lunacy', set up in the Prologue (1, p. 3):

> The word 'idiot' comes from a Greek root meaning private person. Idiocy is the female defect: intent on their private lives, women follow their fate through a darkness deep as that cast by malformed cells in the brain. It is no worse than the male defect, which is lunacy: they are so obsessed by public affairs that they see the world as by moonlight, which shows the outlines of every object but not the details indicative of their nature.

This distinction, mocked by Mary Ellmann for essentialist gender stereotyping,[16] is actually invoked only twice in the book: once, early on, when the writer and her husband disagree about imperialism in gendered terms, she arguing 'like a woman, idiotically' and he like a masculine lunatic (1, pp. 288–9), and once in the Epilogue when she sees some women obliviously weeding a public park during a riot and 'thanked God for the idiocy of women, which must in many parts of the world have been the sole defence of life against the lunacy of men' (2, p. 471). She does also once use the word 'idiot' in a pejorative sense, when she reproaches herself for thinking 'idiotically, as if I were Gerda, imputing worthlessness to them [the Slavs] instead of difference' (2, p. 222); but the point here is *not* that Gerda and she are both females, but that she has momentarily succumbed to Gerda's vice of unthinking contempt for Slav culture.

Nevertheless, Rebecca West's opposition 'lunatic–idiot' does, with whatever qualifications, remain useful for its insistence that human experience is a continuum which can be distorted by two kinds of tunnel vision: seeing only personal details, or only impersonal generalities. Private lives are not 'invaded' by public events; they belong to the same world and are as much subject to history as kings and popes. It is even in her terms 'idiotic' to talk of a private life being 'invaded', as if the individual had a right to an inviolate territory of her or his own. She points out repeatedly that such privacy is a luxury unknown in the Balkans, as when in 'Dalmatia' she imagines the life of a typical citizen (1, p. 54):

> Were I to go down to the market-place, armed with the powers of witchcraft, and take a peasant by the shoulder and whisper to him, 'In your lifetime, have you known peace?', wait for his answer, shake his shoulder, transform him into his father, and ask him the same question,

and transform him in turn into his father, I would never hear the word
'Yes', if I carried my questioning of the dead back for a thousand years.
I would always hear, 'No, there was fear, there were our enemies
without, our rulers within, there was prison, there was torture, there
was violent death.'

This is as true now as in 1941. And as she makes plain throughout the
book, the history of the man's wife or daughter would have been even
grimmer.

It is easy and obvious, and not wrong but too simple, to say that in these
collective memories Rebecca West constantly invokes the grand narratives of Western culture. As Lyotard has shown, Western interpretive
frameworks depend on a narrative, often assumed rather than actually
related, of a triumphalist history whose 'universal' pattern at once makes a
particular idea or event intelligible and defines its terms.[17] Rebecca West
argues in different but related terms that people pattern their own lives in
terms of story, and that such narrative patterning gives a person a
necessary sense of his or her existence as shaped and significant: it is, in
fact, a form of art (1, pp. 54–5):

> As we grow older and see the ends of stories as well as their beginnings,
> we realize that to the people who take part in them it is almost of greater
> importance that they should be stories, that they should form a
> recognizable pattern, than that they should be happy or tragic.

She speculates that it may be as necessary for nations as well as individuals
to identify themselves within a satisfactory story (1, p. 55):

> What would England be like if it had not its immense Valhalla of kings
> and, if it had not its Elizabethan and its Victorian ages, its thousands of
> incidents which come up in the mind, simple as icons and as
> miraculous in their suggestion that what England has been it can be
> again, now and forever?

By arguing that the healthy patriotism of the English is enabled by their
nation's fortunate history (unlike the unhappy Croats, despised and
exploited by the Austrian Empire to which they gave heroic service),
Rebecca West goes beyond invoking historical narrative as good magic,
mental refreshment, to assert that it is necessary to make thought possible.
She represents the Croats' pervasive lack of political intelligence as the
direct result of their hopelessly tangled, depressing past. 'The Croats had a
record of individual heroism that no nation could surpass, but it had never

shaped itself as an indestructible image of triumph that could be turned to as an escape from present failure' (1, p. 55). Nations need such images.

Black Lamb and Grey Falcon tells or invokes several such competing narrative images of European history, directly narrating some and alluding to others. Yugoslavia, whose name meant 'the nation of the South Slavs', was a federation of Catholic, Orthodox and Muslim countries, each including citizens belonging to 'minority' faiths, as well as Jews and gypsies. Each country has a different national history. Dalmatia was subject to and exploited by Venice; Croatia gave its loyalty to the Austro-Hungarian Empire, which despised and exploited it; Bosnia was part of the Ottoman Empire and then of the Austro-Hungarians; Serbia gained its independence from the Ottoman Empire in the early 1800s, against the odds, as a separate kingdom, becoming after the War the core and dominant state of Yugoslavia. All have different – and potent – nationalist narratives which determine their cultures. She observes that 'one can look at nothing in Dalmatia, not even a Flagellation of Christ, without being driven back to the struggle of Slav nationalism' (1, p. 158), and the same is true, *mutatis mutandis*, for the other Yugoslav states. For Rebecca West, the key history is that of Serbia, the only state whose story she tells at length (1, pp. 533–637), supplementing this with detailed if interrupted histories of the medieval Serbian emperors Milutin and Stephen Dushan (2, pp. 223–86). Yugoslavia's recent history (i.e. at the time of writing) is a simple, noble tale of heroic Slavs resisting Turkish imperialism – 'We fought the Turk, and then we fought the Turk, and then we fought the Turk': 1, p. 222), cheated and oppressed by Austrian malignance, almost bloodily defeated in the Great War but finally triumphant as the Serb-led Yugoslavia. This is the narrative of Yugoslav history as understood by 'Constantine', the Serbian Jewish Yugoslav patriot, to which West's long narrative of Serbian history in 'Belgrade', and the shorter histories and anecdotes in 'Old Serbia' and 'Montenegro' Serbia pretty much correspond. The only real difference is that Rebecca West claims and assumes a more wide-ranging view than 'Constantine', arguing that the main enemy of humane civilization in general and Slavs in particular is imperialism, be it Roman, Turk, Austrian or Nazi (she is ambivalent and uncomfortable about the British Empire). Her heroes are brave, democratic rebels, or better still wise, strong princes who give their countries peace and prosperity. Her accounts of the great Serbian emperor Stephen Dushan (2, pp. 258–76), of the nineteenth-century liberal Bishop Strossmayer (1, pp. 105–10) and of 'Gospodin Mac', the admirable Scottish mining engineer in charge of the Trepcha mine (2, pp. 305–20) are all recognizably cast in this mould.

But right from the start she shows that other narratives exist whose assumptions contradict the dominant history and challenge her own liberalism. Constantine's version of Yugoslavia is contested by 'Valetta', a patriotic Croat intellectual who sees the past and present very differently: for him the Christendom which it was the Slavs' glory to defend means the domain of the Catholic Church. Rebecca West presents the man and his arguments sympathetically, but finds them flawed. Valetta admits that he and his friends partly take their orders from some extremely reactionary Catholic clergy, and that they haven't even worked out the principles on which a separate Croat state would be run. (Hence, presumably, the subsequent forced conversions and massacres of half a million Orthodox Serbs in Pavelic's Croatia during the Second World War).[18] Valetta's failings are typical of the general lack of political intelligence which is shown to prevail in Croatia. (In fact, nobody opposed to the Yugoslav state is represented by Rebecca West as reasonable. Later in the book, she describes a Macedonian who naively approves of Hitler as a potential ally of separatist Bulgars: 2, p. 163; and an Albanian cab-driver in Dechani who looks forward to the coming war as an opportunity to kill Serbs: 2, p. 390). The Croat patriots resent Yugoslavia, despise their fellow Slavs, especially the Serbs, and refuse to see that if they separate, they will have no protection against Fascist Italy, which would certainly take them over. The Yugoslav patriots in Dalmatia, including the mayor of Korchula, are admirable, but too old-fashioned to understand the Croats' grievances; besides which they are more used to giving orders than to negotiation. Liberal progressivism in Croatia is represented by the pro-Yugoslav Jews 'Dr and Mrs Y' who run a charity festival which, because it is funded by the Belgrade government, is boycotted by 'all the considerable families in Split'. The couple, happily ignorant of their unpopularity and its implications, are 'buoyant Utopians' who believe that charity festivals and liberal legislation will put an end to poverty, war and misery. Rebecca West observes sadly of these optimists that 'I could only hope that, holding such inoffensive views in our offensive age, they would be permitted to die in their beds' (1, p. 198).

Rebecca West tells plenty of anecdotes about Croatian history, but no full-dress narratives, unless one counts her retelling of the miseries of the later Roman Empire in 'Dalmatia'. Nevertheless, she does, if critically, acknowledge the Croat version of Yugoslav history. For, although Slav nationalists may see their histories differently, they all agree on their 'grand narrative' – namely, the heroic story of the endurance of Western Christendom, defended by the Slavs against the Ottoman Empire and finally victorious. Rebecca West endorses this narrative, arguing that the poverty, division and misery which remain the curse of Yugoslav existence are the result of subjection either to the Turkish empire or to the Christian empires which opposed it. She emphasizes the curse of imperialism early in the book, when she visits the wretchedly poor and sterile Dalmatian island Rab; she explains that the Venetian state, unable to defeat the Turks, survived by bribing them, raising the money by squeezing the poor of Dalmatia and thus ruining their forests, so that most of the Adriatic islands now consist of semi-desert. The citizens of Rab

> gave the bread out of their mouths to save us of Western Europe from Islam; and it is ironical that so successfully did they protect us that those among us who would be broad-minded ... would blithely tell us that perhaps the Dalmatians need not have gone to all that trouble, that an Islamized West could not have been worse than what we are today.

Oh yes it could, says Rebecca West (1, p. 139):

> I had only to shut my eyes and I could smell the dust, the lethargy, the rage and hopelessness of a Macedonian town, once a glory to Europe, that had too long been Turkish. The West has done much that is ill, it is vulgar and superficial and economically sadist; but it has not known that death in life which was suffered by the Christian provinces under the Ottoman Empire. From this the people of Rab had saved me: I should say, are saving me ... Impotent and embarrassed, I stood on the high mountain and looked down on the terraced island where my saviours, small and black as ants, ran about hither and thither attempting to repair their destiny.

Clearly the time of writing is relevant to this vision of Yugoslav history as a tale of Christian soldiers fighting the infidel. The grim history of the Balkans should, she suggests, teach the English what happens to a conquered nation: its citizens for centuries remain oppressed, overtaxed, imprisoned, barred from exercising control, and its past glories vanish into relics and might-have-beens. Resistance demands heroism; it is also the only means of survival: 'A man is not a man if he will not save his seed' (2, p. 398).

At the same time, Rebecca West's historical vision strongly invokes the 'grand narrative' of Christianity: the people of Rab, with their 'faces which recall the crucified Christ' (1, p. 139), become scapegoat-saviours, their suffering mapped on to Christ's. The gospel narrative of Christ's death and resurrection is as important to her interpretive framework as her liberal pro-Slav politics – and not only because her visit takes place at Easter. Her central symbols of 'black lamb' and 'grey falcon' belong, as she acknowledges, to the Christian imagery of blood sacrifice and redemption; the grand narrative of Christianity is thus central to the meaning she finds in Yugoslavia.

Bosnian Muslims presumably had their own version of Yugoslav history, but we do not hear it. Rebecca West has very little to say about the modern history of Slav Muslims, though she is sympathetic and informative about the Bosnians' adherence to the Bogomil sect in 1400, their persecution by the Catholic Church and consequent conversion to Islam (1, pp. 304–11). She is definitely hostile to Islam and to the Ottoman Empire, which she treats as more or less interchangeable, although she insists on distinguishing Turks from Slav Muslims (1, p. 281). She credits Islamic culture with a talent for ease, beauty and elegance, but no more than that. Islam has been intelligently pleasure-loving, good at landscaping cities and designing houses; but, it appears, wholly unintellectual. The Turks' values end with 'ferocity and voluptuousness' (2, p. 453); they are 'so destitute of speculative instinct that they have no word for "interesting" in their language' (2, p. 121). There is no indication anywhere in *Black Lamb* that Islamic intellectual traditions even exist. This racist dismissal of Muslim culture is the only serious blind spot of her otherwise remarkably open-minded book: the shadow side of the 'grand narrative' of the Slav defence of Christendom. It is clear that she didn't know much about Islamic cultures; nor, unlike Western intellectuals today, could she have learnt from the works of post-colonial theorists like Edward Said to avoid such 'Orientalist' dismissive ignorance. And there seems to have been no educated Bosnian Muslim middle class whom she could have learnt from; for the Bosnian intellectuals whom she and her husband meet and admire in Sarajevo are all Jews. The Slav Muslims she encounters all seem to be dirt-poor, 'ground down for centuries by a foreign oppressor to the level of the poor white trash of the southern states or South Africa' (1, p. 280), and have apparently inherited a dying culture. The only Muslims she ever meets who remember the past seem to be ageing Turks who are wardens of museums and whose relative ignorance and political impotence are pathetic (2, pp. 290, 453), or the guide in Trebinje, Herzegovina, who takes her and her husband on a grotesquely disappointing tour of a pasha's house (1, pp. 282–7). When the Turkish Prime Minister visits Sarajevo, the Bosnian Muslims who turn out *en masse* to greet him are deeply disappointed to find that he wears Western clothes, does not mention Islam and is distinctly embarrassed by their fervour (1, pp. 321–2) – an anticlimax which signifies 'the final collapse of the Ottoman Empire' (1, p. 323). It is not, therefore, surprising that she is categorical about the superiority of Christendom, represented both by

Serb-led Yugoslavia and by England: 'My civilization need not die. It must not die. My national faith is valid, as the Ottoman faith was not' (2, p. 453).

Rebecca West's hostility towards Islamic culture is tangled up, in good as well as bad ways, with her enmity towards imperialism and her sympathy for democratic nationalism. She hates all empires for their 'carelessness and cruelty' (1, p. 138), and their exploitation and corruption of subject peoples: 'Empires live by the violation of law' (1, p. 287). She criticizes the Romans, the Venetians and especially the Austrians for the ruinous effects of their rule and their self-serving triumphalism; and she is uncomfortable about the injustice of the British Empire, which has partly corrupted the English because 'Empire makes man own things outside his power to control' (2, p. 453). On the other hand, she does show at least one Briton with a gift for ruling, though not as a proconsul: the 'Gospodin Mac' who manages the Trepcha lead-mine at Kossovska Mitrovska, which she visits in the last quarter of the book.

Another Western narrative, not of romantic nationalism but of economic and cultural development is implied in this account of the British-run Trepcha mine: the story of man's progress from poverty and ignorance through capitalist investment in technologically progressive means of wealth-creation. Trepcha is the only industrial plant they visit in the whole journey, and it is famous: long before they get there, we hear that everyone in Kossovo wants to go there and find a job. (It is today one of the biggest lead-mines in Europe, and is the main economic reason why Serbian-led 'Yugoslavia' has insisted on holding on to Kossovo.) Earlier on, Constantine has lyrically invoked the splendours of industrialism (1, p. 493):

> It would be beautiful if much foreign money came here and bred more money, and if we had factories such as they have in America, splendid white palaces full of machinery so intricate that when it moves it is like symphonies being played in steel, pouring out new and clean things for our people, pouring out golden streams of wages that all could be bought.

This, of course, is naive romanticism. The Trepcha mine, however, managed by the admirable Scotsman known as 'Gospodin Mac', is solid: it has genuinely brought prosperity to previously impoverished people. The chauffeur Dragutin admires the little houses people have there as 'fino, fino' (2, p. 303), and Rebecca West agrees, describing them in terms that charmingly suggest a stylized Byzantine fresco of a housing estate (2, p. 316):

> In the porches of these little houses women were sitting as the blessed in Paradise, with the reinforced satisfaction of those who have known a previous inferiority. . . . 'Running water in each house,' murmured the Gospodin Mac, 'and they keep them like new pins'.

The mine's chief is wise, fair-minded and sensitive, using industrial technology and investment to benefit his workers: 'Here, certainly, Yugoslavia could take the gifts of the West without fearing that they were poisoned' (2, p. 333).

But this does not mean that the mine and projects like it can solve Yugoslavia's problems, first because, however excellent the manager, the mine is owned by a firm which runs it for profit, not for its social value (2, p. 338), and second, because unpolitical, technologically expert engineering of the kind represented by the English officials of the mine is itself subject to and victimized by England's stupidly selfish ruling class (2, p. 335):

> It was childish to suppose that the people of the mine could offer a formula for the well-being of the South Slavs; or even for themselves . . . These people could not save South-Eastern Europe, because they could not save England; which, indeed, would certainly not save them, if their existence were at stake.

Gospodin Mac says that the Foreign Office are not interested in the mine: 'They've never even told me what to do in case of war' (2, p. 337). Which – no doubt deliberately – leaves the reader wondering what did happen to the workers and officials of Trepcha when Yugoslavia was invaded by Hitler's armies.

BLACK LAMB AND GREY FALCON

The black lamb dying on a rock, and the grey falcon tempting a king to defeat, are the two key images – not symbols – of the book. The first is a fertility ritual which Rebecca West witnesses as a tourist, the other refers to a poem recited over a picnic lunch. Each inspires some of the most intense writing in the book, marking the point where the story of the writer's journey becomes a parable about her own self and her country's destiny.

The sacrifice of the black lamb occurs after several descriptions of religious festivals in church, including the Catholic Easter Mass in Shestine, Croatia (1, p. 63), the Orthodox Easter Mass in Skopje a month later (2, pp. 1–13; these churches have different calendars) – and the healing ceremonies at Sveti Naum (2, pp. 114–15). These she finds moving, principally because of the congregation's heroic faith that 'death may last five hundred years yet not be death' (2, p. 13). The climax – and opposite – of these ceremonies is this hateful ritual of the 'black lamb', which consists of cutting the animal's throat over a particular rock in the 'Sheep's Field' on the morning of St George's Day (9 May). After witnessing this sacrifice, she attends no more masses, despite visiting many monasteries to see their architecture and frescos, and to talk and eat with abbots. Although the connection between these Easter Masses and the ceremony of the 'black lamb' is obvious, Rebecca West repudiates the idea of a connection between the irredeemably vile reality of this blood sacrifice and the myth of resurrection celebrated by the Orthodox ceremonies which so much move her, arguing that, on the contrary, the sacrifice of the innocent represents the indulgence of cruelty, and no more.

This sacrifice is the third and last of the fertility rites practised on St George's Day, which are popular as 'magic remedies against the curse of barrenness that lies on Macedonia, partly because of the malaria and partly because of the overwork of the women and the lack of care for childbearing women' (2, p. 182). The first two all-female ceremonies, which Rebecca West finds basically life-affirming, take place on St George's Eve; in one, women come to kiss a sacred stone in one of the mosques and in the other, they come to sleep on the saint's tomb (2, pp. 191–4).[19] Although the 'Sheep's Field' sacrifice is open to both sexes, her husband does not accompany her to it; nor does she afterwards discuss it with him or anyone else, although it dominates her thoughts. (She actually attended it one year later in 1938.[20]) Because her party arrives late, the sacrificial rock is already red and stinking with blood and dead animals when they reach it (2, p. 201):

> The spectacle was extremely disgusting. . . but the place had enormous authority. It was the body of our death, it was the seed of the sin that is in us, it was the forge where the sword was wrought that shall slay us. When it had at last been made visible before the eyes as it is – for we are all brought up among disguised presentations of it – it would have been foolish not to stay for a little while and contemplate it.

This stream of powerful gospel images – body of death, referring to the Eucharist, seed of sin, alluding to the parable of the mustard seed, the sword that slays those who kill by it[21] – invokes Christian symbols and references to attack Christianity's love affair with the blood sacrifice. The spectacle rouses her, unusually, to violent language as well as sacred symbols: she twice uses the abusive phrase 'a letch for cruelty' (2, pp. 204, 208) and even the word 'shit' (2, p. 207).[22]

Yet the cutting of the lamb's throat is definitely a religious scene, not only because the writer reads it through theological history, but because it convicts her – and others – of sin. Its meanings are both intimate – 'I knew this rock well' (2, p. 205) – and universal; for the blood sacrifice of the lamb is at once a re-enactment of Crucifixion and an interpretation of it. Because we perversely desire the rock (that is, blood and death), our theologians have thought up justifications for the Crucifixion and so produced the revolting doctrine of the Atonement (2, p. 205):

> A supremely good man was born on earth ... who could have taught mankind to live in perpetual happiness; and because we are infatuated with the idea of shedding innocent blood to secure advantages, we found nothing better to do with this passport to deliverance than to destroy him ... Our shame would be absolute, were it not that the crime we intended cannot in fact be committed. It is not possible to kill goodness. There is always more of it, it does not take flight from our accursed earth, it perpetually asks us to take what we need from it.

Rebecca West's 'we' is as inclusive as the Calvinist tag 'In Adam's fall/ We sinned all'; it includes not only Christians, not only Europeans, but the entire human race. The self-knowledge which she learns from her own fascination with the rock is that she is all too representatively human: perhaps more conscious and certainly far more learned than most, but not different in kind.

The lamb, the blood, the knife and the rock are, then, both intensely literal and intensely symbolic: Rebecca West's rhetoric works outward from the witnessed event, exploring the way in which human thought has turned the gratuitous death of an animal into complicated lies and intellectual justifications. The sacrifice thus becomes a primal scene dramatizing human's deepest desires: 'It is behind all our lives' (2, p. 334). But its full significance does not become plain until we hear the poem of the 'Grey Falcon' more than a hundred pages later, in 'Plain of Kossovo II'.

Whereas Rebecca West makes a pilgrimage to the Sheep's Field to see the blood sacrifice, the lead-up to the poem is markedly casual. The party has just left Prishtina, a meagre and impoverished town where the inn's tablecloth is stained, the chicken at lunch is 'a ghastly prodigy, lean and twisted in its leanness like one of El Greco's fasting saints' (2, p. 253), and the lavatory is a stinking hole. Rebecca West has been holding forth at length on the brilliance of mediæval Serbian empire and the tragedy of its dissolution, being inspired by the sordid inn to launch into a 25-page history of the great Stephen Dushan (2, pp. 251–77). The medieval drama and magnificence which she evokes so eloquently contrast discouragingly with the miserable present, especially when she observes an Albanian husband walking before his wife, who has a ploughshare tied to her back. No one in Prishtina, including the woman herself, seems to think this is wrong or even surprising.

Meanwhile, the members of the party are getting on badly together. Their Yugoslav guide 'Constantine', depressed by all this evidence of Yugoslav poverty and backwardness, is being irritatingly anti-English; Rebecca West and her husband try, and fail, to mollify him. Their healthy young chauffeur Dragutin, increasingly impatient with Constantine, has virtually taken over running the tour because the latter is now so disorganized and neurotic. They stop for a picnic at Dragutin's suggestion and, as the group converses, the two Slavs are moved to recite this nationalist poem, which Constantine translates into English. The poem, quoted in full, tells how the grey falcon flies to the Tsar and offers him a choice between an earthly and a heavenly kingdom. If he wants the former, he must prepare for war and defeat the Turk; if he wants a heavenly kingdom, he should build a church at Kossovo.

> Build it not with a floor of marble
> But lay down silk and scarlet on the ground,
> Give the Eucharist and battle orders to your soldiers,
> For all your soldiers shall be destroyed,
> And you, prince, with them.

The Tsar ponders, and decides for the heavenly kingdom. So he does as the grey falcon tells him; he and his soldiers all perish, and the glory of Serbia departs for ever: 'All was holy, all was honourable/ And the goodness of God was fulfilled' (2, pp. 293–4).

Rebecca West's response to this parable is deliberately anachronistic: 'I see. Tsar Lazar was a member of the Peace Pledge Union.' She thus identifies the medieval Serbian emperor with a contemporary pacifist organization, whose aims she had previously supported enough to publicly declare herself a pacifist.[23] She links the Tsar with good liberals like H. A. L. Fisher and Gilbert Murray, whose real wish is to be defeated 'and then go to Heaven' (p. 295). This pacifist defeatism is, she suggests, an unconscious glorification of sacrifice: a religious idea which deeply if unconsciously affects the political views of left liberals, including herself. She enlarges this argument in the book's long Epilogue, insisting that Kossovo in 1389 and England in 1939 were in essentially the same situation, differing only in the externals of time and place (2, p. 515). Connecting the revolting image of the blood-stained rock ('its filth and its cruelty and its astonishing power over the imagination': p. 298), with the poem's lyrical celebration of defeat, she draws the moral that liberals and pacifists want to be innocent, passive and martyred, much more than they want to make their ideas win. You can guess this, she says, at left-wing protest meetings where the speakers do not talk as if (p. 296):

> power would be theirs tomorrow and they would use it for virtuous action. And their audience do not seem to regard themselves as destined to rule; they clap as if in defiance, and laugh at their enemies behind their hands, with the shrill laughter of children. They want to be right, not to do right.

She herself is not free of this irresponsible attitude (pp. 297–8):

> I looked into my own heart and I knew that I was not innocent. Often I wonder if I would be ready to suffer for my principles if need came, and it strikes me as a matter of the highest importance. That should not be so. I should ask myself with far greater urgency whether I have done everything possible to carry those principles into effect, and how I can attain power to make them absolutely victorious. But those questions I put only with my head. They do not excite my guts, which wait anxiously while I ponder my gift for martyrdom.

The point of her own intense response is not simply personal, for she exemplifies the standard pathology of 'the left-wing people among whom I had lived all my life . . . We believed in our heart of hearts that life was simply this and nothing more, a man cutting the throat of a lamb on a rock to obtain happiness'. Repudiating violence, such people say 'Since it is wrong to be the priest and sacrifice the lamb, I will be the lamb and be sacrificed by the priest' (2, p. 298). Yet Kossovo's past glories and present miseries show how the price of this virtue is paid not by the sacrificed but, perhaps for centuries, by their unfortunate heirs. 'It is possible that we have betrayed life and love for more than five hundred years on a field wider than Kossovo, as wide as Europe' (2, p. 299).

This wartime critique of the irresponsibility of the intellectual Left (for these meditations are obviously written in retrospect) remains cogent in the 1990s. It is, to my mind, far more searching than Orwell's better-known attack in 'Inside the Whale'. (The point about intellectuals' love affair with martyrdom in the late thirties is, incidentally, confirmed by two well-known literary texts: Rex Warner's *The Professor* (1938) and Stephen Spender's tragedy *Trial of a Judge* (1938), both of which turn on the failure and martyrdom of a liberal hero.) Rebecca West uses the same idea to explain the political passivity of decent technicians like the men who run the mine at Trepcha: 'They listen to the evil counsel of the grey falcon.

They let their throats be cut as if they were black lambs. The mystery of Kossovo was behind this hill. It is behind all our lives' (p. 334).

MICRO-NARRATIVE: REBECCA WEST'S OWN JOURNEY

Right from the beginning, Yugoslavia is represented as beautiful and exhilarating, but not idyllic. When Rebecca West arrives, the spring weather is unseasonably cold, deep snow covering the plum blossom. She avoids any crude symbolism of national promise being nipped in the bud: if the snowy Easter is made to represent anything, it is spiritual survival against the the odds, as when peasants proudly wear their brilliant festival costumes despite the risk of mud and snow. Still, it is a little ominous. There are plenty of signs, too, that all is not well in the Yugoslav state: the disaffection of the Croats, the terrible poverty and sterility of the Dalmatian coast, despite its beauty, and the appearance of some gypsies whose self-hating hostility indicates that 'something alien and murderous had intruded into the Slav pattern, and its virtue had gone out of it' (1, p. 66). Both when the party goes north to Dalmatia and south to Bosnia, they see a country first impoverished by centuries of Venetian and Turkish overtaxing and looting and then exploited by Austro-Hungarian Empire. They then take the train to Belgrade, where they meet Constantine's awful wife Gerda, and things begin to go wrong. The remainder of their journey through Macedonia, Kossovo and Montenegro has many moments of great beauty and intensity, but is increasingly darkened by a combination of threatening political developments and bad relations between the travellers.

Rebecca West's account of this itinerary has a strong fictional component, which is never more pronounced than when it appears to be straightforwardly autobiographical. As well as condensing the results of three journeys in successive years into the story of her 1937 visit, she gives herself an implausibly perfect recall of long conversations, which demand almost as great a suspension of disbelief as that required by Nelly Dean, the narrator of *Wuthering Heights*, who recites forty-page dialogues which she has supposedly overheard a generation ago. Both the 'set-piece' debates, and Rebecca West's prolonged meditations when she sees the sacrifice of the black lamb (2, pp. 200–10) and hears the poem about the grey falcon (pp. 293–301) are very different from the notes in her travel diary. Even without reading her journal, it is obvious that her book differs greatly from a genuine day-to-day record like *Naomi Mitchison's Vienna Diary* (1934) which describes how the writer went to Vienna in March

1934 after Dollfuss' *Putsch*, met Austrian Socialists under cover, gave them what help she could, and visited the prison camps, typing up a nightly diary of these events which Gollancz published, apparently without editing, as a book. Unlike Rebecca West, Naomi Mitchison records hardly any direct speech, apart from one Socialist's poignant 'Es war so schön, Rote Wien!' – 'Red Vienna was so lovely!'[24]

By contrast, the six-page chapter 'Zagreb IV' in *Black Lamb* consists entirely of a lively argument between the Serb patriot 'Constantine' and the Croat patriot 'Valetta' about the justice or otherwise of the Yugoslav state (1, pp. 83–9). Given that both men are arguing furiously over their deepest convictions, one would expect them to fall into Serbo-Croat; but by mentioning Constantine's heaped up negatives (1, p. 87) and guttural mispronunciation of 'honest' as 'chonest' (1, p. 85), Rebecca West indicates that they did talk English and that she has remembered every word. It is clear from an entry in her 1937 travel diary about a lunch at which 'Vinaver ["Constantine"] baited Tribarina ["Valetta"] about Serbia and Croatia', that this recorded conversation refers to a real one; but the entry is far too short[25] to be accepted as proof that the dialogue took place exactly as represented. (It was probably, in fact, a distillation of several debates witnessed by Rebecca West between Croat and Yugoslav patriots.) Similarly, the long analysis of 'Gerda' and the imperialist mind-set which she represents, spoken by 'my husband' with occasional interjections from Rebecca West after 'Gerda' leaves their party (2, pp. 175–182), is clearly fictional. Unmentioned in the 1937 diary (which actually describes her husband as 'speechless' with rage), [26] his analysis is unbelievably long for a recorded conversation. Moreover, his concluding peroration about the exemplary conquered women 'whose fingers never forgot the pattern that an ancient culture had created' (2, p. 182) actually alludes to Rebecca West's *own* unspoken feminist meditation on the creative strength and personal misery of the peasant women of Tserna Gora (2, p. 50).

I am not, of course, suggesting that these arguments and meditations are simply fakes. They are clearly based on conversations or thoughts that actually occurred during or after Rebecca West's Yugoslav trips, though probably not in the same terms and certainly not with the rhetorical elaboration given in her printed text. Their effect is rather like that of debates in Thucydides' *History of the Peloponnesian War*, also loosely based on real speeches, in which the historical actors articulate issues of the conflict with far more self-awareness and clarity than the originals could possibly have done in life.[27] These scenes of largely invented dialogue also help to liven up the narrative and 'flesh out' its characters, especially Rebecca

West's guide 'Constantine' (Stanislas Vinaver) a government official, patriotic Jewish Serb, gifted charmer and Paris-educated poet, and his appalling pro-Nazi German wife 'Gerda', known as 'Mrs V.' in the diary (her real name was Elsa).[28] The relations between this couple and Mr and Mrs Henry Andrews (that is, Rebecca West and her husband), though outwardly trivial, produce most of the book's personal drama.

Gerda is a German of good family, who evidently feels exiled in Yugoslavia, despising Slavs as poor, dirty, backward and – she thinks – uncivilized. Nevertheless, she jealously insists on accompanying 'Constantine', who is to guide Mr and Mrs Andrews around Macedonia, and they are too polite to refuse. Since Gerda's political and emotional allegiances ally her with the enemies of Yugoslavia, she has a paralysing effect on her husband, who is a Jew as well as a Yugoslav patriot. She destroys his self-confidence and undermines his friendship with Rebecca West and her husband, whom she resents partly because they are English (she is a German patriot) and partly because they are liberal cosmopolitans who enjoy the company of intellectual Jews. The first sign of her unpleasantness comes with her snubbing response to their enthusiasm for the delightful people in Bosnia: 'It is twelve years since I saw these people, how can I possibly be interested in them?' The English couple, bewildered, talk this over and work out that the reason must be anti-Semitism: 'Most of the people I mentioned were Jews.' They decide hopefully, however, that 'she is probably a nice woman and has many good points' (1, p. 478).

Needless to say, this charitable optimism proves unjustified. Gerda is deliberately and repeatedly rude, even when silent: 'Every word and movement of hers, and even in some mysterious way her complete inaction, implied that she was noble, patient, industrious, modest and self-effacing, whereas we were materialist, unstable, idle, extravagant, and aggressive' (1, p. 513). She is hostile to the Slav state and wholly insensitive to its history: her comment on the French war cemetery is 'Think of all these people dying for a lot of Slavs' (2, p. 140). She refuses to believe that they can have beaten the Germans and Austrians (as they did) by sheer heroism; they must have won their battles by treachery (2, p. 145). Offered a dish at a picnic, 'her face crumpled up with racial hatred too irrational to find words' (2, p. 148). Even when briefly good-tempered, she casts a blight: to please her nostalgia for Germany, they all have to sit in a boring hotel yard, eating horrible lukewarm liverwurst (1, p. 510).

Although Rebecca West is at some pains to distinguish Gerda from Germans in general, ('Gerda is, of course, not characteristically German': 2, p. 177), it is clear enough that she represents the Nazi mind-set in her rage about her country's defeat in the First World War, her brutal contempt for all those she thinks are her inferiors, and above all in her lack of a 'sense of process' (p. 175). That is, Gerda sees only results, having no notion of what produced them, and wants to grab what she sees. Because she despises her husband Constantine for being a Jewish Serb, he comes to feel that he must be lacking in something vital to be the object of such contempt, and ultimately becomes what she thinks he is: an incompetent Jewish comedian. 'Nobody who is who is not like Gerda', says Rebecca West's husband, 'can imagine how bad Gerda is' (2, p. 176).

Horrible as Gerda may be, she is very good for Rebecca West's narrative. She is a gruesomely comic creation, who leaves the reader waiting for the next grossly rude thing she will do or say, which always turns out to be even more outrageous than one could have imagined. More than this, by provoking a tragicomic drama of alienation between the travellers, her presence turns a travelogue into something more like a novel, whose action first manifests itself in a series of absurdly petty incidents: quarrels over punctuality, accusations of gluttony for indulging in an extra pastry, or tactlessness about the German war cemetery ('here I am, far from my home, and he insults my blood, the German blood!': 2, p. 137). The story of Rebecca West's holiday with her husband in Yugoslavia is not actually much more eventful than a Jane Austen novel about a visit to a country, in which the heroine and her companions visit towns, view landscapes, attend church (Catholic and Orthodox Easter Mass), eat large meals, meet people, and come no nearer to adventure than once being nearly led over a precipice, a disaster which is averted by the heroine's presence of mind (2, pp. 407–10). At the same time, the tragic, heroic context set up by a multitude of historical narratives of Slav oppressions and resistances, meditations on Macedonian Byzantine art, and celebrations of the unsung heroism of ordinary peasants constitutes a vast 'sounding board' against which Gerda's small actions reverberate, at once farcical and sinister. It is as if Rebecca West and her husband were doomed to be accompanied through Macedonia by a Nazi Mrs Elton who hates the ethnic diversity of Yugoslavia, mutters 'They should all be driven out!' at the sight of anyone unconventional (2, p. 33), and constantly threatens by her ill temper and rudeness to turn the tragic intensities of Yugoslav experience into a repetition of the quarrelsome expedition to Box Hill in *Emma*.

When Gerda disappears, her influence remains, for Constantine does not suffer the less from her contempt. After she leaves the party, he goes to pieces; for, though while she was present he and the two English liberals were mostly in agreement, now he feels he has to take her side, even though that means betraying his own allegiances. His friendship with them therefore comes under great strain, and though there are still brief moments of affection and companionship, it does not really survive the journey. Constantine's psychic unwellness is a constant theme of the second volume of the book: he becomes an unreliable guide, he talks inappropriately, he makes them late for occasions they particularly want to attend, he gets times and places wrong so that their chauffeur Dragutin has to take over the organization of all the day-to-day details of the trip, he unjustly accuses them of English arrogance, and at one point is actually reproved by a fellow Yugoslav for spouting Nazi-inspired propaganda against the English-run Trepcha mine (2, p. 328). He gets a fever after being stung by 'a great ferocious insect with huge wings' (2, p. 346), but clearly he has more than insect poison wrong with him. His plight is spelled out at Dechani where a grotesque, sinister little blond monk plagues the visitors, proudly boasting that 'next Whitsuntide we shall have the honour of entertaining at Dechani Herr Hitler and Herr Goering!' (2, p. 381). The party retreats to a nearby wood, where he revives briefly; but then his expression becomes 'a rictus of horror. . . . "I am very ill," he groaned. "I am in great pain. And there is nothing whatsoever the matter with me." ' Rebecca West responds awkwardly because 'I did not know how to say that he was dying of being a Jew in a world where there were certain ideas to which a new star was lending a strange strength' (2, p. 382). Under these intolerable political and emotional pressures, Constantine the gifted, brilliant charmer is disintegrating into neurotic ineffectiveness.

Rebecca West dramatizes the emotional effects of political pressures on Constantine particularly effectively in a scene near the end of the book, when the party is lunching in a Montenegrin restaurant in Podgoritsa. She thinks to please him by admitting that she has underestimated Goethe, whom he admires. But he is not really attending: ' "Yes, yes," said Constantine. But his voice was as distant as his eyes' (2, p. 419). At first she thinks he is refusing to forgive her for having criticized things German; but the reason for his inattention is that he has noticed the restaurant is full of German diplomats. The party has already met two German agents masquerading as tourists on its travels: an odd 'tourist' at Sveti Naum monastery in Ochrid, who doesn't seem interested in the monks, and a self-styled 'Dane' in Petch who speaks perfect German and says Slavs 'are like sheep, like cattle, like swine' (2, p. 392). Constantine suspects – rightly, as it turns out – that 'the Italians are to do something frightful to the Albanians, and their friends the Germans, who do not so greatly love them, wait outside to see how it goes." . . . He shuddered violently and said, "*Ils avancent toujours*" ' (2, p. 420).

One might think that the travellers are united here by their political sympathies. Certainly, Rebecca West's warm response to her Yugoslav friends' plight makes this seem so; and Constantine tries to retrieve the convivial moment by telling them some lively gossip about his friend who writes plays. But he does it 'in a faltering voice', and his story is about artistic failure: the plays are dull, 'weak and *fade*' ('tasteless': 2, p. 420). It is no good: the moment is lost, and so is the friendship. The journey itself ends with Constantine telling bad news from Albania which confirms his earlier fears (p. 463):

> It is very bad. It is a massacre. The officials all are bought by Italian money, and they have taken the four hundred young men who were most likely to give Italy trouble when she takes the country, and they have pretended it is a Communist rising, and they have killed them all. It is all nasty, so nasty, and it will not stop until the end.

So much for the Balkan holiday.

The following Epilogue takes the writer and her husband back through Zagreb, where they witness an anti-Government riot; Budapest, where people express contempt for Slavs; and Vienna, where Rebecca West recalls Dollfuss' brutal suppression of the Socialist Government three years before. In 1942, she did not need to remind her readers that all these cities had been conquered shortly afterwards by Hitler's armies. The story of Rebecca West's own journey cannot, then, be separated from the wider story of Yugoslavia, which is itself a stage for the European crisis. You cannot distinguish private from public: personal friendships express political hope and divisions, no more and no less than the mine at Trepcha, the buildings in the cities, the marketplaces. Yugoslavia is not only a border country; it is a stage where tensions of Europe are acted out, in intimacies as well as in battles.

'Constantine' and 'Gerda' thus become representative figures in the same way as characters in a realist novel, condensing a class, a group, an attitude. Rebecca West writes of her friend with the compassionate authority of a realist, totalizing novelist, making his relations with his wife and friends into a way of staging European hates and enmities. Gerda's nastiness goes beyond rudeness and jealousy to represent the imperialist and Nazi habit of mind, while Constantine's self-hating, self-parodying response to his wife's contempt and his collapse into neurotic hypochondria signify European Jewry's loss of self-confidence and psychological vulnerability to their persecutors: 'He had bared his throat to Gerda's knife, he had offered up his loving heart to the service of hate, in order that he might be defeated and innocent' (2, p. 300). Similarly, the Andrews' polite, ineffectual response to Gerda's shameless rudeness signifies European liberalism's overcivilized failure to deal firmly with Hitler, as the long analysis of her character strongly implies: 'She will snatch power out of hands too well-bred and compassionate and astonished to defend it' (2, p. 179).

These real-life people are thus given the same kind of representative status as the judge and his wife in Spender's *Trial of a Judge* (1938) who stand respectively for defeated liberalism and middle-class Fascism, or Louis Earlham the Labour MP in Storm Jameson's *Mirror in Darkness* trilogy, whose unacknowledged friendship with an industrial magnate represents the corruption of (some) Socialist politicians by a corporatist capitalism with Fascist leanings. Rebecca West's characterization of Constantine as a victim similarly insists on his wider representative significance – though, because she constantly interprets with the compassionate, totalizing authority of a classic realist novelist, he resembles the Spender or Jameson characters less than he does George Eliot's studies of failure like Lydgate or Bulstrode in *Middlemarch*. It is therefore hardly surprising that Rebecca West's friendship with Stanislas Vinaver, the original of 'Constantine' did not survive the publication of *Black Lamb*,[29] which must have been infuriating to him where it distorted the truth, and even worse where it was right. It would be hard to forgive a friend for so publicly anatomizing what breeds about one's heart and one's marriage.

In other words, 'Constantine' and 'Gerda' are not purely fictional characters, but hybrids: part real, part invented, like Sally Bowles and Bernhard Landauer in Isherwood's *Goodbye to Berlin* (1939), whose differences from their originals Jean Ross and Wilfrid Israel I have discussed in Chapter 1 (see pp. 28–30). The main difference between 'Sally Bowles' and 'Bernhard Landauer' on the one hand and 'Constantine' and 'Gerda' on the other is that, because the former appear in a fiction, their qualities can determine or at least be dramatized by the plot: Sally and Bernhard prove their feckless and/or doomed natures by, respectively, drifting for ever around the world and being killed off early, quite unlike the very tough, vigorously anti-Fascist people whom they were based on. This kind of invention is not open to Rebecca West the autobiographer, even though her characterization of 'Constantine' appears to be similarly falsified, especially in the half-prophecy that he is 'dying of being a Jew' (1, p. 382); whereas Vinaver actually survived the war and became a Communist.[30] As I show below, she did edit the events of her journey and considerably altered her own meditations during it, but she was always prevented by her travel-writer's ambiguous but real fidelity to the literal from reshaping the actual events into a fictional narrative.

WRITER AS SUBJECT: DIARY VERSUS BOOK

What is art? It is not decoration. It is the re-living of experience. The artist says, 'I will make that event happen again, altering its shape, which was disfigured by its contacts with other events, so that its true significance can be revealed.'

Vol. 2, p. 524

This statement about art in general exactly corresponds to the practice of Rebecca West's own *magnum opus*. She freely assumed the artist's licence to transform the material of her own experience in the interests of 'revealing its true significance' in her own great book. It is clear to any attentive reader of *Black Lamb and Grey Falcon* that a good deal of editing and rewriting must have gone on to produce this *magnum opus*; but it is not possible to guess just how much 'reshaping' she did without consulting her original 1937 travel diary, now in the Beinecke Library at Yale University. This has only recently become available for consultation because Rebecca West forbade anyone to read it, along with some other personal papers, during the lifetimes of her husband and son.[31]

In terms of content, the travel diary both does and doesn't match the book closely. Most of the events and anecdotes which Rebecca West relates in the first half of the book are to be found, embryonically, in the diary; for instance, the germ of her detailed paean to Korchulan manhood (1, p. 215) is the simple sentence 'Went into shipyards – goodlooking men'.[32] But the record of the second half of her Yugoslav journey through Macedonia and Kossovo in her diary differs considerably from the printed version. Most notably, the diary says nothing about two key scenes: the throat-cutting of the lamb in the 'Sheep's Field', and Constantine's recitation of the 'grey falcon' poem. (The only hint of the long meditations inspired by the 'black lamb' is a single remark 'There is obviously something wrong with innocence as philosophy, look at sheep' [1 April, on Rab], and possibly an anecdote about a café in Belgrade 'where there was a black lamb with a red ribbon around its neck; killed because it ate the tablecloth' [24 April].) The itinerary is different, too, after her party leaves Macedonia. In the book, they follow up the Byzantine glories of Serbian churches in Kossovo with a visit to the lead-mine at Trepcha which enables Rebecca West to meditate on the glories and limitations of Western technological progress (see pp. 196–7); whereas her 1937 diary shows that the party did not in fact go to Trepcha, but straight to Montenegro, to view more Byzantine frescos at Sopocani and Studenica, which she omitted from the book. She did witness the 'Sheep's Field' fertility sacrifice (though not in 1937, but a year later, on her third trip to Yugoslavia; which also, presumably, included a visit to the Trepcha mine); but the scene of the recitation must be a later invention, written in order to integrate the thematically crucial 'grey falcon' poem into her personal travel-narrative. The changes in the narrative of the second half of the journey, her interest in the theme of sacrifice, and the notebooks themselves all indicate that the 'grey falcon' poem came entirely out of her own researches.[33]

There are subtle differences of emphasis between the diary and the book. Vinaver is unwell during the latter part of their trip, but not thought to be heading for a breakdown, and his wife 'Mrs V.' ['Gerda'] is not quite so outrageous as the book represents her, though she behaves badly enough. (For example, Mrs V.'s comment on the French cemetery at Skopje is 'To think of all these people having fallen for Serbia'. This is tactless, but not as brutal as Gerda's 'Think of all these people dying for a lot of Slavs').[34] The mutual resentments between the two couples are much as described in the book, with two significant differences: the tensions are more personal than political (though they are that too), and 'Ric', as Rebecca West calls her husband, actually suffers more than she does from 'Mrs V.'. The latter is furious with him for not chivalrously giving her his place in the motor car, which means that she has to go by bus with the *hoi polloi*, while the rest of Rebecca West's party is driven in comfort.[35] Henry Andrews himself bitterly resents being put under pressure to spoil his trip for an uninvited guest. A row ensues between the two, described almost word for word in the book (2, pp. 136–7), at the German cemetery in Bitolj, after which Rebecca West tries to keep the peace: 'Have rebuked Ric about Mrs V. but plain fact he was so enraged by her conduct at lunch, to say nothing of the whole past week'. After this, Mrs V. puts off her departure yet again, to the Andrews' fury: 'This is the height of all known impudence . . . Ric speechless'. Mrs V. is then rude 'all through dinner – this is an affliction hard to bear. Never have I had to cart about an enemy at my own expense before'.[36]

Henry Andrews presumably became the target of Elsa Vinaver's resentment because, since Rebecca West was the guest of honour and Stanislas Vinaver was her official guide, 'Ric' was the only person who could be asked to give her his seat in the car. And in any case 'Mrs V.' already had reason to be jealous of Rebecca West, since her husband had himself been infatuated with the Englishwoman on her previous trip, and had made a violent but unsuccessful attempt to rape her. The diary alludes to this incident when relating how Mrs V., already described as 'mad and giggly', tells the party 'how the landlord at Debar asked "Are you married or do you want two rooms communicating like Professor Malmowski?" Further joke was that these were the rooms V. had taken for me when he attempted my virtue'.[37] If, as the entry suggests, this 'further joke' was shared with the rest of the party, one can well understand Elsa Vinaver's embarrassment and hostility.

Politically, the diary shows comparatively little of the ever-present awareness of the Axis menace which haunts the book. The writer is certainly alert to 'pure Fascist propaganda' in an Albanian news-sheet in Macedonia, notices in a Montenegrin restaurant a 'table occupied by German tourists – one suddenly recognized by V. as chief German spy in Jugoslavia' and records a comic anecdote about Goering's philistinism;[38] but there is no mention of either the grotesque little blond monk at Dechani, or of the meetings with the Nazi spies whom the travellers encounter in the book. What Rebecca West has on her mind is not so much politics as her own personal unhappiness.

For this travel diary is a remarkably intimate document. It tells more about Rebecca West's private life than she put into her book – more too, evidently, than she told her husband (which explains why she did not want it read when either he or her son Anthony West were alive). The book represents its writer throughout as a public persona characterized by wit, knowledge and authority: Rebecca West both writes explicitly as a woman and a feminist, and claims the traditionally masculine power to judge and define. Even when she examines her inner masochistic darkness during her meditations on the 'black lamb' and 'grey falcon', she defines herself as a 'universal subject' who shares humanity's irrational death wish. As a historian, her style is almost always balanced and judicious. Thus, after relating the story of the unhappy Queen Simonis, daughter of the Emperor of Byzantium, who at six years old was married to King Milutin of Serbia, aged 55, she meditates on the horrific lives of those unfortunate princesses who for dynastic reasons were married in childhood, 'those girl children who held together the fabric of history by leaving their nurseries going into far lands to experience the pains of rape and miscarriage among strangers talking unknown tongues and practising unhomely customs'. Yet she adds, judiciously (2, p. 233):

> Nor is it necessary, in order to feel its horror, to exaggerate the infamy of early sexual activity. It is sheer humbug to pretend that a girl of twelve who is married to a kindly young bridegroom is in worse case than a woman in her forties, of the kind who would like to marry, who is not married.

As throughout the book, her public persona is that of a rational, experienced, objective speaker. Her status as a married woman is, as her critics have noticed, important to producing this balanced, worldly wise effect – which is partly produced by her many conversations with 'my husband', never named as Henry Andrews until the last page. 'My husband' is a crucially important figure: supportive, confident, affectionate, and at one with his wife on all important issues[39] One would never guess from the book how much private pain lies behind these confident assumptions and judgements.

The diary tells a different, unhappier story, in which the writer's erotic and passionate life is miserably separate from her marriage. Like the book, it contains much meditation and self-scrutiny – not about pacifism and the death wish, but about her own frustration as a sexual woman. All through the two month trip, she intermittently broods over a recently ended, unhappy affair with a man she calls 'T.', presumably the surgeon Thomas Pomfret Kilner, named as her lover by her biographers.[40] Their off-and-on affair seems to have begun joyfully at Bad Gastein in 1935, where she went to convalesce from a hysterectomy;[41] since then, 'all intervening period has been agony' (26 March 1937). She decides that 'nothing was for good in that horrible cheating sadistic little creature. There was only his animal warmth, which he loved to withhold' (4 April). Her marriage is certainly affectionate: 'Felt very fond of Ric as walked about', she records in Split on 30 March; and again on 24 April in Belgrade – 'Like being alone with my Ric'[42] – but it leaves her sexually dissatisfied: 'Every night and morning I feel suicidally unhappy. Memory of disaster becomes more and more frustrating, I suppose in view of present frustration' (27 March). Though in Macedonia she and 'Ric' do occasionally have sex[43] in the early morning (the only possible time, given her exhausting programme of sightseeing, diary-keeping and large late dinners), she does not much enjoy it. In Ochrid on 7 May, she records: 'Woke early – Ric playful – for some odd reason I have recrudescence of painful feeling about T.' A later entry is even more depressing: 'Woke early. Ric not entirely successful' (16 May).

Just how deeply she minds about 'T.' becomes plain when, after Ric's 'playful' lovemaking, she visits a church:

> Kissed the tomb of Sveti Naum. Now I knew he had given me what I wanted. I had asked him to give me T. back, that I could stand it whatever T. was like. He gave me back T., against all probability, and I got him as he is[44] – withholding instead of giving, mean, petty and

dishonest. I simply have to take it. Felt deeply moved by the dark magic of church and chapel.

These adulterous prayers are followed by two poignant dreams, the first of which comes while she is still at Sveti Naum. In this dream, she is first rejected by reporters who favour another woman whom she dislikes; and then, alone and ill (8 May):

> felt myself enfolded in somebody's arms, extraordinary, divine, comforting feeling, astonishingly real, c.p. nun's vision. A sweet voice...said 'Do you know why you still love T.?' I was surprised at this but assumed the speaking presence was right. I had no idea of answer. Voice said very tenderly 'Because you are soft as he is'. Surface meaning – your hair and skin are soft as he is, you have the same cuddly quality. Ric woke me telling me it was after six.

Later that day she thinks of a nastier interpretation: 'you are as infantile as he is, you are sexually defective as he is, you are mad as he is. Most curious dream. Felt unhappy.' Another dream four days later is even more revealing (12 May):

> Saw water flowing in the distance and said to myself, 'The trouble is, I want a new lover and I'm 44.' Then was in maternity ward having just had baby, did not worry about it, felt it would be all right, but never enquired if boy or girl – was told that it had died but rather guessed it – was distressed but more distressed when realized Ric had never been to see me.

Although she seems half-tempted to take these dreams as prophecies, comparing the first 'astonishingly real' dream to a 'nun's vision' and interpreting the second as meaning that 'my book will be bad and Ric won't love me' (12 May), they clearly refer both to her present mourning for 'T.' and to her anxiety about being middle-aged and losing out on sexual love. (The reference to the 'nun's vision' may well indicate scepticism, since it seems to refer to the nun who, the day before this entry [7 May], had irritatingly interrupted her conversation with a nice sensitive priest, in order to tell the story of a 'vision' – an incident which reappears in the book [2, pp. 99–101]). The second dream about 'flowing water' and stillbirth is particularly poignant, especially if her affair with 'T.' did start just after her 1935 hysterectomy. The candid statement that 'I want a new lover and I'm 44', combined with the first vanished and then dead baby, condenses several forms of frustrated desire: her general loss of the sexual pleasure that makes babies possible, her particular mourning for the soft-skinned, 'cuddly' lover whose lovemaking is associated with her own loss of fertility, Ric's inadequacy as a lover or comforter, and also perhaps her own failure to give him a child. It is curious to think of this distinguished woman scribbling down these poignant dreams and long-ings in the hotel bedrooms she shared with the apparently oblivious 'Ric'. If he ever did look at her diary, he could have discovered her thoughts; but as they are scattered through a copious record of sightseeing and conversations, a casual reader could miss them. (The diary itself is clearly private; and the fact that Rebecca West prohibited all access to it during Henry's lifetime appears to indicate that she thought him ignorant of this early affair, and wanted him to stay so.) It is equally curious to realize that neither the black lamb nor the grey falcon, named by the book's title as its central images, have any literal connection with the 'journey through Yugoslavia in 1937' (1, p. iii) which they commemorate.

I do *not* mean that these differences from its original version in any way diminish the achievement of *Black Lamb and Grey Falcon*. Readers should anyway be warned against taking the narrative literally by Rebecca West's statement that the true artist does not reproduce reality but transforms his or her own experience so as to display its essential meaning more fully than literal transcription could do (2, p. 524). It would be absurd to complain because the hurried, compressed notes in the diary have been transformed into clear, authoritative prose. It is true that, like all overtly 'realist' writing, Rebecca West's narrative presents itself as a deceptively transparent window[45] through which things may be seen as reliably 'real', effacing the action of her own interpretive mind to show people and scenes 'as they are'. It is also true that, although she constantly reads things and people in terms of a highly expressive symbolism, Rebecca West never says 'This is my interpretation of the scene', but 'This is its meaning'. Thus, describing the lakeside setting of Sveti Naum, the monastery where mentally sick peasants come for spiritual healing as an allegorical 'picture of a man's life', she writes that 'the place itself spells out an argument: that life, painful as it is, is not too painful for the endurance of the mind . . . It presents that argument in a series of symbols' – that is, features of the landscape, which she interprets as she describes them (2, pp. 119–20). The passage is a brilliant exercise in presenting interpretation as fact. Yet it is these interpretations which constitute her own artistry, as when she transforms the brief note 'Beautiful woman in porch' at Easter Mass in Skopje (entry for 1 May) into a brilliantly visualized portrait of a peasant woman (2, p. 6):

She was the very essence of Macedonia, was exactly what I had come back to see. She was the age that all Macedonian women seem to become as soon as they cease to be girls: a weather-beaten fifty. There was a dark cloth about her hair and shoulders, and in its folds, and in her noble bones and pain-grooved flesh, she was like many Byzantine Madonnas to be seen in frescoes and mosaics. In her rough hand she mothered her taper, looking down on its flame as if it were a young living thing; and on the sleeve of her russet sheepskin jacket there showed an embroidery of stylized red and black trees which derived recognizably from a pattern designed for elegant Persian women two thousand years before. There was the miracle of Macedonia, made visible before our eyes.

This unknown woman, Rebecca West emphasizes, can never have had an easy life. The vision of 'the miracle of Macedonia' is followed by a grim account of Macedonia's miserable history of treachery, guerilla warfare and starvation (pp. 6–12).[46] And yet the woman's serenity as she nurses her candle and watches the priests is unimpaired; she might have been painted by Rembrandt. In this scene, and in hundreds of other equally vivid details and incidents, Rebecca West turns her own often messy, painful experience into a work of art which insists that, against all the odds, 'death may last five hundred years yet not be death' (2, p. 13).

Notes

INTRODUCTION

1 See Jameson, *Journey from the North* (Harvill, 1969, 1970), vol. 1, p. 301, on her wish to write a *roman fleuve* on the lines of Proust or Balzac.

2 Women writers are not the only ones ignored. See Andy Crofts, *Red Letter Days* (1990) for an account of the working-class writers neglected by literary historians.

3 Virginia Woolf, 'The Leaning Tower', first published in *Folios of New Writing*, November 1940, reprinted in the *Collected Essays of Virginia Woolf* (Hogarth, 1966–1967), vol. 2. The quotation is from p. 177 of the 1966 text, used for all subsequent quotations from this essay.

4 *The Devil's Decade* is the title of Claud Cockburn's history of the 1930s (Sidgwick & Jackson, 1973).

5 George Orwell, *Inside the Whale and Other Essays* (Gollancz, 1940); Richard Crossman (ed.), *The God That Failed: Six Studies in Communism* (Hamish Hamilton, 1950); Julian Symons, *The Thirties: A Dream Revolved* (Cressett Press, 1960; reprinted by Faber, 1975).

6 See Storm Jameson, *Journey from the North*, p. 291.

7 See Stephen Spender's memoir in *The God That Failed, World Within World: An Autobiography* (Hamish Hamilton, 1951) and *The Temple* (Faber, 1990); Christopher Isherwood, *Lions and Shadows* (Hogarth, 1938), *Kathleen and Frank* (Methuen, 1971) and *Christopher and his Kind* (1977).

8 *Black Lamb and Grey Falcon* was first published in the USA by Viking in New York, 1941. The first English edition was published by Macmillan in 1942.

9 Volume 1 of *Black Lamb* follows Rebecca West's travel-diary very closely. Volume 2's relation to the diary is looser. (See pp. 209–15 for a full discussion of the relation between the book and the diary.)

10 West, *Black Lamb and Grey Falcon*, vol. 1, p. v; vol. 2, p. 532.

11 Eric Hobsbawm, *The Age of Extremes: The Short Twentieth Century* (Michael Joseph, 1994), p. 6.

12 In 1992, the Miners' March for Jobs followed the route taken by the Jarrow Hunger Marchers in 1933 and 1934. So did the earlier People's March for Jobs in 1984. The Right to Work march in 1979 used the slogan 'No Return to the Thirties!'

13   The accusation of 'appeasement' was successfully used by Michael Heseltine to discredit both the Campaign for Nuclear Disarmament and the Labour Party (whose policies then endorsed CND). The accusation certainly contributed to Labour's defeat in the 1987 General Election.

Analogies are often made by journalists between Bosnia in the 1990s and the Munich settlement in 1938. See the article 'Another War, Another Word' by Robert Fisk, which quotes an episode from *The Rise and Fall of the Third Reich* to illustrate the West's indifference to the fate of Bosnia (*Independent*, 7 February 1994, p. 12); also the front page of the 'Outlook' section of the *Guardian*, Saturday 15 July 1995, which features a Rowson pastiche of Picasso's painting *Guernica* adapted for the fall of Srebrenica, and an article by Ed Vulliamy comparing 'ethnic cleansing' with Hitler's Fascism.

14   The first edition of Nancy Cunard's *Negro: An Anthology* (Wishart, 1934) is a rare book, unobtainable in Washington, DC, where this book was drafted. (The Library of Congress, surprisingly, has no copy.) Hugh Ford's 1970 reprint (New York, F. Ungar) is easy to get hold of, but it abridges Cunard's 1000-page original.

1   REMEMBERING THE THIRTIES

1   Walter Benjamin, *One-Way Street* (1979), p. 314.

2   See Christopher Isherwood, *Christopher and his Kind* (Cape, 1976); Edward Upward, *The Spiral Ascent* (Heinemann, 1977); W. H. Auden's ballad 'Sue' (c. 1937, published by Sycamore Press in 1977), his discursive poem 'In the Year of my Youth' (c. 1933), ed. Lucy MacDiarmid, published in the *Review of English Studies* 28 (15), 1978, pp. 281–309, and the early collaborations with Isherwood: 'Enemies of a Bishop', 'The Chase' and 'The Fronny' in *The Complete Works of W. H. Auden*, ed. E. Mendelson (Princeton University Press, 1988), and Stephen Spender's novel *The Temple* (Faber, 1990). The collection of Auden's writings *The English Auden* (Faber, 1977) also prints some previously unpublished poems, including two love-sonnets (pp. 147–8, 149–50) and the autobiographical 'Passenger Shanty' (pp. 233–4).

In the 1970s and 1980s, Virago reprinted a host of mid-century women writers in the 'Modern Classics' series, which helped to transform standard perceptions of twentieth-century writing. The Feminist Press in New York published the dystopian writer Katharine Burdekin's *The End of This Day's Business* (c. 1935) in 1989, as well as reprinting her *Swastika Night* (Gollancz, 1937) in 1985. Valentine Cunningham's anthologies *The Penguin Book of Spanish Civil War Verse* and *Spanish Front* (1980) have also put a lot of previously obscure work back into print.

3   Kathleen Raine's reprinted *Autobiographies*, David Gascoyne's *Collected Journals 1936–1937*, Michael Hamburger's *String of Beginnings: Intermittent Memoirs 1924–54* were all published by Skoob Books in 1991 (Gascoyne previously published by Enitharmon Press, 1980), and Vernon Scannell's *Drums of Morning: Growing Up in the Thirties* appeared in 1992 (Robson Books).

4   Francis Scarfe's *Auden and After* (1941), the first book-length account of the (male) poets of the 1930s, is predated by Orwell's 'Inside the Whale' (title essay of a collection published in March 1940: see Bernard Crick, *George*

Orwell, p. 384) and by Virginia Woolf's lecture 'The Leaning Tower', delivered to the Brighton WEA on 27 April 1940 and published in *Folios of New Writing* in November the same year (*Diaries of Virginia Woolf*, ed. Bell and McNeillie, vol. 5, 1984, pp. 258, 339). C. Day Lewis' *A Hope for Poetry* (1934) might possibly be claimed as the first account of the poetry of the thirties; its argument, however, firmly identifies the contemporary poets it deals with as post-war, not as the product of a decade.

5   See Noreen Branson and Margot Heinemann, *Britain in the Nineteen Thirties* (1971), chapters 1–9, pp. 1–65 and A. J. P. Taylor, 'The Nation Saved: Economic Affairs 1931–3', *English History 1914–1945* (Oxford, 1965), pp. 400–34.

6   Lewis A. Coser in the Introduction to Maurice Halbwachs' *On Collective Memory* (1939; translated and reissued by Chicago University Press, 1992), pp. 6–7.

7   Halbwachs, *op. cit.*, pp. 39–40, 169.

8   Coser, *op. cit.*, p. 22.

9   E. P. Thompson, *The Poverty of Theory* (1978), p. 342.

10   See Virginia Woolf, *Moments of Being* (1976), pp. 139–99.

11   Rebecca West, *Black Lamb and Grey Falcon*, 2 vols (Macmillan, 1942), vol. 1, pp. 530–1. The analogy comes from her 1937 travel diary: 'Dramatisation of failure – might serve for unemployed man from Jarrow, miner from South Wales . . . Mystery of death, of failure, made manifest' (entry for 28 April).

12   Claud Cockburn, *I, Claud* (Penguin, 1967), p. 208.

13   E. R. Gedye, *Fallen Bastions*, pp. 113 and 422; Paul Fussell, *The Great War and Modern Memory* (Oxford, 1975). For the effects of the War on English culture, see especially Fussell's first chapter, 'A Satire of Circumstance' and the last, 'Persistence and Memory'.

14   Virginia Woolf, 'The Leaning Tower' (1940), reprinted in Woolf's *Collected Essays* (1966), vol. 2, p. 177, identified in these notes as *LT*. All subsequent references are from this text.

15   See Orwell, *Collected Essays, Journalism and Letters of George Orwell*, ed. Sonia Orwell (1967), vol. 1, pp. 194–242 (identified in these notes as *CEJL*); Christopher Sykes, *Four Studies in Loyalty* (1948); Isherwood, *Christopher and his Kind* (Methuen, 1977), identified in these notes as *CK*.

16   See Julian Symons, *The Thirties: A Dream Revolved* (Faber, 1975), pp. 113–120, and Samuel Hynes, *The Auden Generation*, p. 176.

17   Stephen Spender, 'The Funeral', in *New Signatures*, ed. Michael Roberts (Hogarth, 1932), p. 95.

18   Woolf identifies the writers as 'Day Lewis, Auden, Spender, Isherwood, Louis MacNeice and so on' (*LT*, 1966, p. 170). Orwell's list is longer: 'Auden, Spender, Day-Lewis, MacNeice, and . . . a long string of writers of more or less the same tendency, Isherwood, John Lehmann, Arthur Calder-Marshall, Edward Upward, Alec Brown, Philip Henderson, and many others' (*CEJL*, vol. 2, p. 511).

19   Samuel Hynes criticizes Virginia Woolf for her factitious self-identification with her WEA audience in 'The Leaning Tower' (*The Auden Generation*, 1976; identified in these notes as *AG*, p. 393). The justice of this attack is confirmed by the publication of Woolf's diaries, in which she expresses dislike of being 'smeared by the village & W.E.A. mind' (entry for 29 May 1940, *The Diaries of*

Virginia Woolf, eds Bell and McNeillie, 1984, vol. 5, 1936–1941, p. 288). Hynes also criticizes Orwell's arguments in 'Inside the Whale' (*AG*, pp. 486–8), but doesn't mention the way Orwell ignores his own educational privilege when attacking public-school writers.

20   A train arrives at a station. A little boy and a little girl, brother and sister, are seated in a compartment face to face, next to the window through which the buildings along the station platform can be seen passing as the train pulls to a stop. 'Look,' says the brother, 'we're at Ladies!'; 'Idiot!' replies his sister, 'can't you see we're at Gentlemen?'
> (Lacan, 'The Agency of the Letter in the Unconscious',
> translated and collected in *Écrits: A Selection*, ed. Alan Sheridan
> (London, Tavistock, 1977), p. 152)

21   See *Spain 1937* in *The English Auden*, ed. Mendelson (1977), p. 211: 'As the poet whispers, startled among the pines/ Or, where the loose waterfall sings, compact, or upright/ On the crag by the leaning tower'.

22   Samuel Hynes, *AG*, p. 393.

23   Virginia Woolf, *A Room of One's Own* (Hogarth, 1929), p. 99.

24   Orwell, *The Road to Wigan Pier*, p. 35.

25   'I was *not* excusing totalitarian crimes but only saying what, surely, every decent person thinks if he finds himself unable to accept the absolute pacifist position' (W. H. Auden in a letter to Monroe K. Spears, 11 May 1963, quoted in Monroe K. Spears, *The Poetry of W. H. Auden*, New York, Oxford University Press, 1963, p. 157).

26   The line cited, 'You're leaving now and it's up to you boys' (Orwell, *CEJL*, vol. 1, p. 511) is the first line of poem 10 of Day Lewis' *The Magnetic Mountain*. A wartime broadcast about contemporary poetry is also careless, alluding to 'Auden's "September 1941" ' (Orwell, *CEJL*, vol. 3, p. 329), which presumably means '1 September 1939'.

27   'At the outset [of the war] Auden had the feeling that life could not be carried on without some kind of union with the Party. So he came out to Spain . . . ' (Claud Cockburn, interviewed in *The Review*, 11–12, 1964, p. 3).
       For the publishing history of Auden's *Spain 1937* in pamphlet form, see Bloomfield and Mendelson, *W. H. Auden: A Bibliography* (University of Virginia Press, 1972), pp. 28–29.

28   Bernard Bergonzi, *Reading the Thirties* (1978), p. 54.

29   I would also add to this list Naomi Mitchison's *Blood of the Martyrs* and Jack Lindsay's *1649* (published in 1939 and 1938 respectively), together with E. R. Gedye's *Fallen Bastions* (1939).

30   See Naomi Mitchison's memoir *You May Well Ask*, 1979, pp. 194–195, for a brief account of her undercover work for Viennese Socialists in 1934, helping political refugees to escape the country and smuggling documents. Storm Jameson, as President of the English PEN Club, worked indefatigably from the late Thirties to help refugee writers (Mitchison, *Among You Taking Notes*, p. 142).

31   Isherwood, *CK*, pp. 124–5, 209; Spender, *World Within World* (1955), pp. 191–205.

32   E. P. Thompson, 'Outside the Whale', collected in *The Poverty of Theory* (1978), pp. 1–33; Andy Crofts, *Red Letter Days*, pp. 17–29.

33　Richard Crossman (ed.), *The God That Failed: Six Studies in Communism* (1950), p. 7.

34　Julian Symons, *The Thirties: A Dream Revolved* (Faber, 1975), p. 40. The quotations from bad or naive left-wing writers are to be found on pp. 26, 67, 74, 102 and 132.

35　Donald Davie's 'Remembering the Thirties' was first published in the collection *Brides of Reason* (1955) and reprinted in *Collected Poems, 1950–1970* (Routledge & Kegan Paul, 1972), pp. 20.

36　Hynes, *AG*, pp. 14–15.

37　Storm Jameson, *Journey from the North* (Harvill, 1969, 1970), vol. 1, p. 142.

38　Robert Graves and Alan Hodge, *The Long Week-End* (1940), pp. 200–1.

39　Richard Johnstone, *The Will to Believe: Novelists of the Nineteen-Thirties* (Oxford University Press, 1922), pp. 20–1.

40　Robin Skelton, Introduction to *Poetry of the Thirties* (1964), pp. 14–15; Julian Symons, *The Thirties*, pp. 114, 127–8.

41　Stevie Smith and Jean Rhys are also mentioned in the chapter about travel-writing, 'Seedy Margins' (*British Writers of the Thirties*, pp. 341–76).

42　See Francis Barker et al. (eds) *1936: The Sociology of Literature*, vol. 1, *The Politics of Modernism* and vol. 2, *Practices of Literature and Politics*, published 1979, a year after the conference at Essex University on the theme '1936' (contains essays on Woolf and Dorothy Richardson in vol. 2, but no other discussion of women writers); Janet Batsleer, Tony Davies and Rebecca O'Rourke, *Rewriting English* (1985); Adrian Caesar, *Dividing Lines: Poetry, Class and Ideology in the 1930s* (1991; discusses Kathleen Raine, but no other woman poet); Jon Clark, Margot Heinemann, David Margolies and Carol Snee, *Culture and Crisis in Britain in the 1930s* (Lawrence & Wishart, 1979; contains Peter Widdowson's discussion of Virginia Woolf on pp. 136–42 of his excellent essay 'Between the Acts? English Fiction in the Thirties', but mentions no other woman writer); Andy Crofts, *Red Letter Days* (1990); Frank Glover-Smith (ed.), *Class, Culture and Social Change: A New View of the 1930s* (Harvester, 1980; discusses no woman writer); John Lucas (ed.), *The 1930s: A Challenge to Orthodoxy* (1978; discusses no woman writer); Alick West, *Crisis and Criticism* (1975; discusses no woman writer).

43　Rachel Blau DuPlessis, *Writing Beyond the Ending* (Indiana University Press, 1985); Jane Miller, *Women Writing About Men* (Virago, 1986); Shari Benstock, *Women Writers of the Left Bank, Paris 1900–1940*, (University of Texas Press, 1986); Jane Marcus, *Virginia Woolf and the Languages of Patriarchy* (University of Indiana Press, 1987); Sandra Gilbert and Susan Gubar, *No Man's Land: The Place of the Woman Writer in the Twentieth Century* (Princeton University Press, 1988–1994, 3 vols); Maroula Joannou, *'Ladies Please Don't Smash These Windows': Women's Writing, Feminist Consciousness and Social Change* (1995).

　　More specialist feminist books include Jean Kennard's study of Vera Brittain and Winifred Holtby in *A Writing Partnership* (University Press of New England, 1989), and Susan Leonardi's elegantly written study of the 'Somerville novelists', *Dangerous by Degrees* (University of Indiana Press, 1990).

44　Alison Light, *Forever England: Femininity, Literature and Conservatism Between the Wars* (Routledge, 1991), pp. 113–35.

45　This assumption was still more widespread in the thirties. Reviewing for the *New Statesman* in August 1939, Anthony West attacked women's novels for being boringly obsessed with personal feelings; he was supported by Cyril Joad (Jill Benton, *Naomi Mitchison*, 1990, p. 113).

46   1930s titles by Bowen, Brittain, Burdekin, Llewellyn Davies, Holtby, Jameson, Lehmann, Milner, Mitchison, Richardson, Smith, Stead, Townsend Warner, West and White have been reprinted by Virago. Three of Katharine Burdekin's books were reissued by the Feminist Press in New York.

47   To give chapter and verse about the omission of women: Julian Symons' *The Thirties* mentions none of these names, and nor do Richard Johnstone's *The Will to Believe: Novelists of the Nineteen-Thirties* (Oxford University Press, 1986), Bernard Bergonzi's *Reading the Thirties* (1978) or Frank Kermode's *History and Value* (1988). Samuel Hynes mentions Storm Jameson for her essay on realism (*AG*, pp. 270–3) but ignores her novels and memoirs. Martin Green discusses Cunard herself as a 'Harlequin' figure and mentions *Negro*'s inclusion of Harold Acton and Norman Douglas as contributors (*Children of the Sun*, pp. 330–1), but does not otherwise discuss the anthology. Valentine Cunningham (*British Writers of the Thirties*, 1988) mentions most of the names on this list apart from Burdekin, Benson, Llewellyn Davies, Stark and West, but gives sustained attention only to Bowen. Paul Fussell's study of inter-war travel writers, *Abroad* (1980), does quote Rebecca West once (p. 12) but discusses no women travel writers at all.

Two admirable exceptions to this rule of neglect are John Gindin's recent *British Fiction of the 1930s* (Macmillan, 1992) and Andy Crofts' *Red Letter Days: British Fiction in the 1930s* (1990), which, despite their titles, cover very different terrain.

48   See Orwell, *The Road to Wigan Pier*, p. 206. Julian Symons sneers at Sylvia Townsend Warner and Edith Sitwell in *The Thirties: A Dream Revolved* (pp. 114 and 127); see also his plain statement, published elsewhere, that women are not the intellectual equals of men (Symons, *A. J. A. Symons: His Life and Speculations*, Eyre and Spottiswoode, 1950, p. 54). Frank Kermode's otherwise generous and sympathetic study of the bourgeois English writers of the 1930s mentions no woman writer, and its final chapter sets up feminist anti-racism as an intellectual Aunt Sally (pp. 114–15, 126). His review of Sylvia Townsend Warner's diaries in the *London Review of Books* (8 July 1994) had a distinctly grudging tone, as did Bergonzi seconding him (letters page, 22 July 1994).

49   Q. D. Leavis, 'Lady Novelists and the Lower Orders,' *Scrutiny* 4(2), September 1935: 112–32; 'Dustier and Dustier' (review of Rosamond Lehmann's *The Weather in the Streets*), *Scrutiny* 5(2), September 1936: 183–5; 'Caterpillars of the Commonweath, Unite!' (review of Virginia Woolf's *Three Guineas*), *Scrutiny* 6(12), July 1938: 203–14. Q. D. Leavis' dismissive judgements have been endorsed by Valentine Cunningham (*British Writers of the Thirties*, p. 247), and by Martin Green, who sees her as a necessary corrective to the cosy literary cliques by whom 'the women writers... in particular were heavily overpraised' (*Children of the Sun*, p. 404).

50   Francis Scarfe, epigraph to *Auden and After*, 1941, p. v.

51   See Michael Roberts, *New Country* (Hogarth, 1933), C. Day Lewis, *A Hope for Poetry* (1934), Louis MacNeice *Modern Poetry* (1938) and Cyril Connolly *Enemies of Promise* (1938).

52   See Louis MacNeice, *Modern Poetry* (1938), p. 152, on the 'virile efficiency' of good poetry, and Herbert Read praising Auden for being 'observant, witty

and masculine' in the Auden Double Number of *New Verse* 26–7, November 1938: 28.

53   See Hynes, *AG*, pp. 11, 14–15; Skelton, *Poetry of the Thirties*, p. 14, for the dating of the 'thirties generation'.

For an excellent account of the literary achievements of working-class writers in the 1930s, see Andy Crofts, *op. cit.*

54   Naomi Mitchison, 'To Some Young Communists from an Old Socialist', *New Verse* 1(1), May 1933: 9. This is the only poem Mitchison published in *New Verse*, which rapidly became the house journal of the Auden Group. Jane Dowson writes in *Into the Whirlwind* (Routledge, 1995) that her poem was written in response to Auden's poem 'A Communist to Others'.

55   Virginia Woolf, *Three Guineas* (1938), p. 3.

56   Distinguished American women writers who were also college alumnae include Marianne Moore, Mary McCarthy and Elizabeth Bishop (Vassar), Gertrude Stein (Johns Hopkins), H.D. (Bryn Mawr), Lillian Hellman (New York University), Laura Riding (Cornell), and Edna St Vincent Millay (Barnard College and Vassar). It is hard to believe that these women's access to higher education did not influence their impressive ambitions and achievements.

57   Claud Cockburn, *I, Claud* (1967), p. 187.

58

INTERVIEWER: Did your political commitments affect the reception of your work?

STW: 'Oh, it affected it very badly. I usually had two or three amazingly good reviews, but I never had reviews from the sort of reviewers that sell books

(Sylvia Townsend Warner in conversation', *PN Review* 26, November–December 1981: 35–6)

59   W. H. Auden, quoted in Skelton, *op. cit.*, p. 41. Auden's editing of his early poems is a complicated story, not yet untangled. For details of the alterations and omissions in Auden's *Collected Shorter Poems 1927–1957* (published by Faber in 1944 and revised again in the subsequent 1966 edition), see B. C. Bloomfield and Edward Mendelson, *W. H. Auden: A Bibliography, 1924–1969* (1964, revised University Press of Virginia, 1972).

60   Spender borrowed this pseudonym from Isherwood, who called Upward 'Chalmers' in the thinly fictionalized memoir, *Lions and Shadows* (1938).

61   Sylvia Townsend Warner, letter to Steven Clark, 6.ix.37, published in her *Selected Letters*, ed. William Maxwell (1982), p. 47, and Claud Cockburn, *I, Claud*, p. 168.

For alternative accounts of Warner and Koltzov, see Corpus Barga, quoted in Claire Harman's biography *Sylvia Townsend Warner*, pp. 162–3, describing STW in Spain comforting a weeping refugee, and the affectionate portrait of Koltzov in Claud Cockburn, *op. cit.*, pp. 168–76.

62   Isherwood, *Kathleen and Frank* (1971), pp. 200ff.

63   Sarah Caudwell (Sarah Cockburn), *New Statesman*, 28 October 1986, pp. 3–4.

64   Rebecca West, *Black Lamb and Grey Falcon* (1942), vol. 2, p. 382. For Vinaver's wartime experiences, see Victoria Glendinning, *Rebecca West* (1987), p. 156.

65   Edward Upward, letter to Janet Montefiore, 2 October 1988.

66   Robin Skelton, *op. cit.*, p. 41.

67 *The Spiral Ascent* retells the anecdote of the butter fight in 'Chalmers' rooms, told in *Lions and Shadows* (1938), pp. 115–16, from the point of view of the victim (Upward, pp. 672–7). The letter from the undergraduate 'Chalmers' – 'If school was unmitigated hell, Cambridge is insidious...' – which Isherwood quotes on p. 72 of *Lions and Shadows* reappears on p. 661. And so on.

68 Edward Upward, *Journey to the Border* (Penguin reprint, 1969), p. 201.

69 Upward, *The Spiral Ascent* (1977), p. 98.

70 'Alan completes his poem as the book ends; thus sharing with a beautiful coda, at last synthesising poetry and communism' (Frank Kermode, *History and Value*, 1988, p. 57).

71 Claud Cockburn, *I, Claud*, p. 70; Storm Jameson, *Journey from the North*, vol. 1, p. 293.

72 Claud Cockburn originally produced three volumes of memoirs: *In Time of Trouble* (Hart-Davis, 1956), *Crossing the Line* (MacGibbon & Kee, 1958) and *View from the West* (MacGibbon & Kee, 1961). These were edited, condensed and brought up to date in his one-volume *I, Claud*, published by Penguin Books in 1967, which is the best version of Cockburn's memoirs. (There is also the late *Cockburn Sums Up*, Weidenfeld and Nicholson, 1980, really a potboiler, which cuts the original heavily, to leave space for a 15,000 word coda.)

73 See T. C. Worsley, *Flannelled Fool* (Alan Ross, 1967; reissued by Hogarth, 1990); Ralph Glasser, *Growing Up in the Gorbals* (Chatto and Windus, 1987) and *A Gorbals Boy at Oxford* (Chatto and Windus, 1988); Kathleen Dayus, *Her People* (1982), *While There's Life* (1985), *All my Days* (1988), *The Best of Times* (1991; all Virago); Helen Forrester, *Twopence to Cross the Mersey* (Cape, 1974), *Minerva's Stepchild* (Bodley Head, 1979); Hilda Hollingsworth, *They Tied a Label to my Coat* (Virago, 1991, published in the US as *Places of Greater Safety*); Margaret Llewellyn Davies (ed.), *Life as We Have Known It, by Co-operative Working Women*, introduced by Virginia Woolf (Hogarth, 1931; reissued by Virago, 1977).

74 J. B. Priestley, *English Journey* (Heinemann/Gollancz, 1934), pp. 235–50; Edwin Muir, *Scottish Journey* (Heinemann/Gollancz, 1935), pp. 100–62.

75 Speaking at Georgetown University in November 1993, Hilda Murrell explained that her memoir of her experiences as an evacuee was deliberately written as if by a child. She originally wrote it to entertain her husband when he was having a nervous breakdown; and because he was a teacher at a primary school, she thought that writing from a child's point of view would best hold his interest (which it did).

76 See Jameson, *JN*, vol. 1, p. 344. Naomi Mitchison records talking in February 1942 to 'Storm Jameson, extremely gloomy, owing to having dealt with refugees, especially Jews, since 1937 about', Dorothy Sheridan (ed.), *Among You Taking Notes* (Gollancz, 1985), p. 184.

77 See Jameson, *JN*, vol. 1, pp. 292–3; Cockburn, *I, Claud*, pp. 207–11.
The question 'What could I have done ?' is the refrain of Kipling's deceptively simple book *Rewards and Fairies* (Macmillan, 1905). Kipling's stories are almost all about the hard choices which kings, citizens and even a Stone Age shepherd had to make for the good of England.

78 Cockburn, *op. cit.*, p. 185. At his trial in 1945, Otto Katz 'confessed' that he had been recruited by 'Colonel Claud Cockburn' into British Intelligence.

Learning Resources
Centre

No evidence was ever produced to confirm this story, which appears to be a fiction produced to satisfy the Soviet inquisitors.

79 See Isherwood, *CK*, pp. 62–3; also Gerald Hamilton, *Mr Norris and I* (Cape, 1955).

80 Julian Symons, *The Thirties*, pp. 118–19.

81 Richard Cockett, *Twilight of Truth: Chamberlain, Appeasement and the Manipulation of the Press* (Weidenfeld and Nicholson, 1989), pp. 84–120.

82 *Ibid.*, p. 65.

83 *Ibid.*, p. 38.

84 Lucy Boston's *Memory in a House* and *Perverse and Foolish* (1979) were published by Bodley Head in 1974, 1979 and collected in the posthumous and privately published one-volume *Memories* (Colt Books, 1992).

Born in 1892, she was almost exactly the same age as Storm Jameson (b. 1891). Coincidentally, these women spent their long old age near one another: Lucy Boston lived from 1939 to 1990 in the Manor House, Hemingford Grey, the original of her well-known 'Green Knowe' books for children, while Storm Jameson spent her old age in Cambridge, twelve miles away. I have no evidence, however, that they ever met.

85 Jameson caricatured Rebecca West viciously in her novel *A Cup of Tea for Mr Thorgill* (Macmillan, 1957) as 'Retta Spencer-Savage' who calls herself 'Athene', a celebrated anti-Communist writer with 'yellow sagging jowls' (p. 7), who has capitalized on an early illicit liaison with a famous man, successfully passing off second-rate writing as masterpieces of tragic insight. Storm Jameson, who habitually recycled her own prose, used the same phrase to describe the 'yellow sagging jowls of a celebrated woman writer' seen at Rose Macaulay's memorial service (*JN*, vol. 2, p. 352). This description can only have meant Rebecca West, the only candidate distinguished, elderly and plump enough to fit it.

The principal cause of this hostility seems to be Jameson's envy of Rebecca West for successfully taking the chance which she herself refused. As she bitterly relates in her autobiography, she yielded to her mother's pressure to refuse a job on Harriet Weaver's *Egoist* after taking her degree ('It's not as if you had a husband to go to'). The post, and with it the opportunity of an early success in London, went to 'Miss Rebecca West' (*JN*, 1969, pp. 78–9), who never looked back.

86 Storm Jameson, *That Was Yesterday* (Heinemann, 1930); *No Time Like the Present* (memoir; 1932), *Company Parade* (1934), *Love in Winter* (1935), *None Turn Back* (1936) were all published by Cassell.

87 Storm Jameson, *JN*, vol. 1, pp. 373–81, 394–402; *Europe to Let* (Macmillan, 1940), pp. 142–7 and 215–23. The post-war scenes in Poland, described in *JN*, vol. 2, pp. 174–97, likewise recycle identical material from the novel *The Black Laurel* (1947).

2 THE PRAM IN THE HALL: MEN AND WOMEN WRITING THE SELF IN THE 1930s

1 W. H. Auden, 'Letter to Lord Byron', part 4, *Letters from Iceland* (1937), p. 201; Stevie Smith, *Over the Frontier* (Cape, 1938), p. 70.

2   See also Jan Montefiore, 'Case-Histories Versus the Undeliberate Dream', in *Difference in View*, ed. Gabriele Griffin (Taylor & Francis, 1994), which forms the basis of this chapter – with considerable modifications, since I have now come to question its central premise.

3   Christopher Isherwood, *Lions and Shadows* (Hogarth, 1938), p. 7.

4   Virginia Woolf, 'The Leaning Tower', *Collected Essays* (1966–1967), vol. 2., p. 177.

5   Louis MacNeice, 'My Case-Book', *Modern Poetry* (1938), part 1, pp. 31–74; Cyril Connolly, 'A Georgian Boyhood', *Enemies of Promise* (1938), part 3, pp. 185–337; Orwell, *The Road to Wigan Pier* (1936), chapters 8 and 9, pp. 156–85,; Graham Greene, *The Lawless Roads* (1939), pp. 1–12; W. H. Auden and Louis MacNeice, *Letters from Iceland* (1937), pp. 201–216; Louis MacNeice, *Autumn Journal (1939), cantos 6–10, pp. 26–43*.

6   MacNeice, *Modern Poetry*, pp. 37–9; Connolly, *Enemies of Promise*, p. 189; Orwell, *The Road to Wigan Pier*, p. 156.

7   The 'Auden Generation' writers whom I discuss here were educated at, respectively, Berkhamstead and Oxford (Greene), Eton (Orwell), Eton and Oxford (Connolly), Gresham's Holt and Oxford (Auden), Marlborough and Oxford (MacNeice), Repton and Cambridge (Isherwood and Upward).

8   Virginia Woolf, *A Room of One's Own* (1929), pp. 26–37, 161–2, and *Three Guineas* (1938), pp. 9–14, on the educational deprivation of middle-class girls; Virginia Woolf, 'The Leaning Tower', *Collected Essays*, p. 169.

9   Julian Symons, *The Thirties: A Dream Revolved*, pp. 34–8; Bernard Bergonzi, *Reading the Thirties*, pp. 10–27.

10 Michael Roberts, Introduction to *New Country* (1933): 9.

11 Robin Skelton makes this point in his Introduction to *Poetry of the Thirties*, p. 15.

12 Samuel Hynes, *The Auden Generation*, p. 9.

13 Greene uses precisely the same adaptation of Wordsworth's line 'Heaven lies about us in our infancy' in evoking the deprived childhood of the boy Pinkie in a Brighton slum: 'Hell lay about him in his infancy', *Brighton Rock* (1938), p. 88.

14 W. H. Auden, 'Sir, no man's enemy', *Poems* (1933 reprint), p. 89.

15 See Isherwood, *Lions and Shadows*, pp. 35, 69, 79, 95, 115, 138, 304 and 305.

16 Virginia Woolf, 'The Leaning Tower', *Collected Essays*, p. 177.

17 See Stephen Spender *World Within World* (1951; Readers Union reprint, 1955), p. 3; Sean Day-Lewis, *C. Day-Lewis: A Biography* (Weidenfeld and Nicholson, 1980), p. 5 and J. Stallworthy, *Louis MacNeice*, pp. 36–9, on Lily MacNeice's mental illness and departure for mental hospital when her son Louis was seven, after which he never saw her again (she died in hospital in 1914).

    For Auden's response to the wartime loss of his father, see Humphrey Carpenter's *W. H. Auden* (1981), pp. 20–1; for Cyril Connolly's early exile from home and the breakup of his parents' marriage, see Clive Fisher, *Cyril Connolly* (1995), pp. 12 and 20.

18 Isherwood, *Christopher and his Kind*, p. 10.

19 Beatrix Campbell, *Wigan Pier Revisited* (Virago, 1984), p. 99. For a subtle analysis of the sexual attraction felt by bourgeois men towards the workers'

'otherness', see Frank Kermode, 'On the Frontier', chapter 2 of *History and Value* (1988), pp. 22–32.

20   Heppenstall, writing to Sir Richard Rees, 29 April 1936. Quoted by Richard Davenport-Hines in *Auden* (Weidenfeld and Nicholson, 1995), p. 166.

21   MacNeice, *Autumn Journal* (1939), p. 49. The writer's First Class in 'Lit. Hum.' (Literae Humaniores; aka Ancient History and Philosophy) in 1929 did indeed get him an immediate appointment as a lecturer in Classics at Birmingham University. See MacNeice, *The Strings Are False* (1965), p. 128.

22   Virginia Woolf, 'The Leaning Tower', *Collected Essays*, pp. 172, 175.

23   I am not aware of any existing account of the post-war psychology of the working-class men who were too young to fight in the First World War. I think that the 'Test' was probably a middle-class obsession, but in the absence of any data about working-class men, this can only be guesswork.

24   See Beatrix Campbell, *Wigan Pier Revisited*, pp. 99–103.

25   The women writers named in Connolly's 'production chart' of Modernist writing from 1923 to 1932 are, in alphabetical order: Elizabeth Bowen, Willa Cather, Ivy Compton-Burnett, Rosamond Lehmann, Anita Loos, Katherine Mansfield, Edith Sitwell, Gertrude Stein and Virginia Woolf.

26   Storm Jameson, *JN*, vol. 1, p. 306.

27   For knowledge of Storm Jameson's erstwhile friendship and subsequent estrangement from Vera Brittain, I am indebted to Beth Foxwell, who drew my attention to Vera Brittain's papers in the library of McMasters University, Ontario. Ms Foxwell kindly showed me photocopies of Vera Brittain's 1941 letters to Storm Jameson pleading with her to preserve their friendship, together with diary entries which mention staying with Jameson 'the night after Winifred died', which implies a close friendship. See also Paul Berry and Mark Bostridge's *Vera Brittain* (Chatto and Windus, 1995), pp. 413–15; also p. 249 on her acquaintance with Naomi Mitchison.

For Storm Jameson's attitude to Rebecca West, see Jameson, *JN*, vol. 2, p. 352. For her friendship with Naomi Mitchison, see the latter's *Among You Taking Notes* (1985), p. 114.

28   Jean Kennard, *Vera Brittain and Winifred Holtby: A Working Partnership* (New England Press, 1989), pp. 187–8.

29   The Rathbone and Zenna Smith novels have been republished in London by Virago (1986), and in New York by the Feminist Press with Afterwords by Jane Marcus, who makes an eloquent case for the importance of Helen Zenna Smith's *Not So Quiet . . . .* Mary Borden's *The Forbidden Zone* (1929) and Enid Bagnold's spare, haunting *Diary Without Dates* (1918), are out of print, probably because they are harder to read and so more difficult to sell.

30   Storm Jameson, *No Time Like the Present* (1932), p. 101.

31   Edward Brittain died in battle, very soon after he had been detected in 'homosexual relations with the men in his company' and was therefore liable to be court-martialled (Berry and Bostridge, *Vera Brittain*, p. 133; see also pp. 128–135 on Vera Brittain's discovery of this fact after *Testament of Youth* was published.)

32   See Jean Kennard, *Vera Brittain and Winifred Holtby*, p. 177; also Berry and Bostridge, *Vera Brittain*, pp. 346–8.

33   Hervey's anger about famine in *Company Parade* (p. 190) is paralleled in *Journey from the North* (vol. 1, p. 156), as is her discovery of the compromising letters

(*Company Parade*, p. 186; *JN*, vol. 1, p. 172), and the memorial service at which she collapses (*Company Parade*, p. 261; *JN*, vol. 1, pp. 189–92). Her second husband's permanent nostalgia for army life in *Love in Winter* (pp. 64 and 354) is also paralleled in *JN* (vol. 1, p. 342).

34   Storm Jameson, *Love in Winter* (1935), p. 249; *None Turn Back* (1936), p. 37.

35   Q. D. Leavis, 'Lady Novelists and the Lower Orders', *Scrutiny* 4(2), September 1935: 112.

36   For the parallels between the novel and NM's life, see Jill Benton, *Naomi Mitchison*, pp. 81–2, 84 and 94. For NM's undercover work in Austria, see her *You May Well Ask*, pp. 193–4.
        The 'prophetic' scene of the Fascist coup in *We Have Been Warned* was not written out of experience, since 'the final chapters of the book were written before the events of summer 1933 in Germany, and before the counter-revolutions of 1934 in Austria and Spain' (Mitchison, p. v).

37   See Richard Stites, *Revolutionary Dreams: Utopian Vision and Experiment in the Russian Revolution* (Oxford University Press, 1989), pp. 111–12, and Boris Kolonitskii, ' "Revolutionary Names": Russian Political Consicousnesss in the 1920s and 1930s', *Revolutionary Russia* 6 (1993).

38   W. Shakespeare, *Macbeth* Act III, scene ii, lines 52–3; Arden edition, ed. Kenneth Muir (1972).

39   Olivia, the heroine of Rosamond Lehmann's *Invitation to the Waltz* (1932) and *The Weather in the Streets* (1936) is another such single woman, divorced and kept as an intermittent mistress by the handsome, rich and obtuse Rollo. See John Gindin's *British Fiction of the 1930s* (Macmillan, 1992) for an admirable analysis of this novel.

40   Virginia Woolf, *The Years* (1937), p. 356.

41   Peter Widdowson, in Jon Clark *et al.*, *Culture and Crisis in Britain in the 1930s*, p. 139.

42   Virginia Woolf, 'On Not Knowing Greek', *The Common Reader* (Hogarth, 1925), pp. 54 and 56.

43   Virginia Woolf, *Three Guineas* (1938), pp. 148, 303n. Maroula Joannou calls these words 'the key to understanding *Three Guineas*' (*'Ladies Please Don't Smash These Windows'*, 1995, p. 178).

44   Stevie Smith, *Novel on Yellow Paper* (1936), p. 103.

45   Bernard Bergonzi has sensitively logged the male writers' variations on the 'frontier' theme in 'Transformations of the Frontier', chapter 4 of *Reading the Thirties*, pp. 66–89.

46   See Valentine Cunningham, *British Writers of the Thirties*, p. 63.

47   The phrase is quoted from Isherwood's Foreword to the first publication of Upward's 'The Railway Accident' in *New Directions in Prose and Poetry: Number Eleven* (New York, 1949), pp. 84–116, reprinted in the Penguin Modern Classic Edition of *The Railway Accident and Other Stories* (Harmondsworth, Penguin, 1969). Isherwood's phrase occurs on p. 34 of the Penguin edition. The paradox of 'fantastic realities' is constantly cited as the 'key phrase' of Peter Widdowson's essay on British novelists in the 1930s (Widdowson, in Clark *et al.*, *Culture and Crisis in Britain in the 1930s*, pp. 134ff.).
        Readers interested in the relations between fantasy, psychoanalysis, and political reality in *Over the Frontier* should consult Lyndsey Stonebridge's subtle discussion of this text in 'Frames, Frontiers and Female Fantasies',

chapter 5 of her study of 1930s writers, *The Destruction Element* (Macmillan, forthcoming 1997), which offers fuller discussions both of Stevie Smith and Marion Milner than I attempt here.

48   This clearly alludes to the death of Philip Quarles in Huxley's *Point Counter Point* (New York, Knopf, 1928). This episode was in fact drawn from Huxley's own conversations with Naomi Mitchison, after the death by meningitis of her son Geoffrey, aged 12. See Jill Benton, *Naomi Mitchison*, p. 54.

49   W. H. Auden, 'Ode to my Pupils', *The Orators* (1932), p. 113.

50   Auden, *The Orators*, p. 108. In the American edition of his *Collected Poetry of W. H. Auden* (New York, Random House, 1945), Auden retitled this poem, appropriately enough, 'Which Side Am I Supposed to Be on?' See Justin Replogle, *Auden's Poetry* (Methuen, 1969), p. 115.

51   Shakespeare, *Macbeth*, Act III, scene ii, lines 52–3.

52   Sigmund Freud, 'The Paths to Symptom-Formation', number 23 of *New Introductory Lectures on Psychoanalysis*, trans. James Strachey, vol. 1 of the Pelican Freud Library (1973), p. 423.

53   Samuel Hynes, *The Auden Generation*, p. 319.

54   When I interviewed Edward Upward in October 1988, I asked him if this resemblance was deliberate. He said no; but he added that *The Pilgrim's Progress* was important to him from his childhood, being the first book he ever read on his own.

55   Freud, 'Paths to Symptom-Formation', p. 424.

56   Edward Upward said this to me during the interview mentioned in note 54 above.

57   Hynes, *AG*, p. 320.

58   Jan Montefiore, 'Case-Histories and Marginal Memories' in *Difference in View*, ed. Gabriele Griffin, p. 71.

59   *A Life of One's Own* received a favourable and thoughtful press, including reviews from Spender in the *Spectator*, and Auden in the *Listener*, quoted by Marion Milner in her Afterword to the 1986 Virago reprint, pp. 218–225. W. H. Auden's description of the book in his *Listener* review is quoted on p. 219 of this edition. All my other quotations from *A Life of One's Own* are taken from the first edition published by Chatto and Windus (1934).

60   Virginia Woolf, 'A great mind is androgynous', (*A Room of One's Own*, 1929, pp. 148).

61   Marion Milner, 'Afterword' to *A Life of One's Own* (Virago reprint, 1986), p. 224.

62   Marion Milner, *Experiment in Leisure* (1937; Virago reprint 1988), pp. 118–119. For a full discussion of these themes, see Lyndsey Stonebridge, 'Frames, Frontiers and Female Fantasies'.

63   Rebecca West, *Black Lamb and Grey Falcon* (1942), vol. 1, p. 1.

64   See Rebecca West, *The Strange Necessity* (Cape, 1928).

65   Both Proust and West edited their lives when they wrote about them. 'Marcel' is represented as an only child who grows up heterosexual, whereas Proust was a homosexual elder son. Similarly, RW mentions her husband and son on p. 2, without admitting that the two men are unrelated except through her. And, though she shows her husband speaking excellent German, she doesn't mention that he learned it in a German prison camp from 1914 to 1919. For more detailed discussion of her omissions, see Chapter 6.

66   Rebecca West, *Black Lamb and Grey Falcon*, vol. 2, p. 403.
67   But see Sidonie Smith, *Women's Autobiographies: Marginality and the Fictions of Selfhood* (Indiana University Press, 1991), for a contrary view.
68   See, for example, Rita Mae Brown's *Rubyfruit Jungle* (Plainfield, VT, Daughters Inc, 1973), Michele Roberts *A Piece of the Night* (The Women's Press, 1977), Lisa Alther *Kinflicks* (1978) and Jeanette Winterson, *Oranges Are Not the Only Fruit* (Pandora, 1984).
69   Valerie Walkerdine, *Schoolgirl Fictions* (Verso, 1990), Liz Stanley, *The Auto/Biographical I* (Manchester University Press, 1992).
70   See Nancy K. Miller, *Getting Personal: Feminist Occasions and Other Autobiographical Acts* (New York, Columbia University Press, 1992); Laura Marcus, *Auto/Biographical Discourse* (Manchester University Press, 1995).

3   VAMPS AND VICTIMS: IMAGES OF WOMEN IN THE LEFT-WING LITERATURE OF THE 1930S

1   Sarah Caudwell, 'Reply to Berlin', *New Statesman*, 23 October 1986, p. 4; Louis MacNeice, *Autumn Journal*, canto 15, p. 57.
2   W. H. Auden, *The Orators* (1932), p. 105; Stephen Spender, 'Oh young men, oh young comrades' in *New Signatures*, ed. Michael Roberts (1932), and *Poems* (1933), 22, p. 36; Geoffrey Grigson, Preface to *New Verse: An Anthology* (1939), p. iv.
3   C. Day Lewis, *A Hope for Poetry* (1934), p. 1.
4   Edward Lear, 'The Jumblies', *Nonsense Poems* (Frederick Warne & Co, 1985).
5   Cyril Connolly, *Enemies of Promise*, pp. 215–16.
6   See Gayatri Chakravorty Spivak, *In Other Worlds* (Methuen, 1987), Edward Said, *Culture and Imperialism* (Chatto and Windus, 1993), especially *passim*, for authoritative critiques of the imperialist assumptions underpinning conventional English literature.
7   For a full account of the Group Theatre's theories and practice, see Michael J. Sidnell, *Dances of Death: The Group Theatre of London in the Thirties* (Faber, 1984).
8   W. H. Auden's ballad 'Sue' was first published as a single poem by Sycamore Press in 1977.
9   On Isherwood's friendships with women, see *Christopher and his Kind* (1976) on his friendships with Rosamond Lehmann and Olive Mangeot (pp. 79–81); on Auden's, see Naomi Mitchison in *You May Well Ask*, 1979, pp. 63–67, Nancy Spender's memoir in the *Auden Newsletter* 10–11, September 1993: 1–3, and Thekla Clark's *Wystan and Chester: A Memoir of W. H. Auden and Chester Kallmann* (Faber, 1995).
10   W. H. Auden, final chorus of *Paid on Both Sides*, published in *Poems* (1933), p. 37; Evelyn Waugh, *Brideshead Revisited* (1945; Penguin edition 1962), p. 206.
11   Samuel Hynes, *AG*, pp. 140, 186.
12   The first, short version of *Paid on Both Sides* was written in 1928; the second, lengthened version was published in the *Criterion* in 1930. See E. Mendelson (ed.), *Plays and Other Dramatic Writings by W. H. Auden and Christopher Isherwood* (Princeton, 1988), Introduction, pp. xiii–xvi, for the textual history of *Paid on Both Sides*. The text which I use in this chapter is that printed in W. H. Auden's *Poems* (1933).

13   Mark Twain, *The Adventures of Huckleberry Finn*, chapters 17 and 18.

14   Mendelson, *op. cit.*, pp. xvi; Auden, quoted in Mendelson, p. xv.

15   Isherwood, *Lions and Shadows*, p. 193.

16   The trial of the Spy was not part of the original play, which was entirely concerned with the feud; see Mendelson, *op. cit.*, pp. 1–13, for the early text. My own account both of the play and its expressionist dream sequence leans heavily on John Fuller's excellent chapter on *Paid on Both Sides* in his *Reader's Guide to W. H. Auden* (Thames & Hudson, 1970), pp. 13–19.

17   Auden and Isherwood, *The Dog Beneath the Skin* (Faber, 1935), reprinted in Mendelson, *op. cit.*, p. 215. The Queen's Speech was written by Isherwood; but Auden maintained the theme of the female death wish against men in the immediately following Chorus in which ladies of the Court admire the handsome bodies of the dead strikers.

18   Robert Graves' *Goodbye to All That* (1928), quoted from the 1960 Penguin edition, p. 189. The text cited by Graves ends with eleven admiring tributes from *The Morning Post*, *The Gentlewoman*, *One Who Has Fought and Bled*, etc., etc. (pp. 190–191), which suggests that the 'Little Mother' was invented by the British propaganda machine. Alternatively, Graves may have written this 'typical document of the time' (p. 188) himself. Although it is described as a bestseller, I have never seen any reference to it outside Graves' autobiography.

19   Rudyard Kipling 'Common Form', from *Rudyard Kipling's Verse: Inclusive Edition 1885–1918*, vol. 2, p. 193.

20   W. H. Auden, 'To Ask the Hard Question is Simple', poem 27 in *Poems* (1933), p. 83.

21   Auden, 'Elegy on Sigmund Freud' (1939), collected in *Another Time* (1940), p. 105.
     The title of *Paid* is taken from *Beowulf*, line 1305: 'That was no good exchange, that they should pay on both sides with the lives of friends' (Mendelson, *Early Auden*, p. 42).

22   For the damaging effect of Dr Auden's absence during the War years, and for the dominating effect of Constance Auden, see H. Carpenter, *W. H. Auden: A Biography* (1981), pp. 20–1, 11–12.

23   Lucy MacDiarmid, *Auden's Apologies for Poetry* (Princeton University Press, 1990), p. 48.

24   *The Dog Beneath the Skin* (1935), reprinted in Mendelson, *Plays*, p. 282.

25   Auden and Isherwood, *The Ascent of F 6*, p. 26.

26   See Samuel Hynes, *AG*, pp. 236–41 for a full account of the notion of the 'Truly Weak Man' and the play's allusions to the life and death of T. E. Lawrence and to George Malory's death on Mount Everest.

27   For the complicated textual history of *The Ascent of F 6*, which exists in several different versions, see Mendelson's *Complete Works of W. H. Auden: Plays*. The speech and song I have quoted first appear in the second edition of the play and were included in all subsequent texts; I have taken them from Mendelson's *Plays*, p. 218. They are not in the 1937 first edition of the play.
     Mrs Ransom's song is recycled (and shortened) from Auden's early play *The Chase*, in which it is sung by a Headmaster 'Augustus Bicknell', when his beloved Olive is revealed as a boy and taken away (*Plays*, pp. 164–5). In both plays, the song thus represents denial.

28   Evelyn Waugh, *A Handful of Dust* (1934; Penguin reprint, 1951), pp. 201–4.

29   In the 1939 versions of the play, Mrs Ransom asks her son's forgiveness; in the still later 1945 version, she herself frees him from the Demon (Mendelson, *Plays*, pp. 642, 651).

30   Mendelson, *Plays*, p. 353. In the 1936 first edition, this collective patriotic outburst appears right at the end of the play, as Ransom's public epitaph (p. 123).

31   Yeats' letter is quoted in Michael Sidnell's *Dances of Death*, p. 198.
     Yeats' proposed image 'Britannia from the penny' may need some explanation to readers unfamiliar with pre-decimal coinage. The reverse side of the old British penny, in use from 1800 to 1970, showed a seated 'Britannia' holding her trident, symbolizing Britain ruling the waves.

32   Hynes, *AG*, p. 240.

33   Auden and Isherwood, *The Dog Beneath the Skin* (1935), Act I, scene i; reprinted in Mendelson's edition of Auden's *Plays*, p. 204. All subsequent references to the play are from Mendelson's text.

34   In the first printed version of the play, Mildred does not shoot Francis, confining her death-wish to telling the 'Lads of Pressan Ambo' that they are being manipulated (Mendelson, *Plays*, p. 579):

> You'll learn to kill whoever they tell you to. And you'll be trained to let yourselves be killed, too . . . I'm glad! What does it matter to me if you're all murdered? My sons were murdered, and they were bigger and stronger and handsomer than you'll ever be, any of you!

35   W. H. Auden, *The Chase*, in Mendelson, *Plays*, pp. 186–7. Unlike the liturgical parodies in Act I, scene iv and Act II, scene iv of *The Dog Beneath the Skin*, Mildred's words are authentic Holy Writ. They are verses 6, 7, 9 and 10 of Psalm 58, one of the 'cursing psalms'.

36   W. H. Auden and Christopher Isherwood, *On the Frontier* in Mendelson, *Plays*, p. 401.

37   Storm Jameson, *Company Parade* (1934), p. 261; Winifred Holtby, *South Riding* (1935; fifth reprint by Fontana/Collins, 1954), pp. 89–90.

38   Isherwood, *The Memorial* (Hogarth, 1932), p. 103.

39   Spender, *Trial of a Judge* (1938), Act II, p. 49–50.

40   W. H. Auden, 'Sue' (c. 1937; published by Sycamore Press, 1977); Orwell, *The Road to Wigan Pier* (1936), p. 18.

41   Auden, 'Sue', stanza 7; 'The Witnesses' in Mendelson, *Plays*, p. 128.

42   *The Dog Beneath the Skin*, reprinted in Mendelson, *op. cit.*, p. 271.

43   Auden, 'The Chase', reprinted in Mendelson, *op. cit.*, p. 159.

44   Louis MacNeice, *Autumn Journal* (1939), canto 22, p. 87; canto 4, p. 20; canto 11, pp. 45–50.

45   Day Lewis, *The Magnetic Mountain*, poem 18, *Collected Poems*, p. 30.

46   Winifred Holtby, *Mandoa, Mandoa!* (1933), p. 385.

47   Day Lewis, *The Magnetic Mountain*, poem 17, *Collected Poems*, p. 31.

48   Upward. *Journey to the Border* (1969), pp. 175–81.

49   John Betjeman, 'Oxford: Sudden Illness at the Bus-Stop', *Old Lights for New Chancels* (John Murray, 1940; reprinted in Betjeman's *Collected Poems*, John Murray, 1958).

50   Alison Light, *Forever England* (Routledge, 1991), pp. 11–19.

51   Cf. Betjeman's own denunciation of 'Tinned fruit, tinned meat, tinned air, tinned beans,/ Tinned minds, tinned breath' in the contemporary poem 'Slough' (*Continual Dew*, 1937, p. 4); also the typist in Eliot's *The Waste Land* who 'lays out food in tins'. Tinned food is also included, along with aspirins and bombs, in Orwell's list of modern horrors ('Inside the Whale', *CEJL*, vol. 1, p. 548).

52   A. J. Tolley, *Poetry of the Thirties* (Gollancz, 1975), p. 196.

53   See also Betjeman's early 'Death in Leamington' and 'The doctor's intellectual wife', both published in his *Continual Dew* (1937).

54   Samuel Hynes discusses Storm Jameson's essay at length in *AG*, pp. 270–3.

55   Orwell, *Road to Wigan Pier*, p. 18.

56   See my essay, 'Socialist Realism and Female Bodies', in *Paragraph* 17(1), March 1994, for a longer discussion of the stories in *Fact*. Other literary representations of working-class men acquiring class-consciousness in 1930s fiction include Lewis Grassic Gibbon's (Leslie Mitchell) *Grey Granite* (Jarrolds, 1934), part 3 of *A Scot's Quair* (published as a single volume by Hutchinson, 1946) in which the radicalization of the proletarian Bob is resisted by his girlfriend, and the less sexist story of Len, the hero of Lewis Jones' *Cwmardy: The Story of a Welsh Mining Valley* (Lawrence & Wishart, 1939) and *We Live: The Story of a Welsh Mining Valley* (Lawrence & Wishart, 1938).

57   Margery Spring Rice, *Working-Class Wives* (Penguin, 1939), pp. 105, 94.

58   See the memoirs of Kathleen Dayus (1991), Hilda Hollingsworth (1991) and Ralph Glasser (1987); also the memoirs in *Voices of Scotland Road*, David Evans (ed.) (private printing, Liverpool, 1974).

59   Allon White and Peter Stallybrass, 'Below Stairs: The Maid and the Family Romance,' in *The Poetics and Politics of Transgression* (London, Methuen, 1986), pp. 149–70.

60   Edgell Rickword, 'To the Wife of a Non-Interventionist Statesman', first published in *Left Review* 3(3), March 1938: 834–6, collected in Rickword's *Behind the Eyes: Collected Poems and Translations* (Carcanet Press, 1976).

61   Valentine Cunningham's Introduction to *The Penguin Book of Spanish Civil War Verse*, p. 71. The advert appeared in *Left Review* 3, March 1938.

62   Dylan Thomas 'The Hand That Signed a Paper' (written 1937; reprinted in Skelton, *Poetry of the Thirties*, p. 154).

63   Spender, 'The Landscape Near an Aerodrome', in *Poems*, p. 45.

64   W. H. Auden, *The Orators* (1932), p. 9.

65   W. H. Auden, 'Love had him fast', *Look, Stranger!* poem 29, p. 62. Reprinted under the title 'Meiosis' in the *Collected Shorter Poems* (1966), p. 77.

66   'Harry Semen' was first collected in Hugh MacDiarmid's *Stony Limits and Other Poems*. The text quoted here is taken from the *Selected Poems* of Hugh MacDiarmid (Penguin, 1970), ed. David Craig and John Manson, p. 88.

67   Spender, 'The Pylons', *Poems*, p. 47.

68   Spender, 'The Express', *Poems*, pp. 43.

69   Stella Gibbons, *Cold Comfort Farm* (Longman, 1932), p. 121.

70   Day Lewis, *From Feathers to Iron*, *Collected Poems*, poem 29, pp. 96. Page references in the text are for the 1935 edition.

71   The poem (*From Feathers to Iron*, *Collected Poems 1929–1933*, poem 29), also anticipates Auden's semi-comic 'Ode' to John Warner as an infant redeemer: 'Roar, Gloucestershire, do yourself proud' (Auden, 1932, pp. 97–106). Its

very 'Audenesque' phrasing and form (a six-line stanza with repeated refrain) also strongly resemble W. H. Auden's 'Prothalamion', written in 1931 (see Lucy MacDiarmid, *op. cit.*, p. 43). The refrain 'Take a whole holiday in honour of this' strongly resembles Auden's imperative 'Fill up glasses with champagne and drink again'. Day Lewis perhaps saw this poem in manuscript?

72 Hynes, *The Auden Generation*, p. 122.
73 'Woman, what have I to do with thee?', John ii, 4.
74 Cf. W. H. Auden, *The Orators* : 'All of the women and most of the men/ Shall work with their hands and not think again' (p. 105).
75 W. H. Auden, *The Orators*. See the 'Ode', 'Roar, Gloucestershire, do yourself proud', and Spender's 'Oh young men oh young comrades', poem 22 of *Poems*, p. 36. First published in *New Signatures: Poems by Several Hands* (1932), ed. Michael Roberts, p. 86.
76 This poem was first published in Michael Roberts' *New Writing* 4, Autumn 1937: 36–8.
77 John Cornford, 'Full Moon at Tierz: Before the Storming of Huesca' (1936); first published in *Left Review*, March 1937: 69–70. It is reprinted in John Cornford, *Understand the Weapon, Understand the Wound*, ed. Jonathan Galassi (1976; reprinted as *Collected Writings*, 1986, pp. 38–9).
78 MacNeice, *Autumn Journal*, part 17, p. 69.
79 From poem 10 of *Look, Stranger!* (1936, p. 29).

4 'UNDESERVEDLY FORGOTTEN': WOMEN POETS OF THE THIRTIES

1 W. H. Auden, 'Reading', *The Dyer's Hand* (Faber, 1954; reprinted by Random House, 1968), p. 10; Sylvia Townsend Warner, writing to Arnold Rattenbury in 1968, quoted in Wendy Mulford's *This Narrow Place* (Pandora, 1988), p. 3.
2 See A. J. Tolley on Raine in *The Poetry of the Thirties* (Gollancz, 1975), pp. 285–8, and Adrian Caesar, *Dividing Lines* (Manchester University Press, 1991), pp. 133–9. Raine's (comparative) visibility probably has to do with the fact that she was the only woman whose poems appeared regularly in Geoffrey Grigson's *New Verse*. Laura Riding is also mentioned respectfully by Robert Graves and Alan Hodge in *The Long Week-End* (1940), p. 200.
3 See Robin Skelton, Introduction to *Poetry of the Thirties* (Penguin, 1964), pp. 14 and 28–30.
4 Edith Sitwell, 'Aubade', *Gold Coast Customs* (Duckworth, 1929), reprinted in *Poems, New and Old* (Faber, 1940), p. 21.
5 Adrian Caesar, *Dividing Lines* (1991), p. 8. This is not really convincing; since, as this chapter shows, women poets did publish in periodicals such as the *Left Review* and the *New Statesman*. Some – for example, Stevie Smith, who published two well-received collections in 1937 and 1938 – even got good reviews.
6 *The Year's Poetry: 1936*, ed. D. Kilham Roberts and John Lehmann (John Lane, 1936) includes two STW poems: 'Some Make This Answer' and 'Song for a Street-Song' (pp. 33–5), and *Poems for Spain*, ed. S. Spender and J. Lehmann (Hogarth, 1939), includes her 'Waiting for Cerbere' and 'Benicasim'.

7   Kathleen Raine, *Stone and Flower* (Nicholson and Watson, 1943), and E. J. Scovell, *Shadows of Chrysanthemums* (Routledge, 1941).

8   See Patricia Jaffé, *Women Engravers* (Virago, 1990).

9   *Boxwood*: a collection of engravings by Reynolds Stone, 'illustrated' with poems by Sylvia Townsend Warner, published by Ruari Maclean of The Monotype Corporation (1957).

10   Readers interested in knowing more of these poets should consult Jane Dowson's anthology *Into the Whirlwind: Women's Poetry of the 1930s* (Routledge, 1996).

11   See Mitchison, Chorus from *The Fourth Pig*, p. 11; Ruth Pitter, '1938', from *A Spirit Watches* (1939; reprinted in *Urania*, Cresset Press, 1950), p. 98.

12   Sylvia Townsend Warner, 'Red Front' *Left Review*, 1(7): 255–7. Omitted by Claire Harman from STW's *Collected Poems* (Carcanet, 1982).

13   STW first came into contact with Nancy Cunard in 1937 over the latter's questionnaire 'Authors Take Sides on the Spanish War', and they later became lifelong friends: 'The bond between them about Spain was so deep, Sylvia said, that they never fell out with each other' (Wendy Mulford, *This Narrow Place*, p. 164).

14   W. H. Auden, 'Ode to John Warner', *The Orators* (1932), p. 105. See also C. Day Lewis' lines 'Men shall know their masters and women their need,/ Mating and submitting, not dividing and defying' in *The Magnetic Mountain* (Hogarth, 1933), poem 29, p. 46.

15   Martin Green has been led by these representations to type Nancy Cunard as a 'Columbine' type (a subspecies of the Dandy), classifying her with Brian Howard as examples of 'socialites . . . [who] developed left-wing views, and a recklessly aggressive and self-destructive pattern of behaviour' (Martin Green, *Children of the Sun*, 1975, p. 292). The parallel is misleading because it ignores Nancy Cunard's very considerable achievements as an editor and publisher.

16   Or so it appears from the printed dates. The 'Hours Press' Paris edition of 'Spain' is dated April 1937, the Faber edition May 1937 (B. C. Bloomfield and E. Mendelson, *W. H. Auden: A Bibliography 1924–1979*, University of Virginia Press, 1972, pp. 28–9). The bibliographers deduce from a letter to Cunard that the Faber edition came out first, but this is not certain.

17   Nancy Cunard, 'Southern Sheriff', *Negro Anthology* (1970 reprint), p. 266.

18   Nancy Cunard, 'To Eat To-Day', *New Statesman*, 1 October 1938; reprinted in Hugh D. Ford (ed.), *Nancy Cunard: Brave Poet, Indomitable Rebel* (1968), p. 177; also in Valentine Cunningham (ed.), *The Penguin Book of Spanish Civil War Verse* (1980), p. 169.

19   Pablo Neruda, 'Almeria',trans. Nancy Cunard, *Left Review*, 3 August 1937: 407, collected in Valentine Cunningham, *op. cit.*, p. 379.

20   Felix Paredes, 'Encarnaciòn Jimenez', trans. Sylvia Townsend Warner, first published in Cunningham, *op. cit.*, 289.

21   S. T. Warner, 'Benicasim' (1937; reprinted in Cunningham, *op. cit.*, p. 150 and STW's *Collected Poems*, ed. Claire Harman, 1982, p. 35).

22   Ackland, 'Instructions from England'; first published in Cunningham (1980), p. 372.

23   W. H. Auden, 'Ode'; Julian Bell, 'Arms and the Man': both in Michael Roberts (ed.), *New Signatures* (1932), pp. 23–9 and 36–47.

24 W. H. Auden, 'Here on the cropped grass of the narrow ridge I stand', *Look, Stranger!* (1936), p. 46; Day Lewis, *A Hope for Poetry* (1934), p. 14.
    Edward Upward is similarly admiring: 'Even in the vile imperialist war of 1914 there were poets. You have always felt a high admiration for the work of Wilfred Owen' (Upward, *Journey to the Border*, 1938, p. 221).

25 Spender, 'Two Armies', *The Still Centre* (1939; reprinted in Cunningham, *op. cit.*, p. 333); C. Day Lewis, poem 22 of *From Feathers to Iron* (Faber, 1932; reprinted in Day Lewis, *Collected Poems 1929–1933*, p. 88).

26 Sassoon, 'Memorial Tablet'; Wilfred Owen, 'Dulce et Decorum est' in *The Collected Poems*, ed. C. Day Lewis (Chatto and Windus, 1963), p. 55.

27 Sylvia Townsend Warner, *T. H. White* (Cape/Chatto, 1964), p. 109.

28 H. C. Engelbrecht and F. C. Haighan, *Merchants of Death: A Study of the International Armament Industry* (Routledge, 1934); Beverley Nichols, *Cry Havoc!* (Cape, 1933); Aldous Huxley, *What Are You Going to Do About It? The Case for Constructive Peace* (Chatto and Windus, 1936); C. Day Lewis, *We're Not Going to Do Nothing: A Reply to 'What Are You Going to Do About It?'* (Left Review Publications, 1936).

29 On the 1935 Peace Ballot and its subsequent diplomatic effects, see Claud Cockburn, *The Devil's Decade* (1973), pp. 132–59.

30 Virginia Woolf, diary entry for 30 September 1938, *The Diary of Virginia Woolf*, vol. 5, 1936–1941, ed. A. O. Bell and Andrew McNeillie (Hogarth, 1984), p. 177. Naomi Mitchison, entry for 29 September 1939, *Among You Taking Notes*, ed. Dorothy Sheridan (1985), p. 42. It would be extremely interesting to know how far working-class men and women shared these feelings.

31 Vera Brittain, 'To my Brother', *Poems of the War and After* (Gollancz, 1934), p. 42.

32 Winifred Holtby, 'Trains', first published in Winifred Holtby's *The Frozen Earth and other Poems* (Collins, 1935), p. 492.

33 Mary Borden figures as a name in Storm Jameson's memoirs (*JN* 1969, vol. 1, p. 204). Wyndham Lewis records staying in her house in 1914, in *Blasting and Bombardiering* (1937).
    She is also, as James Fenton pointed out to me, named in the refrain of John Betjeman's poem 'Dorset', first collected in *Continual Dew* (1937), pp. 18–19: 'While Tranter Reuben, Mary Borden, Brian Howard and Harold Acton lie in Mellstock Churchyard now'.

34 These were written during the War and first published in the *English Review* in 1917. Because they remained uncollected until 1929, I feel justified in discussing them here.

35 Mary Borden, 'The Hill', *The Forbidden Zone*, p. 175.

36 Whitman, 'Song of Myself', section 6, lines 111–113, 119–20, quoted from the *Norton Anthology of American Literature*, vol. 1 (Norton, 1979), p. 1879. Line 118 is quoted below, in the next paragraph.

37 See Luce Irigaray, 'L'Incontournable volume', *Speculum de l'autre femme* (Paris, Minuit, 1979), and 'La Mécanique des fluides', *Ce Sexe qui n'en est pas un* (Paris, Minuit, 1980).

38 Sylvia Townsend Warner, *Opus 7* (Chatto and Windus, 1931), p. 10. Reprinted in STW's *Collected Poems* (Carcanet, 1982).

39 Sylvia Townsend Warner, *T. H. White*, p. 109.

40 Naomi Mitchison, 'New Verse', first published in Jill Benton's 1990 biography *Naomi Mitchison* ('Undated, this poem is found among a batch written in the early 1930s', Benton, p. 90).

41 See Naomi Mitchison, *You May Well Ask* (1979), pp. 117–26, for an account of her friendship with Auden during the 1930s.

42 See C. Day Lewis, *The Magnetic Mountain*, part 34, p. 118; Stephen Spender's 'The Pylons' and 'The Funeral', both printed in *New Signatures* and collected in Spender's *Poems* (1933).

43 'Clemency Ealasaid' was first published as a long epigraph to Naomi Mitchison's Scottish novel *The Bull Calves* (Cape, 1947), pp. 11–15.

44 Ibid., p. 13.

45 Grierson's *Drifters* was first screened in London in 1928, in a double bill, alongside the first showing of Eisenstein's *Battleship Potemkin*: obviously a 'must' for avant-garde liberals of the 1920s. I thank Elizabeth Cowie for this information.

46 Naomi Mitchison, *The Alban Goes Out* (Harrow, Raven Press, 1939), abridged from pp. 6–8.

47 Naomi Mitchison, 'The Bonny Brae', *The Delicate Fire* (1933), p. 195.

48 Naomi Mitchison records her friendship with Stevie Smith in *You May Well Ask*, pp. 153–8.

49 Stevie Smith, 'Eng.', *A Good Time Was Had by All* (Cape, 1937), p. 46.

50 Edith Sitwell, 'I Do Like to be Beside the Seaside', *Façade*, reprinted in *Poems New and Old* (Faber, 1940), p. 46.

51 Stevie Smith, 'Major Macroo', *A Good Time* (1937), p. 79.

52 'We're here to point a moral or adorn a tale' is the last line of 'God and the Devil', *A Good Time* (1937), p. 32. The quotation is from Samuel Johnson's 'The vanity of human wishes'.

53 W. H. Auden, 'Hail the strange electric writing' in *The Dance of Death* (1930; reprinted in *The Collected Works of W. H. Auden: Plays and Other Dramatic Writings 1928–1938*, ed. Mendelson, 1988), p. 105.

54 Stevie Smith, 'To the Tune of the Coventry Carol', *A Good Time*, p. 21; 'In Canaan's Happy Land' and 'And the clouds return after the rain', *Tender Only to One* (1938), pp. 41, 61.

55 C. Day Lewis, 'Carol', *A Time to Dance, and Other Poems* (Hogarth, 1935), reprinted in *Collected Poems*, p. 140. These lines keep very close to the original lines in 'Away in a Manger': 'The stars in the bright sky/ Looked down where he lay/ The little Lord Jesus/ Asleep on the hay'.

Like the 'Coventry Carol' ('Lullay, lullay, Thou little tiny child'), these are traditional Christmas hymns. The other hymns I have mentioned are, in order of citation: number 339, 'Fair waves the golden corn'; 299, 'Come let us join our cheerful songs'; and 281, 'Lead us, heavenly Father, lead us' of *Hymns Ancient and Modern*.

56 Stevie Smith, 'Freddy', *A Good Time*, p. 69.

57 Randall Jarrell, 'Changes of Attitude and Rhetoric in Auden's Poetry,' *Southern Review* (1941; reprinted in *The Third Book of Criticism*, Faber, 1975), p. 145.

58 Stevie Smith, 'Alone in the Woods', 'Little Boy Lost', 'Bag-Snatching in Dublin' and 'The Fugitive Ride', *A Good Time*, pp. 29, 65, 49, 86.

59 See Stevie Smith, 'Bag-Snatching in Dublin', *A Good Time*, p. 86; The Murderer', *Tender Only to One* (1938), p. 31; W. H. Auden 'Sue' (*c.* 1937; Sycamore Press, 1977); William Plomer's 'The Dorking Thigh', title poem of Plomer's *The Dorking Thigh and Other Satires* (Cape, 1945).

60 Hoffmann's translation of Hoffmann's *Struwwelpeter: Pretty Stories and Funny Pictures for Little Children* (Leipzig, 1848); Harry Graham, *Ruthless Rhymes for Heartless Homes* (Edward Arnold, 1909); Belloc's *Cautionary Tales: For the Admonition of Children Between Eight and Fourteen Years of Age* (Eveleigh Nash, 1908).

61 Orwell – in 'Benefit of Clergy: Some Notes on Salvador Dali', written 1944; reprinted in *CEJL*, vol. 3, *As I Please: 1943–1945* (Secker & Warburg, 1968), p. 193.

62 Belloc, Preface to Pitter's *A Mad Lady's Garland*, p. vii; AE, quoted on the back of the dustjacket of the 2nd edition (1936).

63 'She is "traditional" in the bad sense, but her own sensibility and formal intelligence interrupt and occasionally transfigure her delicate, orthodox and reasonably interesting exercises' (Jarrell reviewing Pitter's collection *The Bridge* in 'Verse Chronicle', *The Nation*, 25 May 1946, collected in *Kipling, Auden and Co.*, Carcanet, 1981, p. 138).

64 Ruth Pitter, 'The Earwig's Complaint', *A Mad Lady's Garland* (second edition, 1936), pp. 9–10.

65 Quoted from Elegie 19, 'To his Mistress going to bed'. Pitter's conceit also echoes the preceding Elegie 18, 'Loves Progress', in which the poet imagines the woman's body as a map explored by the poet, travelling southwards past 'the straight *Hellespont* between/ The *Sestos* and *Abydos* of her breasts' towards 'her *India*' (*Complete Poems of John Donne*, ed. C. A. Patrides (Dent, 1985), pp. 184, 181.

66 Stanza 18 of Ruth Pitter's 'The Cygnet', collected in *Urania* (Cresset Press, 1950), p. 127.

67 Boswell's *Life* of Johnson (Oxford University Press, 1922), vol. 2, p. 19 (5 April 1776).

68 Donald Davie, *Under Briggflatts* (1990), p. 232. Short as it is, Davie's five-page essay on Sylvia Townsend Warner's poetry is the best account known to me of its qualities.

69 Entry for 22 September 1957, *The Diaries of Sylvia Townsend Warner*, ed. Claire Harman (Chatto, 1994), pp. 241–242. She was quoting from Psalm 104, verse 24 in the Book of Common Prayer: 'O Lord, how manifold are thy works: in wisdom hast thou made them all; the earth is full of thy riches'.

70 Geoffrey Grigson, *New Verse* 31–32, 1938: 23–4.

71 The poem which I asked permission to quote and discuss was 'Maternal Grief', which was first published in *New Verse* 23–24, April–May 1936, and collected in *Stone and Flower* (1943). Miss Raine, who considers this poem 'a piece of juvenilia', wrote:

> I don't know what you can possibly find of interest in it, there are many better poems in that volume. It is for this reason rather than that your book has a feminist perspective that I really would ask you to leave me out. Although, of course, I would rather be left out for that reason also.
>
> Letter to Janet Montefiore, 17 October 1995

72   Wendy Mulford, *This Narrow Place*, pp. 43–4.
73   STW, 'Drawing you, heavy with sleep to lie closer', *c*. 1935, printed in the *Collected Poems* p. 29. For an analysis of this poem, see my *Feminism and Poetry* (Pandora Press, 1987; revised edition 1994), pp. 158–60.
74   Wendy Mulford, *This Narrow Place*, p. 44.
75   Ruth Pitter, *A Trophy of Arms* (1937), p. 87.
76   E. J. Scovell, 'The Swan's Feet', *Collected Poems*, p. 40.

5   PARABLES OF THE PAST: A READING OF SOME ANTI-FASCIST HISTORICAL NOVELS

1   Sylvia Townsend Warner, *Selected Letters*, ed. William Maxwell (Chatto and Windus, 1982), p. 50. She was describing Professor Shelley Wang telling stories of the 'Chinese revolutionary spirit' to a meeting of the Dorchester Labour Party.
2   See Julian Symons poking fun at 'documentary propaganda' in *The Thirties: A Dream Revolved* (Faber, 1975), p. 64, and Toril Moi's jibe at Socialist novels representing 'strong, happy tractor-drivers and factory workers' in *Sexual/ Textual Politics* (New Accents, Methuen, 1985), p. 8.
3   Lindsay also produced the 'Prelude to Christianity' trilogy (*Rome for Sale*, *Caesar is Dead* and *Last Days of Cleopatra*), and his study of the contradictions of the English Revolution was followed by *Lost Birthright* (1939) about the Wilkesite campaign.
4   For the ways in which the 'mainstream' and Marxist accounts of the 1930s neglect women writers, including STW, see p. 20.
     Andy Crofts' *Red Letter Days* (1990), which discusses both the STW novels I have named, is as usual the honourable exception here.
5   Jan Montefiore, *Feminism and Poetry* (2nd revised edition, 1994), pp. 24–5.
6   Sylvia Townsend Warner's biographer Claire Harman – who edited STW's *Collected Poems* (Carcanet, 1982) and her *Diaries* (1994) as well as writing her biography (1989) – has done much to bring this writer back into public notice. See also Wendy Mulford's *This Narrow Place* (1988), and Crofts, *Red Letter Days* (1990) for good feminist and Marxist readings of STW. There is a good feminist reading of *Lolly Willowes* in Maroula Joannou's *'Ladies Please Don't Smash These Windows'* (1995), though it treats STW's Marxist historical novels rather cursorily.
     Recent articles on *Summer Will Show* include: Terry Castle's important essay, 'Sylvia Townsend Warner and the Counterplot of Lesbian Fiction' in *Textual Practice* 4(2) (1990), collected in her *The Apparitional Lesbian* (Columbia University Press, 1993), which I discuss in this chapter; Robert L. Caserio's 'Celibate Sisters-in-Revolution' in *Engendering Men*, ed. Joseph Boone and Michael Cadden (Routledge, 1991); Sandy Petrey's brilliant essay, '1848: Ideology, *Écriture*, Politics: Sylvia Townsend Warner Unwrites Flaubert' in *Recherches Sémiotiques (Semiotic Inquiry)* 11(2–3) (1991); and my own essay, 'Listening to Minna' *Paragraph* 14(4), January 1991, reprinted in *Volcanoes and Pearl Divers*, ed. Suzanne Raitt (OnlyWomen Press, 1995), which reappears, with some revisions, in the final section of this chapter (see pp. 168–77).
7   Terry Castle, *The Apparitional Lesbian* , p. 91.

8 Isherwood, Foreword to Upward's 'The Railway Accident' in *New Directions in Prose and Poetry: Number Eleven* (New York, 1949); reprinted in the Penguin edition of Upward's *The Railway Accident and Other Stories* (1969), p. 34.

9 Isherwood, *Goodbye to Berlin* (Hogarth, 1939), p. 13; Storm Jameson, 'Documents', *Fact* 4: 'Writing in Revolt: Theory and Examples', July 1937: 15–16.

10 Cunningham, *British Writers of the Thirties*, p. 299.

11 Andy Crofts also defends Marxist writers from the charge of naturalism in his chapter on fantasy in *Red Letter Days*, pp. 268–305.

12 Walter Benjamin, *Understanding Brecht*, trans. Anna Bostock (New Left Books, 1973), p. 5.

13 Peter Hulme has made this point in a review of Barry Unsworth's novel *Sacred Hunger* in *New Left Review* 204 (1994), pp. 138–44.

14 Naomi Mitchison, *The Bull Calves* (1947); African stories: see *When We Become Men* (Collins, 1965).

15 Naomi Mitchison, *You May Well Ask* (1979), p. 179.

16 John Mair in the *New Statesman*, quoted by Andy Crofts, *Red Letter Days*, p. 206.

17 See Andy Crofts, pp. 204 and 218 (on Jack Lindsay discussing Dimitrov's argument in a 1937 *New Masses* article).

18 Lukács wrote that *The Historical Novel* was 'composed during the winter of 1936/7' (1983 reprint, p. 13). The English translation by Hannah and Stanley Mitchell was first issued by Merlin Press (London, 1962); it was reprinted with an introduction by Fredric Jameson, by the University of Nebraska Press in 1983. All quotations from *The Historical Novel* in this chapter are taken from this edition.

19 Naomi Mitchison, *The Blood of the Martyrs* (Constable, 1939), pp. 307 and 380–6.

20 Colin MacCabe, 'Notes on Some Brechtian Theses', *Screen* 17(3), 1974, and chapter 2, 'The End of a Meta-Language', in *James Joyce and the Revolution of the Word* (Macmillan, 1978); Toril Moi, *Sexual/Textual Politics*, pp. 5–8.
   The quotations from Stalin (quoted by Zhdanov) and Bukharin are taken from the Proceedings of the 1934 Writers' Congress, first published in 1935 as *Problems of Soviet Literatur*, ed. H. G. Scott, by Martin Lawrence Ltd, and reprinted in 1977 by Lawrence & Wishart under the title *The Soviet Writers' Congress, 1934: The Debate on Socialist Realism and Modernism in the Soviet Union*.
   See Rita Felski, *Beyond Feminist Aesthetics: Feminist Literature and Social Change* (Hutchinson Radius, 1989), pp. 81–3.

21 Caudwell, *Romance and Realism: A Study in Bourgeois Literature*, ed. Samuel Hynes (Princeton University Press, 1970), pp. 113–16.

22 For a subtle and illuminating study of intertextual relations between Scott, Shakespeare and others, see Professor Michael Ragussis' reading of the representation of Jewish identity in Shakespeare's *The Merchant of Venice* and Scott's *Ivanhoe*, in *Figures of Conversion: The Jewish Question and English National Identity* (Duke University Press, 1995).

23 For Lukács' 'Stalinist views', see Toril Moi, *Sexual/Textual Politics*, p. 6. Catherine Belsey, though less contemptuous of Lukács, similarly places him within that school of 'expressive realism' which is her principal target (*Critical Practice*, p. 14).

24 See my essay, 'The Fourth Form Girls Go Camping' in *Intertextuality and Sexuality* ed. Judith Still and Michael Worton (Manchester University Press, 1993), for a longer discussion of these issues.

25 See Nancy K. Miller, 'Emphasis Added: Plots and Plausibilities in Women's Fiction', chapter 1 of *Subject to Change* (New York, Columbia University Press, 1991) and *The Heroine's Text* (New York, Columbia University Press, 1979), and Rachel Blau DuPlessis' Introduction to *Writing Beyond the Ending* (Indiana University Press, 1985). DuPlessis has since explored this terrain more radically, in *The Pink Guitar* (Routledge, 1990).

   For feminist rereadings of realist novels, see Susan Leonardi, *Dangerous by Degrees* (Univeristy of Indiana Press, 1990); Jill Benton, *Naomi Mitchison* (1990); Jean Kennard, *Vera Brittain and Winifred Holtby: A Working Partnership* (University Press of New England, 1989); Terry Castle, *The Apparitional Lesbian* (Columbia University Press, 1993).

26 As readers may have noticed, I am using Virginia Woolf's words here. See Virginia Woolf, *A Room of One's Own* (1929), chapter 2, p. 53; chapter 6, p. 150.

27 Nancy K. Miller, 'Changing the Subject', *Subject to Change* (New York, Columbia University Press, 1991), p. 106.

28 'Sections 39, 41, 43, 49, 66, 73, 82, 83, 97, 106 and the Endpiece consist of real documents' (Lindsay, Foreword to *1649*, Methuen, 1938, p. xi) .

29 H. Gustav Klaust, 'Socialist Fiction in the 1930s', *The 1930s: A Challenge to Orthodoxy* (Harvester, 1979), pp. 28–29. Klaust argues in the same essay that in concentrating on 'fictive heroes, taken from the anonymous mass of the people', Lindsay 'can claim to have "democratised" the *genre* [of the historical novel]' (p. 37). This overstates Lindsay's achievement, since Scott's novels did the same thing, though not so radically.

30 W. H. Auden, *Poems* (1933 reprint), poem 2229, p. 87.

31 See Ellen Wilkinson, *The Town That Was Murdered* (Gollancz, Left Book Club, 1939), chapter 10, 'N.S.S. Cuts Jarrow's Lifeline', especially pp. 143–149.

32 Ralph Fox, *The Novel and the People* (Cobbett Publishing Co, 1937), pp. 121–7.

33 Claud Cockburn, *I, Claud* (1967), p. 215.

34 Sylvia Townsend Warner, 1945 letter to Nancy Cunard, quoted in STW's *Selected Letters* ed. W. Maxwell (1982), p. 51.

35 This was true when I read it there in 1986. The Lenin Library, now officially renamed the Russian State Library, may possibly have changed its holdings since then.

36 Wendy Mulford, *This Narrow Place*, p. 133.

37 Naomi Mitchison, *The Corn King and the Spring Queen* (Cape, 1931), p.ii.

38 The form of Mitchison's *The Delicate Fire* alternates thematically linked short stories of ancient Greece with obliquely connected lyrics, a structure which closely resembles Kipling's *Puck of Pook's Hill* and *Rewards and Fairies*.

39 Jill Benton, *Naomi Mitchison* (1990), p. 66.

40 D. W. Winnicott, *Playing and Reality* (Tavistock, 1971; reprinted by Penguin, 1980), pp. 18–23.

41 Hélène Cixous, 'The Laugh of the Medusa', trans. Keith Cohen and Paula Cohen, in *New French Feminisms* ed. E. Marks and I. de Courtivron (Harvester Press, 1979); Gloria Anzalduá, 'The Way of the Serpent', in *Borderlands/La Frontera: The New Mestiza* (San Francisco, Spinsters/Aunt Lute, 1989).

42 Sylvia Townsend Warner, *Summer Will Show* (1936), p. 115.

43   Virginia Woolf, *A Room of One's Own* (1929), chapter 5, p. 123.

44   Charlotte Brontë, *Villette* (1853; Penguin Classics edition 1985), chapter 23, 'Vashti', p. 341. 'Vashti' transparently represents the great 'Rachel', the pseudonym of the Jewish actress Elisa Felix, who 'single-handedly revived classical drama'. See Rachel M. Brownstein, *Becoming a Heroine* (1982; Penguin edition, 1984), pp. 176–7.

45   Christopher Caudwell, *Illusion and Reality* (Macmillan, 1937; Lawrence & Wishart edition, 1946), pp. 90–3; Rex Warner, *The Wild Goose Chase* (Boriswood Press, 1937), pp. 250–5.

46   Terry Castle's 'Sylvia Townsend Warner and the Counterplot of Lesbian Fiction' points out the relationship between *Summer Will Show* and other English novels, notably those of Jane Austen. Sandy Petrey's '1848: Ideology, *Écriture*, Politics: Sylvia Townsend Warner Unwrites Flaubert' argues its intertextual relation to Flaubert's *L'Éducation Sentimentale*.

47   STW, note on *Summer Will Show* written in the 1960s, *Selected Letters* (1982), p. 40.

48   Wendy Mulford, *This Narrow Place*, p. 114.

49   Walter Benjamin, 'The Storyteller', *Illuminations* (Fontana, 1977), p. 98.

50   Luce Irigaray, 'Pouvoir du discours, subordination du féminin', *Ce Sexe qui n'en est pas un* (Paris, Minuit, 1974), p. 74.

51   Lukács, *The Historical Novel*, p. 133.

52   I have in mind here Toril Moi's over-valuation, apropos of Virginia Woolf's *Orlando* and *A Room of One's Own*, of the liberation achieved in verbal play (*Sexual/Textual Politics*), pp. 5–6.

53   See Irigaray, 'La Mécanique des fluides', *Ce Sexe qui n'en est pas un*, pp. 105–16.

54   Third stanza of Watts' hymn 'O God, our help in ages past' (a translation of Psalm 90).

55   Terry Castle, *The Apparitional Lesbian*, p. 91.

56   Petrey, '1848: Ideology, *Écriture*, Politics', pp. 66–8.

57   Terry Castle, *The Apparitional Lesbian*, pp. 88–89.

6   COLLECTIVE AND INDIVIDUAL MEMORY: *BLACK LAMB AND GREY FALCON*

1   Rebecca West, *Black Lamb and Grey Falcon* (New York, Viking, 1941; Macmillan, 1942), vol. 2, pp. 481–2 (1982 Papermac reprint, p. 1089).

2   For other hostile references to homosexuality, see also vol. 1, p. 215 and 483. Curiously enough, this attitude is not paralleled in RW's travel diary, which contains an unshocked account of meeting a homosexual monk in the Church of the Patriarchate at Pec, where she notices that 'all through lunch a plump dark Nancy élève was being coy with abbot' (diary entry for 14 May).

3   See Victoria Glendinning, *Rebecca West* (Macmillan, 1987), p. 154, and Carl Rollyson's recently published biography, *Rebecca West: A Saga of the Century* (Hodder and Stoughton, 1995), p. 164.

4   Samuel Hynes, Introduction to *Rebecca West: A Celebration* (1977; reprinted in 1983 by Penguin as *The Essential Rebecca West*), p. xv.

5   Peter Wolfe, *The Art of Rebecca West* (Carbondale and Edwardsville, Southern Illinois Press, 1982), p. 146.

6   Paul Fussell, *Abroad: British Literary Travelling Between the Wars* (1980), p. 203.
7   Fussell is quoting from Samuel Hynes' *The Auden Generation*, p. 229.
8   Christopher Sykes, *Four Studies in Loyalty* (Collins, 1946), quoted in Fussell, *Abroad*, p. 96.
9   This remark was made to me by Felicity Barringer of the *New York Times*.
      For Rebecca West's post-war obsession with Communist traitors, see Victoria Glendinning, *op. cit.*, p. 215.
      Contemporary non-Marxist observers of Eastern European countries in the late 1930s, including Storm Jameson in *Europe to Let* (1940) and in her memoir *Journey from the North* (1969, 1970), and Sheila Grant-Duff in her memoir, *The Parting of Ways: A Personal Account of the Thirties* (Peter Owen, 198), as well as E. R. Gedye in *Fallen Bastions* (1939), took a similar view to RW in regarding Communism as an unimportant factor in the internal politics of pre-War Eastern European countries.
10 George Orwell, 'Inside the Whale' (1940), *CEJL*, vol. 1, p. 567.
11 Claud Cockburn, *I, Claud* (1967), p. 167.
12 The Partido Obrero de Unificacion Marxista (Unified Marxist Workers' Party), which represented (roughly speaking) Spanish Trotskyists, and was suppressed by the Communist Party and its allies.
13 Travel diary: entry for 20 May.
14 Paul Fussell, *Abroad*, pp. 211 and 8.
15 See RW's praise for the Empress Elizabeth: 'Elizabeth's sweetness had not been merely automatic, she had been thinking like a liberal and like an Empress' (vol. 1, p. 4).
16 Mary Ellmann, *Thinking About Women* (New York, Harcourt Brace Jovanovich, 1968; reprinted by Virago, 1979), p. 108.
17 Lyotard, *The Postmodern Condition: A Report on Knowledge* (Manchester University Press, 1984), pp. 27–37.
18 The story of the Croatian persecution of the Serbs during the Second World War is admirably told in Hubert Butler's essay, 'The Sub-Prefect Should Have Held His Tongue', Butler, *Escape from the Anthill* (Gigginstown, Lilliput Press, 1985), pp. 270–85.
19 Rebecca West described these ceremonies in detail in an undated notebook, now in the Yale Beinecke Library.
20 Her biographer Carl Rollyson quotes from a 1938 letter to Denis Saurat describing the 'Sheep's Field' ceremony in *Rebecca West: A Biography* (Hodder and Stoughton, 1995), pp. 164, 402n.
21 The Gospel references invoked here are Matthew xxvi, 26–9 (the Eucharist); xiii, 31 (the mustard seed); and xxv, 52 ('they that take the sword shall perish by the sword').
22 The context of this word is theological history: 'Martin Luther howled against reason, and cried . . . to his hearers to throw shit in her face' (2, p. 207).
23 Earlier in the 1930s, she and other intellectuals, including Naomi Mitchison, Sylvia Townsend Warner and C. Day Lewis, declared herself a pacifist. See Jill Benton, *Naomi Mitchison* (1990), p. 108.
24 Mitchison, *Vienna Diary* (1934), p. 179.
25 The diary records a lunch with Vinaver, Tribarina and Pamacevic (whom she calls 'Pluto' in the book). 'Vinaver baited Tribarina about Serbia and Croatia – about Seton-Watson and about Cuciu. Told how S.W. furious because

Paschitel wd not publish Serbian Sarajevo documents. Told how intellectuals love to be in opposition. Told how Cuciu had altered his sacred text' (RW's travel diary: entry for 27 March).

26   Travel diary: entry for 5 May.

27   I have particularly in mind the 'Catanian debate' in where the Athenians spell out their imperialist *Realpolitik*. See Thucydides, *History of the Peloponnesian War*, book 7.

28   Rollyson, *op. cit.* p. 149.

29   See Victoria Glendinning, *op. cit.*, p. 156.

30   Rollyson reports RW saying, 'Alas, he had become a Communist and was furious with her book' (*op. cit.*, p. 213).

31   Glendinning, *op. cit.*, p. 253.

32   Travel diary: entry for 9 April.

33   The evidence of the Beinecke notebook, slight as it is, also supports the notion that the 'recitation-scene' is invented. The end of the second notebook contains a few notes on Serbian history, laid out as headings: 'the establishment of Serbia as the proper heir of Byzantium . . . the defeat and its consequences – including the poverty of the West/ Something rotten with us – the sacrifice idea'. These thoughts are followed by an almost illegible pencilled prose translation of the 'grey falcon' poem.

34   Travel diary, entry for 9 May.

35   'Mrs V. said people were wondering why she travelled in bus while husband and friends in car – she had explained that we had English guests (!) and they had to have the best seats' (Travel diary: entry for 5 May). The remark is repeated almost verbatim in the book (2, p. 67).

36   Travel diary: entries for 5, 9 and 10 May.

37   See Glendinning, p. 155 on Vinaver falling 'romantically in love' with Rebecca. On the attempted rape, see Rollyson, *op. cit.*, pp. 149–50.

38   Travel diary: entries for 8, 16 and 17 May. The anecdote about Goering tells how he 'complained of Napoleonic glass in villa that was old. Threw old coverlet lace off bed, saying "Look what they've left" – upset whole Hotel Imperial' (17 May: Tsetinye).

39   See Rollyson (quoting Peter Wolfe), *op. cit.*, p. 182.
     Victoria Glendinning suggests that Rebecca West 'may have wanted to aggrandize "my husband" in the eyes of the world and in his own eyes, and to maximize her own feminine wifeliness' (*op. cit.*, p. 183).

40   See Glendinning, *op. cit.*, p. 183; Rollyson, *op. cit.*, p. 141.

41   Glendinning, p. 140.

42   Another entry contrasts 'T.' unfavourably with her husband: 'He could not give. Only Ric can give. His spirit to live generously' (6 April).

43   The 1937 diary contradicts her statement that Henry Andrews stopped making love to her five years after their marriage in 1930 (Glendinning, p. 183). A clue to this discrepancy may be the reminiscence in the 26 March entry that 'I was gloriously happy' at Bad Gastein in August 1935; presumably this is the 'German spa' where she went to convalesce after her hysterectomy (Glendinning, p. 140). It therefore looks as if the affair with 'T.' started then. She may in her old age have unconsciously substituted the date of her own infidelity for the date of her husband's sexual withdrawal.

44   The manuscript reads 'as he was (deleted) is'.

45   On the ideological deceptions implicit in this clarity, see Catherine Belsey, 'Addressing the Subject', *Critical Practice* (1980), p. 69.

46   The notes out of which these meditations grew are relevant but brief: 'Got caught in porch. I was afraid of fire. The Metropolitan used to be a *comitadji* [guerrilla fighter] – spoke of 25 years of freedom. Beautiful woman beside me in the porch. All lovely, but frightening' (1 May).

Select bibliography

The place of publication is London unless otherwise stated.

POEMS

Ackland, Valentine *Whether a Dove or Seagull* Chatto and Windus, 1934 (with Sylvia Townsend Warner).

Auden, W. H. *Another Time* Faber, 1940.

—— *The Ascent of F 6* Faber, 1937 (with Isherwood).

—— *Collected Shorter Poems 1927–1957* Faber, 1966.

—— *The Complete Works of W. H. Auden: Plays and Other Dramatic Writings 1928–1938* ed. E. Mendelson, Princeton University Press, 1988.

—— *The Dog Beneath the Skin* Faber, 1935 (with Isherwood) .

—— *The English Auden: Poems, Essays and Dramatic Writings by W. H. Auden 1927–1939* ed. E. Mendelson, Faber, 1977.

—— *Letters from Iceland* Faber, 1937 (with Louis MacNeice).

—— *Look, Stranger!* Faber, 1936 .

—— *On the Frontier* Faber, 1937 (with Isherwood).

—— *The Orators: An English Study* Faber, 1932 .

—— *Poems* Faber, 1930; reprinted 1933.

—— *The Poet's Tongue: An Anthology* G. Bell, 1935 (with John Garrett).

—— *Spain 1937* Faber, 1937; Cahors, Hours Press, 1937 (pamphlet).

—— *Sue: A Ballad* Oxford, Sycamore Press, 1977 .

Betjeman, John *Continual Dew* John Murray, 1937.

—— *Old Lights for New Chancels* John Murray, 1940; reprinted in *Collected Poems*, John Murray, 1958.

Borden, Mary *The Forbidden Zone* Heinemann, 1929.

Brittain, Vera *Poems of the War and After* Gollancz, 1934.

Campbell, Roy *Flowering Rifle: A Poem from the Battlefield of Spain* Longmans, Green, 1939.

Cornford, Frances *Mountains and Molehills* Cambridge University Press, 1934 .

Cornford, John *Collected Writings* Manchester, Carcanet, 1986 (first published as *Understand the Weapon, Understand the Wound* ed. Jonathan Galassi).

Cunard, Nancy (ed.) *Negro Anthology* made by Nancy Cunard, Lawrence &

Wishart, 1934; reprinted and abridged as *Negro: An Anthology* ed. Hugh D. Ford, New York, F. Ungar Press, 1970.

—— (ed.) *Poems for France* London, La France Libre, 1944.

Cunningham, Valentine (ed.) *The Penguin Book of Spanish Civil War Verse* Harmondsworth, Penguin, 1980.

—— *Spanish Front: Writers on the Spanish Civil War* Oxford University Press, 1986.

Davie, Donald *Collected Poems 1950–1970* Routledge & Kegan Paul, 1972.

Day Lewis, Cecil *Collected Poems 1929–1933* Hogarth Press, 1935.

—— *From Feathers to Iron* Faber, 1932.

—— *The Magnetic Mountain* Hogarth, 1933.

Grigson, Geoffrey *New Verse: An Anthology* Faber, 1939.

Holtby, Winifred, *The Frozen Earth and Other Poems* Collins, 1935.

Isherwood, Christopher *The Ascent of F 6* Faber, 1937 (with Auden).

Jones, David *In Parenthesis* Faber, 1936.

Lewis, Wyndham *Blasting and Bombardiering* Eyre and Spottiswoode, 1937.

MacDiarmid, Hugh (Christopher Grieve) *Second Hymn to Lenin and Other Poems* Gollancz, 1935 .

—— *Stony Limits and Other Poems* Gollancz, 1934.

MacNeice, Louis *Autumn Journal* Faber, 1939 .

—— *Letters from Iceland* Faber, 1937 (with Auden).

—— *Out of the Picture* Faber, 1938 (play).

—— *Poems* Faber, 1934.

Mitchison, Naomi *The Alban Goes Out* Harrow, Raven Press, 1939.

—— *The Delicate Fire* Cape, 1933.

—— *The Fourth Pig* Constable, 1936.

Pitter, Ruth *A Mad Lady's Garland* Cresset, 1934.

—— *The Rude Potato* Cresset, 1941.

—— *A Spirit Watches* Cresset, 1939.

Plomer, William *The Dorking Thigh and Other Satires* Cape, 1945.

Raine, Kathleen *Stone and Flower* Nicholson and Watson, 1943.

Read, Herbert *The End of a War* Faber, 1934.

Rickword, Edgell *Behind the Eyes: Collected Poems and Translations* Manchester, Carcanet, 1976 .

Riding, Laura *Collected Poems* Seizin Press, 1938; reprint Manchester, Carcanet, 1980.

Roberts, Michael (ed.) *New Country: Prose and Poetry by the Authors of 'New Signatures'* Hogarth, 1933.

—— *New Signatures: Poems by Several Hands* Hogarth, 1932.

Scovell, E. J. *Shadows of Chrysanthemums* Routledge, 1941.

—— *Collected Poems* Manchester, Carcanet, 1988 .

Skelton, Robin (ed.) *Poetry of the Thirties* Harmondsworth, Penguin, 1964 .

Smith, Stevie *A Good Time Was Had by All* Cape, 1937.

—— *Tender Only to One* Cape, 1938.

Spender, Stephen *Poems* Faber, 1933.

—— *The Still Centre* Faber, 1939.

—— *Trial of a Judge* Faber, 1938.

—— *Vienna* Faber, 1934.

Warner, Sylvia Townsend *Collected Poems* ed. Claire Harman, Manchester, Carcanet, 1982.

—— *Opus 7* Chatto and Windus, 1931.
—— *Whether a Dove or Seagull* Chatto and Windus, 1934 (with Valentine Ackland)

NOVELS AND STORIES

Brittain, Vera *Honourable Estate* Gollancz, 1936.
Katharine Burdekin (Murray Constantine) *Swastika Night* Gollancz, 1937, 1941;
 reprint New York, Feminist Press, 1990.
Greene, Graham *Brighton Rock* Heinemann, 1938.
Holtby, Winifred *Mandoa, Mandoa!* Collins, 1933.
—— *South Riding* Collins, 1935; Fontana/Collins, 1954 (fifth edition).
Isherwood, Christopher *Goodbye to Berlin* Hogarth, 1939; Penguin, 1945.
—— *The Memorial* Hogarth, 1932.
—— *Mr Norris Changes Trains* Hogarth, 1935; Penguin, 1942.
Jameson, Storm *Company Parade* Cassell, 1934; Virago, 1984.
—— *Europe to Let* Macmillan, 1940.
—— *In the Second Year* Cassell, 1935.
—— *Love in Winter* Cassell, 1935; Virago, 1984.
—— *None Turn Back* Cassell, 1936; Virago, 1984.
—— *That Was Yesterday* Heinemann, 1930.
Lehmann, Rosamond *Dusty Answer* Chatto, 1927; Penguin, 1936 .
—— *The Weather in the Streets* Collins, 1936; Virago, 1981.
Lindsay, Jack *1649: A Novel of a Year* Methuen, 1938.
Mitchison, Naomi *The Blood of the Martyrs* Constable, 1939; reprint Edinburgh,
 Canongate Press, 1990.
—— *The Corn King and the Spring Queen* Cape, 1931; reprinted by Virago, 1983.
—— *The Delicate Fire* Cape, 1933.
—— *The Fourth Pig* Constable, 1936.
—— *We Have Been Warned* Constable, 1935.
—— *When We Become Men* Collins, 1965 .
Rhys, Jean *Good Morning, Midnight* Constable, 1938; Penguin, 1969.
—— *Voyage in the Dark* Constable, 1934; reprint Harmondsworth, Penguin, 1968.
—— *Wide Sargasso Sea* André Deutsch, 1966; Penguin, 1969.
Smith, Stevie *Novel on Yellow Paper* Cape, 1936; Virago, 1986.
—— *Over the Frontier* Cape, 1938; Virago, 1986.
Spender, Stephen *The Backward Son* Faber, 1940.
—— *The Temple* Faber, 1990.
Stead, Christina *The Beauties and Furies* New York, D. Appleton-Century; London,
 Peter Davies, 1936; Virago, 1985.
—— *House of All Nations* New York, Simon and Schuster; London, Peter Davies,
 1938.
Upward, Edward *In the Thirties* Heinemann, 1962; Penguin, 1969.
—— *Journey to the Border* Hogarth, 1938; reprinted in *The Railway Accident and Other
 Stories* Penguin, 1969.
—— *The Rotten Elements* Heinemann, 1969; Penguin, 1972.
—— *The Spiral Ascent: A Trilogy* Heinemann, 1977.
—— *An Unmentionable Man* Enitharmon Press, 1994.
Warner, Rex *The Professor* John Murray, 1938; Penguin, 1944.

—— *The Wild Goose Chase* Boriswood, 1937.

Warner, Sylvia Townsend *After the Death of Don Juan* Chatto and Windus, 1938 .

—— *Summer Will Show* Chatto and Windus, 1936.

Waugh, Evelyn *Black Mischief* Chapman and Hall, 1936; Penguin, 1965.

—— *A Handful of Dust* Chapman, 1934; Penguin, 1961.

Woolf, Virginia *Between the Acts* Hogarth, 1941.

—— *The Pargiters: The Novel-Essay Parts of 'The Years'* ed. Mitchell A. Leaska, Hogarth, 1978.

—— *The Years* Hogarth, 1937

AUTOBIOGRAPHY, BIOGRAPHY AND PERSONAL TESTIMONY

Benton, Jill *Naomi Mitchison: A Biography* Pandora, 1990.

Berry, Paul and Bostridge, Mark *Vera Brittain: A Life* Chatto and Windus, 1995.

Borden, Mary *The Forbidden Zone* Heinemann, 1929.

Brittain, Vera *Testament of Youth* Gollancz, 1933.

Byron, Robert *The Road to Oxiana* Macmillan, 1937; Picador, 1981.

Carpenter, Humphrey *W. H. Auden: A Biography* Allen and Unwin, 1981.

Chisholm, Anne *Nancy Cunard: A Biography* Sidgwick & Jackson, 1979 .

Cockburn, Claud *Crossing the Line* MacGibbon & Kee, 1958.

—— *I, Claud: The Autobiography of Claud Cockburn* Harmondsworth, Penguin, 1967.

—— *In Time of Trouble* Hart-Davis, 1956.

—— (as Frank Pitcairn) *Reporter in Spain* Lawrence & Wishart, 1936.

Cockburn, Patricia *The Years of the Week* Macdonald & Co, 1968; reprint Penguin, 1971.

Crick, Bernard *George Orwell: A Life* Secker and Warburg, 1980; Penguin, 1982.

Crossman, Richard (ed.) *The God That Failed: Six Studies in Communism* Hamish Hamilton, 1950 (memoirs by Stephen Spender, André Gide, Richard Wright, Ignacio Silone, Arthur Koestler and Louis Fischer).

Davenport-Hines, Richard *Auden* Weidenfeld and Nicholson, 1995.

Dayus, Kathleen *The Best of Times* Virago, 1991.

Fisher, Clive *Cyril Connolly: A Nostalgic Life* Macmillan, 1995.

Ford, Hugh D. *Nancy Cunard: Brave Poet, Indomitable Rebel* Philadelphia, Chilton Book Co, 1968.

Forrester, Helen *Twopence to Cross the Mersey* Cape, 1974.

Gedye, E. R. *Fallen Bastions: The Central European Tragedy* Left Book Editions, Gollancz, 1939 .

Glasser, Ralph *A Gorbals Boy at Oxford* Chatto and Windus, 1988.

—— *Growing Up in the Gorbals* Chatto and Windus, 1987.

Glendinning, Victoria *Rebecca West: A Life* Macmillan, 1987.

Greene, Graham *The Lawless Roads* Heinemann, 1939; Penguin, 1947 .

—— (ed.) *The Old School: Essays by Divers Hands* Cape, 1934; Oxford University Press, 1985.

Harman, Claire *Sylvia Townsend Warner* Chatto and Windus, 1989.

Hollingsworth, Hilda *They Tied a Label to my Coat* Virago, 1991; published in the US as *Places of Greater Safety*.

Isherwood, Christopher *Christopher and his Kind* Eyre Methuen, 1977.

—— *Kathleen and Frank* Methuen, 1971.

—— *Lions and Shadows: An Education in the Twenties* Hogarth, 1938.

Jameson, Storm *Journey from the North* 2 vols, Harvill Collins, vol. 1, 1969; vol. 2, 1970; Virago, 1985.

—— *No Time Like the Present* Cassell, 1932.

Koestler, Arthur *Spanish Testament* Gollancz, 1937.

Lewis, Wyndham *Blasting and Bombardiering* Eyre and Spottiswoode, 1937.

Llewellyn Davies, Margaret (ed.) *Life as We Have Known it, by Co-operative Working Women* Hogarth, 1931; reprint Virago, 1977.

MacNeice, Louis *The Strings Are False: An Unfinished Autobiography* ed. E. M. Dodds, Faber, 1965.

Milner, Marion *Experiment in Leisure* Chatto and Windus, 1937; Virago, 1988.

—— *A Life of One's Own* Chatto and Windus, 1934; Virago, 1986.

Mitchison, Naomi *Among You Taking Notes: Wartime Diaries 1939–1945* ed. Dorothy Sheridan, Gollancz, 1985.

—— *Naomi Mitchison's Vienna Diary,* Gollancz, 1934.

—— *You May Well Ask: A Memoir 1920–1940* Gollancz, 1979.

Muir, Edwin *Scottish Journey* Heinemann/Gollancz, 1935.

Mulford, Wendy *This Narrow Place: Sylvia Townsend Warner and Valentine Ackland: Life, Letters and Politics 1930–1951* Pandora, 1988.

Orwell, George *Homage to Catalonia* Secker and Warburg, 1938.

—— *The Road to Wigan Pier* Left Book Editions, Gollancz, 1936.

Priestley, J. B. *English Journey* Heinemann/Gollancz, 1934.

Raine, Kathleen *The Land Unknown* Hamish Hamilton, 1975.

Rollyson, Carl *Rebecca West: A Saga of the Century* Hodder & Stoughton, 1995.

Spender, Stephen *World Within World: An Autobiography* Hamish Hamilton, 1951; Readers Union reprint, 1955.

Stallworthy, Jon *Louis MacNeice* Faber, 1994.

Warner, Sylvia Townsend *The Diaries of Sylvia Townsend Warner* ed. Claire Harman, Chatto, 1994.

—— *Selected Letters* ed. William Maxwell, Chatto and Windus, 1982.

West, Rebecca *Black Lamb and Grey Falcon: A Journey Through Yugoslavia in 1937* 2 vols, New York, Viking, 1941; Macmillan, 1942 .

Woolf, Virginia *The Diaries of Virginia Woolf* vol. 5, 1936–1941, eds Anne Olivier Bell and Andrew McNeillie, Hogarth, 1984.

—— *Moments of Being: Unpublished Autobiographical Writings* ed. Jeanne Schulkind, Sussex University Press, 1976.

Worsley, T. C. *Flannelled Fool: A Slice of Life in the Thirties* Alan Ross, 1967; Hogarth reprint, 1990

LITERARY CRITICISM, THEORY AND JOURNALISM BY WRITERS OF THE PERIOD

Auden, W. H. *The Dyer's Hand* Faber, 1956 .

Benjamin, Walter *One-Way Street and Other Writings* trans. E. Jephcott and K. Shorter, New Left Books, 1979.

—— *Understanding Brecht* trans. Anna Bostock, New Left Books, 1973.

Caudwell, Christopher *Illusion and Reality: A Study of the Sources of Poetry* Macmillan, 1937; Lawrence & Wishart, 1946.

—— *Romance and Realism: A Study in Bourgeois Literature* ed. Samuel Hynes, Princeton University Press, 1970.

Cockburn, Claud *Bestseller: The Books That Everyone Read 1900–1939* Sidgwick & Jackson, 1972.

—— *The Devil's Decade* Sidgwick & Jackson, 1973 .

Connolly, Cyril *Enemies of Promise* Routledge, 1938; Penguin, 1962.

Day Lewis, C. *A Hope for Poetry* Henderson & Spalding, 1934.

—— (ed.) *The Mind in Chains: Socialism and the Cultural Revolution* Frederick Muller, 1937.

Fox, Ralph *The Novel and the People* Cobbett Publishing Co, 1937.

Gorky, Bukharin, Zhdanov et al. *Problems of Soviet Literature* ed. H. G. Scott, Martin Lawrence, 1934; reprinted as *Soviet Writers' Congress 1934: The Debate on Realism and Modernism* Lawrence & Wishart, 1977.

Halbwachs, Maurice *On Collective Memory* ed. and trans. Lewis A. Coser, Chicago/London, University of Chicago Press, 1992.

Jameson, Storm, 'Documents', *Fact* 4, July 1937: 9–17.

Leavis, Q. D. 'Lady Novelists and the Lower Orders', *Scrutiny* 4(2), September 1935: 112–132.

Lukács, Gyorgy *The Historical Novel (A tortenelmi regeny)*, 1937; English trans. Hannah and Stanley Mitchell, Merlin Press, 1962; reprint London/Lincoln, NA, University of Nebraska Press, 1983.

MacNeice, Louis *Modern Poetry* Oxford University Press, 1938.

Muggeridge, Malcolm *The Thirties* Hamish Hamilton, 1940; Fontana reprint, 1971.

Orwell, George *Collected Essays, Journalism and Letters* ed. Sonia Orwell and Ian Angus, 4 vols, Secker and Warburg, 1967 .

Rickword, Edgell (ed.) *Scrutinies, by Various Writers* Wishart, 1928.

Scarfe, Francis *Auden and After: The Liberation of Poetry 1930–1941* Routledge, 1941.

Spender, Stephen *The Destructive Element: A Study of Modern Writers and Beliefs* Cape, 1935.

—— *The Thirties and After: Poetry, Politics, People 1933–1975* Fontana/Collins, 1978.

Spring Rice, Margery *Working-Class Wives: Their Health and Conditions* Harmondsworth, Penguin, 1939.

Symons, Julian *The Thirties: A Dream Revolved* Cressett, 1960; revised edition Faber, 1975; third edition, *The Thirties and the Nineties* Manchester, Carcanet, 1991.

Upward, Edward 'Sketch for a Marxist Interpretation of Literature' in *The Mind in Chains: Socialism and the Cultural Revolution* ed. C. Day Lewis, Frederick Muller, 1937.

West, Alick *Crisis and Criticism* Lawrence & Wishart, 1937; revised edition, 1975.

Woolf, Virginia *Collected Essays* 4 vols, Hogarth, 1966–1967.

—— *The Common Reader* Hogarth, 1935.

—— *A Room of One's Own* Hogarth, 1929.

—— *The Second Common Reader* Hogarth, 1932.

—— *Three Guineas* Hogarth, 1938

PERIOD STUDIES, CASE HISTORIES AND OTHERS

Barker, Francis (ed.) *1936: The Sociology of Literature*, vol. 1, *The Politics of Modernism*; vol. 2, *Practices of Literature and Politics*, University of Essex, 1979. Proceedings of the Essex Conference on the Sociology of Literature, July 1978 .

Batsleer, Janet, Davies, Tony and O'Rourke, Rebecca *Rewriting English: Cultural Politics of Gender and Class* Methuen, 1986.

Beauman, Nicola *A Very Great Profession: The Woman's Novel 1914–39* Virago, 1983.

Belsey, Catherine *Critical Practice* Methuen, 1980.

Bergonzi, Bernard *Reading the Thirties: Texts and Contexts* Macmillan, 1978.

Bowlby, Rachel *Still Crazy After All These Years: Women, Writing and Psychoanalysis* Routledge, 1992.

Branson, Noreen and Heinemann, Margot *Britain in the Nineteen Thirties* Weidenfeld and Nicholson, 1971; reprint Panther Books, 1973.

Caesar, Adrian *Dividing Lines: Poetry, Class and Ideology in the 1930s* Manchester University Press, 1991.

Campbell, Beatrix *Wigan Pier Revisited: Poverty and Politics in the 80s* Virago, 1984.

Castle, Terry *The Apparitional Lesbian: Female Homosexuality and Modern Culture* New York, Columbia University Press, 1993.

Caudwell, Sarah (Sarah Cockburn) 'Reply to Berlin', *New Statesman* 26 October 1986, pp. 3–4.

Clark, Jon, Heinemann, Margot, Margolies, David and Smee, Carol *Culture and Crisis in Britain in the 1930s* Lawrence & Wishart, 1979.

Cockett, Richard *Twilight of Truth: Chamberlain, Appeasement and the Manipulation of the Press* Weidenfeld and Nicholson, 1989.

Crofts, Andy *Red Letter Days: British Fiction in the 1930s* Lawrence & Wishart, 1990.

Cunningham, Valentine *British Writers of the Thirties* Oxford University Press, 1988 .

Davie, Donald *Under Briggflatts* Manchester, Carcanet, 1990.

DuPlessis, Rachel Blau *Writing Beyond the Ending: Narrative Strategies of Twentieth-Century Women Writers* Indiana University Press, 1985.

Ford, Hugh D. *A Poets' War: British Poets and the Spanish Civil War* Oxford University Press, 1965.

Fuller, John *A Reader's Guide to W. H. Auden* Thames and Hudson, 1970.

Fussell, Paul *Abroad: British Literary Travelling Between the Wars* Oxford University Press, 1980.

—— *The Great War and Modern Memory* Oxford University Press, 1975.

Gindin, John *British Fiction of the 1930s: The Dispiriting Decade* Macmillan, 1992.

Glover-Smith, Frank (ed.) *Class, Culture and Social Change: A New View of the 1930s* Brighton, Harvester, 1980.

Graves, R. and Hodge, A. *The Long Week-End: A Social History of Great Britain, 1918–1939* Faber, 1940.

Green, Martin *Children of the Sun: A Narrative of 'Decadence' in England After 1918* Constable, 1975.

Griffin, Gabriele (ed.) *Difference in View: Women in Modernism* Taylor & Francis, 1994.

Hecht, Anthony *The Hidden Law: The Poetry of W. H. Auden* Cambridge, MA/ London, Harvard University Press, 1993.

Hobsbawm, Eric *The Age of Extremes: The Short Twentieth Century 1914–1991* Michael Joseph, 1994.

Hynes, Samuel *The Auden Generation: Literature and Politics in England in the 1930s* Faber, 1976.

—— (ed.) *Rebecca West: A Celebration* Macmillan, 1978; reprinted as *The Essential Rebecca West* Penguin, 1978 .

Jarrell, Randall *Kipling, Auden & Co., Essays and Reviews, 1935–1964* Manchester, Carcanet, 1981.

—— *The Third Book of Criticism* Faber, 1975.

Joannou, Maroula *'Ladies Please Don't Smash These Windows', Women's Writing, Feminist Consciousness and Social Change 1914–1938* Oxford/Providence, Berg Press, 1995.

Kermode, Frank *History and Value* Oxford University Press, 1988.

Light, Alison *Forever England: Femininity, Literature and Conservatism Between the Wars* Routledge, 1991.

Lucas, John (ed.) *The 1930s: A Challenge to Orthodoxy* Brighton, Harvester, 1979.

Marcus, Laura *Auto/Biographical Discourse: Criticism, Theory, Practice*, Manchester University Press, 1995.

Maxwell, D. E. S. *Poets of the Thirties* Macmillan, 1969.

Mendelson, Edward *Early Auden*, Cambridge, MA, Harvard University Press, 1983.

Miller, Jane *Women Writing About Men* Virago, 1986.

Miller, Nancy K. *Subject to Change: Reading Feminist Writing* Columbia University Press, 1991.

Montefiore, Jan 'Case-Histories *Versus* the Undeliberate Dream: Men and Women Writing the Self in the 1930s', in *Difference in View: Women in Modernism* ed. Gabriele Griffin, Taylor & Francis, 1994, pp. 56–74.

—— *Feminism and Poetry* Pandora Press, 2nd revised edition, 1994.

—— 'Listening to Minna: Realism, Feminism and the Politics of Reading', *Paragraph* 14(4), January 1991: 197–216.

—— 'Shining Pins and Wailing Shells: Women's Poetry of the First World War' in *Women in World War I: The Written Response* ed. D. Goldman, Macmillan, 1993, pp. 51–72.

Mulhern, Francis *The Moment of Scrutiny* New Left Books, 1979.

O'Neill, Michael and Reeves, Gareth *Auden, MacNeice, Spender: The Thirties Poetry* Macmillan, 1992.

Oldfield, Sybil (ed.) *This Working-Day World: Women's Lives and Culture(s) in Britain 1914–1945* Taylor & Francis, 1994.

Sidnell, Michael J. *Dances of Death: The Group Theatre of London in the Thirties* Faber, 1984.

Spears, Monroe K. *The Poetry of W. H. Auden* Oxford University Press, 1963.

Stanley, Liz, *The Auto/Biographical I: The Theory and Practice of Feminist Autobiography,* Manchester University Press, 1992.

Stonebridge, Lyndsey 'Taking Care of Ourselves and Looking After the Subject', *Paragraph* 17(2), July 1994: 120–134.

Symons, Julian (ed.) *The Angry Thirties* Eyre Methuen, 1976.

Taylor, A. J. P. *English History 1914–1945* Oxford University Press, 1965; Penguin, 1970.

Thompson, E. P. *'The Poverty of Theory' and Other Essays* Merlin Press, 1978.

Tolley, A. J. *The Poetry of the Thirties* Gollancz, 1975.

Index

UNIVERSITY OF GLAMORGAN
PRIFYSGOL MORGANNWG
Learning Resources Centre